CONFESSING THE IMPASSIBLE GOD

The Biblical, Classical, & Confessional Doctrine of Divine Impassibility

EDITED BY

Ronald S. Baines
Richard C. Barcellos
James P. Butler
Stefan T. Lindblad
James M. Renihan

RBAP
Palmdale, CA

Requests for information should be sent to:

RBAP
349 Sunrise Terrace
Palmdale, CA 93551
rb@rbap.net
www.rbap.net

Printed in the United States of America.

Cover design and formatted for print by Cameron Porter.

Paperback edition.

ISBN-13: 978-0-9916599-2-0
ISBN-10: 0991659929

How is the confessional phrase God is "without . . . passions" to be understood? Is God really without passions? Isn't he like us *or* rather aren't we like God, made in his image? We have passions and emotions, therefore, God must have the same; or so the argument goes. Can God become emotionally hurt or distraught? Does God actually and emotionally change with varying circumstances and situations in human history? After all, doesn't the Bible say that God repented? These are some questions that have been raised in the past century, but with renewed vigor in the last ten years.

The above questions are skillfully answered in this book *Confessing the Impassible God*. It was forged out of the fires of theological controversy within the church instead of in the ivory towers of academia. Rather than letting misguided emotional thinking formulate your beliefs about God and the above questions, this book will drive you back to Holy Scripture. It will take you on a delightful journey of exegetically sound biblical, historical, confessional, and practical teaching through the doctrine of divine impassibility. In a day when most thoughts of God are "too human," this book will cast out empty imaginations, lift your soul to the heights of heaven, and cause you to revel in the glorious God of the Holy Bible. Buy, study, mark, and learn!

Earl M. Blackburn
Heritage Baptist Church, Senior Pastor
Shreveport, Louisiana

No issue is closer to our hearts than that addressed by *The Shorter Catechism* which we taught to our children, to Sunday School students, and to prospective church members: "What is God?" The historic answer is, "God is a Spirit, infinite, eternal and unchangeable . . ." But today there continue to be those who call themselves "Reformed," "Calvinists," or "Evangelicals," who deny that God is unchangeable. Instead they teach that God changes and has changed, in direct contradiction of the Bible: "I am the LORD, I do not change" (Mal. 3:6). Surely we must know whom we worship, who forgives our sins! "The people who know their God shall be strong and carry out great exploits" (Dan. 4:32).

Scripture (Jude 3) exhorts all Christians of all times "to contend earnestly for the faith [i.e., system of doctrine] which was once for all delivered to the saints." That faith is embodied in the word of God delivered by prophets and apostles. Our day cries out for "the faith" to be defended vigorously. This new book was written by a group of ministers and theologians attempting to do just that. As the reader will discover, they have been loyal to the word of God. You will find within these covers profound thought that is not all easy to grasp but well-worth the effort.

I am pleased to commend this volume. May it bring much praise to "Jesus Christ, the same yesterday, today, and forever" (Heb. 13:8).

Walter J. Chantry
Author of *Today's Gospel, Authentic or Synthetic?*,
Signs of the Apostles, and *Call the Sabbath a Delight*

The essays in this volume constitute a wonderful blend of biblical, historical, contemplative, and practical theology all in defense of the doctrine of divine impassibility. The defense mounted is not primarily against the usual cast of detractors—Open Theists and process theologians—but against those evangelicals who imagine that abandoning or reconceiving impassibility can be done with little or no detriment to the edifice of a classical theology proper. The authors are convinced that once one begins to chip away at this crucial piece of the foundation the whole house of orthodox Christian conviction about God and his attributes begins to falter. And they are right.

The trend nowadays is not to deny that God undergoes emotive changes, as the older construal of impassibility maintained, but merely to insist that God controls changes in his emotive state by the sovereign act of his will. It is commendable that the authors resist this realignment of impassibility along Barthian actualist lines. What they offer instead is a recovery of the doctrine that helpfully reintegrates it within the galaxy of other equally indispensable classical doctrines such as God's incomprehensibility, simplicity, immutability, eternity, and perfection of being. The result is a richly rewarding study that magnifies our unchanging God.

James E. Dolezal
Assistant Professor of Theology
Cairn University

_____

Truth sometimes sounds stranger than fiction, which is why *Confessing the Impassible God* is a welcomed, rigorous defense of the traditional and confessional doctrine of divine impassibility. Many in the church have either rejected this vital biblical teaching or have forgotten it because the sands of the hourglass have buried it. The contributors provide a significant exegetical, theological, historical, and practical engagement of the issues, which makes this eminently useful for pastors, scholars, seminarians, and even people in the pews.

J. V. Fesko
Academic Dean
Professor of Systematic and Historical Theology
Westminster Seminary California

_____

Theology is not static. The church has made progress in its understanding of the Trinity, Christology, Soteriology, and Ecclesiology. However, theological development ordinarily comes through the church combating error rather than choosing a research topic for a new book. In responding to error, the church must build upon and enrich her understanding of Scripture, in dialogue with church history, with an eye toward a new generation, rather than jettison the past in the name of theological progress. This book presents the old view of divine impassibility, using old arguments, against new critics. It is precisely this kind of process that the Spirit of God has used through the ages to bring the church to a deeper understanding of and love for the glorious truths of Scripture and of the character of our triune God. Whether or not you agree with everything in this volume, its position should be heard and carefully weighed as you prayerfully search the Scriptures on this vital issue.

Ryan M. McGraw
Associate Professor of Systematic Theology
Greenville Presbyterian Theological Seminary

A spirited reclaiming of the doctrine of divine impassibility, this coherent, well-edited, multi-author project is unique in several commendable aspects. It is decisively Baptist, but advances its argument in ways that recent generations have stopped expecting from Baptist theologians. These authors are committed to the final authority of Scripture in doctrinal matters, but mastery of their tradition's confessional resources gives them uncommon access to depths of theological understanding. In particular, they have chased the doctrine that God is "without passions" all the way down metaphysically, relating it meaningfully to the theology of the divine being as pure act, and steadfastly refusing mere voluntarism, the persistent Scotist reductionist temptation to make everything depend on God's will rather than his nature. Evangelical projects of retrieval are becoming more common as theologians appropriate patristic and medieval resources. *Confessing the Impassible God* stands out for its commitment to a retrieval of the middle distance, the Baptist confessions of early modernity as the nearby trailhead to the great tradition of Christian theology. Good fences make good neighbors, and I think that, paradoxically, the decisively Baptist focus of this project is what will make it useful beyond its own Reformed Baptist confessional borders.

Fred Sanders
Professor of Theology
Torrey Honors Institute
Biola University

Confessing the Impassible God addresses a topic that gets to matters at the heart of our understanding of the living God. Exploring the doctrine of divine impassibility through thorough historical, confessional, systematic, and exegetical studies, the authors make a compelling case that maintaining a robust affirmation of impassibility not only secures our continuity with the long patristic, medieval, and Reformation tradition of theology proper but also guards against falling into a range of errors that entail portraying God as something fundamentally other than the God of classical, biblical Christianity.

This is a bold book in several respects. The contributors not only address radical critics of impassibility but especially consider those we might call friendly critics: revered figures of the past such as Charles Hodge and B. B. Warfield as well as a number of well-known and generally orthodox theologians in contemporary evangelical and Reformed circles. The authors of *Confessing the Impassible God* engage these theologians with a charitable yet firm spirit, and I hope these theologians will reflect carefully on the powerful arguments of this book. I recommend this volume to all thoughtful Christians who wish to know and worship God truly, and I expect they will find here great encouragement to embrace impassibility not as a sterile idea of Greek metaphysics but as profound biblical teaching meant to bolster our faith, hope, love, joy, and confidence in the Triune God.

David VanDrunen
Robert B. Strimple Professor of Systematic Theology and Christian Ethics
Westminster Seminary California

Classical theism is under attack in our day. Specifically such doctrines as divine simplicity and impassibility are deconstructed in an effort to achieve a more believable and accessible God. Unfortunately this more believable and accessible God is not the God of the Bible. It would be bad enough if the enemies of Christ led the attack against classical theism, but it is so-called friends who undermine the classical biblical witness to our great and glorious self-contained triune God. The broader church and Reformed community owe a debt of gratitude to our Reformed Baptist brothers for producing *Confessing the Impassible God*. In this fine book, the classically biblical doctrine of divine impassibility is defined and defended, explored and exposited. *Confessing the Impassible God* confirms my hunch that many attempts to reinvent the wheel of the doctrine of God arise from either ignorance of our great Reformed heritage (especially Reformed Scholasticism) and its biblical *principium* or a facile gloss of the appropriate texts of Scripture and our theological sources. This volume covers the whole spectrum of the theological encyclopedia on divine impassibility. I salute the men who have been involved in the publication of this fine book.

Rev. Jeffrey C. Waddington
Stated Supply & Ministerial Adviser — Knox Orthodox Presbyterian Church Lansdowne, PA
Ministerial Adviser — Calvary Church of Amwell (OPC) Ringoes, NJ
Panelist & Secretary of the Board — The Reformed Forum
Articles Editor — The Confessional Presbyterian Journal
Book Series Editor & Fellow — Alliance of Confessing Evangelicals

---

There was a time when it was my opinion that the Doctrine of God or Theology Proper was settled. It seemed to me that, except for the debates over God's eternal decree between Reformed and Arminian Christians, the Doctrine of God was of little polemic interest. If that was ever really the case, it is surely not the case now. The onslaught of Process and Open Theism, the claims that the classical Christian doctrine of God was seriously infected with Greek philosophical ideas, and the consequent and widespread proposals to modify the traditional Theology Proper of classical Christian theism are provoking widening discussion. *Confessing the Impassible God* provides an important, deep, and thoughtful response to the proposed revisions to the doctrine of divine impassibility — one of the hot-spots in the polemic furor among Reformed evangelicals over the Doctrine of God. I am grateful for the theologically careful and historically informed hermeneutics and exegesis of the present volume. I am grateful especially for the reminder that this book contains of the importance of recognizing the revelation of Scripture as analogical, and sometimes anthropopathic, and the importance of recognizing this in our teaching. *Confessing the Impassible God* deserves close study and appreciative discussion among Reformed Christians.

Sam Waldron
Dean of Covenant Baptist Theological Seminary
Pastor of Grace Reformed Baptist Church
Owensboro, KY

_____

Contents

Introduction

Part I: Theological and Hermeneutical Prolegomena

Part II: Biblical Foundations

Part III: Historical Theology

Part IV: Systematic Theology

Part V: Confessional Theology

Part VI: Practical Theology

Part VII: Conclusion

Appendices

List of Abbreviations

2LCF   Second London Confession of Faith 1677/89

BDAG   *A Greek-English Lexicon of the New Testament and Other Early Christian Literature.*

CNTUOT   *Commentary on the New Testament use of the Old Testament.*

Commentaries   John Calvin, *Calvin's Commentaries*, Twenty-Two Volumes.

Dictionary   Richard A. Muller, *Dictionary of Latin and Greek Theological Terms: Drawn Principally from Protestant Scholastic Theology.*

JETS   *Journal of the Evangelical Theological Society*

JIRBS   *Journal of the Institute of Reformed Baptist Studies*

NIDOTTE   *New International Dictionary of Old Testament Theology and Exegesis*, Five Volumes.

NPNF   *Nicene and Post-Nicene Fathers*, First and Second Series, Twenty-Seven Volumes.

PRRD   Richard A. Muller, *Post-Reformation Reformed Dogmatics*, Four Volumes.

RD   Herman Bavinck, *Reformed Dogmatics*, Four Volumes.

RBTR   *Reformed Baptist Theological Review*

TDOT   *Theological Dictionary of the Old Testament*, Fifteen Volumes.

TWOT	*Theological Wordbook of the Old Testament,* Two Volumes.
WCF	Westminster Confession of Faith
Works	John Owen, *The Works of John Owen*, Twenty-Three Volumes.
WSC	Westminster Shorter Catechism
WTJ	*Westminster Theological Journal*

FOREWORD

To many readers, *Confessing the Impassible God* will be a surprising book. It articulates and defends the impassibility of God by Baptists, taking seriously the statements of Baptist confessions of faith of the seventeenth century! Such surprise is due largely to the custom of identifying Baptists exclusively with the culture and theology of modern evangelicalism, the temper of mind of which is concerned with modifying and supplanting the theological heritage of Protestantism with innovations of various kinds. The contributors to this book are well aware of such deviations. Furthermore, many Baptists have been taught to believe that it is altogether alien to the Baptist outlook to formulate and adhere to confessions of faith. Confessions of faith, it is customarily believed, are uncharacteristic of the Baptist mentality, which is strongly inclined to think that adherence to confessions cramps the mind and spirit of the Christian church. The idea is that Baptists, being independents or congregationalists in their polity, are marked by an individualism which fosters in each congregation and each minister their own ways of expressing their faith. But history is not on their side at this point. The authors of this book take a different view.

I

So the first thing to be said is that *Confessing the Impassible God* is not an exercise in antiquarianism. All the essays which form it have a positive theological stance, and one with distinctive practical and pastoral consequences. The writing is at one and the same time impassioned about classical Christian theism, and careful and serious about the application of this confessional position to the contemporary church. For a modern evangelical Baptist to adopt these recommendations will require fresh thinking.

Before we consider the book's approach to God and his impassibility, let us reflect a moment on the meaning of 'impassible' as applied to God. The word is often mistaken for others, and given a meaning that it does not have. For example, it is often confused with *impassable*. If the road is blocked by an avalanche we may say that as a consequence it is 'impassable'; no one can get through. But divine impassibility has nothing that gets in the way of God being accessible or available. Impassibility sets up no barriers. The authors fervently believe that God has revealed himself in Scripture, and that the disclosure of his own impassibility is a fundamental feature of this revelation. But the impassible God may meet us in our need, deliver us from our sin, and bring us unfailingly to glory. He is the very reverse of the impassable road, blocked up after a rockslide.

Another misconception is that an impassible God is *impassive*, unfeeling and uncaring in the face of suffering and need. This suggestion has links with the caricature of the impassible God as psychotically withdrawn, indifferent to the needs of his creation. But no one in orthodox Christianity has ever said such a thing, that God is blocked off either psychologically or in other ways from his creation or from his people.

'Impassible' is a negative term. As 'impossible' means 'not possible,' so 'impassible' means 'not passible.' So if God is impassible, then he is not passible, not subject to the onset of passions or moods, and of changes of mind. It is not simply that he is not in fact subject to the onset of passions, like a Stoic, but he is *not able* to be made to have a passion. Paradoxically, being impassible does not denote a deficiency or lack in God, but it testifies to God's fullness, to his undiminishable goodness, to his eternal will. The goodness of God is such that while the creation of the universe and the redemption of his people is a consequence of his goodness, God cannot be affected by or molded by his creation, and especially not by his human creation. It is as we, creatures in time and space, change or are changed that this fullness of God comes to us in one form or another, according to our different circumstances, and God's unchanging purposes operate upon us, as we exercise faith, or are disobedient, or careless, or defiant, or forgetful. So God may be understood as a savior, a guide, or a judge, as he is understood as the eternal upholder and governor of his creation.

Impassibility is closely connected with God's immutability. When in Hebrews 6 the author states that it is impossible for God to lie, he grounds this statement in God's own being. This immutability is not something that God has decided to be—unchangeable—but it is rooted in his nature, as the writer of the letter goes on to explain. "For when God made a promise to Abraham, since he had no one greater by whom to swear he swore by himself, saying, 'Surely I will bless you and multiply you.'" Impassibility is an aspect of such immutability. So God does not simply decide to be constant in his character; it is his being (or essence) to be such, an aspect of his greatness, his perfection. He cannot waver. And so he cannot change his care, his love, his justice and so on, nor can he be changed, for he expresses his character in accordance with his eternal purposes. The connectedness of impassibility with other aspects of God's being or essence is therefore important, and we shall return to it.

II

When the Second London Confession of Faith asserts, as an aspect of the God it confesses, that he is "without body, parts, or passions," the Baptist authors unashamedly copy the wording of earlier confessions of the English Reformation. That language, in turn, borrows from the thought of the medieval church and of patristic theology, going back to Augustine and beyond. In working in this way those confessional Particular Baptists avowed that their congregations are in direct line with the theology of the Christian church from her inception.

Note the rather brave and gracious way that these men worked. During the times when Baptists were persecuted and discriminated against in England (John Bunyan put in Bedford jail for preaching Christ, and so forth), they nonetheless appropriated for their own confessions the language of the XXXIX Articles of Religion of the persecuting Church of England. (And the same would have been true, I reckon, had the English Parliament of the 1640's had its way, and its anti-blasphemy legislation had been implemented. Baptists would then have been on the receiving end of Westminster Confession-style discrimination and persecution. But Cromwell intervened.) They deliberately followed this wording both of the Articles, and of the Westminster Confession of Faith, and of the Savoy Declaration (so long as conscience permitted them to do so) because they wanted it to be known that they had the same doctrinal pedigree.

The Reformation was not a revolution, the discovering or inventing of a new kind of Christianity, but a re-formation, a protest against a corrupt church. This meant that wherever there were grounds for agreement and continuity, the Reformers upheld the ancient faith. Thus in asserting God's transcendence, the trinitarian character of the Godhead, the incarnation in which the Logos took on human nature, the creation of the universe out of nothing, the ancient theological landmarks were left undisturbed. But where there was corruption — over the denial of justification by faith alone, by the promotion of human merit, the invention of acts of supererogation, and so on — the Reformers vigorously opposed the Roman Church.

The English Particular Baptists adopted this same stance; opposing paedobaptism, episcopacy, certain liturgical practices, and the intolerance of the Church under the Stuarts, and later on that of the Presbyterians of the Long Parliament. As is shown in this book, they were resolute in upholding the theology and the doctrines of grace of Augustine and the Reformers, and of their Anglican and Puritan successors. To underline the point, they steadfastly confessed this theology in very similar and often identical words. Unfortunately, later Baptists who have acknowledged their confessions have often done so without a great deal of enthusiasm or conviction regarding this abiding theology. This book is an expression of a renewed enthusiasm and commitment for this confessional position.

III

We have already noticed the close connection between divine impassibility and divine immutability, that one is an aspect of the other. They are together linked to divine eternity. God is the Creator of all creatures in time, but is not himself in time, but is timeless, "before the ages began" (Titus 1:2). Not being in time he is not liable to change; he does not age, nor is part of his life over, as parts of all our lives are over. For him time does not pass away. He has no memory, and he "only has immortality" (1 Tim. 6:16). So there is no time in which he changes, changing his mind, experiencing onsets of moods, and so forth. The divinely-created universe is contingent in the sense that it is dependent on this God, who sustains and governs all that he has made.

Being the Creator, he is not created, and so he is not dependent on anything else. No one or no thing has created the Creator, nor does he simply happen to be. He exists independently, in the purest and most basic sense. "Who has measured the Spirit of the Lord, or what man shows him his counsel?" (Isa. 40:13). He is pure spirit: "God is spirit, and those who worship him must worship in spirit and truth" (John 4:24), and so not constituted out of parts, as the creation is, parts composed of atoms and grains and cells, or a stream of consciousness. That would be an absurd idea in the case of the Creator; for where would these parts come from? And if we could answer that question, how could we avoid the conclusion that these parts, out of which God is composed, whatever they were, were more basic than God himself? No. God is independent, and not composed; he has a simple unity. "Hear, O Israel: The Lord our God, the Lord, is one" (Deut. 6:4). And so, God being one simple essence, the Trinity is not a tripartite being, but each member of the Trinity is the wholly indivisible Godhead, not partitioning the one God, but distinguishing it in ways that are basic to the Christian religion—the Father, the Son, and the Holy Spirit. Ways of thinking that do justice to God's eternal being run like a golden thread through the confessions of the church, including the Baptist Confession elaborated in *Confessing the Impassible God.*

Those in the past who confessed this God, and those who now do the same, recognize that such a God is incomprehensible. This term does not mean that talk of such a God is gibberish, incoherent, but that the being of God is so extraordinary that we cannot fully get our minds around it. We cannot *comprehend* God, but we can *apprehend* him from what he reveals to us about himself in Scripture. Nevertheless, to think and to talk of God in these ways requires development of the mental discipline that is also a part of the historic religion of Christianity.

So here we have a family of ideas—simplicity, independence, necessity, eternity, immutability, impassibility—each interconnected with the others in our understanding of God's transcendence. Divine impassibility is not some arbitrary invention, due to the quirkiness of theologians, but it points instead to the intensely mysterious character of God. Understanding even a little of such grandeur taxes our minds, and stretches our thinking, leading us to use language that Scripture itself uses — *negative* language, to say what God is not, and *metaphorical* language to portray the ways that God deals with us in creation and redemption, and *stretched* language to attempt to do justice to God's supreme eminence.

IV

What is especially noteworthy about this book is the care and respect with which the writers handle this biblical and confessional heritage. This is not a case of ancestor worship, or of mere antiquarianism, but it arises from a renewed appreciation of "historic catholic theology," as one contributor puts it. It has often been claimed that such theology was the result of the influence of Hellenistic philosophy on the early thinkers of the church, with the consequent smothering of the pure biblical teaching. But the doctrine of divine impassibility is not affirmed as a result of philosophical speculation. Rather as this book shows more than once, the doctrine of God of which his impassibility is an aspect has a firm basis in sound hermeneutical principles and doctrinal exegesis in both the Old and New Testaments. Included in this outlook is the drawing of the distinction between literal language about God, such as that he is the "only wise God," immutable and so forth, and the metaphorical language according to which God changes, and has passions and bodily states, culminating in his supreme act of accommodation, in which he becomes incarnate as the Christ. Both the words of God and the coming to us of the incarnated Word of God are aspects of God's work of sovereign grace.

This exegetical tradition arises from a deep conviction that Scripture is one word of God, possessing a theological unity. There are not many, diverse theologies in Scripture. The Creator is not a creature, nor does he have creaturely features. As we have been noting, unlike the gods of classical antiquity he is the origin of all that is in time and space, but is himself not subject to it. A natural question that arises is: But what about the incarnation? Does God not enter time and space at that point? The key to thinking clearly about the incarnation is to bear in mind that in it God became man not by 'morphing' into a human being, but by the person of the Logos taking on human nature and so becoming the two-natured Mediator, the God-man, the Savior. For in the incarnation God did not change in his essence, but took on human nature. This also is seriously mysterious. We shall never come near to understanding what happened, least of all if we try to imagine what it was like to be Jesus. As the definition of Chalcedon, formulated in A.D. 451, put it:

> The properties of each nature are conserved and both natures concur in one "person" and in one *hypostasis*. They are not divided or cut into two *prosopa*, but are together the one and only begotten Logos of God, the Lord Jesus Christ.[1]

The seventeenth-century Particular Baptist confessions adopted the disciplines of thinking about the incarnation developed by the early church.

V

Finally, the commitment to this pure Christian theism, of which divine impassibility is an aspect, has a practical outworking, a practical theology, issuing in a distinctive piety. To know God is to know this God, and so to know our own creatureliness; to know something of his majesty and grace, and so by reflex to be aware of our own insufficiency, guilt and unrighteousness. This eternal God works out our salvation in space and time in various ways, without in any way diminishing his goodness. And "If we are faithless, he remains faithful, he cannot deny himself" (2 Tim. 2:12-13). Belief leads to action, and distinctive beliefs lead to distinctive actions. As a consequence of who he is, such a God is not at our every beck and call.

On July 10th, 1666, the house of Anne Bradstreet, the wife of a

---

[1] John Leith, *Creeds of the Churches* (New York: Anchor Doubleday, 1963), 36.

colonial administrator, burned down at night. The fire awoke the family, and all escaped from the building and watched the fire engulfing everything. In the poem that she wrote in memory of this occurrence these words occur:

> And when I could no longer look,
> I blest His name that gave and took,
> That layd my goods now in the dust,
> Yea, so it was, and so 'twas just.
> It was his own: it was not mine;
> Far be it that I should repine.[2]

She recognized herself to be in the hands of her eternal God, and believed that what he willed was best. God's gracious purposes for his people remain unchangeable even if the reasons why he permits difficulties are often not presently disclosed to them.

VI

This book can be said to present an interdisciplinary exposition and so a cumulative defense of divine impassibility and of the doctrine of God of which that is an aspect. Each line of argument strengthens and supports the other. Its foundation in Scripture, and the hermeneutics employed, show the doctrine to be not speculative or abstract but to have its foundation in the varied data of both Testaments of the Bible. The chapters on history show that divine impassibility is not a recent whimsy or the peculiar invention of a Christian sect, but the historic catholic faith. Those on the confession and the doctrine of God set out its Baptist pedigree, and the connectedness of impassibility with other distinctions made in the doctrine of God, and their overall coherence. Each line of enquiry sensitizes the palate to taste the others. There is a polemical strand throughout the book, contrasting this view with those of

---

[2] Anne Bradstreet (c.1612-1672), "Here followes some verses upon the burning of our House," in *Seventeen Century American Poetry*, ed. with an Introduction, Notes, and Comments by Harrison T. Meserole (Garden City, NY: Anchor Books, 1968), 35.

Open Theism and aberrant statements from contemporary Calvinists and others. But these arguments are used not to score points but to set forth and make even clearer the positive, historic teaching on divine impassibility, by contrasting it with other currently-held views.

I am honored to have been asked to write this Foreword, and delighted with what I have read. *Confessing the Impassible God* is heartily recommended.

Paul Helm
Former Professor of the History and Philosophy of Religion
King's College
London

PREFACE

> . . . We have no itch to clog religion with new words, but do readily acquiesce in that form of sound words which hath been, in consent with the Holy Scriptures, used by others before us . . .[1]

These humble words come from the seventeenth-century signatories to the Second London Confession of Faith (1677/89). We heartily agree with them. We propose nothing new, neither methodologically nor theologically. To cite one of the endorsers of this work, "This book presents the old view of divine impassibility, using old arguments, against new critics." We are not offering our exposition to readers in order to discover something never understood before, nor to offer a new twist on an old doctrine. The contents seek to rediscover, recover, and remind readers of an ancient theological truth, confessed by Christians for many centuries across various ecclesiastical lines. It utilizes words and concepts that have a long history. This has been a truly collaborative work and it is our conviction that the doctrine of divine impassibility is, in the true sense of the word, a catholic doctrine. It is also our conviction that the doctrine of divine impassibility is gravely misunderstood and falsely maligned in our day and in need of clear explication and defense if we are to uphold what has been the common confession of classical theism in its various ecclesiastical and historical expressions.

The book is structured as follows. The Introduction presses home the importance of the doctrine of divine impassibility. Readers will be challenged to recognize that tinkering with divine impassibility as classically understood has implications that always end up compromising other fundamental articles of the Christian faith.

The main argument is contained in seven parts. Part I addresses vital issues of prolegomena. Prior to providing a positive

---

[1] "To the Judicial and Impartial Reader," in *The Baptist Confession of Faith and The Baptist Catechism* (Birmingham, AL and Carlisle, PA: Solid Ground Christian Books and Reformed Baptist Publications, 2010), xiii. This is a modern reprint of the original 1677 edition.

explication of the doctrine, we outline our theological method. Chapter 1 discusses the theological grammar of the doctrine of divine impassibility. Important concepts such as biblical metaphysics, act and potency, and the analogy of being are discussed. These are basic and crucial concepts to understand at the outset. Chapter 2 offers an introduction to the hermeneutical method employed throughout. These two chapters together reflect our commitment to the traditional language of classical theism and the hermeneutics of the Reformed tradition as articulated in the English Reformed Confessions of the sixteenth and seventeenth centuries. As readers will become aware in reading the subsequent sections, the issue of method is crucial and foundational in this discussion.

Part II (chapters 3-7) covers the Old and New Testaments. Though all potential passages of Scripture are not discussed, the most important texts on the subject of divine impassibility are addressed. The order of these chapters reflects our hermeneutical method: we consider texts on the nature of God first, texts which speak of immutability and impassibility next, concluding with those texts that appear to indicate some sort of passibility in God. Each testamental section ends with a brief conclusion.

Part III (chapters 8-9) surveys the history of the doctrine of divine impassibility. We seek to demonstrate that what was once a catholic doctrine has become muddied as scholars of various theological traditions have reformulated, modified, and in some instances rejected classical theism's commitment to divine impassibility.

Part IV (chapters 10-12) offers a systematic-theological approach to the subject. It assumes Parts I-III and builds upon them. Careful discussion is provided on such issues as the relationship of divine impassibility to the essence and attributes of God, the divine affections, and the incarnation of the Son of God. Our goal is for readers to realize the significance of divine impassibility in relation to many other essential doctrines of the Christian faith. It is part of the system of doctrine contained in our Confession; tinkering with impassibility has far-reaching ramifications.

Part V (chapter 13) offers an overview of the doctrine of divine impassibility as contained in the Second London Confession of Faith (1677/89). This confessional document asserts the same doctrine as the Westminster Confession of Faith (1647) and the Savoy Declaration (1658) on the issue of divine impassibility. The place of the doctrine in the Confession as well as its relationship to other confessed truths is presented.

Part VI (chapter 14) seeks to explicate the practical theology of divine impassibility. It draws out implications of the doctrine under the topics the saving knowledge of God, the Christian life, worship, and pastoral ministry.

Part VII (chapter 15) offers closing comments and a list of affirmations and denials in light of the entire study.

Additionally, we have included two appendices, containing book reviews of contemporary attempts to modify the classical doctrine of divine impassibility.

We offer this book, not as the end of discussion on this vital issue, but as a continuation of an older discussion that has been largely lost in our day. As readers will soon notice, we quote favorably many older theologians who affirm the classical doctrine of divine impassibility. Prior to the eighteenth century, among Reformed theologians, there was uniformity of thought on this issue. Since the Enlightenment, however, there have been diverse opinions represented by theologians of various traditions, even among those claiming to be confessional and Reformed. We are of the firm opinion that the methodological, hermeneutical, and theological shifts that took place after the ascendancy of the Enlightenment steered theology in the wrong direction.

The editors wish to thank several readers who assisted us along the way. Their insights helped tighten the over-all argument and presentation of the book. We are especially grateful to Paul Helm for writing the Foreword. We asked Professor Helm to write it because we knew he would read carefully and provide a very informed and helpful perspective for prospective readers. Cameron Porter deserves special recognition for his stellar work on the cover and formatting the book for print.

It is our prayer that the following pages will contribute to fruitful thought and discussion concerning the doctrine of divine impassibility and other related doctrines of the Christian faith.

The Editors
June 2015

An Introduction to
the Doctrine of Divine Impassibility
Why is this Doctrine Important?
James M. Renihan

Then Moses said to God, "Indeed, *when* I come to the children of Israel and say to them, 'The God of your fathers has sent me to you,' and they say to me,'What *is* His name?' what shall I say to them?" 14 And God said to Moses, "I AM WHO I AM." And He said, "Thus you shall say to the children of Israel, 'I AM has sent me to you.'" 15 Moreover God said to Moses, "Thus you shall say to the children of Israel: 'The LORD God of your fathers, the God of Abraham, the God of Isaac, and the God of Jacob, has sent me to you. This *is* My name forever, and this *is* My memorial to all generations.' 16 "Go and gather the elders of Israel together, and say to them, 'The LORD God of your fathers, the God of Abraham, of Isaac, and of Jacob, appeared to me, saying, "I have surely visited you and *seen* what is done to you in Egypt. (Exod. 3:13-16)[1]

For I *am* the LORD, I do not change; Therefore you are not consumed, O sons of Jacob. (Mal. 3:6)

Do not be deceived, my beloved brethren. 17 Every good gift and every perfect gift is from above, and comes down from the Father of lights, with whom there is no variation or shadow of turning. 18 Of His own will He brought us forth by the word of truth, that we might be a kind of firstfruits of His creatures. (James 1:16-18)

It is agreed by all that those expressions of "repenting,

---

[1] Unless otherwise noted, all English Bible quotations are taken from the New King James Version (NKJV).

"grieving," and the like, are figurative, wherein no such affections are intended as those words signify in created natures, but only an event of things like that which proceedeth from such affections. (John Owen, commenting on Hebrews 6:17)

Two Words: "without . . . passions"

This book has been written because there is debate over the sense of two words contained in Chapter 2, paragraph 1, of the Second London Confession of Faith. Those two words are "without . . . passions."[2] Some might say that, in the grander scheme of a long Confession, these two words are unimportant. Others might argue that the sense of the terms is flexible and not fixed. Still others might simply think the matter is not serious enough for debate. To the contrary, it is our assertion that these words are of great significance, and altering them or adjusting their meaning has serious consequences for both confessionalism and, more importantly, the Christian faith itself. The following chapters are intended to demonstrate from Scripture, systematic theology, historical theology, confessional theology, and practical theology that the matter is of great weight and is worth a serious and firm defense.

It is not difficult to illustrate from the history of theology how important apparently small matters may be. At the time of the Reformation, one word characterized the difference between the Lutherans and Reformed on one side and Rome on the other — the four letters that spell the Latin word *sola*.[3] The Roman Catholic system of salvation incorporated grace and faith into its doctrine, recognized the great importance of Scripture, and upheld the true deity and humanity of Jesus Christ, acknowledging that he is Savior of the world. Yet in each of these, the Romanists failed to proclaim

---

[2] The words "without . . . passions" are a part of the larger phrase "without body, parts, or passions." See chapter 13, "Confessional Theology and the Doctrine of Divine Impassibility" below. This phrase occurs in the Forty-Two Articles of the Church of England (1552), the Thirty-Nine Articles of the Church of England (1563), the Westminster Confession of Faith (1647), and the Savoy Declaration (1658).

[3] Translated into English as 'alone.'

aloneness, i.e., that salvation is by faith alone apart from works, by grace alone apart from human merit, that the Scriptures alone are the infallible rule for the church apart from the canon law developed in the previous centuries, and that Jesus Christ is the only Mediator apart from any others. In a very important sense, the recovery of gospel truth rested on this word *alone*.

We might also remember that one letter once made the difference between orthodoxy and heresy. In the fourth century, some theologians were unable to understand how the eternal God could become man in the person of Jesus Christ. Can the infinite and the finite come together in one person? Because they could not conceive of this notion, and because there were some Scriptures that seemed to support their objections, they suggested that Jesus Christ was the first-born of all creation—the highest and best and first—but still a being created by the one true God. They argued that he was ὁμοιούσιος, of a similar substance to God, though not fully and completely God. The reply was that Christ was actually ὁμοούσιος, of the same substance as the Father, and therefore really and truly deity. The difference between these two positions is the Greek letter "ι," the equivalent of our letter "i." One letter made the difference.

It is our hope that this book will help those with questions to understand these two words, "without . . . passions," and their significance for the doctrine in our Confession, recognize the importance of the doctrine, and stand together in its defense. We understand that all Confessions, as human documents, may be subject to revision in the light of Scripture. We believe, however, that the classical doctrine of divine impassibility as stated in these two words is of great importance and thus a matter of confessional integrity. We believe Herman Bavinck is correct, when he says:

> Those who predicate any change whatsoever of God, whether with respect to his essence, knowledge, or will, diminish all his attributes: independence, simplicity, eternity, omniscience, and omnipotence. This robs God of his divine nature, and religion of its firm foundation and assured comfort.[4]

---

[4] Bavinck, *RD*, 2:158.

Definition of the Confessional Doctrine by Opponents

The doctrine of our Confession of Faith has been widely understood, by its use of the words "without . . . passions," to teach the ancient doctrine of divine impassibility, defined as

> that divine attribute whereby God is said not to experience inner emotional changes, whether enacted freely from within or effected by his relationship to and interaction with human beings and the created order.[5]

This is especially clear in the writings of its critics who oppose this doctrine. Here we cite several examples.

Jeff Pool

In his book, *Against Returning to Egypt: Exposing and Resisting Credalism in the Southern Baptist Convention*, Jeff B. Pool, critiquing the 1994 Southern Baptist "Report of the Presidential Theological Study Committee," writes about the "'Second London Confession' of 1677" in these terms:

> The "Second London Confession" of 1677, [is] a confession based upon and, in both form and substance, with some variations almost identical to the Calvinistic "Westminster Confession of Faith." . . . As easily perceived . . . the "Westminster Confession of Faith" clearly supplied its Baptist imitation with much of its exact wording: God is "a most pure spirit, invisible, without body, parts, or passions, immutable, immense, eternal, incomprehensible, almighty, most wise, most holy, most free, most absolute." While the "Second London Confession" certainly remains part of the larger Baptist heritage, the SBC did not produce this confession, nor any confession fully consistent with it. Moreover, the SBC's confessional statements have never infused the doctrine of God with the meaning ascribed by

---

[5] Thomas G. Weinandy, "Impassibility of God," in *New Catholic Encyclopedia*, 2nd ed., 15 vols., ed. Thomas Carson and Joann Cerrito (Detroit; Washington, D.C.: Thomson/Gale, 2003), 7:357.

the concepts of either divine immutability or divine impassibility, as confessed by both the "Second London Confession" and its parent, the "Westminster Confession of Faith. . . ."

. . . God gave humans freedom to sin. Contrary to the divine desire for human life, humans betrayed God through the very power with which God has endowed them. According to the book of Genesis, prior to the "flood of the world," the pervasiveness of human sin grieved God; according to [sic] book of Isaiah, Israel's betrayal of God's loving mercy also grieved God. Even Pauline writings in the New Testament refer to the abilities of reconciled people to limit the indwelling Holy Spirit's work: reminding both Thessalonian Christians not to quench the Spirit and Ephesian Christians not to grieve the Holy Spirit of God. The scriptures do not describe God as "without . . . passions."[6]

For Pool, the language of the Confession, "without . . . passions," is clearly that of the classical doctrine of God. While he rejects this doctrine, his acknowledgement of the meaning of the phrase is important to note. Modern modifications, alterations, and rejections do not fit into the sense of the confessional statement.

Clark Pinnock

Clark Pinnock, a famous theologian who began his teaching career as a Calvinistic Baptist and ended it as an Open Theist, wrote

---

[6] Jeff B. Pool, *Against Returning to Egypt: Exposing and Resisting Credalism in the Southern Baptist Convention* (Macon, GA: Mercer University Press, 1998), 182-86. The ellipsis at the end of the citation is in the original. Later in the book, Pool argues against divine impassibility on the basis of Christology. Stating that classic Chalcedonian Christology requires the doctrine of divine impassibility, he then says, "Baptist Christians can remain most biblical only by refusing to affirm the *Substance* of orthodox Christologies," 192ff., emphasis original. Pool understands that Chalcedonian orthodoxy — the doctrine about our Lord Jesus Christ which states "that two whole, perfect, and distinct natures, were inseparably joined together in one *Person*: without *conversion, composition,* or *confusion*" (the quotation is from 2LCF 8.2) — is intimately related to the doctrine of divine impassibility. To deny one necessitates denial of the other. Thankfully, many are inconsistent at this point.

extensively on the topic of divine impassibility. Pinnock's theological journey is of great interest, as it illustrates the dangers associated with revisions to this doctrine. In the definitive biography, *Clark H. Pinnock: Journey Toward Renewal*,[7] author Barry L. Callen describes the path followed by Pinnock. The most significant period for his movement from Calvinism to Arminianism and Open Theism was during the 1970s. From 1974-77, he taught at Regent College in Vancouver, B.C., and there "began to review carefully and revise cautiously his inerrancy views."[8] Callen's comments are important:

> During the early 1970s Clark Pinnock thought that he had only entered into a process of making some select theological adjustments to his received theological tradition. This tradition was the scholastic paradigm[9] that supported a deterministic mindset and its strict view that biblical inerrancy is the necessary foundation for a sound pattern of Christian believing and witnessing. He later came to understand that something more extensive was in process in his case. Specifically:
>
> > I was also moving away from the larger framework of Calvinism itself to more dynamic ways of thinking theologically. I was being drawn to a new orientation which sees God as love, away from the view of God as authoritarian and austere judge. I was giving up the view according to which God is thought to relate primarily to us as all-determining monarch and law-giver and shifting to the paradigm in which God relates to us primarily as parent, lover, and covenant partner.
>
> He was coming to realize that the quest for certainty in

---

[7] Barry L. Callen, *Clark H. Pinnock: Journey Toward Renewal* (Nappanee, IN: Evangel Publishing House, 2000). Pinnock himself contributed an "Afterword," in which he says, "Dr. Callen has created a convincing interpretation of my work, and I do not challenge it in any way" (269).

[8] Callen, *Pinnock*, 57.

[9] In the book, language like this is functionally equivalent to Reformed theology.

faith, typically evidenced by the insistence on inerrancy of the biblical text, is but one key reflection of the creed of Reformed scholasticism. . . . He realized that there was one faulty assumption at the very beginning of the Calvinistic chain of logic—a misfocused perception of God.[10]

Pinnock's published writings came to detailed expression of this early change in several volumes, including *The Openness of God* and *Most Moved Mover*. Each of these must be noticed. In the first book, Pinnock contributed the third chapter, titled "Systematic Theology." There we read such things as these:

> Impassibility is the most dubious of the divine attributes discussed in classic theism, because it suggests that God does not experience sorrow, sadness or pain.
>
> The theme of suffering strongly brings out God's openness to the world. Not aloof and impassive, God does not just imagine what it would be like to suffer, he actually suffers because of his decision to love.
>
> . . . We could say that God is impassible in his nature but passible in his experience of the world. Change occurs in the world and affects God when he becomes aware of it.[11]

In his monograph, *Most Moved Mover*, Pinnock seeks to demonstrate the inconsistency of modern evangelicals who modify the doctrine of divine impassibility while holding onto a view of divine sovereignty.

> Of special interest is the way in which conservative Calvinist authors now want to say that God responds to us and is unhappy when things go badly. They are trying to work such themes into their work. They know that evangelicals believe these truths and try to co-opt them, even

---

10 Callen, *Pinnock*, 89-90, 94. The citation from Pinnock is provided as "Clark Pinnock, foreword to *Clark Pinnock on Biblical Authority*, by Ray Roennfeldt, (Berrien Springs, MI: Andrews University Press, 1993), xx-xxi."

11 Clark H. Pinnock, Richard Rice, John Sanders, William Hasker, and David Basinger, *The Openness of God: A Biblical Challenge to the Traditional Understanding of God* (Downers Grove, IL: InterVarsity Press, 1994), 118-19.

though divine changeableness is incompatible with theological determinism. Many are taking advantage of the rhetoric of the open view of God, which Bible readers find compelling, and are trying to work it into their own language.

. . . Impassibility is undoubtedly the Achilles heel of conventional thinking. It was as self-evident to our ancestors as it is out of question for us, but as soon as one tinkers with it the edifice trembles.

. . . Most evangelical theists, however, do not acknowledge a problem, or, if they do, respond to it with half measures. Like Arminius himself, they know modifications have to be made but draw back from making them — at least coherently. Typically, Calvinists reject impassibility and therefore, modify immutability but hold onto timelessness, all-controlling sovereignty and exhaustive foreknowledge. Tiessen denies timelessness and impassibility but sticks to all-controlling sovereignty — but why would God grieve if he were meticulously sovereign? McLeod upholds divine passibility and redefines immutability in terms of faithfulness but continues to defend all-controlling sovereignty, which makes nonsense of these moves. . . . (A theologian is not obliged to be logically consistent but there is a price to pay for exempting oneself from laws of rationality, it is intelligibility.)

. . . The conventional package of immobility attributes is very tight. If you retain one, you might as well retain them all. Retaining all-controlling sovereignty, for example, hinders reforms needed in other areas from doing any good. . . . It remains a mystery how one can say that God acts and feels in response to different situations whilst saying that he causes everything and knows everything.

These developments show that many evangelicals are half-hearted about the need of reform, even though they see that it is necessary. . . . One cannot just introduce dynamic and relational features into the doctrine of God without reconsidering undynamic and unrelational features of it like meticulous sovereignty and exhaustive foreknowledge.

The conventional package of attributes is tightly woven.

You cannot deny one, such as impassibility, without casting doubt cast [sic] on others, like immutability. It's like pulling on a thread and unraveling a sweater. A little boldness is required; tentative changes will not do. Wolterstorff comments

> Once you pull on the thread of impassibility, a lot of other threads come along with it. Aseity, for example—that is unconditionedness. The biblical witness seems to me clearly to be that God allows himself to be affected by the doings of the creatures God created. What led the traditional theologians to affirm aseity was their philosophical argument that the world is such that it can only be explained if we postulate a being which is the condition of everything itself, itself being conditioned by nothing. To give up aseity then is to give up an argument for God's existence—an argument which is questionable in any case. One also has to give up on immutability and eternity. If God really responds, God is not metaphysically immutable and, if not metaphysically immutable, not eternal.

The conventional package of attributes is tightly drawn. Tinkering with one or two of them will not help much.[12]

This is an important diagnosis from an opponent of the classical doctrine of divine impassibility. Pinnock understood that alterations to this doctrine have profound influence on other important doctrines. His own journey exemplifies the dangers inherent in modifying the classical doctrine. Theological changes have serious consequences.

---

[12] Clark H. Pinnock, *Most Moved Mover: A Theology of God's Openness* (Carlisle: Paternoster, 2001), 75-78. The citation from Wolterstorff is given as N. P. Wolterstorff, 'Does God Suffer?', *Modern Reformation* 8.5 (1999): 47. Pinnock is correct in pointing out these inconsistencies.

Richard Rice

Another contributor to *The Openness of God*, Richard Rice, may add to our argument. In his chapter, "Biblical Support for a New Perspective," we read:

> The Old Testament attributes to God a wide range of feelings, including joy, grief, anger and regret. Many references involve divine pleasure. The repeated exclamation of Genesis 1, "And God saw that it was good," seems to express warm personal satisfaction. A number of passages speak of God as taking delight in various things.[13]

Speaking of the book of Hosea, he writes:

> This powerful poem tracks a succession of feelings, from jealousy and anger to hope and joy. God's response to Israel runs the gamut of emotion a betrayed husband would feel, with the significant exception that God longs for reconciliation beyond rejection.
> . . . 'When God is portrayed as betrayed husband,' one scholar observes, 'then God's own frustrated desires and suffering are brought into focus.' 'Through this imagery, the people of Israel are enabled to *feel* God's agony.'[14]

And on the next page, he says:

> . . . Some people believe that monotheism makes God directly responsible for everything that happens in the world, but Tikva Frymer-Kensky draws a completely different conclusion. She asserts that 'the reactivity of God' that we see in his powerful emotions for Israel is essential to monotheism, and shows that the one God grants human beings a central role in determining the course of history. God is the ultimate power in reality, but God's activity

---

[13] Pinnock, et al., *The Openness of God*, 22.

[14] Pinnock, et al., *The Openness of God*, 23-24, emphasis original. According to the endnote, the citation is from Tikva Frymer-Kensky, *In the Wake of the Goddesses: Women, Culture and the Biblical Transformation of Pagan Myth* (New York: Fawcett Columbine, 1992), 147.

consists in large measure in responding to human decisions and actions. What he actually decides to do depends directly on the actions of human beings. Far from detracting from the significance of human initiative, then, monotheism heightens and enhances it.[15]

We shake our heads in wonder at these ideas. Does God indeed have frustrated desires? Does he sit on the edge of his seat, waiting for his creatures to act so he may respond? This is the logical conclusion of the denial of divine impassibility, and these scholars demonstrate powerfully its fatal consequences.

This is not a slippery slope argument. It is sober reality. Jeff Pool is deeply concerned with what he perceives to be credalism in the Southern Baptist Convention, and he realizes that when this credalism touches the doctrine of God, it teaches divine impassibility. Clark Pinnock, *within our lifetime*, migrated from a view of God's sovereignty which we would have recognized and rejoiced in to an Open Theism outside the bounds of orthodoxy, and central to his movement was his rejection of divine impassibility. Richard Rice cites the same passages of Scripture that are cited by others in our day who are seeking to modify the classical doctrine, and draws consistent anti-impassibilist conclusions from them. Does God react or respond to events in the world? We would urge the reader to reexamine these quotations and notice what is said about God. Pinnock is correct: "The conventional package of attributes is tightly drawn. Tinkering with one or two of them will not help much." To argue that the statement "without body, parts, or passions" is unclear or may have alternate interpretations flies in the face of all the evidence.

The reformulation of the doctrine of God that Pinnock claims is needed and unavoidable is underway in evangelicalism. It is evident in numerous ways. Evangelical theologians have not only advanced propositions denying or modifying God's impassibility, but have also proposed reformulations of divine immutability, divine eternity, divine omnipresence, divine knowledge or foreknowledge, and Chalcedonian Christology and its implications

---

[15] Pinnock, et al., *The Openness of God*, 25. There is no endnote marking the citation from Frymer-Kensky.

for trinitarian suffering. We interact with some of these reformulations and modifications to the doctrines of God and Christ in this book. Pinnock's claim is demonstrated by the presence of these proposals. A reformulation of the doctrine of God is underway within evangelicalism, and a trickle of professed Reformed confessionalists within the broader evangelical world are adopting these reformulations in whole or in part. This is deeply troubling, and has profound, far-reaching implications for Reformed theology. Some of these implications are explained in this book.

Our Theological Method

Our theological method is quite simple and straightforward. We provide a prolegomenon to the doctrine of divine impassibility (chapter 1) to introduce readers to some of the technical issues that will be addressed in subsequent chapters. Along with this is an introductory chapter on hermeneutics. We address the topic directly from the text of Scripture on an exegetical level in chapters 3-7. We seek to do so with a canonical, or whole-Bible, consciousness. We allow the Word of God itself first place in our understanding of texts and the doctrines contained therein. We synthesize our exegetical conclusions within the context of the entire canon of Scripture, allowing the Bible to check our exegetical method and conclusions. We believe this method is an application of what we confess in 2LCF 1:9-10. We briefly survey the history of Christian thought on the doctrine of divine impassibility (chapters 8-9). We discuss the doctrine from the perspective of systematic theology (chapters 10-12), providing a theology of divine impassibility. We analyze our Confession, showing that the doctrine is an essential part of the entire system of theology in it, and demonstrating how it fits within this overall system (chapter 13). We examine the practical and pastoral implications of divine impassibility (chapter 14). The entire book is brought to its end with a conclusion, including affirmations and denials, and two appendices.

Conclusion

The language of our Confession is understood consistently by friend and foe. We believe that modifications are necessarily incompatible with the theology expressed by these terms. We will do well to hearken to the words of Albert Mohler, where he says, "When a denomination begins to consider doctrine divisive, theology troublesome, and conviction inconvenient, consider that denomination on its way to a well deserved death."[16] Or, in the words of Charles Spurgeon:

> To say that "a creed comes between a man and his God," is to suppose that it is not true; for truth, however definitely stated, does not divide the believer from his Lord. So far as I am concerned, that which I believe I am not ashamed to state in the plainest possible language; and the truth I hold I embrace because I believe it to be the mind of God revealed in his infallible Word. How can it divide me from God who revealed it? It is one means of communion with my Lord, that I receive his words as well as himself, and submit my understanding to what I see to be taught by him. Say what he may, I accept it because he says it, and therein pay him the humble worship of my inmost soul.[17]

Spurgeon is correct. Our Confession wonderfully expresses the truth of Scripture, drawing us ever closer to our majestic God. We must never think that careful and precise adherence to it hinders our love for Christ or each other—rather, it stimulates each, simply because it does confess the truth.

We close with this plea: this is a matter of great importance. We ask our readers to study prayerfully the entire book. It is closely argued. Please do not read it partially, nor presume familiarity with its arguments. We hope this provides clear support in defense of the classical and confessional doctrine of God.

---

[16] Albert Mohler, "What Mean these Stones: Convention Sermon," 2; *Annual of the SBC* [1995]: 93. As cited in Pool, *Against Returning*, 173.

[17] Charles Haddon Spurgeon, "The Baptist Union Censure," *Metropolitan Tabernacle Pulpit* 34 (London: Passmore and Alabaster, 1888), 1ff.

Writing 335 years ago, John Owen could say of the doctrine of divine impassibility:

> *It is agreed by all* that those expressions of "repenting," "grieving," and the like, are figurative, wherein no such affections are intended as those words signify in created natures, but only an event of things like that which proceedeth from such affections.[18]

Our prayer is that these words may be written again today.

---

[18] Owen, *Works*, 21:257.

Chapter 1

Analogy and
the Doctrine of Divine Impassibility

Charles J. Rennie

The 2LCF affirms the classical and orthodox doctrine of divine impassibility with two words: "without . . . passions" (2.1). This weighty phrase is faithfully defined by Thomas Weinandy:

> Impassibility is that divine attribute whereby God is said not to experience inner emotional changes of state, whether enacted freely from within or effected by his relationship to and interaction with human beings and the created order.[1]

Does God have passions? When we hear the word *passion*, we might think of the "passion of Christ," which refers to the suffering of Christ. To say that God is impassible, or without passions, is to say that God, as God, cannot suffer. But merely to equate passion with a passive, suffering victim, or impassibility with the inability to suffer, would be an understatement.[2] As the above definition indicates, impassibility, as understood by the classical Christian tradition, does not merely exclude negative emotional changes in God, such as sorrow or pain, but any emotional change whatsoever. God's love and joy cannot grow or become further aroused. The idea is not merely that God cannot suffer, but that he cannot, in any sense, *undergo* inner emotional changes of state, "whether enacted freely from within or effected by his relationship to and interaction with . . . the created order."

---

[1] Weinandy, "Impassibility of God," in *New Catholic Encyclopedia*, 2nd ed., 7:357.

[2] For a brief and helpful discussion of the terms "affection" and "passions," see James E. Dolezal, "Still Impassible: Confessing God without Passions," *JIRBS* (2014): 127–29.

In recent days, the doctrine of divine impassibility has undergone intense criticism, particularly as it has been caricatured as a scholastic dogma rooted in metaphysical and philosophical speculation apart from Scripture. While such a criticism has a certain emotional appeal, it has no footing in reality.[3] It is without doubt that the church in all ages has used philosophy, but not for the purpose of imposing it upon the Scripture. It was used as a handmaiden in the theological task of more fully understanding the revealed truths of Scripture. Philosophy was not used to establish faith, but as a tool for faith as it seeks understanding. The Scripture itself reveals a certain metaphysic, a kind of Christian philosophy, which calls for believing reflection and Christian rationality.

The classical and confessional doctrine of divine impassibility is not the result of philosophical speculation, but is instead founded upon the revealed Word and formulated in the way of believing reflection. One look at the context in which the Confession mentions impassibility demonstrates that it flows out of the biblical conviction that

> The Lord our God is but one only living and true God; whose subsistence is in and of himself, infinite in being and perfection; whose essence cannot be comprehended by any but himself; a most pure spirit, invisible, without body, parts, or passions . . . who is immutable. (2LCF 2.1)

Therefore, impassibility is intimately related to, and a necessary consequence of, the biblical truths of God's aseity (Exod. 3:14), infinity (Psalm 147:5), perfection (Job 11:7-10), incomprehensibility (Psalm 145:3), simplicity (Deut. 6:4), spirituality (John 4:24), immutability (Mal. 3:6), and so on. Herman Bavinck notes that orthodox

> theology proceeds from these dogmas as its first principles and tries by reasoning to trace their interconnectedness, to penetrate more deeply into the knowledge of revealed truth, and to defend them against all opposition.[4]

---

[3] Bavinck, *RD*, 1:607-10. Bavinck discusses Dogma and Greek Philosophy on these pages.

[4] Bavinck, *RD*, 1:145.

The scope of Scripture (which is the glory of God) and the particular scriptural affirmations above lead to certain metaphysical conclusions that must, in turn, govern how we interpret other scriptural affirmations of a secondary sort. In other words, God's love, grief, joy, sorrow, and so forth, must be understood in a manner logically consistent with God's aseity, infinity, perfection, and the like, unless we wish to aver that God is self-contradictory, either in his essence or in his revelation. Bavinck states the matter clearly and cogently:

> Finally, it is the task of the thinking theological mind to gather up and recapitulate all truth in one system. System is the supreme desideratum in all science. Also theology does not rest until it has discovered the unity underlying revelation. It may not impose that system from without, nor press the truth into a philosophical system that is foreign to its nature. But it keeps searching until the system that is present in the object itself has been reproduced in the human mind. In all this theology operates like other sciences. Like these other sciences, it is bound to its object. In the process of thinking, it is subject to the laws that apply to this process. It too cannot violate the laws of logic with impunity.[5]

The question, therefore, regards how we are to interpret those passages of Scripture that predicate changing emotions of God in light of the metaphysical truth-claims of Scripture. It needs to be stressed that those who reject the classical understanding of impassibility on the grounds that it is too philosophical and instead adopt a biblicist approach in the name of *sola Scriptura* do not escape their own philosophical and metaphysical presuppositions, whether stated explicitly or implied. Millard J. Erickson's remark with regard to both process theologians and open theists is pertinent to the present context as well:

> Repeatedly, they criticize the traditional view, or classical theism, for adopting the Greek philosophy of a Plato or an Aristotle, but do not ask what philosophical view underlies

---

[5] Bavinck, *RD*, 1:618.

their own theology. It may well be that modern dynamic or process philosophy is preferable to Greek metaphysics. That, however, is what must be debated, rather than simply criticizing the latter view, while giving the impression that their view is not based upon an alternative philosophy, but is simply the way things are.[6]

The conclusion that God is capable of emotional changes of state *unwittingly* presupposes certain unbiblical and philosophically dubious conclusions about God, namely, that he is mutable, finite, perfectible, composite, and comprehensible. This may not be the intention of those who have sought to modify the doctrine of divine impassibility, but motives and intentions notwithstanding, this is the logical implication of the rejection or modification of this confessional doctrine. The sound principles of logic cannot be violated with impunity. Ideas have consequences.

A biblical metaphysic must cohere, or be consistent with what we know on the basis of revelation. We believe and know that God is incomprehensible, immutable, simple, infinite, and perfect, and therefore we must seek to understand God's emotions or affections within that biblical and logical framework. As such, we must recognize that, because God precedes our knowledge of God, metaphysics precedes epistemology; our theory of knowledge, and therefore our hermeneutical approach, rests upon certain metaphysical conclusions. We will argue that, because God is incomprehensible and fundamentally different from us (metaphysical assumptions), those passages which predicate changing emotions or affections of God must be understood in the mode of analogy (epistemological conclusion).

Before developing these claims, an additional word of introduction is in order. By the very nature of the topic under consideration, the use of certain technical philosophical and theological terminology is unavoidable. Like any other field of study, philosophy and theology have historically employed certain words and concepts that are designed to communicate truth with precision and clarity. The aim is to explain these in a

---

6 Millard J. Erickson, "God and Change," *Southern Baptist Journal of Theology* 1/2 (1997): 51.

straightforward manner, while at the same time recognizing that we have entered the proverbial deep waters. God, indeed, is incomprehensible, and yet knowable.

By way of prolegomenon, we will consider the real distinction between act and potency as a way of accounting for *both* permanency *and* change, or being *and* becoming. God is pure actuality, whereas every creature is composed of act *and* potency. There is, therefore, a real distinction between the Creator's mode of being (i.e., infinite) and the creature's mode of being (i.e., finite). This will inevitably lead to a discussion about analogical predication, since the distinction between Creator and creature necessarily raises the question of how language which is drawn from the creature's experience and knowledge can be predicated of God. For example, to what extent is God's love like the creature's love? If God's being is not of the same order, should we assume that his love must be of the same order? Or is God's love and being impassible? It would be difficult to address such questions in a manner consistent with both the Reformed tradition and the biblical distinction between Creator and creature without a theological understanding of God as pure act (*actus purus*), or as our Confession puts it, "a most pure Spirit" (2LCF 2.1).

Act and Potency

The concept of act-potency is simple, but has far-reaching theological implications. We will leave the reader to explore its many implications and seek only to present it here with a broad stroke. Insofar as the concept was integrated into the church's theological discourse, we may rest assured that it was not imposed upon the Scriptures, but rather introduced as a handmaiden to help the church better understand what it had already believed on the authority of Scripture alone (i.e., faith seeking understanding).[7]

---

[7] For a brief discussion of how sixteenth- and seventeenth-century Reformed theology selectively and critically employed the philosophy of Aristotle, and particularly the distinction between act and potency, see T. Theo J. Pleizier and Maarten Wisse, "'As the Philosopher Says': Aristotle," in Willem J. van Asselt, with T. Theo J. Pleizier, Pieter L. Rouwendal, and Maarten Wisse, *Introduction to Reformed Scholasticism*, trans. Albert Gootjes (Grand Rapids: Reformation Heritage

Aristotle began his book on metaphysics in dialogue with the well-known philosophical differences over the nature of being (i.e., permanence) and becoming (i.e., change). How can something cease to be what it is and become something else? Previously, philosophers had argued that change would require being to arise out of non-being, and since non-being is nothing and being cannot come out of nothing, change must be impossible.

Aristotle agreed with the premise that being cannot come from non-being, but disagreed with the assumption that change was therefore impossible. Rather, according to Aristotle, change involves one sort of being arising out of another sort of being. Take, for instance, the slab of marble Michelangelo used to make the sculpture of David. As a slab, it was a *being-in-act*, what it *actually* was, but as such, it also had *being-in-potency* with respect to the slab's *potential* to become a sculpture. When Michelangelo sculpted the slab into the likeness of David, its potential was actualized (or realized); its potential to become a sculpture was perfected. One sort of being (the sculpture in act) arose from another sort of being (the slab in potency for becoming a sculpture).

A real distinction must be made between being-in-potency and being-in-act. It is a real distinction because the difference exists in reality, in truth, and in the object itself, and not merely in how we think about the object. This real distinction is a reminder that potency must be grounded in actuality. Even though the Michelangelo sculpture did not have *actual* being prior to being sculpted, it did have *potential* being (i.e., potency for being actually sculpted). There is some*thing* inherent in the nature of a marble slab that gives it the potential to become an actual sculpture of a man, while at the same time lacking the potential to become an actual living man. The possibility of change, and the nature of that change, is therefore limited by a thing's potency, and a thing's potency is always grounded in actuality. In other words, the range of change that a thing may potentially undergo is determined and limited by the nature and mode of the thing *that actually is*. Given the nature of *what a man actually is*, he has the potential to have his compassion grow and his love aroused, but by virtue of the same nature, he

---

Books, 2011), 27-44. Se Muller, *PRRD*, 1:360-82; and Carl. R Trueman, *The Claims of Truth: John Owen's Trinitarian Theology* (Carlisle: Paternoster, 1998), 29-44.

does not have the potential *to be* love. Likewise, given *what God actually is*, infinite, simple, and immutable in perfection, not only must we say that God *is* infinite, simple, and immutable love, but that he has no potential to be otherwise. God is pure act, pure being without becoming. He is infinite in perfection. If he were to have potency for greater compassion or greater affectional capacity, he would not have been, or yet be, perfect. Likewise, if his joy were at any moment displaced by sorrow, he would no longer be perfect. Indeed, if he were to have the potential to change in any regard whatsoever, he would not be immutable.

The issue at stake in the doctrine of divine impassibility is not an issue of whether or not God has something similar to emotions, though the very language itself is anthropopathic; the issue is whether or not such affections in God essentially, relationally, or in any other way change. Likewise, the issue is neither merely whether the change is negative or positive nor whether it comes from without or within. The fundamental issue is whether or not passive potency of any kind is predicated of God.[8] Given *what he actually is*, infinite and immutable, and all other divine perfections, there can be no passive potency in God to be other than he is. He says clearly, "I AM WHO I AM" (Exod. 3:14).

The pure actuality of God underscores the decisive distinction between the Creator and creature.

> Of old You laid the foundation of the earth, And the heavens *are* the work of Your hands. 26 They will perish, but You will endure; . . . And they will be changed. 27 But You *are* the same . . . (Psalm 102:25-27)

---

[8] Thomas Aquinas' third definition of so-called passions (*pati*) demonstrates that "passion" can refer to any change, positive or negative, from act to potency. To say that God is "without passions" means that he cannot undergo any kind of change. "Thirdly, in a wide sense (*communiter*) a thing is said to be *pati*, from the very fact that what is in potentiality to something receives that to which it was in potentiality, without being deprived of anything. And accordingly, whatever passes from potentiality to act, may be said to be *pati*, even when it is perfected. And thus with us to understand is to be *pati*." *Summa Theologica*, trans. Fathers of the English Dominican Province (Notre Dame, IN: Christian Classics, 1981), I.a q.79 a.2.

He effects change in all things, but is himself not changed, nor does he have the need or the potential to do so. Bavinck concludes:

> Nevertheless, the doctrine of God's immutability is highly significant for religion. The difference between the Creator and the creature hinges on the contrast between being and becoming. All that is creaturely is in process of becoming. It is changeable, constantly striving, in search of rest and satisfaction, and finds this rest only in him who is pure being without becoming. . . . Christian theology frequently also expressed this last point in the term "pure actuality" (*purus actua*).[9]

The Analogy of Being

The question arises, however, "How can we speak, or make predications, of a God who is pure act, infinite, and essentially different from us?" To be sure, true knowledge of God is possible only on the basis of his self-revelation in Scripture, but it is not enough simply to say, "The Bible says this or that about God." The question that always remains is, "When the Bible says this or that about God, what does it mean?" The question is one of language and being, or language predicated of this or that being. This will be fleshed out below, but it may be observed at the outset that generally there are three modes or kinds of predications: univocal, equivocal, and analogical.

A quality or property is said to be predicated of two beings univocally when the predicate is used in an identical way, with the same sense, in both cases. For example, "Bilbo is a hobbit," and "Frodo is a hobbit." Hobbitness is predicated of both, and what it means for Bilbo to possess hobbitness is univocally the same for Frodo. Conversely, a word may be equivocal when it is used in an unrelated way with regard to two or more beings. Zanchi uses the example of the different senses of the word ram, which may refer to an "animal, and a ram for the means by which the walls of the city are razed, and a ram for the stars of heaven," to which we may also

---

[9] Bavinck, *RD*, 2:156-57.

add the memory of a computer.[10] Although the word is the same in each case, the definitions and senses are not only different, but unrelated. Analogical predication, on the other hand, is neither univocal nor equivocal in identity, but analogical in similarity. An analogy may be defined generally as the affirmation of a similarity "between some feature common to two different realities that extends or expands our knowledge of one or the other, or both of them."[11] In other words, while the predication does not imply an identical sense for both realities, neither are they unrelated; there is a similar sense proportionate to the mode of each being. Edward Feser explains:

> The notion of a proportionate similarity can be illustrated by the analogical use of a term like "seeing," as when one says "I see the tree in front of me" and "I see that the Pythagorean theorem is true." These are obviously not univocal uses, since the way one sees with one's intellect is radically different from the way one sees with one's eyes. But they are not completely unrelated, as the meanings of equivocal terms are. For the eyes are to a tree as the intellect is to the Pythagorean theorem.[12]

The eye's relationship to the tree not only provides the foundation for the similarity of the intellect's relationship to the Pythagorean

---

[10] Girolamo Zanchi, *De Natura Dei seu de divinis attributis, lib.* V, (Heidelberg: Jacob Mylius, 1577), *1.x.q.8* (p. 25). *Aequivoca sunt, quorum etsi idem nomen est; alia tamen longé; diuersa est ratio & defintio, ut aries, animal: & aries pro machinamento, quo moenia ciuitatis diruuntur: & aries pro sydere coelesti.*

[11] Robert Masson, "Analogy as Higher-Order Metaphor in Aquinas," in *Divine Transcendence and Immanence in the Works of Thomas Aquinas*, eds. Harm Goris, Herwi Rikhof, and Henk Schoot (Walpole, MA: Peeters Leuven, 2009), 115.

[12] Edward Feser, *Scholastic Metaphysics: A Contemporary Introduction* (Germany: Editiones Scholasticae, 2014), 259. The same illustration was given by the Scottish Reformer Robert Baron, *theologi ac philosophi celeberrimi, Metaphysica generalis accedunt nunc primum quae supererant ex parte speciali : omnia ad usum theologia accommodata, opus postumum, ex muséo Antonii Clememtii Zirizaei* (London: R. Danielis), 422, concluding that "the similitude is proportional, and similarity of these perceptions is to say, that as the perception of the eye to the eye, so, too, a mental to the mind." *similitudinem proportionalem, similitudo autem illarum perceptionum est, quod sicut se habet ocularis perceptio ad oculum, ita etiam mentalis ad mentem.*

theorem, but also expands our knowledge of the nature of that relationship. All predication of the divine essence and attributes is of this sort, that is, analogical predication.

Richard A. Muller has pointed out that there was a general consensus among the early and late Reformed orthodox regarding the doctrine of analogy, or analogical predication, understood predominantly from a Thomistic perspective which resisted the notion of a core of univocity in the language of predication with regard to God and creatures. The doctrine of analogy was stock-in-trade in the sixteenth and seventeenth centuries, enjoying a relatively precise and established meaning.[13] In today's theological context, however, although it is popular to cite the analogical proviso, its precise meaning can no longer be assumed. As a result of ambiguous formulations and inconsistency in fleshing out the doctrine, what was once employed in defense of divine impassibility is now marshaled by evangelicals and Reformed alike in defense of its revision.[14] Not surprisingly, the result has been a

---

[13] Richard A. Muller, "Not Scotist: Understandings of being, univocity, and analogy in early-modern Reformed thought," *Reformation & Renaissance Review* 14:2 (2012): 127-50. It is not our intention to minimize the various developments and nuances among the Reformed Scholastics. Relative to the present state of theological discourse, however, there was an undeniable consensus with regard to the doctrine.

[14] Such a trend is neither limited to the doctrine of divine impassibility nor confined to the evangelical and Reformed contexts. For example, Gregory Boyd, in his defense of Open Theism, ironically purports that his view is the one that emerges from a consistent application of the doctrine of analogy. It could be pointed out that he obscures the distinction between proper and improper analogies and flattens the hermeneutical principles which would identify them respectively, but our point here is merely to illustrate how analogy is used as a kind of univocal catch-all category of gradual steps between the Creator and the creature. Boyd writes, "There is, of course, a sense in which all of language about God is analogical. When we say God loves, judges or foreknows aspects of the future, for example, we are saying that he does things like what we do when we love, judge or know things ahead of time—but he does so without any attendant imperfections. Still, the classical tradition holds that language about, say, God's changing his mind was nonliteral in a way that, say, language about God's foreknowing the future was not. The latter describes God as he really is; the former does not. My argument is simply that the second motif describes God as he really is just as much as the first motif does. God really does love, judge and foreknow aspects of the future. In this sense we should take Scriptures that depict God as loving, judging and foreknowing 'literally.' God really does change his mind, regret decisions and anticipate open possibilities in the future. We should take

drift toward univocity, or a so-called univocal core.[15]

Kevin Vanhoozer recites the objection of Nicholas Wolterstorff with sympathy:

> [I]f God cannot be affected by anything other than himself, then how are we to understand God's knowledge of human suffering and human loss? Is this something that God can know, or not? Can a God who does not experience suffering in some sense be said to "know" particular instances of suffering in our world? More pointedly: can a God who is unable to sympathize be said to love?[16]

Elsewhere, he attempts to hedge this assumption by an appeal to the doctrine of analogy, but one that, in practice, is ambiguous enough to surrender to univocal assumptions about God's emotions. Perfected human love involves sympathetic suffering in the face of human suffering. Therefore, if God's love is to mean anything at all, it must involve the same sort of thing. With the same pervading assumption, but with far less ambiguity, Donald Macleod writes:

> Consequently, when the New Testament appeals to the moral force and constraint of Calvary, it is on the involvement of God the Father that it frequently focuses. The cross is the expression of his love and of *his* pity (John 3:16, Rom. 8:32). *He* is the One whose conduct is the model

---

these Scriptures just as 'literally' as we take those supporting the first motif." See "The Open-Theism View," in *Divine Foreknowledge: Four Views,* ed. James K. Beilby and Paul R. Eddy (Downers Grove, IL: IVP Academic, 2001), 23, n. 12.

[15] For example, in *Covenant and Eschatology* (Louisville: Westminster John Knox Press, 2002), 88, Michael S. Horton locates the univocal core in Christ: "Consequently, we could say that Jesus was and remains the univocal core of divine action, discourse, and being."

[16] Kevin J. Vanhoozer, *First Theology: God, Scripture, & Hermeneutics* (Downers Grove, IL: InterVarsity Press, 2002), 75. Vanhoozer later concludes that God is impassible in precisely the way Jesus is impeccable, unwittingly predicating a univocal relationship between God as God and Jesus as man (93). The weight of this argument, which is cited favorably by Horton as well, will be evaluated when we consider the relationship between impassibility and Christology. It is sufficient for our purpose here to note that such an argument unhappily presupposes a univocal core.

of self-denial and cross bearing. *He* is the One who bore the cost of redemption. Indeed, if he is so immobile and so passionless that Calvary cost him nothing, all talk of him must cease because our language about him is meaningless. If Calvary was painless for him, we are not made in his image and he does not love with our love. When Abraham offered Isaac, there was pain; when Jacob lost Joseph, there was pain; when David lost Absalom, there was pain. If things were different when God gave up his Son then either he does not love his Son or his love is so radically different from ours as to be meaningless. . . . But he suffered seeing the Son suffering and the even greater (and quite unfathomable) agony of being the One who had to bruise and forsake him.[17]

Macleod's premise is there must be a univocal core, such that God the Father suffered the same kind of pain that Abraham must have suffered when he proceeded to offer Isaac. If not, Macleod assumes, all talk of God's love is meaningless. God's love is different from our love, but if it is so different (because God is so different) that it doesn't involve such suffering as we suffer when we lose a son, then it must be meaningless. In other words, divine love and human love are analogical until they're not; if there is no univocal core, such predications of love must be equivocal. With rhetorical flare, Macleod tells us that either the Father felt agony and pain as the one who bruised the Son, or else the text is meaningless. But what is to prevent us from forcing the same univocal assumptions upon texts like Isaiah 53:10: "Yet it pleased the LORD to bruise Him." Was the Father bereaved or pleased (delighted!)? Are we to conclude from Isaiah 53 that if the Father doesn't delight in the death of his Son, in the sort of way we experience delight, that the text is meaningless?

William Placher argues that this drift toward univocity has been one of the primary causes of what he calls "the domestication of transcendence."[18] Perhaps this has never been more apparent than with regard to the doctrine of divine impassibility. Language about

---

[17] Donald Macleod, *From Glory to Golgotha* (Fearn, Ross-Shire, Scotland: Christian Focus Publications, 2002), 107-08.

[18] William Placher, *The Domestication of Transcendence: How Modern Thinking about God went Wrong* (Louisville, KY: Westminster John Knox Press, 1996), 10.

God that would have traditionally been considered either analogical or metaphorical is now commonly interpreted according to a "hierarchical series of gradual steps between creatures and their Creator," an analogical-until-it's-not proviso.[19] This "domestication of transcendence" and the revisionist approach to divine impassibility find their roots in an ambiguous doctrine of analogy. This has opened the door to a view of a God who, at least with regard to impassibility, has begun to resemble more of our image than *vice versa*. But neither has this revision of analogy, one that has practically drifted toward univocity, appeared out of nowhere. Feser is surely correct that such a drift toward univocity is the inevitable result of either an explicit or implicit rejection (perhaps neglect) of the real distinction between act and potency.[20] As Aquinas argued long ago, "potency and act are a complete division of being. Hence, whatever is must be either pure act or a unit composed of potency and act," so that there can be no univocal core of being predicated of the Creator (who is pure act) and creature (who is composed of act and potency).[21] Neglect of this distinction, or dismissing it altogether, will inevitably produce a view of analogy that will eventually surrender divine discourse to a univocal concept of being, in which the infinite God is nothing more than a greater version of ourselves, a god in our image.

Analogy and Mode of Being

In order to understand why the Reformed approach to the predication of divine attributes has historically rejected the shift toward a univocal core, we must first consider the general concept of the analogy of being (*analogia entis*).[22] The importance of this exercise can be seen in the common, though erroneous, assumption

---

[19] Gregory Rocca, "'Creatio ex nihilo' and the Being of Creatures: God's Creative Act and the Transcendence-Immanence Distinction in Aquinas," in *Divine Transcendence and Immanence in the Works of Thomas Aquinas*, 2.

[20] Feser, *Scholastic Metaphysics*, 262.

[21] Bernard Wuellner, *Summary of Scholastic Principles* (Chicago: Loyola University Press, 1956), 120.

[22] For a brief and accessible exposition of Aquinas' argument for the *analogia entis*, see Joseph Bobik, *Aquinas on Being and Essence: A Translation and Interpretation* (Notre Dame, IN: University of Notre Dame Press, 2004), 115-18.

stated by D. A. Carson:

> But this way of wording things [i.e., that God is impassible in the sense that he has no passions, or emotions, that make him vulnerable from the outside or cause him to lose control] guards the most important values in impassibility and still insists that God's love is real love, of the same genus as the best of love displayed by God's image-bearers.[23]

The idea that God's love and man's love are of the same genus necessarily assumes that God's being and man's being are also of the same genus. The resulting conclusion is that what may be predicated of love in man may be predicated of love in God, albeit more perfectly. Notwithstanding the differences, the result of such univocity is a view of God that is nothing more than the creature writ large. Conversely, we will argue, after a brief consideration of the place of "being" within a logical taxonomy, that "being" cannot refer to, or fall within, a genus. Moreover, since God's love is identical to his being, neither can God's love and man's love be considered within the same genus. Love stands in a different relationship to the divine being than it does to the creature's being—a difference which is neither univocal nor equivocal, but analogical.

Taxonomy, whether logical or biological, is the branch of science concerned with the classification of beings according to the whatness or essence of one being relative to other beings. Created beings (i.e., what-exists or something-out-there) are identified and distinguished one from another by gradual steps from the more general to the more specific, ultimately from genus to species. For example, a logical taxonomy with regard to man might identify the genus as animal and differentiate the species of man from others within the same genus as a *rational*-animal. For our present purposes, it is important to note that the genus does not determinately express the *whole* essence that is signified by the species. Animal, taken as the genus, does not exclude the *whole* essence of what it means to be a rational-animal, but neither does it

---

[23] D. A. Carson, *The Difficult Doctrine of the Love of God* (Wheaton, IL: Crossway Books, 2000), 61.

determinately signify it, for there are other non-rational species within the same animal genus (i.e., canines, bovines, etc.). Therefore, the essence of the species man is its genus (i.e., animal) *and* its species' specific difference (i.e., rational), thus a rational-animal. In other words, the genus only signifies *part* of the essence which is more precisely signified and differentiated by the species. It is noteworthy that the genus animal may be predicated univocally of dogs, cows, and man according to their undifferentiated modes of being; they are all animals, and none are more or less an animal than the other. The specific difference among the species (e.g., rational and non-rational) is left undetermined by the genus and is a distinction *extrinsic* to that which is signified by the genus. Yet there is nothing that may be *more* than, or extrinsic to, being, and therefore being is unique in that it cannot be considered a genus.

As Feser rightly points out:

> There is nothing that can serve as a specific difference to mark out something as a species within being considered as a purported genus, because the only thing extrinsic to being is non-being or nothing, and non-being or nothing cannot differentiate anything, precisely *because* it is nothing.[24]

That which differentiates the species is outside or beyond the genus, for it is not determinately signified by the genus. And although we may speak of different beings, the differences are not something outside of or beyond what is signified by being. "Only *nothing* is outside being, and nothing cannot be added to being so as to constitute an ultimate genus of being."[25]

What being expresses cannot be a genus, and therefore we must always consider that which is predicated proportionate to its *particular* mode of being. The significance of this may be illustrated with the word *life*, or *existence*. Life may be predicated of different beings: God, angels, and man, etc. If being were considered the ultimate genera under which every "thing" else is differentiated, being would be predicated univocally of God, angels, and man, just as animal is predicated univocally of dogs, cows, and man. Therefore, life also would be predicated univocally of each, for each

---

[24] Feser, *Scholastic Metaphysics*, 258.
[25] Bobik , *Aquinas on Being and Essence*, 116-17.

would partake of life according to the same general mode of being. This is not the case, however. Life, or existence, has a different relationship to each mode of being (i.e., the essence/nature of each). For example, the existence of men and angels is not identical to their respective essences, but is contingent upon the will of God (Acts 17:28; cf. Rev. 4:11). Moreover, the existence of man actualizes the essence of something that is both material and immaterial, whereas the existence of angels actualizes the essence of something purely immaterial. Life is predicated of both, but its relationship to each differs according to its particular mode of being, proportionate to the distinct nature of their being, and therefore cannot be univocal.

That being cannot be predicated univocally is all the more evident when we are speaking about God, in whom existence and essence are identical. God *is* his existence and has life in himself (John 5:26); it is not of the essence of men or angels to exist, but it is for God. Moreover, unlike created beings, God is not identified, or composed, of a genus and species. He is not part of a divine genus within which he may be differentiated from, and identified relative to, other species.

> Though creatures bear the image of God's existence and attributes, their similarity to God is better understood as analogical rather than univocal. The manner in which God exists and possesses attributes is so radically unlike anything found in creatures that he cannot be classified together with them in a single order of being or as the highest link on a great chain of being. As the one who ultimately accounts for being in general, as its first and final cause, God does not stand within that general ontological order.[26]

He does not belong to any genus or taxonomy, for he says, "To whom will you liken Me, and make *Me* equal and compare Me, that we should be alike?" (Isa. 46:5). There is no genus "God." God is that being which is unlike every other being, who is pure act and infinite in perfection (Exod. 15:11; 2 Sam. 7:22; Psalm 50:21; Isa. 46:5). There is infinitely greater difference between God and man,

---

[26] James E. Dolezal, *God without Parts: Divine Simplicity and the Metaphysics of God's Absoluteness* (Eugene, OR: Pickwick Publications, 2011), 29.

than between man and beast. Therefore, the mode of God's being and the mode of the creature's being differ, not simply by a hierarchy of qualitative and quantitative steps between them, but *quidditatively*, being utterly different in essence. Likewise, life, love, goodness, and so forth can no more be predicated univocally of God and man than can being, for God's life, love, etc., are as different from ours as his being is from ours.[27]

Yet, neither is life and being predicated of God and man equivocally, for neither is predicated in an unrelated sense. There is a similarity or analogy that is grounded in creation *ex nihilo* and the image of God (more on this below), *so that the divine life stands in relation to the divine nature in a mode proportionately similar to the way human life stands in relation to human nature.* In the same way, we must understand divine and human love, goodness, wisdom, and so forth, the nature of each predication being proportionately understood according to its peculiar mode of being.

Analogy and Proper and Improper Proportionality

Although all scriptural analogies convey some truth about God, they do not all do so in the same way. There are two kinds of analogies that should be considered, proper and improper (metaphorical), and two elements that define them. The first element is common to both, in that the thing predicated is intrinsic to both analogates.[28] For example, life is intrinsic (and proper) to God and creatures. What may be less obvious, however, is how that which is improper, or metaphorical, predicates something intrinsic to both analogates. Suffice it to say for the moment that the distinction between proper and improper predication is not *whether* that which is predicated exists intrinsically in both analogates, but in *how* it exists in them. Thus the second element, and that wherein

---

[27] Zanchi, *De Natura Dei, 1.x.q.8* (26).

[28] Two things should be noted. First, intrinsic does not mean univocal. Second, this distinction distinguishes both kinds of analogies of proportionality from analogies of attribution. It doesn't serve our present interest to elaborate on the latter sort of analogy. An example of an analogy of attribution, however, would be "George is healthy" and "This diet is healthy." Healthy is predicated intrinsically of George, but not of the diet. Health is attributed to the diet because it is the sort of diet that will produce health in George.

they differ, is the question of whether or not that which is intrinsic to both analogates exists in them *formally* or *figuratively*. If that which is predicated exists figuratively in one of the analogates, it is an improper predication; and if it exists formally in both it is a proper predication. Life is predicated properly of God and man because life exists formally in both. If we were to say, however, "That is a lion," referring to the animal at the zoo, and "George is a lion," referring to your friend George, although that to which "lion" refers is predicated of both intrinsically, it does not exist in both formally. While that to which lion refers exists in the animal formally, it exists within the man figuratively (or metaphorically).[29] There is, after all, something in George that corresponds to the likeness of a lion (i.e., fierceness, strength; cf. Gen. 49:8-9), although the form, or nature, of a lion is not actually in him.[30]

It would be a mistake, therefore, to assume that metaphorical or improper predication, if not taken literally, must be meaningless.[31] Rather, metaphors relax the ordinary rules of meaning in order to communicate, not what God *is*, but what he *is like*. Traditionally, such metaphors have been classified as either anthropomorphisms (i.e., attributing to God human shape or body) or anthropopathisms (i.e., attributing to God human passions). Regarding the former, but applicable to both, Stephen Charnock observes:

> All such representations are to signify the acts of God, as they bear some likeness to those which we perform by those members he ascribes to himself. So that those members ascribed to him rather note his visible operations to us, than his invisible nature; and signify that God doth some works

---

[29] An example of this manner of speech among the Protestant Scholastics is Robert Baron's illustration of the "smiling meadow" (cf. Isa. 35:1), where he concludes that the nature of a smile is "in it metaphorically." Baron, *Metaphysics*, 423.

[30] Feser, *Scholastic Metaphysics*, 256-58.

[31] This is a common objection among liberals and evangelicals alike, though the latter's objection is typically and inconsistently confined to biblical anthropopathisms. Gregory Boyd, "The Open-Theism View," in *Divine Foreknowledge: Four Views*, 192, criticizes evangelicals for being inconsistent. For an example within the evangelical camp, see Rob Lister, *God is Impassible and Impassioned: Toward a Theology of Divine Emotion* (Wheaton, IL: Crossway, 2013), 107-22.

like to those which men do by the assistance of those organs of their bodies.[32]

For example, Scripture frequently attributes eyes to God. Given *what God actually is*, a most pure Spirit, eyes are not predicated of God *formally* (or properly), but *figuratively* after the manner of men. Thus, God's "eye" signifies God's omniscience (Prov. 5:21; Zech. 4:10) and his watch care over his people (Psalm 34:15a; Prov. 15:3).

> Therefore, we must not conceive of the visible [descriptions of the] Deity according to the letter of such expressions, but the true intent of them. . . . We must not conceive of God according to the letter, but the design of the metaphor.[33]

In the same way, Scripture frequently attributes to God a changing array of emotions after the manner of men. For instance, God is said to be afflicted (i.e., sympathetic suffering) in the affliction of his people (Isa. 63:9). Given *what God actually is*, infinite and immutable (Mal. 3:6; James 1:17), it should be obvious that affliction is not predicated of God *formally* (or properly), but *figuratively*, for if affliction were in God *formally* it would require potency in God *for* affliction. Such language does not describe God as he is (i.e., his invisible nature), but what he is like toward his people (i.e., his visible operations). His love for his children is *like* that of a father who is afflicted in the affliction of his children, in that he acts so as to deliver them from their affliction as surely *as if* it were his own. All such representations signify the visible operations of God, as they bear some likeness to those which we perform under similar conditions, so that the *form* of affliction itself is not in God. However, because God's visible operations (i.e., the effects) reveal God's invisible nature (i.e., the cause), we must also affirm that such affliction is in God *figuratively*, that is, it *signifies* the unfailing and unchanging love of God for his people even in their affliction. Likewise, all other passions that would imply change in God (e.g., grief, sorrow, anger, etc.), should be interpreted, not

---

[32] Stephen Charnock, *The Existence and Attributes of God*, 2 vols. (1853; reprint, Grand Rapids: Baker Book House, 2000), 1:189.

[33] Charnock, *Existence and Attributes*, 1:190.

according to the letter, but the design of the metaphor, and in a manner both consistent with the whole of Scripture and suitable to the divine perfections.[34] They reveal to us, not what he *is*, but what he *is like*.

Herein lies the genius of analogies of improper (metaphorical) proportionality. They should not be thought of as an inferior mode of revelation, for in a most accessible manner they convey truth about God as well as man. Metaphors communicate something about God according to the manner of men, so that if God were a man, such a man he would be. Although affliction is only *figuratively* in God, the metaphor presupposes that it may be *formally* in man. When he is said to be afflicted in the affliction of others, should we therefore not especially learn what it means for us to love our neighbor as ourselves? And when he is said to grieve over sin, should we not especially learn to do likewise? Moreover, metaphorical predication is more befitting the sort of knowledge we have of God in this life. It reminds us that what is obviously true of metaphor is in fact true of all predication about God, that

> what He is not is clearer to us than what He is. Therefore similitudes drawn from things farthest away from God form within us a truer estimate that God is above whatsoever we may say or think of Him.[35]

Analogies of *proper* proportionality differ from those which are *improper* insofar as that which is predicated exists formally in each analogate. For example, love is properly predicated of God and of man because it is both intrinsic to and formally in both. Whereas proper (i.e., non-figurative) predication, however, can easily give us the impression that we can know God as he is, improper (i.e., figurative) predication reminds us that this is not so. Although love is proper to both God and man, it stands in relation to the divine nature in a mode proportionately similar to the way human love stands in relation to human nature. Precisely for this reason, we

---

[34] Owen, *Works*, 12:111. Such metaphors must be "understood . . . in such a sense as may answer the meaning of the figurative expression, assigning them their truth in the utmost, and yet to be interpreted in a suitableness to divine perfection and blessedness."

[35] Aquinas, *Summa Theologica*, I.a q.1 a.9.

may expect that every proper analogy between God and man will convey more dissimilarity than similarity, insofar as God's being is more dissimilar than similar to our being. Therefore, one thing remains to be considered, namely, how we are to interpret analogies of proper proportionality so as to adequately account for both the similarities and the dissimilarities.

Analogy and the Threefold Way of Knowing God

The Reformed orthodox approached the problem of knowledge and language concerning God according to a threefold biblical pattern: the way of causation (*via causalitatis*), the way of negation or removal (*via negationis*), and the way of eminence or perfection (*via eminentiae*).[36] The way of causation provides the metaphysical foundation for all the similarities between Creator and creature so that knowledge and language of God can be possible. The way of negation accounts for the dissimilarities that arise on account of the distance between the Creator and creature, whereas the way of eminence reminds us that the Creator is always infinitely greater than the creaturely predications that reveal him. Muller explains:

> The "way of causation" understands that a cause can be known in some manner from its effects. . . . By the "way of eminence" we attribute eminently to God all of the "perfections" known from creatures—while by the "way of negation we remove from God the imperfections known from creatures."[37]

This threefold way of knowing God is not a means for speculative and philosophical deductions that explain away the Scripture, but, as will be shown, a biblical pattern of classification that aims at better understanding what the Scripture says about God. It is not a means for undermining the revealed "language of

---

[36] For a thorough introduction to this topic see Gregory P. Rocca, *Speaking the Incomprehensible God: Thomas Aquinas on the Interplay of Positive and Negative Theology* (Washington, D.C.: Catholic University of America Press, 2004).

[37] Muller, *PRRD*, 3:166. The last part of Muller's statement is a quotation of Turretin.

faith," but rather a threefold means of interpreting that language faithfully.

> All three ways are at work in any statement we make. All we say of God is grounded in divine causality, seeks to remove creaturely imperfections from him, and intends to eminently affirm unlimited perfection. When we call God 'good,' for instance, we recognize (by way of causality) that he is the ultimate cause of goodness in creatures, and (by way of negation) that he is not good in the limited mode of creatures, and (by way of eminence) that he is good in a surpassing way.[38]

The Via Causalitatis

Our consideration naturally begins with the metaphysical foundation of all our language about God, the way of causation, or creation. Without a point of similarity between Creator and creature that is grounded in reality, we have no assurance that the analogies we use are appropriate for an incomprehensible God, or whether a knowledge of the one will lead to a knowledge of the other.[39] Without such a foundation, the analogy itself becomes equivocal, and our knowledge of God swings as the proverbial pendulum into nothing more than a univocal, yet empty, projection of ourselves.

Contemporary theology has tended to agree with the conclusion that our language for God must have a metaphysical foundation if it is to mean anything at all, and it must mean something. What becomes problematic is how this foundation is often conceived. Recognizing the need for such a foundation, Michael S. Horton, an otherwise ardent defender of the doctrine of analogy, concludes:

> Without a univocal core, critics have correctly insisted, there is no way of determining whether the analogies we use for an unknown God are apt. But the New Testament represents

---

[38] Michael Dodds, *The Unchanging God of Love: Thomas Aquinas & Contemporary Theology on Divine Immutability* (Washington, D.C.: Catholic University of America Press, 2008), 138.

[39] Zanchi, *De Natura Dei*, 26.

Jesus Christ as the univocal core of God.[40]

It is often assumed, if not stated, that a univocal core between the Creator and creature is more than a mere possibility, but rather is of the utmost necessity in order for our language about God to have any meaning at all. It is precisely this assumption that unintentionally opens the door to a view of analogy that, when pressed with regard to God's so-called emotions, surrenders to a univocal gradation of hierarchal steps between God and man. To suppose a univocal core as the foundation for analogy is to lose analogy altogether; or, our language about God is analogical until it is not!

Rejecting the possibility — much more the need — for a univocal core, the Reformed orthodox, drawing upon a long-standing tradition, maintained a principle of causation affirmed in the Scripture and grounded in creation *ex nihilo*. This principle of proportionate causality affirms that "[w]hatever is in an effect must be in its *total* cause in some way or other, whether *formally*, *virtually*, or *eminently*."[41] Simply put, we may know something about the cause (i.e., God) from the effect (i.e., creation). The Reformed orthodox observed that Jesus' statement in Matthew 7:16 presupposes a principle of causation, so that one's heart (i.e., the cause) is revealed by one's conduct (i.e., the effect); "You will know them by their fruits." Likewise, Paul affirmed the same principle on a higher level:

> For the wrath of God is revealed from heaven against all ungodliness and unrighteousness of men, who suppress the truth in unrighteousness, 19 because what may be known of God is manifest in them, for God has shown *it* to them. 20 For since the creation of the world His invisible *attributes* are clearly seen, being understood by the things that are made, *even* His eternal power and Godhead, so that they are without excuse (Rom. 1:18-20)

---

[40] Horton, *Covenant and Eschatology*, 97. Dr. Horton has pointed out, through personal correspondence, that he intentionally omitted any reference to Christ as the univocal core in his more recent work, *The Christian Faith: A Systematic Theology for Pilgrims on the Way* (Grand Rapids: Zondervan, 2011).

[41] Feser, *Scholastic Metaphysics*, 154-59.

Therefore, the doctrine of creation *ex nihilo* provides the metaphysical foundation for all of our language about God, as he has revealed what he is like by what he has made. Like an artist, he has ordered and designed creation according to his own likeness so that his invisible attributes can be understood by the things that are made. Citing Aquinas, Gregory Rocca explains:

> The divine wisdom 'has carefully devised the order of the universe, which consists in the distinction of all things', and 'all created realities are therefore compared to God as products of art are to an artist, but the artist brings forth into being the products of art through the direction of his wisdom and understanding.' Since God creates from nothing, there is nothing 'out there' to function as a template for God's creativity, nor is there anything 'out there' that can compel or drive that creativity. God's loving will chooses from eternity whether to create and directs God's understanding and wisdom to look to the divine essence for patterns of divine imitability.[42]

There is no such thing as *pure* potency. All created reality is a composition of act and potency, and potency only exists *in* something that is already actual; it is the *potential* of some *actual* thing. Therefore, being-in-act must be prior to being-in-potency. When God actualized creation, he did not actualize the pure potency of some stuff that was co-eternal with him. There was nothing "out there" with inherent and independent potential waiting to be actualized, for he made all things out of nothing. There was nothing to consult as a template for his creative work, therefore in love he looked to his own essence as the archetypal pattern for his ectypal creation. Psalm 94:9 speaks in these very terms, saying, "He who planted the ear, shall He not hear? He who formed the eye, shall He not see?" The cause is thus revealed in the effect, though never univocally, for the cause is always greater than the effect. In this case, the cause is infinitely greater than the effect since God's being is infinitely greater than ours.

---

[42] Rocca, "'Creatio ex nihilo' and the Being of Creatures: God's Creative Act and the Transcendence-Immanence Distinction in Aquinas," in *Divine Transcendence and Immanence in the Works of Thomas Aquinas,*," 11-12.

It must be observed that this in no way diminishes the preeminence of Christ. It is, however, to argue that it is creation *ex nihilo*, not Christology, that provides the metaphysical foundation for analogical discourse, for the latter assumes the former. "Had he not shown himself in his creatures, he could never have shown himself in his Christ; the order of things require it."[43] To be sure, Christ is the express image of God, the image of the invisible God, who has declared the Father whom no one has seen (John 1:18). The Son incarnate is the fullest and final revelation of God, and indeed is God. Nonetheless, he is God *in the flesh*, and as such preeminently reveals God to us through the *via causalitatis*, according to his creaturely mode of being.

It must also be observed, moreover, that this in no way detracts from the necessity of special revelation for a true knowledge of God. The issue here does not revolve around the priority of general revelation over special, or reason over faith. Rather, the *via causalitatis* speaks to the heart of special revelation itself. General revelation is insufficient; apart from special revelation, we could not know God as we ought.

> As God is known only of himself, so we must only learn of him, what he is. As for man, he knoweth no more what God is, than the unreasonable beasts know what man is; yea, and so much less, as there is more difference between God and man, than between man and beast.[44]

When God reveals himself in his Word, he tells us authoritatively which analogies are appropriate, drawing upon familiar "effects" rooted and grounded in creaturely knowledge and experience in order to draw our minds to heaven to contemplate the God who far exceeds such knowledge and experience. Rather than telling us what he is, he tells us what sort of God he is toward us and how the things he has made are related to him. Take for instance, "God is love" (1 John 4:8). Love is primarily predicated of God and only secondarily of the creature. God *is* love, such that love existed in God even when there was no creature of which love could be

---

[43] Charnock, *Existence and Attributes*, 1:86.

[44] Roger Hutchinson, *The Image of God or Layman's Book* in *The Works of Roger Hutchinson*, ed. John Bruce (Cambridge: The University Press, 1842), 16.

predicated. However, the order in which we come to know love is different from the order in which it exists. We first come to know what love is in the creature, and only by that prior knowledge of the creature are we led by way of similitude to the knowledge of love as it is in God. In his Word, the Lord uses the knowledge of that which is more familiar to lead us to a knowledge of that which is unfamiliar.

> To such as are better acquainted with the less than with the greater, the less may illustrate the greater. If a man have all his life been enclosed in a dark dungeon, where he never saw the light of sun or day, but only used candle-light, by that candle-light one may set out the excellency of the light of the sun.[45]

Therefore, he does not speak to us in his own language, but in ours. In a sermon on Deuteronomy 5:22, Calvin asks, "For if he should speak in his own language; should it be understood [by] mortal creatures?" He replies:

> Alas no. But how is it that he hath spoken to us in the holy Scripture? As nurses do to their little babes. . . . So then, GOD did as it were stoop, because we should not have understood what he said, unless he had lowered himself unto us.[46]

Hutchinson adds:

> Because our understandings be weak, and not able to perceive God, if he should use such words as become his majesty, he borroweth common and plain words to declare a difficult matter unto us: and even as mothers, before they can teach their young babes to speak, are fain as it were to lisp, stammer, and stut with them; so God, to teach our

---

[45] William Gouge, *Commentary on Hebrews*, 2 vols. (1866; reprint, Birmingham, AL: Solid Ground Christian Books, 2006), 1:214 (Heb. 3:2).
[46] John Calvin, Sermon 42 (on Deut. 5:22), *Sermons on Deuteronomy*, trans. Arthur Golding (Edinburgh; Carlisle, PA: Banner of Truth, 1987), 249, modernized language.

capacities, useth these familiar manner of speeches.[47]

If he had not used our language, we would not understand; furthermore, if he had used our language without a metaphysical ground for doing so, we "would be unable to answer the arguments of those who claim our knowledge of God is nothing more than a projection of ourselves."[48] Instead, he accommodates the revelation of himself to us on the basis of the *via causalitatis*. "Everything from above comes from below."[49]

The Via Negationis

The presupposition that lies behind the way of negation is the conviction that, while the creature is in some way like God, God is in no way like the creature. With the *via negationis* in mind, Aquinas wisely points out:

> Although it may be admitted that creatures are in some sort like God, it must nowise be admitted that God is like creatures. . . . For, we say that a statue is like a man, but not conversely; so also a creature can be spoken of as in some sort like God, but not that God is like a creature.[50]

"To whom will you liken Me, and make *Me* equal and compare Me, that we should be alike?" (Isa. 46:5). Indeed, when Moses reiterated the second commandment to the people before they entered the land, he set it in the context of God's incomprehensibility and the limitations of our infinitesimal knowledge, saying, "And the LORD spoke to you out of the midst of the fire. You heard the sound of the words, but saw no form; *you* only *heard* a voice" (Deut. 4:12; cf. John 1:18). Indeed, the Lord revealed himself to Moses, but not as he is in himself, nor in the form or likeness of any created thing. Because of the infinite distance between the Creator and the creature, Charnock

---

[47] Hutchinson, *The Image of God*, 18.

[48] Dodds, *Unchanging God of Love*, 137.

[49] Mark-Robin Hoogland C.P., *God, Passion and Power: Thomas Aquinas on Christ Crucified and the Almightiness of God* (Walpole, MA: Peeters Leuven, 2003), 231.

[50] Aquinas, *Summa Theologica*, I.a .q.4. a.3.

asserts that making images of God in the likeness of any of his creation

> impairs the reverence of God in the minds of men, and by degrees may debase men's apprehensions of God, and be a means to make them believe he is such a one as themselves; . . . He being more above a man, though the noblest creature, than man is above a worm, a toad, or the most despicable creeping thing upon the earth. To think we can make an image of God of a piece of marble, or an ingot of gold, is a greater debasing of him, than it would be of a great prince, if you should represent him in the statue of a frog.[51]

When the Lord revealed himself more fully to Moses, moreover, it is noteworthy that he revealed his hindquarters, not his face. And when Moses went atop the mountain to meet with God, "the people stood afar off, but Moses drew near the thick darkness where God *was*" (Exod. 20:21). He came to know God in the darkness, so that what he discovered was God shrouded in mystery. "For I *am* God, and not man, The Holy One in your midst . . ." (Hos. 11:9).

If by the *via causalitatis* we acknowledge the necessary foundation that enables us to make analogical predications, insofar as creation *ex nihilo* provides the basis for similarities between Creator and creature, by the *via negationis* we remember that the dissimilarities are always greater than the similarities. Because our language about God is first drawn from his likeness in the creature, it is therefore necessary to *negate* anything that would imply an imperfection in God, lest our reverence of God be impaired in our minds and we futilely project our image upon him.

> Wherefore that rule which we have used elsewhere, is to be held, that whatsoever imperfection we find in our affections, we are first to take that away, and then the same affections, love, and mercy, being purged as it were from all imperfection, is to be attributed to God.[52]

---

[51] Charnock, *Existence and Attributes*, 1:194.

[52] Jerome Zanchi, *Life Everlasting: or, the True Knowledge of One Jehovah* (Cambridge: John Legat, 1601), 358.

It is absolutely critical to understand that the *via negationis* is not an attempt to go beyond what the Scripture says. In the first place, it is more a confession of what God is *not* than speculation about what he is. The Scripture speaks of God as immortal (1 Tim. 1:17), invisible (Col. 1:15), infinite (Psalm 147:5), and so forth. These are apophatic, or negative, predications. Given the straightforward yet lofty language and the affirmative manner in which it is predicated of God, moreover, there is a danger of assuming that we have therefore learned what God is. In reality, we know nothing about what it is to be infinite, invisible (i.e., not merely unseen, but unseeable), or immortal. We do, however, know what it is to be finite, visible, and mortal, so when the Scripture says God is infinite, it is telling us he is *not* finite, and so on. We thereby are enabled to receive a greater knowledge of God, not in such a way that explains away the mystery, but rather enables us to apprehend the mystery itself more fully. Such knowledge is not comprehensive, but it is sufficient. "We cannot know him otherwise as we live now, nor do we need to know him otherwise to live well."[53]

In the second place, the *via negationis* is not an attempt to go beyond what the Scripture says, but rather a modest attempt to allow Scripture to interpret Scripture, so as to rightly divide the Word of truth. For example, after Saul had turned his back on the Lord, we hear the Lord say, "I greatly regret that I set up Saul *as* king" (1 Sam. 15:11). The word "regret" could be translated "repent" and seems to imply that the Lord has changed his will towards Saul. However, using the same word a few verses later, we are told, "the Strength of Israel will not lie nor relent. For He *is* not a man, that He should relent" (1 Sam. 15:29; cf. Num. 23:19). However we are to interpret God's "regret," we must take into account *what it does not mean*; it cannot mean for God what it means for us, for God is not a man. Thus, whatsoever would imply an imperfection in God, even if it were considered a perfection in the creature, must be removed. In doing so, we interpret Scripture in the manner in which it was intended, no more and no less.

Particularly relevant to the present discussion is the *via negationis* with regard to divine love. In the first place, although it is

---

[53] William Ames, *The Marrow of Theology*, trans. John Dykstra Eusden (1968; reprint, Grand Rapids: Baker Books, 1997), I.iiii.

not itself an apophatic term, it must be confessed that we no more know what divine love *is* in itself than we can understand infinity, invisibility, and immortality. We do, however, have the ability to know what human love is, and from an understanding of that which is familiar we may come to a better understanding of that which is unfamiliar. In the second place, we must also remember that God and man are more dissimilar than similar. The analogy itself is based upon a proper proportionality, such that divine love stands in relation to God's nature in a mode proportionate to how human love stands in relation to human nature. Whatsoever there is in human love that would imply an imperfection in relation to the divine nature, therefore, must be removed. With the *via negationis* in mind, Owen concludes:

> They differ in this also: — *The love of God is like himself, —equal, constant, not capable of augmentation or diminution; our love is like ourselves, —unequal, increasing, waning, growing, declining.* His, like the *sun*, always the same in its light, though a cloud may sometimes interpose; ours, as the *moon*, hath its enlargements and straightenings.[54]

The Via Eminentiae

All three ways of knowing God are applicable to every predication of God. Near the beginning of this section we cited Dodds' observation: "All we say of God is grounded in divine causality, seeks to remove creaturely imperfections from him, and intends to eminently affirm unlimited perfection." For instance, when we ascribe to God the name *love*, we recognize by way of causality that he is the ultimate cause of love in creatures thereby establishing a point of similarity; by way of negation, we are reminded that his love is not defined according to the limited and changing mode of creatures. That which remains, after it has been purged from all imperfection, is that love which is properly and positively attributed to God according to the *via eminentiae*, in the way of preeminence or perfection. God's love is not only *not* unequal, increasing, waning, growing, or declining; it *is* infinitely greater than all we can conceive as love.

---

[54] Owen, *Works*, 2:29-30.

Once again, it is tempting to think we have now arrived at what God *is* by way of rational deduction. However, the *via eminentiae* reminds us that God *is* infinitely beyond all that we can conceive, so that it stresses the limitations, not the achievements, of our knowledge. The fact remains that we have no idea what it is *to be* love, though we must affirm such of God by way of the *via eminentiae*. We *have* love as an accidental property, so that our love may grow or diminish without our becoming more or less human. God's love is himself, an essential attribute, so that his love cannot change any more than his being can change. God's love is identical to his being, something we know nothing about, though it must be affirmed nonetheless. In the *via eminentiae* we are confessing our knowledge of a love that surpasses knowledge (Eph. 3:19).

In other words, the *via eminentiae* cannot be separated from the *via causalitatis* or *via negationis*. Failing to locate the metaphysical ground for similarity between God and man in the *via causalitatis*, Carson implicitly rejects the *via negationis*, and thereby domesticates the *via eminentiae*. He is at least broadly representative of the evangelical modification of impassibility when he writes, "Doubtless God's love is immeasurably richer than ours, in ways still to be explored, but they belong to the same genus, or the parallelisms could not be drawn."[55] If God's love and our love are of the same genus, then God's being and our being are of the same genus, for God's love is identical to his being. As a result, the *via eminentiae* becomes nothing more than a gradation of hierarchal steps between God and man. His love is identical to ours in kind, though not in perfection. Simply put, his love becomes a far more perfect version of our own. But, as we have already shown, God's love and human love are no more of the same genus than God's being and our being, nor need they be (cf. Matt. 19:17). Dodds' criticism of such an approach is worthy of serious consideration. He writes:

Without the *via negationis*, which underlines the radical difference between God and creatures, the God affirmed in the *via eminentiae* would become nothing more than a beneficent creature 'writ large.'[56]

---

55 Carson, *The Difficult Doctrine*, 48.
56 Dodds, *Unchanging God of Love*, 137.

The irony is that certain modern approaches that portend to exalt God's perfections end up domesticating his transcendence.

The *via eminentiae* does not merely imply that God is the most perfect being, but that he is perfection and being itself of an altogether different order. "Transcendence that fits our categories has been domesticated."[57] For this reason we are reminded by way of the *via eminentiae*, understood alongside the *via causationis* and *via negationis*, that God is always infinitely greater than the revelation (i.e., words or names) of himself. When applied to God, there is a sense in which superlatives become diminutives. Once we have purged all imperfection (by way of negation) and have positively affirmed that God is love (by way of eminence), we have raised the meaning of the name love to a higher order, beyond our categories of language.

> We should say that, because our intellect is not equal to the divine substance, what God's substance is remains beyond our intellect, and so we do not know it. And so the ultimate human knowledge about God is that one knows that one does not know God, inasmuch as one knows that what God is exceeds everything we know about him.[58]

Thus, the point of such language is not that we should know God as he is, much less conceive of him as though he fit within our categories, but to cause us to worship him with reverence and awe. Following Anselm's dictum, "God is that, than which nothing greater can be conceived," Bullinger writes:

> But whatsoever may be thought of him shall still be less than he; and whatsoever in speech is shewed of him, being compared with him, shall be much less than he. . . . For if you call him Light, then do you rather name a creature of his than him, but him you express not. . . . Say all of him whatsoever thou canst, and yet thou shalt still rather name something of his than himself. For what canst thou fitly

---

[57] Placher, *The Domestication of Transcendence*, 10.

[58] Thomas Aquinas, *The Power of God*, trans. Richard J. Regan (New York: Oxford University Press, 2012), 209.

think of him that is above all loftiness, higher than all height, deeper than all depth, lighter than all light, clearer than all clearness, brighter than all brightness, stronger than all strength, more virtuous than all virtue, fairer than all fairness, truer than all truth, greater than all greatness, mightier than all might, richer than all riches, wiser than all wisdom, more liberal than all liberality, better than all goodness, juster than all justice, and gentler than all gentleness? . . . so that God may truly be said to be such a certain being as to which nothing may be compared. For he is above all that may be spoken.[59]

So also Charnock:

So we should endeavor to refine every representation of God, to rise higher and higher, and have our apprehensions still more purified; separating the perfect from the imperfect, casting away the one, and greatening the other; conceive him to be a Spirit diffused through all, containing all, perceiving all. All the perfections of God are infinitely elevated above the excellencies of the creatures; above whatsoever can be conceived by the clearest and most piercing understanding. The nature of God as a Spirit is infinitely superior to whatsoever we can conceive perfect in the notion of a created spirit. Whatsoever God is, he is infinitely so; he is infinite Wisdom, infinite Goodness, infinite Knowledge, infinite Power, infinite Spirit, infinitely distant from the weakness of creatures, infinitely mounted above the excellencies of creatures: as easy to be known that he is, as impossible to be comprehended what he is. Conceive of him as excellent, without any imperfection; a Spirit without parts; great without quantity; perfect without quality; everywhere without place; powerful without members; understanding without ignorance; wise without reasoning; light without darkness; infinitely more excelling the beauty of all creatures, than the light in the sun, pure

---

[59] Heinrich Bullinger, *The Decades of Henry Bullinger*, 2 vols., ed. Thomas Harding (Grand Rapids: Reformation Heritage Books, 2004), 2:127-28.

and unviolated, exceeds in the splendor of the sun dispersed and divided through a cloudy and misty air: and when you have risen to the highest, conceive him yet infinitely above all you can conceive of spirit, and acknowledge the infirmity of your own minds. And whatsoever conception comes into your minds, say, This is not God; God is more than this: if I could conceive him, he were not God; for God is incomprehensibly above whatsoever I can say, whatsoever I can think and conceive of him.[60]

The more we know God, the more we understand that his "essence cannot be comprehended by any but himself" (2LCF 2.1). Ironically, the more we come to know what God is, the more we come to know that he cannot be known univocally.

Conclusion

The doctrine of divine impassibility could be alternatively referred to as the doctrine of God's absolute perfection; God is not undergoing a process of perfection, nor could he be. He is infinitely and incorruptibly perfect in his eternal essence. The issue at hand, therefore, is not whether something like emotion can be predicated of God, but which are proper to God and which are not. Likewise, the issue is not merely whether God's affections can be changed for the worse, but whether they may undergo any change at all. For how can a God who is pure actuality, without passive potency, either grow or diminish? How can a God who is the negation of all becoming (*via negationis*) become anything other than he is, and how can a love that is infinite in perfection (*via eminentiae*) be any more perfect than it is? He is "most holy" because he could not be any more or any less holy. He is "most wise" because he could not be any more or less wise. Likewise, he is "most loving" because he could not be any more or less what he is (2LCF 2.1). To be infinitely and immutably perfect is no point of imperfection; it is the height of perfection.

---

[60] Charnock, *Existence and Attributes*, 1:200-01.

Chapter 2

HERMENEUTICS

Analogia Scripturae *and* Analogia Fidei

Ronald S. Baines

As *confessional* Reformed believers, the starting point of all theology is affirmed to be "The Holy Scripture [which] is the only sufficient, certain, and infallible rule of all saving Knowledge, Faith and Obedience" (2LCF 1.1).[1] The Confession recognizes itself as a subordinate authority or norm to the absolute and prior authority or norm of the Word of God.[2] It further acknowledges that all theological or religious controversies are to be "determined, and all Decrees of Councils, opinions of ancient Writers, Doctrines of men, and private Spirits, are to be examined" by the Holy Scriptures as "[t]he supreme judge" (1.10). Thus, it is to the text of Scripture that we will turn in the next section.

Hermeneutical Foundations

The introductory comments above draw attention to the foundational importance of the interpretation and use of Scripture

---

[1] By *confessional* Reformed believers we intend those who subscribe to one of the historic Reformed confessions. This is not to suggest that other evangelicals have a different starting point than that of *sola Scriptura*. It is simply to recognize the common ground within Reformed confessionalism.

[2] For a helpful discussion of the place of subordinate authorities see esp. Francis Turretin, *Institutes of Elenctic Theology*, 3 vols., ed. James T. Dennison, Jr., trans. George Musgrave Giger (Phillipsburg, NJ: P&R Publishing, 1992-97), 2.21.1-18 (1:162-67). Though Turretin deals with the Reformers' use of the church fathers, his discussion applies more broadly to the use of subordinate authorities in general. Cf. See Muller, *Dictionary*, 284. For a recent book on this subject, we recommend Michael Allen and Scott R. Swain, *Reformed Catholicity: The Promise of Retrieval for Theology and Biblical Interpretation* (Grand Rapids: Baker Academic, 2015).

in the formulation and defense of any doctrine, no less than in the context of doctrinal differences. With regard to the doctrine of divine impassibility, the exegetical material is not generally in dispute, in terms of what texts need to be considered. In other words, the parties largely agree that the Scriptures speak of God repenting (e.g., Gen. 6:6-7) and of God not repenting (e.g., Num. 23:19). Differing doctrinal conclusions result from differing interpretations of the sense or meaning of such texts, considered both individually and in their necessary interrelation. In other words, hermeneutics is at the heart of the debate.

D. A. Carson recognizes this important consideration when he characterizes classical impassibilists and open theists as fundamentally differing in their harmonizing or hermeneutical paradigm.[3] Critical of classical impassibilists in biblical doctrine and interpretive practice, Carson simplistically mischaracterizes their use of Scripture as follows:

> The methodological problem with the argument for divine impassibility is that it selects certain texts of Scripture, namely those that insist on God's sovereignty and changelessness, constructs a theological grid on the basis of those selected texts, and then uses this grid to filter out all other texts, in particular those that speak of God's emotions. These latter texts, nicely filtered out, are then labeled "anthropomorphisms" and are written off.[4]

Carson is equally critical of Open Theism:

> Unfortunately, almost without exception, they commit the opposite error. They begin with all the texts that depict God

---

[3] We have chosen Carson because he specifically challenges the hermeneutical method of classical impassibility. Cf. Robert R. Gonzales Jr., *Where Sin Abounds: The Spread of Sin and the Curse in Genesis with Special Focus on the Patriarchal Narratives* (Eugene, OR: Wipf and Stock Publishers, 2009), 80, who considers Carson to be a "fitting rebuttal" to the "interpretive approach" of the classical impassibility of John Calvin in particular and classical impassibilists in general. In terms of the larger argument of this book this evidences a hermeneutical difference between Carson/Gonzales and the 2LCF's affirmation of classical impassibility.

[4] D. A. Carson, *How Long, O Lord?: Reflections on Suffering and Evil* (Grand Rapids: Baker Publishing Group, 2006), 165.

as a suffering God, create a theological grid on this basis, and filter out the texts that point in another direction. The result is a picture of God who is vulnerable, halting, suffering, sympathetic, ever-changing, in process of growth. But the cost is great. At least those who defend divine impassibility had a category for explaining the texts that were difficult to them: they labeled them "anthropomorphic." But these new theologians have no such excuse. They simply ignore them, or so subordinate them to the "suffering" passages that the texts are no longer allowed to mean what they say.[5]

What is perplexing with Carson's objections to both classical impassibility and present day versions of passibility is that he fails to provide a hermeneutical framework for dealing with the biblical material. He offers no alternative "category of explaining the texts" of Scripture which need to be understood in order to formulate a coherent doctrine of God.[6]

What is objectionable, however, is Carson's unwillingness to engage the central hermeneutical questions related to the doctrine of divine impassibility in a serious and substantive fashion. For instance, to suggest that texts are "labeled 'anthropomorphisms' and are written off" is simply not the case, nor is it accurate to suggest that classical impassibilists teach the following:

---

[5] Carson, *How Long, O Lord?*, 166.

[6] Carson acknowledges that "metaphors litter the descriptions" of God in Scripture which are "suggestive of his profound emotional life." Unfortunately, he provides little to no framework for dealing with these "metaphors" in a way that makes sense of the whole of scriptural revelation. As with many present day evangelicals, he further confesses that God suffers, but that "God's suffering is not exactly like ours" (166). The problem with such claims is that he is critical of classical impassibilists for calling the language anthropopathic (a form of metaphor) while acknowledging them to be metaphorical. Nor does he ever explain how they can be metaphorical and yet speak directly to God's "profound emotional life." Furthermore, he does not adequately address the passages that speak of God in emotive terms, such as his relenting, while Scripture also declares that God does not relent. We cannot simply ignore these apparently contrary affirmations, but must seek to harmonize them in a logically and theologically defensible way. In his own case, Carson ultimately offers an approach that is similar to that of Rob Lister and others by affirming that "God is never controlled or overturned by his emotions" (167).

You may then rest in God's sovereignty, but you can no longer rejoice in his love. You may rejoice only in a linguistic expression that is an accommodation of some reality of which we cannot conceive, couched in the anthropopathism of love. Give me a break. Paul did not pray that his readers might be able to grasp the height and depth and length and breadth of an anthropopathism and know this anthropopathism that surpasses knowledge (Eph. 3:14–21).[7]

While we will deal with this in greater detail below, no classical impassibilist that we have encountered reads Paul this way. Doesn't Paul affirm that the love he wants the Ephesians to know is that which "surpasses knowledge"? Classical impassibility seeks to maintain that God's love is not dismissed nor diminished, while at the same time affirming that it is infinite, eternal, and unchangeable, something human love can never be. Further, it affirms that God's love is essential while love in us is accidental, and that the differences are not quantitative but quidditative. The doctrine of classical impassibility does not diminish or make meaningless the love of God, but places it in the larger context of God's glorious transcendence. For this reason, Carson's misrepresentation of classical impassibility is deeply unfortunate.

At the foundation of the confessional doctrine of divine impassibility are principles of interpretation that, when applied consistently, necessitate the conclusion that God is "without body, parts, or passions" (2LCF 2.1). To these principles we now turn.

The Analogy of Scripture (Analogia Scripturae)

One of the most important hermeneutical principles affirmed by the Confession is the analogy of Scripture. Muller defines this as:

. . . the interpretation of unclear, difficult, or ambiguous passages of Scripture by comparison with clear and unambiguous passages that refer to the same teaching or event.[8]

---

[7] Carson, *The Difficult Doctrine*, 59.
[8] Muller, *Dictionary*, 33.

This critical Reformed hermeneutical principle is summarily expressed in 2LCF 1.9.

> The infallible rule of interpretation of Scripture is the Scripture itself; and therefore when there is a question about the true and full sense of any Scripture (which is not manifold but one) it must be searched by other places that speak more clearly.

The importance of *analogia Scripturae* for the 2LCF's doctrine of divine impassibility cannot be overstated. The supposed methodological problem that Carson posits above is, at best, a misrepresentation of the classical and confessional approach to the interpretation of the biblical texts in question. The grid through which the confessional doctrine is viewed is not selected *a priori*, after which the biblical texts are viewed through this preconceived lens.[9] The challenge is that Scripture, when taken as a whole, speaks in such a way as to require viewing certain texts literally and certain texts metaphorically or anthropopathically; otherwise, we are left with seemingly contradictory propositions respecting the doctrine of God. Thus the clearer passages, having been interpreted according to their divinely-intended sense or meaning, serve as the foundation for interpreting the less clear passages. It must be remembered that not only do individual texts have one divine sense, but so also does the whole of Scripture. A simplistic biblicism or dialectical approach portends that Scripture may have competing senses, while the interpretive model of the analogy of Scripture confesses what Scripture itself teaches, namely that properly understood, the sense of Scripture on any given doctrinal topic is not manifold, but one.

Perhaps an example of two texts which inform the doctrine of impassibility will help illustrate this point. When texts that posit divine repentance (e.g., Gen. 6:6-7) are compared with texts that deny the very same thing (e.g., Num. 23:19), the exegete is left with few options. If we are to maintain a right view of scriptural

---

[9] This at least appears to be the way Carson represents what classical impassibilists have done. He gives no examples to justify his assertion, and consequently his characterization of classical impassibility comes across more as a straw man argument than a real engagement with the proponents of the doctrine.

authority and infallibility, we cannot simply take both texts literally in some form of contradictory or dialectical biblicism. These texts will be dealt with at greater length below, but they highlight the interpretive challenge in that they cannot both be true at the same time and in the same way.[10] To suggest that giving precedence to the texts which speak of God ontologically (i.e., Num. 23:19) is methodologically flawed, as Carson does, simply does not follow. Treating certain texts metaphorically or anthropopathically is not a hermeneutical failure but a necessary conclusion from the texts and their respective contexts.

The Analogy of Faith (**Analogia Fidei**)

Alongside of the analogy of Scripture, the 2LCF also recognizes the Reformed principle of the analogy of faith (*analogia fidei*). Muller, again, helpfully defines this concept as

> . . . the use of a general sense of the meaning of Scripture, constructed from the clear or unambiguous *loci* . . . as the basis for interpreting unclear or ambiguous texts. As distinct from the more basic *analogia Scripturae* . . . the *analogia fidei* presupposes a sense of the theological meaning of Scripture.[11]

The clear places of Scripture yield clear theological conclusions, or a summary of the faith once delivered. Thus when the 2LCF suggests that the "true and full sense of any Scripture" (1.9) must include the theological priority of clear texts, it recognizes that more than grammatical and lexicographical principles are necessary for rightly dividing the Word of God. One must interpret the texts of Scripture theologically. Muller helpfully points us to the Puritan William Perkins' explanation of the analogy of faith:

---

[10] It is important to note that the texts do not make affirmations that need reconciliation; i.e., God is "A" and God is "B." They actually make opposite affirmations, or better, an affirmation on the one hand and a denial on the other; i.e., God repented and God does not repent; God is "A" and God is "not A."

[11] Muller, *Dictionary*, 33.

. . . but in doubtfull places Scripture it selfe is sufficient to declare his owne meaning: first, by the analogie of faith, which is the summe of religion gathered out of the clearest places of Scripture: second, by the circumstance of the place, the nature and signification of the words: thirdly, by conference of place with place. By these and the like helps contained in Scripture, we may judge what is the truest meaning of any place. Scripture itselfe is the text and the best glosse. And the Scripture is falsely termed the matter of strife, it being not so of itself, but by the abuse of men.[12]

The analogy of Scripture and the analogy of faith require that we compare Scripture with Scripture, but not in a theological vacuum. When biblical texts speak to the doctrine of God, we must understand them in light of the whole. Muller goes on to assert:

It is important to note this, given the tendency of modern writers to identify the *analogia fidei* as a credal grid placed over the text. But the analogy is made from the text in question to the broader theological meaning of the whole of Scripture. . . . The Protestant orthodox were certain of the unity and coherence of the biblical message — and they were also convinced of an intimate relationship between the various forms and levels of theology, from the basic exegesis of the sacred page, to the exposition of its fundamental articles in catechesis, to the more elaborate forms of positive, polemical, and scholastic theology. The analogy of faith is connected, explicitly, with the identification of fundamental articles of faith . . .[13]

The Scriptures must be interpreted both exegetically and theologically. Therefore, impassibility cannot be divorced from the rest of the doctrine of God, especially God's incomprehensibility, immutability, aseity, and simplicity, to which the 2LCF gives rich

---

[12] Muller, *PRRD*, 2:494. The expanded version of this quote is taken from, William Perkins, *Works of that Famous and Worthy Minister of Christ at the University of Cambridge, Mr. William Perkins* (London: John Legatt, Printer to the University of Cambridge, 1612), 1:583.

[13] Muller, *PRRD*, 2:494–95.

evidence. While Carson and Gonzales[14] may be critical of the methodology of classical impassibility as some sort of "grid" placed over the text of Scripture, neither the Scriptures, nor confessional Reformed theology in general, nor the 2LCF, in particular, allow for such a simplistic misrepresentation.

We are convinced that the 2LCF rightly points to the interpretive practice of comparing Scripture with Scripture, exegetically and theologically, so as to understand all that it teaches respecting the doctrine of God. Furthermore, we are convinced that this necessitates taking the Scriptures which speak of God in the language of human passions as anthropopathic, since this alone does justice to the one, unified sense of Scripture.

From Hermeneutics to Exegesis and Theology

In what follows, we have endeavored to deal with the texts respecting divine impassibility exegetically and theologically in the light of the whole of scriptural revelation. We have incorporated the hermeneutical principles richly advocated by the Reformers and affirmed by the 2LCF with a view to faithfully representing the doctrine of God. While we will not address every possible text of Scripture relative to the doctrine of divine impassibility, we have sought to cover the major texts of both the Old Testament and the New Testament which are associated with this important doctrine. Additionally, what follows supplies a sufficient framework within which to address other texts that may contain language respecting the presence or absence of passions or affections in God.

---

[14] See footnote 3 above.

Chapter 3

THE OLD TESTAMENT ON
THE DOCTRINE OF DIVINE IMPASSIBILITY

(I) Texts on the Nature of God

Steve Garrick with Ronald S. Baines

It is often difficult to interpret what a particular biblical text may be teaching about God without a proper framework drawn from the entire canon. On account of our finitude, the Scriptures disclose certain truths about God by using language borrowed from common human experience, some of which portrays him as changing. That is, Scripture speaks of the manifestation of God's infinite nature, though from our perspective it appears as change. The central issue when interpreting these passages is methodological. Such language of change must be understood metaphorically or anthropopathically, rather than in a literal or univocal fashion. This is the best and time-proven method of interpretation.

There are three basic approaches that have been posited to interpret these kinds of biblical passages. In the classical view, Scripture is seen as using the common experiences of men to convey the ideas of God's omniscience, wrath, and judgment. In this view, the language of change or mutability is understood metaphorically, anthropopathically, or analogically, rather than in a literal or univocal fashion.[1] At the opposite end of the spectrum, the literal or univocal view (generally associated with Open Theism) teaches that God really does see, grieve, feel pain, and change his mind—all due to limitations or changes in his essential nature. In this view, God really does change, because he is essentially finite in some respect. Finally, in the relational-mutability view, the biblical language

---

[1] For further discussion of analogical versus univocal language concerning God, see chapter 1, "Analogy and the Doctrine of Divine Impassibility."

for God is understood as "semi-literal." That is to say, while such language depicts real changes in God as he responds to events, these changes are not caused by these events, nor do they stem from limitations in God's essential nature or alter it. They are construed as the result of God's own voluntary covenantal condescension to relate to his creatures.[2]

An example of the latter view is articulated by John Frame. In his response to Open Theism's overly-literal approach to those Bible passages where God is said to relent, Frame writes:

> Contrary to Open theists, God does have an unchanging purpose, described in Ephesians 1:11 and other texts noted earlier. That purpose is unchanging, but it ordains change, including the divine relentings mentioned in the above passages.[3]

According to Frame, God ordains all things—even his own change of mind. Later, Frame concludes that

> [God] does what is appropriate in each situation, responding to one situation one way, to another another way. This is, as Open theists emphasize, a kind of change . . . God is both fully omniscient *and* responsive to creatures.[4]

---

[2] There is no consensus among present evangelical reformulations of God's passibility as to the language used to describe the semi-literal understanding of language depicting God. Rob Lister, for instance, distinguishes between anthropomorphisms and anthropopathisms via the literal/non-literal spectrum. He affirms "divine incorporeality leads us to the conclusion that *anthropomorphisms are analogical and nonliteral* (though nevertheless truth bearing), whereas *anthropopathisms are analogical and literal*" (emphasis original). Statements such as this cause one to wonder how careful Lister is with analogical predications of God. Be that as it may Lister's distinction does appear to be, at least in some degree, begging the question. Doesn't one have to presuppose passions on the part of God in order to view anthropopathisms as "analogical and literal"? By treating anthropopathic language in this fashion, Lister largely avoids engaging the important discussion of proper and improper predications of God. Cf. Lister, *God Is Impassible and Impassioned*, 187.

[3] John M. Frame, "Open Theism and Divine Foreknowledge," in *Bound Only Once: The Failure of Open Theism*, in ed. Douglas Wilson (Moscow, ID: Canon Press, 2001), 90.

[4] Frame, "Open Theism and Divine Foreknowledge," 91.

Similarly, K. Scott Oliphint, while not using the language of "relational-mutability," sees God as assuming created, covenantal properties as he condescends to relate to his creation in a manner that involves relenting and change on God's part.[5] Oliphint writes:

> [W]hatever kind of "assumption" this is, we can affirm that in his condescension Yahweh relented, while in his essential deity Yahweh does not change. Not only so, but whatever relenting Yahweh does, it is always done in the context of his sovereign plan.[6]

Deciding which of the three views is correct begins with careful exegesis of the Scriptures. The purpose of the chapters on the Old and New Testaments is to examine several key texts in order to determine a proper understanding of them in their context and to place them in a theological system. This will aid in determining which of the above approaches is scriptural. The following will argue that while the view of Open Theism mistakenly permits the less clear texts of Scripture to interpret the clear texts and the relational-mutability or modified classical view tends to interpret each passage in relative isolation, leading to an incoherent (i.e., dialectical or dualistic) doctrine of the divine attributes, the classical and confessional Reformed approach necessarily invokes the Bible's own principles of interpretation in such a way as to lay the proper exegetical foundation for a true, though analogical, doctrine of the divine attributes, including the doctrine of divine impassibility.[7]

Texts on the Nature of God

Exodus 3:14

> And God said to Moses, "I AM WHO I AM." And He said, "Thus you shall say to the children of Israel, 'I AM has sent me to you.'" (Exod. 3:14)

---

[5] K. Scott Oliphint, *God with Us: Divine Condescension and the Attributes of God* (Wheaton, IL: Crossway, 2012), 110. We will interact with Oliphint in various chapters of this book.

[6] Oliphint, *God with Us*, 186.

[7] See chapter 2, "Hermeneutics: *Analogia Scripturae* and *Analogia Fidei*."

As Moses is commissioned by God to bring his message to Israel and Pharaoh, he asks what seems to be an unusual question. He assumes that, upon hearing his report that the God of their fathers has appeared to him, the Israelites will ask him, "What is his name?" This question is most likely not an indicator that Israel had forgotten God or his revealed name. After all, since they remembered the stories of their fathers, they would have likely remembered God's revealed name as well. Also, if the name of God had been erased from their recollections, then hearing it would hardly have elicited a faithful response. But a god's name (e.g., Dagon, Molech, or Baal) often reveals something of the realm of his power and of his character. Moses is likely anticipating that the Israelites would want to know about the power and nature of the God of their fathers. Keil and Delitzsch write:

> The question, "What is His name?" presupposed that the name expressed the nature and operations of God, and that God would manifest in deeds the nature expressed in His name. God therefore told him His name, or, to speak more correctly, He explained the name יהוה, by which He had made Himself known to Abraham at the making of the covenant (Gen 15:7), in this way: אֶהְיֶה אֲשֶׁר אֶהְיֶה, "*I am that I am*," and designated Himself by this name as the absolute God of the fathers, acting with unfettered liberty and [independence].[8]

God's name reveals at least two things. First, it declares the immutability of his eternal nature. Second, it shows that this eternally immutable God interacts with his creation. That is, God is both essentially transcendent and immanent.

God's self-declared name reveals his unchanging, eternal

---

[8] C. F. Keil and F. Delitzsch, *The Pentateuch*, vol. 1, *Commentary on the Old Testament in Ten Volumes*, trans. James Martin (1949; reprint, Grand Rapids: Eerdmans Publishing Co., 1983), 442. The English translation reads "self-dependence." We have consulted the original German text and German language resources prior to making this change of translation. See the *Oxford Duden German Dictionary*, s.v., Selbständigkeit (which is the term employed in the original German text). Thanks to Dr. James M. Renihan for assisting in clarifying the translation at this point.

nature. As the I AM, God doesn't become; he is.[9] This name shows "the constancy and certainty of his nature, and will, and word. The sense is, I am the same that ever I was."[10] As Stephen Charnock notes, it is improper, therefore, to speak of God in terms of what he used to be or what he has or will become.

> If his essence were mutable, God would not truly be; it could not be truly said by himself, "I Am that I Am" (Exod. 3:14), if he were such a thing or Being at this time, and a different Being at another time. Whatsoever is changed properly is not, because it doth not remain to be what it was; that which is changed was something, is something, and will be something.[11]

Matthew Henry explains God's name as signifying what "he is in himself." Specifically, Henry exposits God's name as teaching us that he is "self-sufficient, eternal and unchangeable," ultimately incomprehensible, and immutably faithful to all his promises.[12] Elaborating on the aseity of God manifest in his name, Oliphint writes:

> To move no further than the etymological sense of the phrase "I AM," all that God is, he is as the only genuine, essential, fundamental one. . . . God, and God alone, is original. He is the "I AM." Because this is such a central and nonnegotiable aspect of God's character, we can say that God, and God alone, is *Eimi*.[13]

---

[9] John Currid rightly shows the implications of Exod. 3:14 for the doctrine of God. Though "YHWH appears in the imperfect" it should not be translated as a future. Noting that the "imperfect in Hebrew actually can appear in any tense, past, present, or future" he affirms that God's name "means that he is immutable or unchanging. He is not in the process of becoming something else. God is the same yesterday, today and for ever."Cf. John D. Currid, *A Study Commentary on Exodus: Exodus 1–18*, vol. 1, EP Study Commentary (Darlington, England; Carlisle, PA: Evangelical Press, 2000), 91.

[10] Matthew Poole, *A Commentary on the Holy Bible*, 3 vols. (London: Banner of Truth Trust, 1962), 1:122.

[11] Charnock, *Existence and Attributes*, 1:320.

[12] Matthew Henry, *Commentary on the Whole Bible*, 6 vols. (New York: Funk & Wagnalls Co., n.d.), 1:166.

[13] Oliphint, *God with Us*, 90. For a review of Oliphint's book and interaction

Seventeenth-century New England divine John Norton rightly addressed the implications of Exodus 3:14 which further reflect the simplicity of God. Arguing that "[a]ll the Attributes in God are one and the same Perfection," he explains in greater detail:

> Simplicity is God, one meer and perfect act without all composition. God calleth his Name, I am, Exod. 3.14. that is, meer Essence, wherein is nothing past nor to come. Because spirits are inmixt in respect of bodies, to shew that he is not compounded, he saith he is a Spirit, Iohn 4.24. When we say that God is a meer and perfect Act, the meaning is, that God is a cause without any Cause, a Being that is not from any Being; not compounded of an Act, by which he is; and Possibility, by which he might not have been, or may not be: of whom it never could nor can be said, that any thing was to be in him, which was not; or cannot be, that is.
>
> That God is a pure simple Act without all composition, is evident, Because of his Perfection; all composition supposeth imperfection, because he is the first Being. Were there any composition in God, it would follow there were first and second in God: Something in God that were not first, or that there were more first Beings. . . . Composition supposeth Succession . . .[14]

God's name, then, reveals his transcendence. The name YHWH shows God's eternality, unchangeableness, and self-existence. But it is also the foundation for God's relation to Israel, and, indeed, to the world. Oliphint says that "the I AM is utterly transcendent, beyond all categories of creation."[15] Without qualification, however, this may imply that God in his eternal being is *so* transcendent that in himself he cannot relate to man. The name YHWH reveals more than just God's transcendence; it simultaneously discloses his immanence — and without conceiving of his transcendence as a

---

with some of his proposals with which we disagree, see appendix 1.

[14] John Norton, *The Orthodox Evangelist* (London: Printed for John Macock, and Henry Cripps, and Ludwick Lloyd, 1654), 5. We are indebted to Sam Renihan for this source.

[15] Oliphint, *God with Us*, 90.

problem that his immanence must overcome.[16] Moses, pronouncing that God had now undertaken to act on Israel's behalf — to remove them from bondage, to constitute them a special nation by his covenant, and to fulfill the promises to their fathers — does so by invoking the name of the great self-existent One. While the revelation of God's name to Israel, as well as Israel's relation to him, is via a mediator, the foundation of both this revelation and this relation is God's name. That is, because he is the eternal, infinite, I AM, God relates to Israel as such. Indeed, as Henry observes, the name I AM also denotes "what he is to his people."[17]

---

[16] Rob Lister does not view God's transcendence as a problem per se, but it is hard to see his formulations as satisfactory to the text of Scripture and to the transcendence and immanence of God advocated by classical theism. In attempting to counter the ways in which Open Theism conceives of God's immanent relations, Lister addresses God's immanence similarly to Oliphint, via covenantal condescension. He notes, "When we turn to examine the nature of divine condescension more closely, it becomes apparent that the immanental realities of God's condescension (e.g., inhabiting the creatures' time and space, relating to his creatures volitionally and affectively) are all contingent on God's free decision to create in the first place. That is to say that creation was the logically necessary precursor to the expression of these immanent attributes." What Lister appears to be saying is that God's immanence must be accounted for apart from his transcendence. In other words, transcendence for God is essential but immanence is volitional. This conclusion is hard to escape when he makes statements such as, "It is crucial to the task at hand, therefore, to note that God's immanence is a product of divine freedom and not divine necessity." By making immanence contingent and volitional in God, Lister divides the two in ways that are not biblically defensible. For instance, is it conceivable for Lister that God might choose not to "inhabit the creatures' time and space" thus removing himself from time and space? Are time and space like a box: outside the box God exists transcendent but then he chooses to covenantally condescend and enter the box thereby becoming immanent? Do time and space really become God's habitation? Exodus 3:14 mitigates against such a view. The transcendent I AM is simultaneously immanent in the bush burning before the shoeless Moses. Exodus 3:14 does not expose when God entered time and space, but the burning bush becomes an instrument in revelation, revealing the transcendent God who has all along been simultaneously immanent. Cf. Lister, *God Is Impassible and Impassioned*, 225, 197.

Thomas G. Weinandy, *Does God Suffer?* (Notre Dame, IN: University of Notre Dame, 2000), 57, helpfully explains that divine immanence is not to be conceived of as if it were conflicting with divine transcendence: "Equally, to speak of God's immanence is not to speak of God in himself as if there were aspects of him which are a part of the created order, but rather 'immanence' specifies that he who is not 'a part' of the created order is nonetheless present to and active within it."

[17] Henry, *Commentary*, 1:166.

Later, in Exodus 32, Israel violates the commandments they have just received by God's voice. Moses, acting the part of national mediator, pleads for Israel's existence. In verse 11, Moses "reminds" God that he acted "with great power and a mighty hand" (attributes normally ascribed to God's transcendence) to bring Israel out of Egypt. Through Moses' intercession, "the LORD [i.e., YHWH] relented from the harm he said he would do to his people" (Exod. 32:14).[18] This relenting comes from the same YHWH—eternal, immutable, and self-existent—who revealed himself in the burning bush. The text grounds God's decree to act toward Israel in mercy in his eternal, essential being. God's *immanent* relationship to Israel is based on his being the unchangeable I AM.

Finally, in Exodus 34, granting Moses' request to see his glory, God passes before the prophet. Again, the name YHWH is intoned and expounded. God himself exegetes the meaning of his name.

> And the LORD passed before him and proclaimed, "The LORD, the LORD God, merciful and gracious, longsuffering, and abounding in goodness and truth, 7 "keeping mercy for thousands, forgiving iniquity and transgression and sin, by no means clearing *the guilty*, visiting the iniquity of the fathers upon the children and the children's children to the third and the fourth generation." (Exod. 34:6-7)

Here, God's mercy, grace, patience, infinite goodness, truth, and covenant faithfulness are all disclosed by the name YHWH. Those actions of God by which he most closely relates to his people all derive from the eternal essence of God's self-existence. Rather than seeing God's transcendence as related to his essence and his immanent relations with his people stemming from covenantal properties, Scripture portrays both as directly originating in the eternal God. Put another way, it is *because* God is transcendent that he is also immanent. Because God is omniscient, he knows the intentions and thoughts of our hearts. Because God is omnipotent, he can deliver and save with his mighty hand. Because God is infinitely merciful and faithful, he is gracious to those whom he wills to be gracious who yet deserve justice. Because he is I AM, he

---

[18] On God's relenting see chapter 5, "The Old Testament on the Doctrine of Divine Impassibility: (III) Texts on Apparent Passibilism and Conclusion."

is our God, even God with us. It is only by virtue of his aseity, his existence in and of himself, that God is, in himself, all that we need.

In Jonah 4:2, the prophet laments that he knew God would be merciful to Nineveh. "I know that You *are* a gracious and merciful God, slow to anger and abundant in lovingkindness, One who relents from doing harm." Rob Lister says, "It seems that Jonah was quite familiar with the principle of what we are calling God's relational mutability."[19] However, Jonah's knowledge of God is based on God's own self-revelation of his nature as the self-existent One. Jonah is quoting from Exodus 34:6-7, where God expounds the meaning of YHWH as he passes before Moses. God's relenting from evil is the personal experience of Israel in Exodus 32:14, after Moses' intercession with God. Jonah does not derive his prediction of God's mercy to Nineveh from a knowledge of covenantal properties or relational mutability, but from God's personal revelation of what it means that he is I AM. It is not relational mutability that grounds Jonah's knowledge, but the eternal immutability of God as infinitely merciful and gracious.

Exodus 3 teaches us that God is the great, eternal, self-sufficient, and transcendent God. It teaches us also that this same transcendent God—in virtue of his infinite perfection—is the merciful, gracious, and faithful God of Israel. God's relationship to his people is based on his eternal, essential existence as I AM. He need not assume relational properties. Similarly, the Psalms show us that the eternal I AM is the protector and sustainer of his people (Psalm 3:3-5; 18:2; 31:23); the one who hears our weeping (Psalm 6:8); the judge and ruler of the nations (Psalm 7:8; 22:28); a refuge for the oppressed (Psalm 9:9); the one who sees all the human race (Psalm 14:2-4; 33:13); the one who shows tender mercy (Psalm 25:6; 40:11; 69:16; 145:9); and who fills the earth with his goodness (Psalm 33:5). All of these—and many more—are attributed to the eternal I AM. God is both essentially transcendent and immanent.

Exodus 15:11

> Who is like you, O LORD, among the gods? Who is like you, majestic in holiness, awesome in glorious deeds, doing

---

[19] Lister, *God is Impassible and Impassioned*, 211.

wonders? (Exod. 15:11, ESV)

After the Red Sea crossing, Moses and the children of Israel break out into song, praising God for the display of his marvelous power on their behalf. Because God has chosen Israel, he acts *for* Israel. Moses' song focuses on the distinctions God makes between Israel and the other nations, particularly Egypt. There is a relationship between God and Israel that God does not have with other nations. So, Moses declares that "He *is* my God, and I will praise Him; My father's God, and I will exalt Him" (Exod. 15:2). Similarly, in verse 13, it is by God's covenant love that he leads Israel. God will bring them into the land and establish them there. By contrast, God is a warrior against the other nations. His majestic power destroys Pharaoh and his chariots. God overthrows his enemies (Exod. 15:7), so that other nations and peoples hear and tremble (Exod. 15:14-16). The same actions from God are both deliverance for Israel and, at the same time, judgment upon others. The Red Sea that delivers Israel, destroys Egypt. The same act is both one of covenant love and power.

The doxological climax of Moses' song is verse 11. "Who is like you, O Lord, among the gods? Who is like you, majestic in holiness, awesome in glorious deeds, doing wonders?" Moses emphatically and rhetorically declares to God his own incomparability, indirectly challenging any to name a god who is like YHWH. God is utterly different from all who may claim the title of "majestic" — whether angels, men, or idols. Moses amplifies his rhetoric, naming three facets of God's matchlessness: his holiness, his deeds, and his miracles.

Holiness is God's separateness, his distinctiveness. God is not just different from others, as if on the far end of the same spectrum. "The word '*sanctitas*,' holiness, expresses that glory which separates God from all His creatures."[20] He is *holy*, unlike and distinct from any other gods. His distinctiveness, in fact, is noble and majestic. His holiness is a glorious holiness. God's providential acts in history also show his transcendence, causing men to compose or lift up praises to him. These praises are not mere adulations, like the flatteries that idol worshippers bring to their idols. Rather, they are

---

[20] Calvin, *Commentaries*, 2:259.

full of awe and fear, honest in their exultation of God as supreme. Finally, God's acts are sometimes miraculous works, working "without, above, or against" the ordinary means as he ordains (cf. 2LCF 5.3). Such miraculous works go beyond the curious or magical displays of others. God's miracles leave men with no room to deny that the God of Moses and Israel *is* God (Exod. 8:10; 10:2). No men or so-called gods have performed such mighty works.

In all of this, God is shown to be utterly transcendent, distinct, supreme, peerless, and incomparable. Yet, his transcendence is his immanence — that is, the acts of God which demonstrate his transcendence are also those acts which work in human history in a way that proves he is without peer or comparison. His covenant faithfulness to his people is based on his incomparability.

While confessing that he is infinite in his essence and transcendence, the relational-mutability view asserts that God relates to his people through covenantal properties — properties he assumes in order to relate to the created order. But Exodus 15:11 declares that God's transcendence itself is the basis for his acts on his people's behalf. His mighty deeds manifest that his transcendence and his immanence are not separable, but both are based on the same, eternal, and infinite nature of the LORD. Again we see that God's relationship to his people is based directly on his eternal, essential self-existence as YHWH.

Psalm 90:2

> Before the mountains were brought forth, Or ever You had formed the earth and the world, Even from everlasting to everlasting, You *are* God. (Psalm 90:2)

Psalm 90, ascribed to Moses, is another song by God's great prophet. Verse 2 declares that "from everlasting to everlasting, You *are* God." Here the psalmist teaches us not just that God is eternal, but that he is eternally *God*. He is the unchangeable God "from everlasting to everlasting," neither increasing nor diminishing in any way. Immutability and eternality are woven together in this description of God.

There are two complementary lines of thought in Psalm 90

which testify to God's immutability and its relationship to men. The first speaks of God's transcendence in his relationship to time and judgment. In verse 4, God's working in relation to time is above our experience and knowledge. A thousand years, longer than the lifespan of any man, is portrayed as a memory of an already-past day. "With [God] there is neither succession of Counsels and purposes, nor yet plurality, but as with one opening of his eye, he beholds all things as they are."[21] Time is seen by God in a manner somewhat like our reflecting upon a memory, being comprehended in a single thought. In verse 11, God's wrath and anger are above our knowledge, so that, as dying sinners, we stand before God in danger of eternal and infinite justice.

The second line of thought in Psalm 90 speaks of God's relationship to men. He is our dwelling place (Psalm 90:1). He decides the length of our brief lives (Psalm 90:3-6). He holds his righteous wrath over all who sin, for God knows even our secret sins as if done in full light before his face (Psalm 90:6-11). Yet, God is merciful, so that his works for his people surpass the afflictions of their short lives. God is glorious and beautiful, and makes the work of their hands to be not in vain.

Here again, the utter transcendence and immanence of God are interconnected. Because God is not subject to time, he is our true dwelling place. Because the events of human history are like a single thought to him, he knows eternally every single event — even our secret sins. Because God is infinite, so his justice is frighteningly infinite, his wrath already abiding on sinners. Because God is transcendent, he is merciful toward sinners, and his infinite mercy can satisfy us in a way that our frail, finite lives never can. Our beauty is but the quickly fading flower of the grasslands; God's beauty is forever.

In conclusion, God's closest, most immanent of relationships to his creation are based directly on his eternal, unchangeable nature as the everlasting God. God relates to his people on the very basis of his eternal, essential being, such that there is no need to posit a duality in God between his transcendence and his immanence.

---

[21] Hugh Binning, *The Common Principles of Christian Religion* (Glasgow: Printed by R.S., 1666), 169, as quoted in Samuel Renihan, ed., *God without Passions: A Reader* (Palmdale, CA: RBAP, 2015), 117.

Psalm 94:9

> He who planted the ear, shall He not hear? He who formed
> the eye, shall He not see? (Psalm 94:9)

In Psalm 94, the psalmist seeks God's retribution on the proud of the land. The proud are wicked, who speak insolently, and do not cringe from oppression and murder of the most righteous or helpless. Their fixed religious perspective is that God does not see what they do, nor does he hear their words or even the prayers of the righteous who are oppressed. In Psalm 94:8-9, the psalmist, calling such men stupid and foolish, shows the complete irrationality of their unbelief. "Understand, you senseless among the people; And *you* fools, when will you be wise? He who planted the ear, shall He not hear? He who formed the eye, shall He not see?" That God created man with the ability to hear and see proves that he, who is infinitely above us, must also be possessed of infinitely greater abilities than we are. Therefore, he surely sees the evil act and hears the prayers of his oppressed people.

On this passage, Robert Gonzales writes:

> As the *imago Dei*, man is an analogue of God. Hence, when we approach "anthropomorphic" language biblically, we won't place all the emphasis on discorrespondence. That's not where the Bible places the emphasis! Listen to the language of Psalm 94:9: "He who planted the ear, does he not hear? He who formed the eye, does he not see?" The psalmist is certainly not implying that God has physical ears or physical eyes. He's assuming a certain discontinuity between Creator and creature. Nevertheless, the emphasis of the text is on continuity or correspondence. Our hearing ear and our seeing eye are visible replicas of God's invisible and spiritual ability to perceive.[22]

This interpretation is problematic, however. First, the point of Psalm

---

[22] Robert Gonzales, "The Passionate Impassible God: Toward a Biblical View of Divine Emotions," *http://drbobgonzales.com/2012/biblical-balance-affirming-gods-emotivity-and-his-impassibility/*. Accessed 23 March 2012.

94:9 is not on correspondence between God's abilities and man's abilities. The fact that the Creator must be possessed of infinitely superior capabilities than he crafts in his creatures is not, in itself, a statement of correspondence between God's abilities and those of the creature. The above interpretation mistakenly concludes that if a certain faculty is found in the creature, it must of necessity be found in a greater way in the Creator. The *context* and *logic* of the passage, however, point to discontinuity rather than correspondence. The claim of the oppressors (v. 7) is one of certainty, not probability. To them, God does *not* see or hear. They are certain that his faculties are either totally absent or limited (like man's) to the point of ineffectiveness. Contrariwise, the psalmist replies that God most certainly sees and hears. He even knows the futile thoughts of men (v. 11). If God's knowledge were either incorrect or incomplete, there could be no certainty. The only way such certainty can be ascribed to God's knowledge is if it is infallible and exhaustive — characteristics that are not analogous to the type of seeing and hearing of which men are capable. Thus, the point of the passage hinges on the *discorrespondence* between God and man.

Second, the context makes plain that God is the Creator, and man is the creature. God's "seeing" and "hearing" must therefore be uncreated, infinite, and thus *eternally* infallible and exhaustive — again showing that God's knowledge is of a nature distinct from our own. God, as a rational being, marked by infinite knowledge, created us also as rational beings and capable of knowing. In this way, the *imago Dei* extends to the existence of the faculty in us. However, man's mode of existence is distinct from God's mode of existence, and so our knowledge is distinct from God's knowledge. God knows inherently, eternally, infallibly, and infinitely. Our knowledge is learned or acquired, derived, temporal, fallible, and very limited.

The point of Psalm 94, then, is not to declare that God's knowledge is analogous to ours. Rather, it is to show that the distinction between God and man makes his knowledge infallible and certain — thus condemning the proud for their intentional suppression of the truth.

Psalm 94 shows us that God relates to us from his eternal nature. There is nothing in the passage that indicates God's knowledge and judgment is based on anything other than his essential, infinite nature. It is God's omniscience that "sees" and "hears" all the deeds and thoughts of men. He relates to us as the all-seeing and all-knowing I AM.

Conclusion

The texts examined above show that God is eternal, unchangeable, and self-existent. None of this is denied, of course, by those proposing a relational-mutability view of God's relationship to man. Yet these verses also show that, when God relates to men, he does so as the same eternal, transcendent I AM who is infinite in being and perfection. We should not separate transcendence and immanence into two separate orders of divine being — one eternal, and the other temporal or covenantal — as if God's transcendence is a problem that only a temporal mode of existence, falsely termed immanence, must somehow overcome. Rather, every attribute of God is transcendent *and* immanent. His knowledge, love, compassion, and justice are all infinite and eternal. And it is just because they are so that they can reach to every person individually and directly.

Chapter 4

THE OLD TESTAMENT ON
THE DOCTRINE OF DIVINE IMPASSIBILITY
(II) Texts on Immutability and Impassibility
Ronald S. Baines and Steve Garrick

There are several Old Testament passages that relate directly to the doctrine of divine impassibility. What follows is an exegetical and theological assessment of four important and related passages—Numbers 23:19; Deuteronomy 28:63; 1 Samuel 15; and Malachi 3:6.

Numbers 23:19

> God *is* not a man, that He should lie, Nor a son of man, that He should repent. Has He said, and will He not do? Or has He spoken, and will He not make it good? (Num. 23:19)

Numbers 23 continues the narrative of the encounter of Israel with Balak, who has enlisted Balaam to curse Israel. On the first encounter, Balaam received the word of the Lord which came as a word of blessing for Israel, rather than cursing as Balak had hoped. Assuming that somehow the numerical size of Israel or some other alterable element was at the heart of the problem, Balak convinced Balaam to try a second time, hoping to reverse the favor of God toward Israel. In the opening declarations of the second of Balaam's oracles, he proclaims the word of God to Balak:

> Rise up, Balak, and hear! Listen to me, son of Zippor! [19] God *is* not a man, that He should lie, Nor a son of man, that He should repent. Has He said, and will He not do? Or has He spoken, and will He not make it good? [20] Behold, I have received *a command* to bless; He has blessed, and I cannot reverse it. (Num. 23:18b-20)

God's opening call for Balak's attention reveals that his most foundational problem was a decidedly corrupt conception of Israel's God. Like all who "suppress the truth in unrighteousness," Balak conceived of YHWH after the order of "the creature rather than the Creator, who is blessed forever" (cf. Rom. 1:18-25). To assume simply changing physical locations or limiting the visibility of Israel (and thereby possibly the size of Israel) would somehow empower Balaam to convince or enable God to curse them, and so reverse the previous unfortunate (in Balak's estimation) blessing, was the height of folly and wickedness.

God, through the wicked prophet Balaam, forcefully comes forward to disabuse Balak of any such notion by declaring that he "*is* not a man . . . Nor a son of man," thereby calling his attention to the Creator/creature distinction.[1] God's blessing is irreversible, Balak is informed, because it does not originate in either the willingness of God to bless or in the lack of God's willingness to curse. It is not simply volitional, although God is clearly unwilling to withdraw his blessing. Rather, God declares that his act of blessing Israel is grounded in his very essence or nature; because he is God, and "not a man . . . Nor a son of man," the blessing is irrevocable. In other words, it is not that God *will not* revoke his blessing; it is that he *cannot* revoke his blessing. This is further underscored by what follows in verse 21 and following. God's relationship with Israel is covenantal, and Israel's covenant status had not changed since God's pronounced blessing in Numbers 22.

The Fact of the Creator/Creature Distinction

In rebuking Balak, God first sets himself apart from mankind

---

[1] The forcefulness of the Lord's address to Balak is found first in the three introductory imperatives directed at Balak. As Timothy Ashley, *The Book of Numbers*, The New International Commentary on the Old Testament, ed. Robert L. Hubbard, Jr. (Grand Rapids: Wm. B. Eerdmans Publishing Co., 1993), 476-77, points out, commanding Balak to rise when he was already "standing" (v. 17) fails to do justice to the construction if one assumes this is a simple command to stand up. The forcefulness is further underscored by the use of the Hebrew negative particle לֹא (lō') not, no. See Paul Joüon and T. Muraoka, *A Grammar of Biblical Hebrew* (Roma: Pontificio Istituto Biblico, 2006), §160.c.

ontologically by way of negation and then expresses the consequences of this foundational theological reality in several ways. By doing so, God himself makes evident in his Word the necessary distinctions between God and man, the Creator and the creature.[2]

It is important at the onset, however, to note that God is providing for us a way or method of naming himself. While "God *is* not a man . . . Nor a son of man" is the fundamental starting point for what follows, Balak's folly was in thinking God was "a man," that there was a level of essential identity between God and man. By confronting Balak this way, God is establishing the practice of describing the Creator/creature distinction negatively, i.e., by what God is not.[3] The result is a declared distinction that must be maintained. As Psalm 50:21 confirms, our sinful tendency is to think God is "altogether like" us. While there are ways that the *imago Dei* reflects our likeness to God in certain limited respects, this biblical truth does not permit attributing all that is true of the image-bearer to the infinite Creator. That is, the *imago Dei* also highlights those ways in which God and man are not alike. It is to these dissimilarities that God turns as the direct consequences of his foundational theological declaration that he "*is* not a man."[4]

---

[2] Joüon and Muraoka, *Grammar*, §169 b, identifies the two jussive verbs with *waw* following the oracle's opening negative clause as expressing consequence. See also A. B. Davidson, *Hebrew Syntax*, 3rd ed. (1901; reprint, Edinburgh: T&T Clark, 1958), §150.

[3] This provides ample foundation for the practice of using negatives to describe God, such as "without body, parts, or passions." See Muller, *Dictionary*, 326.

[4] In describing God's knowledge in Isa. 55:8-9, God distinguishes between his "thoughts" and man's "thoughts." This text confirms that God's knowledge transcends the created order, not just in extent (infinite vs. finite), but in kind (Creator vs. creature). But it also confirms a level of correspondence. Man's thoughts are in some fashion analogous to God's; God and man both have "thoughts" (Heb. מַחֲשָׁבָה, *maḥăšābâ*, thought). In Num. 23:19, however, God does not offer a comparison/contrast between something both mankind and God share. Rather, using the *via negationis*, he denies attributing what is characteristic of man (i.e., to repent and to lie) to God. Thus we can say that "thoughts" are predicated of God properly yet analogically/anthropomorphically, while to "repent" is applied to God analogically/anthropomorphically but improperly, because, as Num. 23:19 asserts, "God *is* not a man, that He should lie, Nor a son of man, that He should repent." On the distinction between *proper* and *improper* when delimiting analogical

The Consequences of the Creator/Creature Distinction

The clauses which follow this basic negative declaration give greater clarity to the implications or consequences of the Creator/creature distinction revealed by God. The text does not leave us to speculate in what ways God is not like a man. The first consequence is that God does not lie.[5] All the major modern English versions reflect this translation. The rest of the Old Testament richly attests to this reality. Psalm 116:11 affirms not only that mankind lies, but that this is a universal and ongoing experience for man; "All men *are* liars."[6] This distinction cannot be overstated: God and mankind bear no similarity here.

Nevertheless, it is likely that there is more to God's declaration than simply that he does not lie. What follows God's assertion that he does not lie nor repent is the avowal that what he has spoken stands; he will make good on his word. Embedded in this further clarification is the awareness that the Creator does not lie because whatever he purposes, whatever he says, must certainly come to pass. It cannot fail: first, because it is ontologically impossible for God to lie (cf. Heb. 6:18) and second, because he will sovereignly and infallibly ensure that it "stands."[7] God not only cannot lie, he cannot fail to keep his promises. There is nothing in the universe that can inhibit his declared promises and purposes. He is not a man. The blessing previously pronounced on Israel is as certain as the very being of God.

This fuller explication is confirmed by the use of this verb rendered "fail" in Isaiah 58:11.

---

language, see the discussion in chapter 1, "Analogy and the Doctrine of Divine Impassibility."

[5] The Hebrew verb is וִיכַזֵּב (conj.-pi. impf. 3 m.s., jussive in meaning).

[6] The durative or ongoing character of men as liars (כֹּזֵב) is captured by the qal participle. See Eugene Carpenter and Michael A. Grisanti, "כָּזַב (kāzab)," in *NIDOTTE*, 2:619-21.

[7] This is reflected at the end of Num. 23:19, "Or has He spoken, and will He not make it good?" The verb is in the hiphil stem; literally "God will cause his word to stand" (cf. Isa. 40:8). This use of קוּם (vb. arise, stand up, stand), has covenantal overtones indicating the word of covenantal ratification spoken by God in Gen. 6:18; 9:9, etc.

The LORD will guide you continually, And satisfy your soul in drought, And strengthen your bones; You shall be like a watered garden, And like a spring of water, whose waters do not fail. (Isa. 58:11)

The final word of verse 11 is the same verb translated as "lie" in Numbers 23:19. Timothy Ashley captures this well:

> *God is not a human that he should fail* (*lō' 'îš 'ēl wîḵazzēḇ*). The first part of the line establishes a basic tenet of Hebrew thought: God and humankind are not the same. The assertion is even more vivid than that: God is not to be confused with a creature. The word used here is *'îš*, which does not generally mean humankind, but a single example of it, a man (even a male). God is definitely not a man. He is the Creator, not a creature. Of the many predications that could have been chosen here, *that he should fail* points to a very basic distinction between the Creator and a creature. Although the translation *lie* is common, the context shows that the primary thought is not that God does not utter untruths (although that is true), but that his purposes are utterly true and reliable, and that his nature does not disappoint or fail, as is the case with human creatures.[8]

False prophets lie (Ezek. 13:19; Mic. 2:11), because they have no power to effect what they prophesy and God has no intention of honoring their words; they will fail. Humans lie, but they also find themselves unable to bring to fruition their plans and purposes because of things beyond their control. Human purposes fail. It cannot be so, however, with the word of the Lord, because it is spoken by the Lord God, who is not a man. As Isaiah declares:

Remember the former things of old, For I *am* God, and *there is* no other; I *am* God, and *there is* none like Me, ¹⁰ Declaring the end from the beginning, And from ancient times *things* that are not *yet* done, Saying, 'My counsel shall stand, And I

---

8 Ashley, *The Book of Numbers*, 477.

will do all My pleasure,' [11] Calling a bird of prey from the
east, The man who executes My counsel, from a far country.
Indeed I have spoken *it*; I will also bring it to pass. I have
purposed *it*; I will also do it. (Isa. 46:9-11)

God's word is inseparably connected to God's essence; his word
cannot fail because he cannot lie. The implications for this
respecting God's impassibility come to center in the parallel
construction that God uses to underscore this distinction. God treats
the possibility of his telling a lie to be of the same cloth with the
possibility of his repenting.

The second consequence of God's affirmation that he is "not a
man . . . Nor a son of man" is that he does not repent. This divine
negation provides some challenges reflected not least in the split
between versions that translate the Hebrew word as "repent" (KJV,
NKJV, NASB,) or as "change his mind" (ESV, NIV, NRSV).[9] The
challenge is further underscored by the use of the verb elsewhere of
God where he is said to "repent." Of the slightly more than 100 uses
of this verb in the Hebrew Old Testament, some 35 are predicated of
God. Numerous passages mention God's repentance (Gen. 6:6, 7;
Exod. 32:12, 14; Judg. 2:18; 1 Sam. 15:11, 35; 2 Sam. 24:16; 1 Chron.
21:15; Psalm 90:13; 106:45; 135:14; Jer. 15:6; 18:8, 10; 26:3, 13, 19;
42:10; Ezek. 5:13; Joel 2:13-14; Amos 7:3, 6; Jon. 3:9, 10; 4:2), while
others assert that God does not repent or change his mind (Num.
23:19; 1 Sam. 15:29; Psalm 110:4; Jer. 4:28; 20:16; Ezek. 24:14; Zech.
8:14). What are we to make of this data?

One issue that warrants care is that, as Butterworth
acknowledges, the "classification of the meanings of this root is
difficult."[10] This confirms that simple lexicography will not supply
sufficient materials to iron out all the wrinkles, although it does
provide the important starting point. According to Wilson, the

---

[9] The Hebrew verb is נָחַם (*nāḥam* — hithpael imperf., 3ms jussive in meaning)
and is used just over 100 times in the OT. Though the verb predominantly occurs in
the niphal and piel stems (the qal is lacking), the rare use of the hithpael stem in
this text probably reflects better the stem's reflexive emphasis (See Psalm 119:52 for
another example of the reflexive nature of the verb in the hithpael stem.).

[10] Mike Butterworth, "נָחַם (*nāḥam*)," in *NIDOTTE*, 3:81-83.

primary meanings are "to repent" or "to change one's mind"[11] and "to comfort" or "console."[12] Simian-Yofre captures well both a subjective and an objective character to the word:

> The twin factors of decision/effect and emotion/affect are thus the rule in *nhm*; they are indissolubly interwoven, even when in individual cases there may be greater emphasis on one element or the other.[13]

Here, however, we must remember that the word is negated in the Hebrew text, reflecting how God, because he is not "a son of man," undergoes neither the subjective affect nor the objective effect underscored by "repent." As Simian-Yofre notes with reference to Numbers 23:19 and 1 Samuel 15:29, "its use in negation is absolute: ultimately Yahweh does not change his mind."[14] The core idea here is one of objective change and the subjective human emotional aspects that apply to it, neither of which, according to these two texts, can be properly predicated of God.

This drives us to the conclusion that the doctrine of divine impassibility is a subset of at least two foundational theological premises fleshed out by Numbers 23:19. The first is the ontological foundation of the Creator/creature distinction: "God *is* not a man." He is "a most pure spirit" (2LCF 2.1) and therefore is unchangeable, both subjectively and objectively. He does not change, not because he chooses not to, but because it is contrary to his being. He cannot change any more than he can lie. In other words, God does not claim *volitional* reasons but *ontological* reasons for his own immutability and impassibility.

The second foundational premise is that divine impassibility is a necessary theological consequence of divine immutability. In other words, divine impassibility is an extension of God's

---

[11] M. R. Wilson, "נָחַם (*nāḥam*)," in *TWOT*, 2:570-71. This meaning is found predominately in the niphal stem.

[12] Wilson, "נָחַם (*nāḥam*)," in *TWOT*, 2:570-71. This sense is predominately represented in the piel stem, although this meaning may also be present in the niphal, pual, and hithpael stems.

[13] Simian-Yofre, "נחם (*nhm*)," in *TDOT*, 9:342.

[14] Simian-Yofre, "נחם (*nhm*)," in *TDOT*, 9:344.

incommunicable attribute of immutability. If, as Numbers 23:19 insists, God is incapable of change, then he is incapable of repentance in the proper sense. This is the very point of Numbers 23:19. Balak misunderstood both the essence of God as a whole and the immutability of God, specifically. He projected idolatrous views of his own making back onto his view of YHWH—a fatal flaw.[15]

It seems pertinent in the light of the discussions of divine impassibility taking place within evangelical and Reformed circles to note further that this text informs us not only that repentance is not a divine attribute, but that it most certainly *is* a human trait. In other words, God is not distinguishing between human and divine traits, between human repenting and divine repenting. The text does not say "God does not repent like men."[16] But rather "repentance" is not to be found in God; it is contrary to the very essence of God. Conversely, we are to understand also that God is confirming that repentance *is* of the essence of the creature, but *cannot* be in the Creator properly. More specifically, repentance is of the created anthropological realm; repentance belongs properly to man but not properly to God. Therefore, all references elsewhere in Scripture that speak of God as repenting (see the references above)

---

[15] Because impassibility is a subset of immutability, it is frequently handled under the doctrine of divine immutability in theological treatises on the attributes of God. This is especially so in pre-twentieth-century theologies.

[16] This is the understanding of Lister. He claims a *"similarity* between divine and human repentance" and thus concludes, *"because God is not a man,* he does not repent like one" (Lister, *God is Impassible and Impassioned,* 210, italics original). This is a major theological misstep by Lister. He goes on to claim that repentance in God is an example of God's relational mutability, a term he seems to have adopted from Bruce A. Ware, "An Evangelical Reformulation Of the Doctrine of the Immutability of God," *JETS,* Vol. 29, No. 4, (December 1986): 431-46. While Ware appears to agree largely with Lister's modification of classical impassibility, he denies firmly that repentance can be predicated of God as an example of relational mutability. If Num. 23:19 and 1 Sam. 15:29 allow that God can repent, they would also necessitate that God can lie—an exegetically inescapable conclusion. Ware rightly denies this conclusion and so denies that repentance can belong properly to God. See Bruce A. Ware, *God's Lesser Glory; The Diminished God of Open Theism* (Wheaton: Crossway Books, 2000), 86-91. Lister never addresses this implication. Lister claims to be advocating a modified form of classical impassibility; however, the form of his advocacy of repentance in God leads one to suspect his position may be better considered "qualified" passibility. See James E. Dolezal, "Review: *God is Impassible and Impassioned,*" *WTJ* 76 (Fall 2013): 414-18. This review is reprinted with permission as an appendix to this book.

must be understood as God reveals them to be in this text—as anthropopathisms.

In light of this, it is hard to fathom why a number of present-day evangelicals decry the assignation of texts such as Genesis 6:6-7, which affirm God's repentance, by Reformed expositors as anthropomorphisms or anthropopathisms.[17] Numbers 23:19 (and also 1 Sam. 15:29) calls for just such a conclusion. Further, Numbers 23:19 (and 1 Sam. 15:29) suggests exegetically that to deny these texts are anthropopathic means a number of present-day evangelicals are confusing texts that assert God's nature with texts that describe God's actions. In other words, it is not a pre-commitment to some philosophical ideal of an Aristotelian Unmoved Mover or a belief that God is "apathetic" that brings Calvin to say the following in his interpretation of Genesis 6:6-7:

> The repentance which is here ascribed to God does not properly belong to him, but has reference to our understanding of him. For since we cannot comprehend him as he is, it is necessary that, for our sake, he should, in a certain sense, transform himself. That repentance cannot take place in God, easily appears from this single consideration, that nothing happens which is by him unexpected or unforeseen. The same reasoning, and remark, applies to what follows, that God was affected with grief. Certainly God is not sorrowful or sad; but remains for ever like himself in his celestial and happy repose: yet, because it could not otherwise be known how great is God's hatred and detestation of sin, therefore the Spirit accommodates himself to our capacity. Wherefore, there is no need for us to

---

[17] E.g., Gonzales, *Where Sin Abounds*, 80-81 and Carson, *The Difficult Doctrine*, 58-59. It is certainly counter-productive when some of these same men misrepresent the classical impassibility of the historic confessions as holding God to be "apathetic" or distant and cold. Foundational to God's rejection of Balak's frustrated attempts to have Israel cursed is not a cold, indifferent, or apathetic God, but one who is fundamentally committed to faithfulness in covenant with Israel. Certainly no Israelite would view this covenant faithfulness as apathy or indifference. The beauty of God's declaration in Num. 23:19 is not that God is emotionally cold, but that he is infinite, eternal, and unchangeable in his covenantal commitments and care for Israel; hence, his purposes to bless Israel were unalterable.

involve ourselves in thorny and difficult questions, when it is obvious to what end these words of repentance and grief are applied; namely, to teach us, that from the time when man was so greatly corrupted, God would not reckon him among his creatures; as if he would say, 'This is not my workmanship; this is not that man who was formed in my image, and whom I had adorned with such excellent gifts: I do not deign now to acknowledge this degenerate and defiled creature as mine.' Similar to this is what he says, in the second place, concerning grief; that God was so offended by the atrocious wickedness of men, as if they had wounded his heart with mortal grief. There is here, therefore, an unexpressed antithesis between that upright nature which had been created by God, and that corruption which sprung from sin. Meanwhile, unless we wish to provoke God, and to put him to grief, let us learn to abhor and to flee from sin. Moreover, this paternal goodness and tenderness ought, in no slight degree, to subdue in us the love of sin; since God, in order more effectually to pierce our hearts, clothes himself with our affections. This figure, which represents God as transferring to himself what is peculiar to human nature, is called ἀνθρωποπάθεια.[18]

Robert Gonzales accuses Calvin here of being guilty of two logical inconsistencies, neither of which proves to be a correct understanding of Calvin.[19] First, Gonzales claims Calvin is "willing to allow the emotions [Calvin does not use this term here] of anger and detestation but not the emotions of regret and sorrow." But here Gonzales fails to account for Calvin's point; he is not affirming "anger and detestation" while denying "regret and sorrow." Calvin considers all of these to be in God analogically. But his point is that within this analogical context repentance and grief do not *properly* belong to God; they are inconsistent with his nature. In contrast, whether one calls them emotions or not (and Calvin does not), hatred and detestation of sin are properly predicated of God because they are necessary manifestations of his essential holiness

---

[18] Calvin, *Commentaries*, 1:270.
[19] Gonzales, *Where Sin Abounds*, 80-81, n. 83.

and justice with respect to sin (Deut. 12:31; 16:20-22; Psalm 5:6; 11:5; 45:8; Prov. 6:16; Isa. 1:13-17; 61:8; Jer. 44:4; Hos. 9:15; Amos 5:21-24; Zech. 8:7; Mal. 1:3). God has infinitely, eternally, and unchangeably hated and detested sin. However, to assume that because they are analogical they are emotional responses also is to say more than Scripture would have us to acknowledge; "God *is* not a man" (Num. 23:19; 1 Sam. 15:29). Calvin's distinction is not an inconsistency. He distinguishes rightly between those analogical expressions which are proper (hatred and detestation of sin) and those which are improper (repentance and grief). Contra Gonzales, Calvin is interpreting Genesis 6:6-7 consistently. God's holiness and justice require a judicial response to sin which in the larger flood narrative is described in human emotional terms so that we may understand better the ways of God himself.

Second, Gonzales accuses Calvin of the inconsistency of using "descriptive language that, on the one hand is untrue of God in order to, on the other hand, make known to us what 'could not otherwise be known.'" Again, Gonzales misconstrues Calvin. If biblical anthropopathisms are "untrue" then are not also biblical anthropomorphisms? If God has no arms, then is Deuteronomy 32:27 using "descriptive language that [is] on the one hand, untrue of God in order to, on the other hand, make known what 'could not otherwise be known'"? Gonzales does not explain why anthropomorphisms are valid but anthropopathisms are not. This is critical, especially since anthropopathisms are essentially a subset of anthropomorphisms. It seems that Calvin is actually the more consistent here.

It appears the options here are two. One, it may be that Gonzales is affirming that the terms used in Genesis 6 apply to God properly, and they mean, basically, that God had these emotions in himself. This appears to be his point when he affirms, "This exposure of emotional turbulence in the heart of an infinite, eternal, unchangeable God is one of the greatest indicators of the colossal proportions of human sin."[20] If this is the case, he is reformulating the doctrine of God by insisting that repentance and grief belong properly to God, directly contradicting Numbers 23:19 and 1 Samuel 15:29. The other option appears to be that Gonzales is

---

[20] Gonzales, *Where Sin Abounds,* 81.

denying Calvin's correct understanding and helpful exposition of analogical language. Analogies are not "untrue," neither are they one-to-one correspondences. Calvin is acknowledging that these terms tell us something of God, "his hatred and detestation of sin," but they are communicating this reality in human terms that reflect emotions which do not properly belong to God, i.e., "regret and grief." In either case, Gonzales has not represented Calvin accurately.

What Calvin is doing in his comments on Genesis 6 is invoking the analogy of Scripture and the analogy of faith, thereby allowing certain clear predications regarding God's essence to be the lens through which he explains other texts which speak of God's actions. This is underscored by his comments on Numbers 23:19, where he says:

> In order, therefore, that we may learn to lift up our minds above the world, whenever the faithfulness and certainty of God's word are in question, it is well for us to reflect how great the distance is between ourselves and God. Men are wont to lie, because they are fickle and changeable in their plans, or because sometimes they are unable to accomplish what they have promised; but change of purpose arises either from levity or bad faith, or because we repent of what we have spoken foolishly and inconsiderately. But to God nothing of this sort occurs; for He is neither deceived, nor does He deceitfully promise anything, nor, as James says, is there with Him any "shadow of turning" (James 1:7.) We now understand to what this dissimilitude between God and men refers, namely, that we should not travesty God according to our own notions, but, in our consideration of His nature, should remember that He is liable to no changes, since He is far above all heavens.[21]

The "dissimilitude between God and men," as Calvin refers to it, compels the conclusion that Numbers 23:19 and 1 Samuel 15:29 teach that repentance does not properly belong to God, but does

---

[21] John Calvin, *Commentaries on the Four Last Books of Moses Arranged in the Form of a Harmony*, vol. 4 (Edinburgh: The Calvin Translation Society, 1860), 211.

belong to man. It is anthropological in nature and so must be treated as such. We must assume, therefore, that the predication of repentance to God in passages such as Genesis 6 is an example of analogically applying a term to God which is proper only to humans—a term which does not properly belong to God. Such terms are equal in nature to terms which apply physical arms (Deut. 32:27) to God. This is not an imposition of philosophy onto theology, nor does it empty the "terminology of significance."[22] Rather, it is the necessary consequence of comparing Scripture with Scripture.

Deuteronomy 28:63

> And it shall be, *that* just as the LORD rejoiced over you to do you good and multiply you, so the LORD will rejoice over you to destroy you and bring you to nothing; and you shall be plucked from off the land which you go to possess. (Deut. 28:63)

Deuteronomy 28:63 is an important text for the biblical doctrine of impassibility. The Hebrew verb translated "rejoice" occurs four times in Deuteronomy; two in our text and two times in 30:9. In all four occurrences it is God who is rejoicing and it is Israel over whom God rejoices.[23]

---

[22] Gonzales, *Where Sin Abounds*, 80.

[23] The Hebrew verb is שׂוּשׂ (*śûś*), to rejoice or exult. In each of the four occurrences in Deuteronomy (28:63 twice and 30:9 twice) God is the subject and it is followed by the preposition עַל ('al) upon, over, on account of, and has Israel as the object of the preposition. Three of these four occurrences reflect God's positive rejoicing over Israel to bless them nationally (יַטַב yāṭab, in the hiphil expressing a causative relation, to cause good to come to Israel) while one occurrence (Deut. 28:63) reflects God's judicial rejoicing over them to bring them to nothing (lit. with the Hebrew verb אָבַד 'ābad, in the hiphil expressing a causative relation, to cause Israel to be destroyed as a nation). Overall, the verb שׂוּשׂ (śûś) occurs 27 times in the Hebrew OT, most often in Isaiah (nine times) and Psalms (seven times). In eight of the 27 occurrences, the verb has God as the subject (Deut. 28:63 twice; 30:9 twice; Isa. 62:5; 65:19; Jer. 32:41; Zeph. 3:17). The thematic connections between the uses of the verb in Isa. 62:5 and Deut. 28:63 are numerous; the same is true for Isa. 65:19; Jer. 32:41; and Zeph. 3:17. Each and every case of God rejoicing over his people involves him bringing them back to the land of promise and under his blessings.

It is important to set our discussion of verse 63 into the larger context of Deuteronomy. Israel is about to enter the land, and Moses is giving final instruction to this second generation regarding their covenantal status with God. Moses commands that Israel, after entering the land, gather at the conjunction of Mount Ebal and Mount Gerizim to recount graphically the covenant curses that will come upon them if they do not "obey the voice of the LORD your God" (Deut. 27:10) and the covenant blessings that shall accrue to them if they are faithful to the covenant and "obey the voice of the LORD your God." The curses to be proclaimed from Mount Ebal were recorded by Moses in Deuteronomy 27:11-26. The covenant blessings promised by God were recorded by Moses in Deuteronomy 28:1-14. Moses follows the blessings with a second round of covenant curses that God will bring upon Israel, including their ultimate expulsion from the land, which he is ready to bring about, should they be covenantally unfaithful to him (Deut. 28:15-68). Our text falls in the midst of the second round of curses.

It is in this second round of covenant curses that God prophetically expresses his demeanor as the covenant Lord in executing his curses if Israel disobeys the covenant and in bestowing his blessings if they obey the covenant. Pivotal to understanding Deuteronomy 28:63 is the foundational requirement for Israel to "fear this glorious and awesome name, THE LORD YOUR GOD" (Deut. 28:58). If Israel gives due fear to his glorious (better "honored," NASB) and awesome name by expressing their covenant faithfulness to God, then he will "rejoice" over them and cause them to prosper. If they fail to fear his honored and awesome name and disobey the covenant, he will "rejoice" over them to banish them from the land. Their covenant faithfulness is directly connected to the honor they accord to God's name.[24]

Michael A. Grisanti is certainly correct to see the use of "rejoice" in Deuteronomy 28:63 as an "indicator of the status of Israel's

---

Further, the only negative occurrence of the verb with respect to God is in Deut. 28:63.

[24] The NKJV and ESV translate the Hebrew verb כָּבֵד (kābēd, a niphal participle) as "glorious." However, the idea of weighty is at the heart of the meaning and thus the NASB "honored" appears the better translation. Israel's honor for God's name was directly connected to their covenant obedience.

covenant relationship."[25] Not only does "rejoice" occur in the midst of the instructions to renew the Sinai covenant after Israel has entered the land, it harkens back further to the foundation of Israel's relationship to God in the Abrahamic covenant (cf. Deut. 26:5).[26] In this light, for God to "rejoice" is for him to express his unfailing commitment, as covenant Lord, to the stipulations of the covenant. God's commitment to Israel is via covenant and he is assuring Israel that his response to their covenant faithfulness is the manifestation of his unfailing commitment to bless; his covenant response to Israel in the face of their covenant unfaithfulness would be likewise the manifestation of his unfailing commitment to display his justice and to curse them. He delights in expressing his own goodness toward Israel and he will delight in expressing his own justice toward them should they disobey the covenant.[27]

What is important here for the doctrine of divine impassibility is that, while God uses language that is certainly emotion-laden, it is

---

[25] Micahel A. Grisanti, "שׂוּשׂ (śûś)," in *NIDOTTE*, 3:1223-26.

[26] The link to the Abrahamic covenant is established via the word in Deut. 28:63 translated "destroy." The Hebrew verb אָבַד (ʾābad) "perish, be destroyed," appears in Deut. 26:5 with direct reference to Abraham, "a perishing Aramean" whom God promised to make a great nation. That this passage is linked to the Abrahamic covenant is further underscored by God indicating that Israel, under God's blessing, was as numerous "as the stars of heaven in multitude" (Deut. 28:62, cf. Gen. 15:5; 22:17; 26:4; Exod. 32:13; Deut. 1:10; 10:22). Duane L. Christensen, *Deuteronomy 21:10-34:12*, Word Biblical Commentary, ed. John D. W. Watts and James W. Watts (Dallas: Word Incorporated, 2002), 6b:701, aptly notes, "The wording 'to cause you to perish' implies a strong contrast to 26:5, where the same verbal root appears (אבד, 'to perish'). God took a single 'perishing' (אבד) Aramean and made from him a people of vast numbers, so long as they were obedient. If they proved to be disobedient, he would diminish those numbers again by making his people 'perish' (להאביד)."

[27] This is underscored by the use of two comparative clauses linked by the combination of comparative particles כַּאֲשֶׁר + protasis—כֵּן + apodosis. God's response of delight in blessing Israel's faithfulness is compared to God's delight to bring justice on Israel through exile. The two clauses reflect the same response of delight from God. Note especially in this place that while God's delight is expressed in either case, it is Israel who shifts between faithfulness and unfaithfulness. God as covenant Lord has not changed; in fact, his unchanging nature is the very foundation of this promise of blessing or cursing depending on Israel's faithfulness or lack thereof. On the comparative in Deut. 28:63, see Bruce K. Waltke and Michael Patrick O'Connor, *An Introduction to Biblical Hebrew Syntax* (Winona Lake, IN: Eisenbrauns, 1990), §38.5.a, 641.

clear that he is warning Israel that he will not undergo emotional conflict should they prove covenantally unfaithful. Their status before God is conditioned by the covenant, and not because there are any emotional shifts in God, since there are none. He is equally delighted to bless or curse; to express delight in his goodness in the face of Israel's covenant faithfulness or to express delight in his holiness and justice in the face of Israel's covenant unfaithfulness. In essence, this text underscores the psalmist's understanding of God in Psalm 45:6-7a, which reads, "Your throne, O God, *is* forever and ever; A scepter of righteousness *is* the scepter of Your kingdom. You love righteousness and hate wickedness." Israel would be tempted to think the nation was the centerpiece, that God loved Israel and hated Gentiles. God puts Israel on notice that his love is for righteousness and holiness and so, in the face of Israel's unfaithfulness, his love of righteousness and hatred of sin, or love of his own justice, would necessitate Israel's chastening and ultimate exile. God suffers no emotional conflict in executing his covenant Lordship.

Two important elements warrant comment at this point. First, God has not changed emotionally. His love of righteousness is unwavering and so Israel in faithfulness is showered with blessings (God delights to do them good) but in unfaithfulness they are cursed (God delights to be just, to bring Israel to nothing). God is not emotionally conflicted. He is unchanged and impassible as covenant Lord.

Second, God uses language that is reflective of human rejoicing so as to emphasize this point. This is underscored by God using the same Hebrew word for rejoice in Isaiah 62:5 to represent the joy of newlyweds. "For *as* a young man marries a virgin, *So* shall your sons marry you; And *as* the bridegroom rejoices over the bride, *So* shall your God rejoice over you" (Isa. 62:5). God has couched the revelation of his covenantal actions toward Israel in language that is richly anthropopathic so as to emphasize the nature of his commitments to himself and to the covenant he has established with Israel. God is using the comparison of a bridegroom's rejoicing over his bride to express metaphorically the depth of his covenantal commitment. Calvin aptly remarks:

But although it is only by a metaphor that God is said to

rejoice in destroying the wicked, yet it is not without good reason that this expression is applied to Him; that we may know that He can no more fail to be the defender of His Law, and the Avenger of its contempt, than deny Himself.[28]

In his sermons on Deuteronomy, Calvin gives greater explication to God's metaphorical use of rejoicing.

Here Moses first of all shows what affection God bears toward those whom He has chosen for Himself and intends to take for His flock. It is certain that God is not subject to any human passions, yet He is not able sufficiently to manifest either the goodness or the love that He has toward us, except by transfiguring Himself, as if He were a mortal man, saying that He would take pleasure in doing good to us.

Let us understand therefore that God holds us dear, as if a father should delight and rejoice to do good to his children. . . . God likens Himself to mortal men, and says that He will delight to do us good. And therefore we cannot magnify the inestimable goodness of our God too much, seeing He stoops so low as to tell us that His whole delight is in making us to enjoy His benefits. . . . But on the other side let us consider also that He must likewise delight to do us evil. And why? Certainly because He is just . . .[29]

---

[28] John Calvin, *Commentaries on the Four Last Books of Moses Arranged in the Form of a Harmony*, vol. 3 (Edinburgh: The Calvin Translation Society, 1860), 264. The comparative nature of the analogy in Isa. 62:5 is proven by the rare use of כִּי (*kî*). See Joüon and Muraoka, *Grammar*, §174. e. note 4. Poole, *Commentary*, 1:392, concurs with Calvin:

> *Rejoice over you to destroy you;* his just indignation against you will be so great, that it will be a pleasure to him to take vengeance on you. For though he doth not delight in the death of a sinner in itself, yet he doth doubtless delight in the glorifying of his justice upon incorrigible sinners, seeing the exercise of all his attributes must needs please him, else he were not perfectly happy.

[29] John Calvin, *The Covenant Enforced; Sermons on Deuteronomy 27 and 28*, ed. James B. Jordan (Tyler, TX: Institute for Christian Economics, 1990), 250-52.

Calvin affirms that God reveals himself to us, in both his "inestimable goodness" and in his unalterable justice, in human language which we can comprehend. Nevertheless, while Calvin confesses that "God is not subject to any human passions," to represent his confession of God's impassibility as portraying God as apathetic or numb in the face of man's sinfulness or in the light of his covenant faithfulness is to seriously misunderstand or misrepresent both God and Calvin.

Thomas Scott, concurring with Calvin on Deuteronomy 28:63, notes:

> The miseries of his creatures are not in themselves pleasing to the Lord; but he is pleased with that display of his justice, truth, wisdom, and power, which become him as the Judge of all the earth. (Note Jer. 32:39-41).[30]

Furthermore, to appreciate fully all that is indicated in this text, Scott rightly suggests we must look to the prophets, especially Jeremiah, and to the future expression of its richest fulfillment in the new covenant in Christ. The remaining four instances of "rejoice" where God is the subject appear in Isaiah 62:5 and 65:19, Jeremiah 32:41, and Zephaniah 3:17. These four texts acknowledge that God's judgment had fallen on Israel in accord with Deuteronomy 28:63. Their covenant unfaithfulness had brought upon them God's rejoicing to jealously guard his own holiness and justice and to remove Israel from the land, dispersing them among the nations.

This reveals the sober truth that the covenant God had ratified with Israel at Sinai, and which Moses in Deuteronomy had instructed was to be renewed at Mount Ebal and Mount Gerizim, was, in some respects, a republication of the covenant of works. It was left to Israel to choose life or death.

> I call heaven and earth as witnesses today against you, *that* I have set before you life and death, blessing and cursing; therefore choose life, that both you and your descendants

---

[30] Thomas Scott, *The Holy Bible, Containing the Old and New Testaments, with Explanatory Notes and Practical Observations and Copious Marginal References*, 3 vols. (New York: W. E. Dean, 1846), 1:364.

may live . . . (Deut. 30:19)

To be sure, blessings came upon them at rare times for covenant obedience (principally under Joshua and David), but ultimately Israel proved unfaithful and God expelled them from the land.

As Israel's history so sadly proved, what she needed was not another opportunity to prove her faithfulness. As with all who are born in sin, faithfulness was not to be found in Israel. What was needed was a new covenant, established on better promises (Heb. 8:6). The faithfulness lacking in Israel must be found in the promised Mediator of the covenant of grace rather than with the nation of Israel in a further republication of the covenant of works. As Jeremiah 32 confirms, only then would the people of God never again fear God's rejoicing over them for evil. Rather, they could expect that all God's rejoicing over them would be to bring them blessings.

> 'They shall be My people, and I will be their God; 39 'then I will give them one heart and one way, that they may fear Me forever, for the good of them and their children after them. 40 'And I will make an everlasting covenant with them, that I will not turn away from doing them good; but I will put My fear in their hearts so that they will not depart from Me. 41 'Yes, I will rejoice over them to do them good, and I will assuredly plant them in this land, with all My heart and with all My soul.' (Jer. 32:38-41)[31]

As is evident from this new covenant promise, all four of the prophetic references to God's delighting in his people are with

---

[31] It is important at this juncture to underscore that the word *delight* in Jer. 32:41 is the same as in Deut. 28:63. In fact, a comparison between the two texts reflects Jeremiah's dependence on Deuteronomy in that the verb for delight in both texts is followed by the preposition עַל (*'al*, upon, over) with the second (Deut. 28:63) or third (Jer. 32:41) person pronominal suffix followed by יָטַב (*yāṭab*, be good, be well, be glad, be pleasing) in the infinitive construct and prefixed with לְ (*lĕ*, to, at). The dependence of Jeremiah on Deuteronomy is further underscored by his reference to permanence in the land; "I will assuredly plant them in this land, with all My heart and with all My soul" (Jer. 32:41b). Under the new covenant, the blessings are delightfully bestowed and no curses are feared because of the merits of its Mediator, our Lord Jesus Christ.

respect to the future new covenant blessings of God and contain no caveat of possible future curses. Anticipating Paul's declaration in Romans 8:28, the new covenant promises of Jeremiah guarantee that God will ensure only good will flow to his people. Moreover, as Isaiah 65 confirms, it shall be eternally so in the new heavens and the new earth. How will God bring about this unchanging delight to do good to his chosen people? God brought the covenant curses due to us on Christ. He also gives us all the new covenant blessings in Christ who alone has merited God's delight. Moreover, God promises to remove the covenant unfaithfulness of his people by giving them a new heart so that they fear him forever (cf. Deut. 28:58).

This unambiguously points to what Christ, as the Mediator and head of the covenant of grace, would win for us in his life, death, resurrection, ascension, and second coming. Using the language of Deuteronomy 28:63 we can rightly say God rejoiced to exact his justice on Christ as if he was covenantally unfaithful—he became sin for us (2 Cor. 5:21) and "He bore our sins in his body on the tree" (1 Pet. 2:24). But unlike Israel under the old covenant, we can rightly also say that God's rejoicing over us is in Christ alone and will always and only be to do us good because the faithfulness he demands of us was richly and perfectly provided for by the righteousness of Christ.

Though, as Calvin and others correctly assert, the language of delight is metaphorical (i.e., anthropopathic), this is no expression of distance or apathy on God's part. That anyone could think God could be so in respect to Christ, his own Son, is unfathomable. It is in fact the case that, precisely because God is impassible, his goodness shall never fail us in Christ. God reveals that he will be to us as one who rejoices over his bride; a metaphor, to be sure, but one that all eternity shall not exhaust.

1 Samuel 15

"I greatly regret that I have set up Saul *as* king, for he has turned back from following Me, and has not performed My commandments." And it grieved Samuel, and he cried out to the Lord all night. (1 Sam. 15:11)

And Samuel went no more to see Saul until the day of his death. Nevertheless Samuel mourned for Saul, and the LORD regretted that He had made Saul king over Israel. (1 Sam. 15:35)

And also the Strength of Israel will not lie nor relent. For He *is* not a man, that He should relent. (1 Sam. 15:29)

First Samuel 15 is an important text in the discussion of divine impassibility if for no other reason than its double declaration that God "regretted" or "repented" (vv. 11 and 35) and its assertion that God does not "relent" (v. 29, "repent," KJV). In all three cases, the Hebrew word is the same as in Numbers 23:19. In fact, the construction in 1 Samuel 15:29, as Ralph W. Klein notes, "is virtually a verbatim quotation from the oracles of Balaam (Num. 23:19) and hence rooted in ancient Israelite tradition."[32] In light of this, we will build upon the exegetical and theological foundation of Numbers 23:19 established above.

The narrative affirmation that God "regretted that He had made Saul king" (1 Sam. 15:35) comes at a point in the history where it looks like a major change in the purpose and plan of God is being revealed.[33] He is about to judicially reject Saul, his sons, and his whole tribe (the Benjamites) from the future royal plans for Israel. In this instance, the repentance ascribed to God in verses 11 and 35 stands within the narrative in a similar way to that of Genesis 6, describing from a human perspective the major shift in direction God initiates in the light of Saul's sin and his judgment on that sin.

This underscores an important point often ignored in the handling of this and similar texts by modified passibilists, especially those who wish to translate "relent" or "repent" as an emotionally-laden term with respect to God. The incursion of sin in the redemptive-historical narrative is front and center to the expressions of God's repentance in Genesis 6:6-7 and 1 Samuel 15:11

---

[32] Ralph W. Klein, *1 Samuel*, Word Biblical Commentary, ed. John D. W. Watts (Dallas: Word Incorporated, 1998), 10:154.

[33] For some reason, the NKJV adds the adverb "greatly" to the declaration of regret by God in 1 Sam. 15:11. There is not a shred of textual evidence for the inclusion and neither the older KJV nor any of the more recent translations include the adverb. The Hebrew text warrants no such adverbial inclusion.

and 35. Nonetheless, what God repents of in these four uses of the term is his own action. If God is emotionally upset, we must assume he is upset with himself for what he has done. Notice carefully Genesis 6:6, "The LORD was sorry that He made man . . .," Genesis 6:7, "for I am sorry that I have made them," 1 Samuel 15:11, "I greatly regret that I have set up Saul *as* king . . .," and 1 Samuel 15:35, "The LORD regretted that He had made Saul king over Israel."[34] In each context, there is both the third person narrative expression of God's regret and the first person confession of God's regret.[35]

By refusing to see these texts as anthropopathic expressions that give context to the revelation of major changes in God's redemptive dealings with creation (Gen. 6) or Israel's king (1 Sam. 15:11, 35), we are left to see them as expressions of God's emotionally-charged response to his own actions. We must assume, therefore, the sequence of God's action, man's sin, and then God's emotionally-

---

[34] The four occurrences of נָחַם (*nāḥam*) in Gen. 6:6-7; 1 Sam. 15:11, and 35 are all followed by the Hebrew particle כִּי (*kî*) showing the cause of God's change in the unfolding redemptive-historical narrative. In Gen. 6:6-7 the cause is that God had made man. In 1 Sam. 15:11 and 35, the cause is that God had made Saul king. The Hebrew is very clear in each of these four instances that the cause of God's נָחַם (*nāḥam*) is his own action antecedent to the rebellion of his creatures.

[35] Gonzales, *Where Sin Abounds,* 81, would be an example of one who attributes emotionally-charged language to God but ignores the text's assertion that God is upset with himself. Rejecting Calvin's impassibilist interpretation of Genesis 6 (see above), he notes, ". . . [I]n response to man's change from *very good* (1:31) to *very evil* (6:5), Yahweh genuinely feels a mixture of extreme disappointment and anger, which in turn produces a profound heart-felt sorrow, something any reader who has felt the pangs of the curse can to some degree identify with. The exposure of emotional turbulence within the heart of an infinite, eternal, unchangeable God is one of the greatest indicators of the colossal proportions of human sin." Gonzales also quotes, with approval, the emotional assessment of the acknowledged Open Theist and Process theologian, Fretheim, who claims, "God is caught up in the matter; and in some respects will never be the same." He likewise approvingly quotes von Rad, "Precisely in this way, by referencing the Creator's bewilderment, he has communicated something of the incomprehensibility of the incursion of sin." To be sure, one appreciates Gonzales' emphasis on the "colossal proportions of human sin," and his rejection of the Open Theism and Process Theology of Fretheim, but in his affirmation of Fretheim's description of God's emotional responses to sin, he never addresses the text's clear declaration that God's "extreme disappointment and anger" is with himself.

charged frustration with himself as expressing the main point of the narratives.

What these occurrences better reflect is that how we handle biblical expressions of God's repentance directly relates to our doctrine of God; that is, hermeneutics and theology dovetail. Either God is undergoing some sort of emotional turmoil for what he has done, or he is using such language, language that would be expressive of a man's emotional turmoil at the frustration of his own purposes, to give expression to a major shift in the narrative's trajectory. God is about to judge mankind and start over with Noah, and God is about to judge Saul and start over with David. From a human perspective, these are redemptive-historical moments that come to us as major shifts. But for God, they were part and parcel of his redemptive plan all along. A man might be emotionally frustrated with the unalterable circumstances in which he finds himself, especially if his purposes and plans were frustrated by the sin of others and he was forced to put an alternative plan in place. To read this of God is to assume that somehow God is frustrated with himself while executing his perfect plan for the eternal redemption of his elect. Given these two options, reading these texts anthropopathically does not "empty the terminology of its significance" (as Gonzales suggests[36]) but becomes a necessity. To do otherwise is to alter significantly the biblical and theological representation of the being and nature of God.

As with the Balaam narrative, the issue in 1 Samuel 15:29 is the immutability of God's word as it is grounded in his own immutable essence. When Israel initially asked for a king, God revealed to Samuel their motivation:

> And the LORD said to Samuel, "Heed the voice of the people in all that they say to you; for they have not rejected you, but they have rejected Me, that I should not reign over them." (1 Sam. 8:7)

In the formal selection process that soon followed, Samuel reiterated this fact to the nation at large.

> But you have today rejected your God, who Himself saved

---

[36] Gonzales, *Where Sin Abounds*, 80.

you from all your adversities and your tribulations; and you have said to Him, 'No, set a king over us!' Now therefore, present yourselves before the LORD by your tribes and by your clans. (1 Sam. 10:19)

The verb *reject* is in the forefront of both of these verses. Notably, its only occurrence in the books of Samuel is in the narrative surrounding the selection and rejection of Saul as king. It appears first within the narrative where Israel has asked for a king "like all the nations" (1 Sam. 8:5), indicating that Israel had "rejected" God (8:7). Its final appearance comes with the rejection of David's older brother Eliab as God's choice for king in 1 Samuel 16:7, making way for God's acceptance of David as the man after his own heart (cf. 1 Sam. 13:14 and 16:7). Thus, we cannot understand the nature of the declaration of repentance respecting God without placing the rejection of Saul into this larger narrative context. Israel asked for a king like the other nations and, in doing so, revealed they had already rejected God. Therefore God gave them that for which they asked.[37]

There is an additional component to the narrative that weaves its way throughout: Saul's refusal to obey the word of the Lord. Actually, Saul's rejection of God's word (the same Hebrew word is used in 15:23 and 26) is the foundation of God's rejection of Saul. Saul's kingship had been conditioned on obedience from the first, as Samuel proclaimed:

Now therefore, here is the king whom you have chosen *and* whom you have desired. And take note, the LORD has set a king over you. 14 If you fear the LORD and serve Him and obey His voice, and do not rebel against the commandment of the LORD, then both you and the king who reigns over you will continue following the LORD your God. 15 However, if you do not obey the voice of the LORD, but rebel against the commandment of the LORD, then the hand of the LORD will be against you, as *it was* against your fathers. (1 Sam. 12:13-15)

---

[37] The verb for *reject* in these verses is מָאַס, (*mā'as*, to reject or despise). The several uses in Samuel are 1 Sam. 8:7 twice; 10:19; 15:23 twice, 26 twice; and 16:1 and 7.

Samuel refers back to this day of anointing when he commanded Saul, by the word of the Lord, to attack the Amalekites. "Samuel also said to Saul, 'The LORD sent me to anoint you king over His people, over Israel. Now therefore, heed the voice of the words of the LORD'" (1 Sam. 15:1).[38]

This warning also reflected more deeply the instructions and warnings of Deuteronomy respecting kingship in Israel.

> When you come to the land which the LORD your God is giving you, and possess it and dwell in it, and say, "I will set a king over me like all the nations that *are* around me," ¹⁵ you shall surely set a king over you whom the LORD your God chooses; *one* from among your brethren you shall set as king over you; you may not set a foreigner over you, who *is* not your brother. ¹⁶ But he shall not multiply horses for himself, nor cause the people to return to Egypt to multiply horses, for the LORD has said to you, "You shall not return that way again." ¹⁷ Neither shall he multiply wives for himself, lest his heart turn away; nor shall he greatly multiply silver and gold for himself. ¹⁸ Also it shall be, when he sits on the throne of his kingdom, that he shall write for himself a copy of this law in a book, from *the one* before the priests, the Levites. ¹⁹ And it shall be with him, and he shall read it all the days of his life, that he may learn to fear the LORD his God and be careful to observe all the words of this law and these statutes, ²⁰ that his heart may not be lifted above his brethren, that he may not turn aside from the commandment *to* the right hand or *to* the left, and that he may prolong *his* days in his kingdom, he and his children in the midst of Israel. (Deut. 17:14-20)

The narrative declaration of God's repenting that he had made Saul king (1 Sam. 15:11, 35) comes on the heels of Saul's rejection of

---

[38] The Hebrew verb translated "obey" in 1 Sam. 12:14 is שָׁמַע (*šāma* '). This is the same verb translated "heed" in 1 Sam. 15:1. This alone confirms that Samuel is connecting the condition of Saul's anointing as king in 1 Sam. 12 to his obedience in removing the Amalekites in 1 Sam. 15. Samuel is exhorting Saul to give attention to his calling as Israel's king. Framed this way, 1 Sam. 15:1 presages the judicial removal of Saul later in the chapter.

God's word. In other words, it reflects God's unchanging commitment to his word grounded in his unchanging nature. For God not to reject Saul would have entailed his failing to keep his word and would thus have made God a liar, an ontological impossibility affirmed by 1 Samuel 15:29. From the human perspective, it looked like God changed his mind respecting Saul, but from the divine perspective, God remained unchanged.

Certainly verse 29 confirms that God's declaration of judgment on the kingship and dynasty of Saul is irrevocable. The irrevocability of this declaration is not anchored in God's will, but in God's essence: "because He is not a man."[39] His word of judgment cannot fail, not because God chooses for it not to fail, but because ontologically he cannot go back on his word. To do so would be tantamount to God denying himself! Thus, in the final analysis, God has not changed but acted in perfect consistency with his own unchangeable nature and according to his own unchangeable word. Additionally, to assume that the repenting in 1 Samuel 15:11 and 35 is proper to God is to assume he is emotionally conflicted with honoring his word and removing Saul from the kingship, none of which the text itself teaches.

Rob Lister misses this point entirely in his comments on 1 Samuel 15:29. Taking only a portion of the verse, he reformulates the text to say, "*because God is not a man, he does not repent like one*" (emphasis original). But if this is the true intent of the passage, then we must apply the same theological methodology to the whole verse. It would then read, "And also the Strength of Israel will not lie [like a man] nor relent [like a man]. For he *is* not a man, that he should relent [like a man]" (1 Sam. 15:29). The whole point of the verse is to declare that God neither relents nor lies. He can no more do one than the other because he is not human—he is God. Lister

---

[39] The Hebrew is כִּי לֹא אָדָם. This is the author's translation as all the major versions use the English word "for" to express the Hebrew causal particle. The clause "He is not a man" is introduced with the Hebrew particle (כִּי, *kî*) expressing a causative relationship between the two. For this reason, Waltke and O'Connor, *Biblical Hebrew* Syntax, § 38.4.a, suggest "because" is an effective translation of the causative nature that exists between the two concepts. It is unquestionably *because* God is not a man that he cannot repent. Note further that the clause "He is not a man" is framed both before and after with the word for "repent." In a linguistic sense, this is a doubly emphasized reality.

attempts to distance himself from the implications of this in the paragraphs that follow, assigning a "certain and constant character" to God. But in attempting to find some middle ground for what he calls "relational mutability," he opens the door for theological confusion and contradiction. If God cannot lie, then the corollary is also true—he cannot repent. Declarations of ontology take theological priority over statements of narrative description.[40]

Thus the narrative descriptions of God's repenting in 1 Samuel 15:11 and 35 frame the judicial rejection of Saul in human terms. From a human perspective, it looks like God changed his mind. But the larger narrative reflects that Saul's kingship was Israel's attempt to be like the other nations and constituted a rejection of God's dominion over them from the start. This rejection was personified in the choice of Saul, who proved to be what Israel wanted, not a man after God's own heart, but a man like the kings of the nations. When Saul failed to obey the word of the Lord, God, in judgment, did what he previously proclaimed he would do—he removed the kingship from Saul and moved forward to the kingship of David. Nor does God emotionally regret this decision, for that would put him in conflict with his own judgment and prophetic word. As this was God's plan and purpose all along, it is impossible to imagine that God is ontologically, volitionally, or emotionally conflicted here. In other words, he is not passible.

Indeed, the text specifically distances itself from affirming some form of internal emotional conflict within God as it contrasts his judicial rejection of Saul with Samuel's mourning over the rejection of Saul (1 Sam. 15:35). When God moves forward, in 1 Samuel 16, to begin the process of selecting the king he had chosen to replace

---

[40] Cf. Lister, *God is Impassible and Impassioned*, 210. Other evangelicals also refer to "God's relational mutability." One can only assume that such references derive from the thesis put forward by Bruce Ware noted above. But, like Lister, they do not account for the fact that Ware denies "repentance" to be within the bounds of God's "relational mutability." His conclusion is actually based upon this text. Thankfully, Lister also affirms "God's essential immutability." Nonetheless, the challenges here are not small. To postulate that God is ontologically unchanged by the change in Israel's kingship necessitated by Saul's disobedience and yet God is simultaneously truly emotionally grieved posits a certain dissonance in the Godhead (what Gonzales considers an "emotional turbulence within the heart of an infinite, eternal, unchanging God," Gonzales, *Where Sin Abounds*, 81) that 1 Sam. 15:29 clearly denies.

Saul, he even chastises Samuel for still mourning over Saul, on account of God's judicial rejection of him as king. In other words, the narrative reflects Samuel as laden with emotion, not God.[41]

Finally, let us not read some form of numbness in God into the narrative of Saul's rejection. God's interaction belies such false assessments. He has been extremely patient with Israel and careful to warn and exhort Saul. Furthermore, God is, and has been all along, moving toward the establishment of the Davidic kingship, the precursor to the arrival of the future Davidic king who would reign on the throne of David forever (Isa. 9:7; Jer. 33:17; Luke 1:32). God's eternal purpose and plan for the monarchy in Israel was moving forward according to his eternal decree and sovereign will. To suppose he was somehow emotionally conflicted at this point is to misread the text and to misrepresent God. The expressions of God's repentance may look like human emotional responses, but their purpose is revelational. They prepare us, as human readers, for the redemptive-historical shifts that are about to come in the biblical narrative. But are we to assume that God is emotionally conflicted when remaining true to his eternal decree and revealed word? No such conclusion is warranted by the text. In fact, the opposite must be maintained.

Malachi 3:6

For I, the LORD, do not change; therefore you, O sons of Jacob, are not consumed. (Mal. 3:6, NASB)

Malachi's prophecy is composed of six disputations between God and his people. Malachi 3:6 opens the fifth of these, focusing on the people's robbing God by withholding their tithes, thus not supporting the worship of God. Yet despite Israel's long-running record of disobedience, God never abolished the nation. Thus, on behalf of God, Malachi writes, "For I, the LORD, do not change; therefore you, O sons of Jacob, are not consumed" (Mal. 3:6, NASB).

Malachi 3:6 is parallel in structure, each term of the first clause

---

[41] The verb for mourning here (Hebrew אָבַל, 'ābal, I mourn, lament) occurs some 36 times and is never predicated of God in Scripture.

corresponding to one in the second. Thus "I" corresponds to "you," "the LORD" corresponds to "sons of Jacob," and "do not change" corresponds to "are not consumed." Further, the clauses relate to each other as cause and effect. The first clause gives the cause; the second, the effect. This is shown by the first word of the verse ("for") and the logical conjunction ("therefore") that introduces the second clause. It is because the LORD does not change that the sons of Jacob are not consumed.[42]

God's claim of changelessness is not limited by the text. It is not any one attribute in particular to which he refers. Rather, God is speaking of his one, simple nature as God, YHWH. Calvin comments:

> Here the Prophet more clearly reproves and checks the impious waywardness of the people; for God . . . now claims to himself what justly belongs to him, and says that he changes not, because he is God. Under the name Jehovah, God reasons from his own nature; for he sets himself, as we have observed in our last lecture, in opposition to mortals; nor is it a wonder that God here disclaims all inconsistency, since the impostor Balaam was constrained to celebrate God's immutable constancy—"For he is not God," he says, "who changes," or varies, "like man." (Numbers 23:19.) We now then understand the force of the words, *I am Jehovah.* But he adds as an explanation, *I change not,* or, I am not changed. . . . God continues in his purpose, and is not turned here and there like men who repent of a purpose they have formed, because what they had not thought of comes to their mind, or because they wish undone what they have performed, and seek new ways by which they may retrace their steps. God denies that anything of this kind can take

---

[42] The cause and effect of the Hebrew construction is established by the use of the subordinating conjunction כִּי (*kî*) as the first term in the first clause, followed by the conjunction וֹ (*wĕ*) leading the second clause. Christo H. J. van der Merwe, Jackie A. Naudé, and Jan H. Kroeze, *A Biblical Hebrew Reference Grammar* (Sheffield: Sheffield Academic Press, 1999), 301, elaborate helpfully on this construction: "The reason that the clause referring to the cause comes first in the clause is that the speaker/narrator wishes to remove any doubt about the specific cause of a situation."

place in him, for he is *Jehovah*, and *changes not*, or is not changed.[43]

God himself, then, through the prophet, declares in clear, stark terms his own infinite and absolute immutability. Moreover, he states that his immutable nature is the basis for his dealings with his people. God relates to Israel, not in reactionary response to Israel's behavior, but in love, according to his unchanging nature.

---

[43] Calvin, *Commentaries*, 15:579.

Chapter 5

THE OLD TESTAMENT ON
THE DOCTRINE OF DIVINE IMPASSIBILITY
(III) *Texts on Apparent Passibilism and Conclusion*
Steve Garrick, James P. Butler, Charles J. Rennie

One of the more pressing challenges encountered in addressing the complex doctrine of divine impassibility from a classical and confessional perspective is that there are many biblical texts which use emotive language in describing God's relationship to his creation. This chapter will address several of the more prominent Old Testament texts which ascribe emotive language to God. We trust that it will also provide an example of how similar texts encountered in Scripture should be interpreted in light of the whole of scriptural revelation and in accord with the classical and confessional doctrine of divine impassibility.

Genesis 6:1-7 (God and His Grief)

Now it came to pass, when men began to multiply on the face of the earth, and daughters were born to them, 2 that the sons of God saw the daughters of men, that they *were* beautiful; and they took wives for themselves of all whom they chose. 3 And the LORD said, "My Spirit shall not strive with man forever, for he *is* indeed flesh; yet his days shall be one hundred and twenty years." 4 There were giants on the earth in those days, and also afterward, when the sons of God came in to the daughters of men and they bore *children* to them. Those *were* the mighty men who *were* of old, men of renown. 5 Then the LORD saw that the wickedness of man *was* great in the earth, and *that* every intent of the thoughts of his heart *was* only evil continually. 6 And the LORD was sorry that He had made man on the earth, and He was grieved in His heart. 7 So the LORD said, "I will destroy man whom I have created from the face of the earth, both man and beast, creeping thing and birds of the air, for I am sorry that I have made them." (Gen. 6:1-7)

In Genesis 6:1-7, Moses pulls back the veil to show his readers God's view of the deluge. The descendants of Abraham had undoubtedly heard stories of the flood from their fathers. Other cultures had their own versions as well. Moses gives us the infallible interpretation of the event that radically changed the earth's ecology.

In this account, Moses portrays God as perceiving man's thorough and incessant wickedness (v. 5), and therefore as "sorry" or regretting having created him. This regret grieves God to his heart.[1] He then declares that he will act in such a way as to "un-create" the world, destroying man, beasts, birds, and creeping things from the face of the earth. God will act in a manner that is the reverse of his creative acts in Genesis 1 in light of the far-reaching effects of the fall in Genesis 3-5.

When Moses tells us that "the LORD saw the wickedness of man *was* great in the earth," he uses the generic term for seeing that is used to describe either physical sight (e.g., Gen. 18:2) or perception/realization (e.g., Gen. 3:6; 16:4; 40:16). Moses describes God as seeing man's sin, comprehending the extensiveness of it. God then reacts with sorrow or repentance that he has made man,

---

[1] The Hebrew verb translated "grieved" in Gen. 6:6 is עָצַב (*'āṣāb*) and appears in the hithpael stem only here and in Gen. 34:7. Holladay recognizes that the verb can carry the idea of outrage in the hithpael stem while Meyers affirms its "tendency to prefer reflexive forms may be due to the verb's introspective, personal, and emotional semantic content." William L. Holladay and Ludwig Kohler, *A Concise Hebrew and Aramaic Lexicon of the Old Testament,* (Leiden: Brill, 2000), 280. C. Meyer, " עָצַב *'ā ṣāb*," in *TDOT,* 11:278. Gordon Wenham translates this verb in such a way as to carry forward both the anger of Jehovah and the introspective nature of the verb: "He felt bitterly indignant." He goes on to explain, "The root עצב is used to express the most intense form of human emotion, a mixture of rage and bitter anguish." Gordon J. Wenham, *Genesis 1–15*, vol. 1, Word Biblical Commentary (Dallas: Word, Incorporated, 1998), 144. The occurrences of the nominal forms in Gen. 3:16 and 17 as well as 5:29 are surely intentional and instructive.

to the degree that it pained him at his heart. Finally, God responds by saying he will undo all he has done in populating the earth. Due to the emotion-laden language of the narrative in Genesis 6, this text has become a focal point for discussions of the doctrine of divine impassibility among Open Theists (divine passibility), classical theists (divine impassibility), and a number of evangelicals who can be classified as modified impassibilists/passibilists. Our main interaction will be with evangelical and Reformed authors who advocate a modification to the classical doctrine of divine impassibility.

Applied to Genesis 6, the modified impassibility/passibility view understands each of the descriptions of God as if they are said in some fashion properly of him. While there is some variation among the evangelical advocates as to how this language may be properly predicated of God, they seem to agree that the classical view which understands this language as improperly predicated of God and therefore necessarily anthropomorphic/anthropopathic is inadequate. In their opinion, classical explanations fail to do the biblical accounts justice.

K. Scott Oliphint, for instance, views such language through the lens of covenantal condescension. According to Oliphint, emotion-laden language in depictions such as Genesis 6, reflects God's sovereign decision to take on non-essential "contingent (accidental?) properties."[2] In other words, God is capable of a range of emotions but these emotions are never wrung from him by his creatures, he sovereignly controls them and enters fully into them with his covenant children. Further, not only can God thus be considered as sovereignly owning and expressing an array of human-like emotions in his covenantal condescension, but other covenantal characteristics are evident as well. Thus when God "saw," there is a sense in which this must be taken to reflect God's entering into the circumstances along with his creatures. For example, while speaking of God's testing of Abraham in Genesis 22, Oliphint claims:

> Once God condescends, we should recognize that, in taking
> to himself covenantal properties, he takes to himself as well

---

[2] Oliphint, *God with Us*, 154.

the *kind* of knowledge . . . that accrues to these properties. Or, to put it another way, one of the covenantal properties that he takes to himself is the development of knowledge that is conducive to his interaction with his creation generally, and specifically with his people.[3]

Thus, Oliphint allows room in God's assumed covenantal properties for "the development of knowledge." Though omniscient essentially, God sometimes has a new assessment in his covenantal condescension, a different evaluation of man. This different evaluation from God is followed by an emotional-affective response which is construed as an emotional change in God. Looking to the hypostatic union of the two natures of Christ as paradigmatic, God is understood to have decreed a change in himself within the confines of his covenantal condescension and in response to a change in creation. Oliphint can then hold to the premise that passages such as Genesis 6, with their strong emotive language, reflect the idea that God, though essentially impassible, is covenantally passible and truly grieved.[4]

Another example of an evangelical modification to the doctrine of divine impassibility is Rob Lister's *God is Impassible and Impassioned*. As the title suggests, there is a decided attempt in Lister's work to advocate a both/and paradigm with respect to God. In this case, God is understood as impassible in his essence and yet impassioned in his relations. When discussing God's grief in passages like Genesis 6, Lister carefully qualifies it as "not something true of the eternal metaphysical fabric of the Trinity."[5] That is, God's sovereign choice to enter into the economy of creation means God chooses to take on impassioned relationships that did not exist previously. But, while Lister allows for grief in God, it is

---

[3] Oliphint, *God with Us*, 194.

[4] In using the hypostatic union as his paradigm, Oliphint goes on to affirm: "Thus, as we discussed above, it is legitimate to ascribe real emotions and passions to God (focused in the Son). . . . It is, to be sure, beneath God, until and unless he freely decides to condescend to us and to take on properties that are not essential to him but are of an entirely different nature than who he is essentially. Once he has decided to condescend and has done so, however, he really and fully takes on those properties, not metaphorically or figuratively." Oliphint, *God with Us*, 153-54. For a fuller examination of Genesis 22 see below.

[5] Lister, *God is Impassible and Impassioned*, 256.

not "constitutive of God's very nature."[6] The result gives Lister room to declare that God's grief is a genuine emotion. He says:

> It follows from divine incorporeality (John 4:24) that God can experience neither bodily suffering nor physical death. And since God exhaustively knows and determines the future, he never faces situations in which the outcome is uncertain.
>
> Having said all that, we should nevertheless affirm with Scripture that God can be grieved by his creatures as they transgress his revealed will (Gen. 6:6; Isa. 63:10; Eph. 4:30). . . . [T]here is nothing improper about acknowledging God's grief over sin in the economy, provided that we simultaneously understand that he transcends all of his relationships in the economy.[7]

In Genesis 6, then, according to Lister God's response is genuine, heart-felt grief, to the point of remorse over having made man. Though God is essentially impassible, yet in his relationship to men he is truly impassioned, responding emotively to the event of man's wickedness. The sovereign yet grieving God issues his judgment to destroy man from the face of the earth. Lister concludes his evaluation of scriptural designations of repentance in God with a comment on Genesis:

> So even when Genesis 6:6 adds to the statement of divine repentance one of divine grief over the wickedness of mankind, it is not difficult to understand on these terms.

---

[6] Lister, *God is Impassible and Impassioned*, 257.

[7] Lister, *God is Impassible and Impassioned*, 256-57. As Lister notes, one of the fundamental distinctions between the classical and confessional doctrine of divine impassibility and the evangelical modifications being presented of late is the nature of proper and improper predication of emotions or passions to God. While we will deal with this more fully in the material on systematic theology below, the classical doctrine of divine impassibility recognizes that passions cannot be predicated properly of God. In Lister's reformulation, God can be properly said to experience passions. In the modified view the question is whether or not God chooses to express his passions; he is always in sovereign control and therefore only expresses them when and how he wills. In the classical doctrine of divine impassibility it is affirmed that God, because he is God, does not and cannot have passions.

God both foreknew the wickedness into which the world would devolve (cf. Acts 2: 23–24) and, when it came to pass in time, responded with the perfectly fitted emotional response. The foreknowing and even foreordaining of sin for the sake of some larger purpose do not in the least diminish God's displeasure in that sin when it occurs.[8]

Another contemporary advocate of modified divine impassibility, Robert Gonzales, expresses this emotional event more starkly in *Where Sin Abounds*. Gonzales suggests Genesis 6 reflects the "exposure of emotional turbulence within the heart of an infinite, eternal, unchangeable God."[9]

What are we to make of these reformulations? While there are a number of problems with them, we will limit ourselves to three reasons why the modified doctrine of divine impassibility view of Genesis 6 should not be adopted. In summary, 1) it is based on an inconsistent interpretation of the passage, 2) it requires that the passage teach an eternal conflict within God's own decree, and 3) it results in a relationship to God based on attributes that are, in fact, the exact opposite of his eternal nature.

First, this view inconsistently interprets Genesis 6. Genesis 6:6 says God "was grieved in His heart." The phrase "in His heart" directly qualifies or describes the grief that God is said to feel. And yet, it is readily admitted that "in His heart" is anthropomorphic in that God does not have a heart properly speaking. When used of men, the heart has both a literal and figurative meaning. Figuratively it reflects the "inner man." Speaking of the different variations of this term, Alex Luc notes, "In the OT, the words have a dominant metaphorical use in reference to the center of human psychical and spiritual life, to the entire inner life of a person."[10] By its very nature, therefore, the term heart reflects man as a composite being having identifiable inner and outer characteristics. However, God is not a composite being: unlike man he is not made up of inner and outer parts. The classical and confessional doctrine of God affirms unequivocally God's simplicity.

---

[8] Lister, *God is Impassible and Impassioned*, 211.

[9] Gonzales, *Where Sin Abounds*, 81.

[10] Alex Luc, "לֵב, לָבַב (לֵב, לָבַב), heart," in *NIDOTTE*, 2:749.

This is further underscored in this instance as the term heart is used of God in verse 6 only after referencing the sin of man as located in his "heart" in verse 5.[11] In other words, there is a clear parallel here; man's sin is viewed internally and God's grief is referenced after the same fashion. However, to assume that the text is not using the term anthropomorphically respecting God is to lose the parallelism and to fashion God after the image of man. We either must view the expression as anthropomorphic and thus reflective of God's revelation or we must view God as having parts in some fashion or another. Classical divine impassibility views this language anthropomorphically and thus carefully guards against any such redefinition of God.[12]

It follows further that if God truly feels grief, then he must (according to Gen. 6:6) truly feel it "in His heart." If, on the other hand, the phrase "in His heart" is acknowledged as anthropomorphic, then the natural question arises as to whether the entire affirmation is anthropomorphic as well. Most interpreters would readily agree that God does not have a physical heart on the basis of clear teaching of God's incorporeality elsewhere in Scripture. It seems odd, then, that the principle of using the clearer portions of Scripture to interpret the less clear is employed to classify one part of a clause as metaphor, all the while contending that doing the same thing for the rest of the very same clause is somehow to be guilty of ignoring its plain and full meaning. One phrase being obviously anthropomorphic, the most natural interpretation of the whole clause would be that it is also anthropomorphic. It reflects God's disposition in such a way that we can readily comprehend.

Second, from a confessional and Reformed perspective the modified doctrine of divine impassibility view results in an eternal conflict within God regarding his own decree. Genesis 6:6 begins with the statement that God was grieved that he had made man on the earth. While the immediate cause of God's grief is man's sin, verse 6 reveals the ultimate cause was God's own decree to create man and the execution of that decree in man's creation recorded in

---

[11] These are the first two occurrences of this word in BHS.

[12] Luc notes, "Direct anthropomorphic use of 'heart' for God is infrequent in the OT and is found a total of only 26x (Fabry, 448)." *NIDOTTE*, 2:750.

Genesis 1. God is grieved, or repents, that he created man. This cannot be overstressed. If God is truly feeling grief in Genesis 6, it is grief ultimately over *his own decision to create man*. Yet the complexity grows even beyond this conundrum. Certainly, God's decision to create man is eternal, part of his eternal decree. Similarly, the modified doctrine of divine impassibility view insists that God's grief in Genesis 6 was also ordained in eternity past since his emotional expressions such as grief are sovereignly controlled.[13] Thus, when these two ideas are juxtaposed, the modified doctrine of divine impassibility view presents God as eternally ordaining to create man and also eternally ordaining that he will one day repent of that very decision. It is hard to escape the conclusion that from eternity past, God would be holding to two conflicting decrees. It is one thing to say God decreed one thing and then another; it is quite a different thing to say God decreed to create and then decreed (or sovereignly chose) to be grieved with his decision to create. The first reflects the unfolding plan envisioned in the decree, the second reflects a conflict in the one who decrees. God's declaration of grief and sorrow in Genesis 6 is much more consistently harmonized with the decree of God when understood in the long stream of classical and confessional theology respecting God's impassibility.

Third, the modified view of Genesis 6 ultimately presents God relating to man on the basis of properties that are the antithesis of his eternal nature. In this view, God is said to be essentially omniscient and impassible, and yet he evaluates and assesses man's increasing wickedness and is emotionally conflicted by what he sees. God is essentially impassible, yet he emotively responds to man's sin and his own decree to create. God is essentially sovereign, yet he decides to destroy the world based on his evaluation and emotive response. In the end, man's relationship to God is based on properties that are the opposite of God's essential nature. To be sure, the Lord reveals his assessment of this wicked generation. Yet this does not imply that he has been brought to a state of new knowledge or undergone an emotional change of state. Moreover, to assume that the revelation of his assessment of the change in the

---

[13] This is at least certainly true for Oliphint, Lister, and Gonzales. Acknowledging God's sovereign control over his own emotions and the circumstances under which they rise and fall is largely what separates these men from Open Theism and Process Theology.

creature entails an emotionally responsive change in God, or in God's relationship to the creature, is to compromise not only divine immutability, but divine aseity. In the modified doctrine of divine impassibility view, God does not relate to us directly (i.e., essentially), that is, according to his eternal, unchangeable nature, but rather from within an array of covenantal properties, assumed by God in his relationship with man. But one wonders what the gain is here. If God's essential nature is virtually hidden from man behind his covenantally acquired attributes, some at least of which are opposite to his essential attributes, then does man ever encounter the essential, impassible God? Or for that matter the essential, immutable God?

What, then, does Genesis 6:5-7 mean? The anthropomorphisms of this text are not empty, but serve to highlight and communicate something of the truth regarding the infinite God. When the wicked acts of men became constant and universal, did God know? Indeed, for we are told that "God saw the wickedness of man." This is not a new evaluation of man based on his digression further into sin. Rather, it is a statement that the independent, immutable, omniscient God knows even the unexpressed thoughts and intentions of our hearts. Moreover, the sins of man are not neutral to the immutable and most holy God. He who eternally loves righteousness must similarly be eternally disposed to judge evil. Thus, Moses depicts the action of God as analogous to a man who undoes all he had begun. John Gill captures this rich expression well:

> Because of the wickedness of man, the wickedness of his heart, and the wickedness of his life and conversation, which was so general, and increased to such a degree, that it was intolerable; wherefore God could have wished, as it were, that he had never made him, since he proved so bad; not that repentance, properly speaking, can fall upon God, for he never changes his mind or alters his purposes, though he sometimes changes the course and dispensations of his providence. This is speaking by an anthropopathy, after the manner of men, because God determined to do, and did something similar to men, when they repent of anything: as a potter, when he has formed a vessel that does not please

him, and he repents that he has made it, he takes it and breaks it in pieces; and so God, because of man's wickedness, and to show his aversion to it, and displicency [dissatisfaction] at it, repented of his making him; that is, he resolved within himself to destroy him, as in the next verse, which explains this. "And it grieved him at his heart" — this is to be understood by the same figure as before, for there can no more be any uneasiness in his mind than a change in it; for God is a simple Being, uncompounded, and not subject to any passions and affections. This is said, to observe his great hatred to sin and abhorrence of it.[14]

The actions God was about to undertake in destroying the race of men, indeed, the world that then was, are likened to the actions of a man who had been greatly and unjustly grieved. God reveals this in an anthropopathic manner, not only because it resonates with our own sense of justice, but also for the sake of our instruction. He would teach us that he inviolably and immutably hates our sin, so that we might in like manner hate our sin and understand how contrary sin is to his intentions for his creation. As Calvin well noted:

The repentance he is speaking of is to horrify us at ourselves and not to indicate that God is changeable. So it ought to astonish us that God says he repents of having made man and that he is grieved and saddened in his heart for doing so. It is certain, as I have said, that there is no passion in God . . . It is very certain Moses did not intend to change God's image and say that he is subject to passion, that he is subject to repentance the way we are, but he wanted to touch us with horror when he said God repents. The term means that God disavows us as his creatures because we are no longer those whom he made and formed.[15]

Repentance, therefore, is not attributed to God properly, but

[14] John Gill, *Exposition of the Old and New Testaments*, 9 vols. (reprint, Paris, AR: The Baptist Standard Bearer, Inc., 1989), 1:47.

[15] John Calvin, *Sermons on Genesis, Chapters 1:1-11:14*, trans. Rob Roy McGregor (Edinburgh; Carlisle, PA: The Banner of Truth Trust, 2009), 563-64.

according to the manner of men. Henry Ainsworth summarizes the force of the text along these very lines:

> This is spoken not properly, for God *repenteth not*, I. Sam 15. 29. but after the manner of men, for God changing his deed, and dealing otherwise then before, doeth as men doe when they repent. So I. Sam 15. 11. . . . The Scripture giveth to God, *joy, grief, anger,* &c. not as any passions, or contrary affections, for he is most simple and unchangeable, Jam. 1. 17. but by a kinde of proportion, because he doeth of his immutable nature and will, such things, as men doe with those passions and changes of affection...& *if he be sometime angrie & sometime joyful, then is he changeable. But all these things are not found save in persons obscure and base, that dwell in houses of clay, whose foundation is in the dust: but he the blessed God is blessed and exalted above all these.*[16]

Genesis 22:12 (God and His Knowledge)

In Genesis 22, God tests Abraham, instructing him to offer his son, Isaac, as a sacrifice. As Abraham raises the knife to obey God's command,

> . . . the Angel of the LORD called to him from heaven and said, "Abraham, Abraham!" So he said, "Here I am." [12] And He said, "Do not lay your hand on the lad, or do anything to him; *for now I know* that you fear God, since you have not withheld your son, your only *son*, from Me." (Gen. 22:11-12, emphasis added)

Taken literally, the verse would indicate that God had just then learned that Abraham truly feared and trusted God. So John Sanders, the Open Theist, says:

> God needs to know if Abraham is the sort of person on whom God can count for collaboration toward the

---

[16] Henry Ainsworth, *Annotations upon the first book of Moses, Called Genesis* (Amsterdam: Imprinted by [Giles Thorp], 1616), n.p., emphasis original.

fulfillment of the divine project. Will he be faithful? Or must God find someone else through whom to achieve his purpose? God has been faithful; will Abraham be faithful? Will God have to modify his plans with Abraham?[17]

Rejecting the Open Theism of Sanders, Bruce Ware lists several inconsistencies and problems with this view. First, it shows that God, as well as not knowing the future, doesn't even know the present condition of Abraham's heart. Second, Abraham's track record of obedience beforehand clearly shows his heart; how could God not know *already* of Abraham's faithfulness? Third, in the Open Theist view, this test would still fail to bring to God a sure knowledge of Abraham's future actions. Abraham could still turn out to be unfaithful. God could not say he knew for certain that Abraham would be faithful in the future.[18]

Though Ware's criticisms of Open Theism are cogent, he is no proponent of classical divine impassibility for in formulating his relational mutability response he affirms:

> Just because God knows in advance that some event will occur, this does not preclude God from experiencing appropriate emotions and expressing appropriate reactions when it actually happens. So, although God may have known that the world would become morally corrupt (Gen. 6:5-6), that Nineveh would repent (Jonah 3:5-10), that Moses would plead for his people (Ex. 32:11-14), and that Saul would fail as king (1 Sam. 13:8-14; 15:1-9), nonetheless God may experience internally and express outwardly appropriate moral responses to these changed situations when they occur in history. That is, he may literally change in emotional disposition and become angry over increasing moral evil and flagrant disobedience, or he may show mercy in relation to repentance or urgent prayer. And, this may occur in historical interaction with his human creatures even though he knows, from eternity past, precisely what would occur and what his response would be.[19]

---

[17] John Sanders, *The God Who Risks: A Theology of Providence* (Downers Grove, IL: InterVarsity Press, 1998), 52-53.

[18] Ware, *God's Lesser Glory*, 67-72.

[19] Ware, *God's Lesser Glory*, 91-92.

Oliphint argues that, while God is essentially omniscient, he nonetheless has assumed certain "covenantal properties" for the sake of condescending to us, to relate to us. It is this condescension on God's part that explains how God, in Genesis 22, can say, "now I know." That is, in Oliphint's proposal, God is essentially omniscient, and yet he takes to himself properties that include the kind of knowledge that develops and grows, and so God does not know what we will do until we act.

> So, why does God say of himself, "Now, I know . . ."? He says this . . . to take seriously [his] condescension. Once God condescends, we should recognize that, in taking to himself covenantal properties, he takes to himself as well the *kind* of knowledge . . . that accrues to those properties. Or, to put it another way, one of the covenantal properties that he takes to himself is the development of knowledge that is conducive to his interaction with his creation generally, and specifically with his people. . . .
>
> So the lack of knowledge that God has, as given to us in Genesis 22:12, is a covenantal lack; it is a lack in which God's relationship to his people includes his real and literal interaction with us. . . . And since contingency is real in God's creation, it is not until we act/react that God, as condescended to that contingency, sees/knows what we will do (even though he always knows it, as who he is essentially).[20]

There are several problems and concerns with this approach to God's knowledge. First, in contrast to the classical doctrine of divine impassibility, Open Theism and Oliphint's covenantal condescension have the same result in terms of how God relates to men. That is, both Open Theism and the modified doctrine of divine impassibility portray God as waiting to see what Abraham will do in order to learn about him. The distinction between these views is that, in Open Theism, the lack of knowledge is inherent in the essence of God; whereas in the modified view of Oliphint, God is essentially omniscient and his lack of knowledge is rooted in the

---

[20] Oliphint, *God with Us*, 194-95.

covenantal properties he chooses to take to himself. Put another way, in Open Theism, God's ignorance of the future choice of Abraham is *natural* to God. In Oliphint's modified view, God's ignorance is found *only* in what he takes to himself, out of his own sovereign choice. But in terms of God's relationship to Abraham, both views see that relationship predicated on a God who watches Abraham in order to learn.

Second, other attributes become open for reformulation. For instance, Ware presents God as relating to Abraham through a form of relational mutability. In his reformulation God is immutable essentially and ethically but not relationally. He explains as follows:

> But if this statement [Gen. 22:12] cannot refer to a literal acquiring of knowledge that Abraham fears God— knowledge of which God was ignorant until Abraham raised the knife to kill Isaac—what can this statement mean? . . . God is changeable *in relationship* with his creation. . . . In this relational mutability, God . . . does interact with his people in the experiences of their lives as these unfold in time. God actually enters into relationship with his people, while knowing from eternity all that they will face. . . . When the angel of the LORD utters the statement, "for now I know that you fear God," this expresses the idea that *"in the experience of this action, I [God] am witnessing Abraham demonstrate dramatically and afresh that he fears me, and I find this both pleasing and acceptable in my sight.* Through Abraham's action of faith and fear of God, God sees and enters into the experience of this action of obedience, which action and heart of faith he has previously known fully and perfectly.[21]

At that stage of progressive revelation, Abraham could not have interpreted his relationship to God through the lens of clearer Scripture or revelation. Upon hearing the Angel of the LORD declare "now I know . . ." (Gen. 22:12) the only conclusion Abraham could have drawn, then, is that (at least sometimes and in some ways) God's relationship to Abraham changed: God had "now" come to

---

[21] Ware, *God's Lesser Glory*, 73-74, emphasis original.

know.[22] In the relational mutability view, Abraham's experience with God could not but lead him to a conclusion about God which, in part at least, was errant (i.e., God's acquired knowledge through a changing relationship). This means God's acts in relating to Abraham, that he entered "into the experience of this situation of obedience," could not be truly revelatory of the God who is infinitely and eternally immutable.[23]

Third, Oliphint states that God takes on covenantal properties that are "conducive to his interaction with his creation generally, and specifically with his people." Does this not imply that the eternal attributes of God are not conducive to interaction with his creation? Is Oliphint stating that, in order to relate to men, God must covenantally take to himself characteristics or properties which are different—even opposite—from what he is ontologically? This would seem to say that, in the modified doctrine of divine impassibility view, the best way for God to relate to men is to become different from what he is essentially. Abraham is confronted with the covenantally condescended God who is quite different from God in his essence.

Genesis 22:11-12 does not teach us that God grows or acquires knowledge in any sense. This would contradict the clear teaching of such passages as Psalm 44:21, Proverbs 15:3, Isaiah 40:28, Romans 11:33, Hebrews 4:13, etc. In Genesis 22, Moses is using a figure of speech to declare that God knows Abraham's act as an evidence of his faith. Accordingly, Charles Simeon, in his *Horae Homileticae,* comments on this passage as follows:

> THERE are in the Holy Scriptures many expressions, which, if taken in the strictest and most literal sense, would convey to us very erroneous conceptions of the Deity. God is often pleased to speak of himself in terms accommodated to our

---

[22] The adverb translated "now," Heb. עַתָּה (ʿattâ, now, at this time, henceforth) is an adverb of time. Leonard J. Coppes indicates that there is implied in Gen. 22:12 the sense of "after what has happened . . ." In other words, God is portrayed as being involved as a part of the narrative sequence and his knowledge as acquired in a before/after sequence. Coppes, "עַתָּה (ʿattâ)," in *TWOT*, 2:680-81.

[23] Ware's relational mutability is just one example. There are other examples of God's attributes of time and space being reformulated by those who would modify the classical doctrine of divine impassibility as well.

feeble apprehensions, and properly applicable to man only. For instance: in the passage before us, he speaks as if from Abraham's conduct he had acquired a knowledge of something which he did not know before: whereas he is omniscient: there is nothing past, present, or future, which is not open before him, and distinctly viewed by him in all its parts. Strictly speaking, he needed not Abraham's obedience to discover to him the state of Abraham's mind: he knew that Abraham feared him, before he gave the trial to Abraham: yea, he knew, from all eternity, that Abraham would fear him. But it was for our sakes that he made the discovery of Abraham's obedience a ground for acknowledging the existence of the hidden principle from which it sprang: for it is in this way that we are to ascertain our own character, and the characters of our fellow-men.[24]

Similarly, John Calvin, in his Genesis commentary, states that God is here speaking to us "according to our infirmity. Moses simply means that Abraham, by this very act, testified how reverently he feared God."[25]

Judges 2:18 (God and His Pity)

There are two passages in the book of Judges that seemingly present a challenge to the classical doctrine of impassibility. The two passages will be discussed below; however, it will be helpful to get an overview of the book as a whole.

The books of Joshua and Judges describe Israel's attempt to dispossess Canaan of its inhabitants in accordance with the commandment of God in Deuteronomy 7:1-5. Joshua portrays a relatively positive picture of Israel's holy war with the Canaanites; Judges portrays a consistently negative picture of the effort. In the book of Judges, chapters 1:1-3:6 are introductory in nature. The geographical description of the land division in chapter 1 indicates

---

[24] Charles Simeon, *Horae Homileticae, Or Discourses Now First Digested Into One Continued Series and Forming a Commentary Upon Every Book of the Old and New Testament*, 21 vols., (London: Holdsworth and Ball, 1832), 1:179-80.

[25] Calvin, *Commentaries*, 1:570.

the overall inability of Israel to dispossess the land of the Canaanites and thus highlights the failure to comply with the instructions given in Deuteronomy 7:1-5. Judges 2:1-3:6 is a thematic introduction to the book: the author gives the reader an overall view of life in Israel during the period of the judges. The nation would sin against God; God would deliver them over to oppressors; the nation would cry out in distress (not in repentance); and God would raise up a judge or a deliverer to save his people from their oppression. Judges 3:7-16:31 is the largest section of the book, and describes the various men[26] whom the Lord raised up to deliver Israel from her oppressors. Chapters 17-21 are appendices, and probably cover the time prior to the installation of the first judge, Othniel. These chapters give a general view of life in Israel prior to the judges.

Let us look at Judges 2:18. The chapter highlights Israel's disobedience to the Lord (Jdg. 2:1-6), indicates the timeframe of Israel's apostasy (after the death of Joshua, Jdg. 2:7-10), and comprehensively describes the cycles that will later be described in more detail in the book of the deliverers (Jdg. 3:7-16:31). The nation of Israel would sin against God (Jdg. 2:11-13), be rejected by the Lord as a result (Jdg. 2:14-15a), and would then express their distress (Jdg. 2:15b) to God. The Lord would then undertake on their behalf: he would raise up judges who would deliver them from oppression. The reader should appreciate the graciousness of God in such a situation: Israel cries out because of distress, not in repentance. That God raised up deliverers indicates something of his goodness and mercy to his wayward people. It is a revelation of his saving kindness and a foretaste of new covenant blessing: each of the earthly judges typifies the Lord Jesus and the salvation from the oppression of sin that he would ultimately achieve for his people. In Judges 2:18, the author states:

> And when the LORD raised up judges for them, the LORD was with the judge and delivered them out of the hand of their enemies all the days of the judge; for the LORD was moved to pity by their groaning because of those who oppressed them and harassed them. (Jdg. 2:18)

---

[26] Deborah was neither a judge nor a co-judge, but a prophetess.

The doctrine of impassibility indicates that God does "not . . . experience inner emotional changes, whether enacted freely from within or effected by his relationship to and interaction with human beings and the created order."[27] Verse 18 seems to indicate the contrary: the "LORD was moved to pity." Does the text teach that God does, in fact, experience inner emotional changes? Does God react to his people's oppression as men might react in similar situations? No, God is impassible. The language employed in verse 18 is anthropopathic. The Lord God does not react. He does not fluctuate. He is not governed by forces outside of his being or conflicted by that which is *ad intra*. The author is giving the reader information concerning the nature of God; not giving information concerning the *changing* nature of God. As 2LCF 2.1 teaches, God is "most loving, gracious, merciful, longsuffering," etc. He does not become more so because of external influences. Judges 2:18 is anthropopathic language designed to reveal the gracious actions of our God.

Some suggest that such an approach to these types of verses empties the biblical narrative of its meaning. We think it does just the opposite. By employing language that the creature is familiar with, the biblical author is able to convey truth about God, truth that communicates his unchanging affections toward his people. What changes is not God's being, but his providential dealing with his people. John Gill comments:

> *for it repented the Lord because of their* groanings . . . the Lord being merciful had compassion upon them, when they groaned under their oppressions, and cried unto him, then he received their prayer, as the Targum, and sent them a deliverer; and so did what men do when they repent of a thing, change their conduct; thus the Lord changed the outward dispensation of his providence towards them, according to his unchangeable will; for otherwise repentance, properly speaking, does not belong unto God.[28]

---

[27] Weinandy, "Impassibility of God," in *New Catholic Encyclopedia*, 2nd edition, 7:357.

[28] Gill, *Exposition*, 2:286.

It is important to notice that Gill says, "properly speaking." This is helpful language in the debate concerning impassibility. There are times when authors speak of things that pertain to God improperly—for instance, the predicating of hands, feet, eyes, and in the case of Judges 2:18, repentance. Therefore, as Gill notes, repentance is an improper predication and hence, Judges 2:18 does not detract from the classical doctrine of divine impassibility.

Judges 10:16 (God and His Soul's Endurance)

So they put away the foreign gods from among them and served the LORD. And His soul could no longer endure the misery of Israel. (Jdg. 10:16)

Judges 10 provides a brief account of two minor judges, Tola and Jair.[29] After the death of Jair, Israel "again did evil in the sight of the LORD" (Jdg. 10:6) and hence the cycle described in the overview in chapter 2 begins again. Because Israel sinned, they would face the judgment of God as specified in the curses of the covenant (Deut. 28), specifically, oppression from the Philistines and Ammonites. Israel cried out in distress, expressed confession and contrition (Jdg. 10:15), and they "put away the foreign gods from among them and served the LORD" (Jdg. 10:16a). It is just here that the Lord again reveals to the people of Israel something of his great grace and mercy, "And His soul could no longer endure the misery of Israel" (Jdg. 10:16b).

That the text should be interpreted anthropopathically is evident for several reasons. First, God communicates to his children using language and concepts they can understand. In verse 14, God tells Israel, "Go and cry out to the gods which you have chosen; let them deliver you in your time of distress." We certainly do not understand this text to mean that God actually validates the existence of Baal and his cohorts and that God recognizes their ability to save Israel. Second, the Lord Jesus describes God as "spirit" in John 4:24, and we do not understand a spirit being as having a soul. Third, the expression in verse 16 fits the narrative: the

---

[29] They are minor, not in importance, but because there is not nearly as much written material concerning them as there is for the "major" judges in the book.

author is explaining the series of events so that man can understand it; he is not describing essential change in the being of God. Gill comments:

> *and his soul was grieved for the misery of Israel;* which is to be understood after the manner of men; for grief properly does not belong to God, there being no passions in Him; but it denotes a carriage or behavior of His, which shows what looks like sympathy in men; a love and affection for Israel, notwithstanding their ill behavior to Him, and a change of His dispensations in providence towards them, according to His unchangeable will.[30]

Note again Gill's use of "properly does not belong to God." As noted above, there are many things predicated of God in Scripture which are not proper to his being: hands, feet, eyes, and repentance, for just a few examples. The Scriptures use anthropopathic language in order to reveal God to us; not to describe actual changes in his being. John Calvin comments on this convention in a statement calculated to show the folly of the anthropomorphites.

> The Anthropomorphites, also, who imagined a corporeal God from the fact that Scripture often ascribes to him a mouth, ears, eyes, hands, and feet, are easily refuted. For who even of slight intelligence does not understand that, as nurses commonly do with infants, God is wont in a measure to "lisp" in speaking to us? Thus such forms of speaking do not so much express clearly what God is like as accommodate the knowledge of him to our slight capacity. To do this he must descend far beneath his loftiness.[31]

Judges 2:18 and 10:16 are prime examples of this type of accommodation of language. God is immutable and impassible; he does not change in his being, but rather condescends through such language to "lisp" to his children something of the incomprehensible truth of his infinite nature.

---

[30] Gill, *Exposition*, 2:336.

[31] John Calvin, *The Institutes of the Christian Religion,* ed. John T. McNeill and trans. Ford Lewis Battles, *Library of Christian Classics,* vols. 20-21 (Philadelphia: Westminster Press, 1960), I.xiii.1 (121), hereafter *Institutes.*

Deuteronomy 5:29 and Hosea 11:8-9
(God and His Desires)

Then the LORD heard the voice of your words when you spoke to me, and the LORD said to me: 'I have heard the voice of the words of this people which they have spoken to you. They are right *in* all that they have spoken. 29 'Oh, that they had such a heart in them that they would fear Me and always keep all My commandments, that it might be well with them and with their children forever! (Deut. 5:28-29)

How can I give you up, Ephraim? *How* can I hand you over, Israel? How can I make you like Admah? *How* can I set you like Zeboiim? My heart churns within Me; My sympathy is stirred. 9 I will not execute the fierceness of My anger; I will not again destroy Ephraim. For I *am* God, and not man, The Holy One in your midst; And I will not come with terror. (Hos. 11:8-9)

Does God have wishes? Does he pine for something which he has ordained will not happen? Or does God ever wish for something and, as a result, change his course of action based on his desire?

In Deuteronomy 5, Moses is recounting the event of Mount Sinai. The manifestation of God is so overwhelming for the Israelites that they plead with Moses to hear the rest of God's instructions and to relay them as a mediator. They wanted no more of the glory of God! In this passage, Moses reminds them that God heard their request. God told Moses that the people were right in what they had said. His glory was, indeed, overpowering; the people had truly been awed and frightened by it. However, God knew that their promised obedience based on this fear would be short-lived. He expresses his knowledge of their shallow reverence by means of an optative: "Oh, that they had such a heart in them that they would fear me and always keep all my commandments . . ." The question is: Is God here wishing for a different heart for Israel, when he has the power to give it? Does he yearn for something which he has ordained will not happen?

Similarly, in Hosea 11, God's desires for Israel are expressed as a heart-churning compassion which cannot bring judgment on the people of Ephraim again, even though they certainly deserve his wrath. Is God here showing us that his emotions change his mind? Does he alter a course of action based on his wishes or passions?

Calvin explains Deuteronomy 5:29 as a figurative expression:

> God signifies that they would not be so firm and faithful in keeping their promises, as they were ready and willing to make them; and thus that hypocrisy was not altogether banished, or purged from their minds. Moreover, He figuratively (*improprie*) assumes a human feeling, because it would be vain and absurd for him to desire what it was in His power to confer. Certainly He has the power of bending and directing men's hearts whithersoever He pleases. Why, then, does He wish that it were given to the people from some other quarter, that they should be always kept in the path of duty, except that, speaking in the character of a man, He shows that it was rather to be wished than hoped that the people would constantly persevere in their fidelity? . . . But here we must consider God's will as it is set before us in His word, not as it is hidden in Himself; for, while by His word He invites all promiscuously to (eternal) life, He only quickens by His secret inspiration those whom He has elected.[32]

Calvin classifies the passage as figurative, based on two arguments. First, he declares it would be "vain and absurd" for God only to wish for what he could bring about. After all, says Calvin, God has the power to change hearts; why would he ask who could give such a change, as if seeking someone else to do it? The only explanation is that God must be speaking "in the character of a man" (i.e., figuratively). Second, Calvin argues that, since we know God has a will of decree (a secret will "hidden in himself") and a will of command (a revealed will "set before us in His word"), we must see Deuteronomy 5:29 as an expression of the latter (cf. Deut. 10:16). God here shows his perfect knowledge of the true nature of Israel's heart and, by the analogy of a human wish, is setting before Israel their need to seek for themselves a new heart.

Likewise, the Hosea passage portrays God as so moved with love and compassion for Israel that he commutes the sentence of

---

[32] Calvin, *Commentaries*, 2:337.

judgment and refuses to give Ephraim over to it. A literal reading would see God's desires as *overriding* his justice. This would set one aspect of God in opposition to another, destroying divine unity and simplicity. Again, however, the passage may be interpreted in light of other scriptural information about God, seen as a figurative (and poetic) expression of his mercy. As Calvin notes:

> But when he says that his *heart was changed,* and that his *repentings were brought back again,* the same mode of speaking after the manner of men is adopted; for we know that these feelings belong not to God; he cannot be touched with repentance, and his heart cannot undergo changes. To imagine such a thing would be impiety. But the design is to show, that if he dealt with the people of Israel as they deserved, they would now be made like Sodom and Gomorra. But as God was merciful, and embraced his people with paternal affection, he could not forget that he was a Father, but would be willing to grant pardon; as is the case with a father, who, on seeing his son's wicked disposition, suddenly feels a strong displeasure, and then, being seized with relenting, is inclined to spare him. God then declares that he would thus deal with his people.[33]

It should be noted that the basis for God's actions is a *dissimilarity* between God and man. "For I *am* God, and not man, The Holy One in your midst; And I will not come with terror" (Hos. 11:9). A man might not act in compassion, but give vent to his anger. God, on the other hand, is unchangeable and faithful. He is immutably compassionate to his people. Rather than being a proof text for God's emotivity, the passage actually teaches the vast disjunction between the perfect nature of God and that of finite man. This difference is so great that God must reveal it to us by means of an analogy.

In the end, if God were seen as wishing for what he had not ordained, or changing his determined course of action based on his emotions, there would be implications for the entire doctrine of God. The 2LCF closely connects God's spirituality, simplicity, and

---

[33] Calvin, *Commentaries*, 13:402.

impassibility. For God to wish for what he has not ordained implies disunity in God, where one "part" of God is wishing for something which another "part" of God had chosen not to ordain. The resultant view of God would come dangerously close to denying his unity and simplicity, seeing God as composed of parts and attributes, rather than being one, simple, spiritual, perfect being whose essence is not a conglomeration of attributes but a unified and singular whole. God is as much "without . . . parts" as he is "without . . . passions," and the two are inextricably linked.

Jonah 3:10 (God and His Will)

> Then God saw their works, that they turned from their evil way; and God relented from the disaster that He had said He would bring upon them, and He did not do it. (Jon. 3:10)

When the correlation between God's will and man's freedom is discussed, the focal point is usually that of personal responsibility. But another issue needs to be discussed as well—that of genuine contingency. If God has decreed everything from eternity, can a man's decisions genuinely alter either his personal future, or the general future of his world? Put another way (for the sake of our verse), does God's decree in any sense depend upon the will of man?

In Jonah 3:10, we must consider the relationship between the repentance of the Ninevites from their evil and the repentance of God from the disaster he said he would bring on them. The classical view interprets God's repenting as figurative or anthropopathic, describing from man's vantage point what God's action looks like. That is, from our perspective, God's action has the same appearance as when a man changes his mind. Furthermore, as God ordains all things, he ordains the means as well as the end, including all secondary causes, whether necessary, free, or contingent. Thus, the 2LCF asserts:

> God hath decreed in himself, from all eternity, by the most wise and holy counsel of His own will, freely and unchangeably, all things, whatsoever comes to pass; yet so as thereby is God neither the author of sin nor hath

fellowship with any therein; nor is violence offered to the will of the creature, nor yet is the liberty or *contingency* of second causes taken away, but rather established; in which appears His wisdom in disposing all things, and power and faithfulness in accomplishing His decree. (2LCF 3.1, emphasis added)

Thus, God not only ordained that he would spare Nineveh (the end), but that Jonah would preach, the people would heed the preaching and subsequently repent and turn (contingent secondary causes), and that God would thus accomplish his purpose of sparing them.

All of this requires taking God's repentance as figurative or anthropopathic. Oliphint, however, proposes a different understanding from the classical view, wherein God's relenting is not figurative but more literal:

> It should be obvious by this point in our discussion, however, that there *is* a literal way in which we can apply the notion of relenting to God; that is, by virtue of his taking on covenantal properties. The Lord relents in that, as he interacts with us covenantally, his interaction allows for (because he has decreed it) the reality and responsibility of our choices, and of contingency generally. Thus, he may determine (covenantally) to respond to his people or his creation in a particular way, but may "change his mind" with respect to his initial response.[34]

Oliphint continues:

> When the Lord tells us in his Word that he relented from the disaster that he had threatened, we need not explain this in such a way as to diminish the clear, covenant implications of his actions. In condescending to interact with his people, the Lord really did relent from what he would otherwise have done. This is in no way an improper or metaphorical way of speaking. It is, in fact, a way of speaking that takes

---

[34] Oliphint, *God with Us*, 219.

seriously the condescension of the Lord from the beginning . . . that is part and parcel of the Lord's interaction with his people from Genesis 3 into eternity.[35]

Both the modified doctrine of divine impassibility view and the classical view see the outcome and means as sovereignly ordained. Nevertheless, Ware and Oliphint see the primary difference between them in the genuineness of the change in God. But this requires some interesting contrasts between the essential, unchangeable God and his covenantal properties. We must remember that the modified doctrine of divine impassibility view claims that God is unchangeable and immutable *in his essence*. As such, he has ordained "all things, whatsoever comes to pass," including ordaining the change of his own covenantal properties. That is, God has eternally ordained to change, not in his nature, but in his covenantal properties.

But for a change to be genuine, the alteration must be measurable and real. That is, in the case of Nineveh, if according to his covenantal properties God changed "his mind" regarding what was to be done with Nineveh, then the original intention must have been to destroy Nineveh. If the original intention was to spare Nineveh all along, then there is no measurable or real change. Furthermore, for the change to be genuine, the original intention must have been truly chosen and willed, otherwise the change of mind would not be genuine. So God, in his *eternal essence*, decrees that Nineveh will be spared. God, in his *covenantal properties*, truly intends that Nineveh be destroyed, but then relents upon Nineveh's repentance.

The proponents of the modified view claim that it is necessary for God to make just such a real change, based on his eternal nature. Rob Lister writes:

> Because God is not a man, he does not repent like one. That is to say, that God does not repent/regret/change his mind on account of sin, error, or lack of foresight. Again, Bruce Ware helpfully explains this phenomenon by pointing out that God's relational mutability . . . is, as we have also seen

---

[35] Oliphint, *God with Us*, 220.

above, an expression of his own immutable being and promises.[36]

That is, because he is immutably holy, righteous, good, etc. in his eternal being, when men change in relation to him, God *must* respond differently. Otherwise, it is claimed, God would have to change his essential nature.

But this is not a necessary conclusion. The classical view has always maintained the immutability of God's essence and that, as men change, they stand in a different relationship to God. God does not change in his relationship to men, but men change in their relationship to God. As such, God manifests his eternal attributes differently to them. To men, this different manifestation of God's attributes *appears* as change, and is often figuratively depicted as such in Scripture. Yet classical theism insists that the change is solely in man; there is no change in God. This explanation of the scriptural data has not only the weight of history and the Confession behind it, but avoids the complications of the modified doctrine of divine impassibility view that has God creating and assuming certain covenantal properties which often display the very opposite nature of God himself. In summary, it is *not* necessary that a change in men elicit a change in God. The classical view, in which there is no change in God at all, better accounts for the scriptural data.

Isaiah 63
(God and His Anger, Fury, Affliction, and Grief)

Who *is* this who comes from Edom, With dyed garments from Bozrah, This *One who is* glorious in His apparel, Traveling in the greatness of His strength? — "I who speak in righteousness, mighty to save." 2 Why *is* Your apparel red, And Your garments like one who treads in the winepress? 3

---

36 Lister, *God Is Impassible and Impassioned*, 210. The reference to Bruce Ware is to his "An Evangelical Reformulation of the Doctrine of the Immutability of God," 440. Though Lister adopts Ware's concept of relational mutability, it is important to remember that Ware does not agree with Lister's exegetical conclusion regarding God's repentance though, as we noted above, he does see relational and emotional changes in God.

"I have trodden the winepress alone, And from the peoples no one *was* with Me. For I have trodden them in My anger, And trampled them in My fury; Their blood is sprinkled upon My garments, And I have stained all My robes. ⁴ For the day of vengeance *is* in My heart, And the year of My redeemed has come. ⁵ I looked, but *there was* no one to help, And I wondered That *there was* no one to uphold; Therefore My own arm brought salvation for Me; And My own fury, it sustained Me. ⁶ I have trodden down the peoples in My anger, Made them drunk in My fury, And brought down their strength to the earth." ⁷ I will mention the lovingkindnesses of the LORD *And* the praises of the LORD, According to all that the LORD has bestowed on us, And the great goodness toward the house of Israel, Which He has bestowed on them according to His mercies, According to the multitude of His lovingkindnesses. ⁸ For He said, "Surely they *are* My people, Children *who* will not lie." So He became their Savior. ⁹ In all their affliction He was afflicted, And the Angel of His Presence saved them; In His love and in His pity He redeemed them; And He bore them and carried them All the days of old. ¹⁰ But they rebelled and grieved His Holy Spirit; So He turned Himself against them as an enemy, *And* He fought against them. (Isa. 63:1-10)

If there were ever a chapter that seemed to imply that God is capable of passions or emotional changes of state, it would be Isaiah 63. In the span of a single chapter, God is described as angry (vv. 3, 6), furious (vv. 3, 5, 6), afflicted (v. 9), and grieved (v. 10). In many respects, Isaiah 63 epitomizes several of the conclusions and observations that have already been made and provides a relatively comprehensive example of the richness of a classical and Reformed hermeneutic.

The structure of the book of Isaiah can be identified according to three Messianic portraits: the Lord (chapters 1-37), the Servant (chapters 38-55), and the Anointed Conqueror (chapters 56-66).[37] J. Alec Motyer very helpfully summarizes the context in which Isaiah 63 appears:

---

[37] J. Alec Motyer, *The Prophecy of Isaiah: An Introduction & Commentary* (Downers Grove, IL: InterVarsity Press, 1993), 13.

[The] theme is announced in 56:1. Historically, the people are back from Babylon (48:20-22); conceptually, they are the redeemed of the Lord, his servants, clothed with the righteousness of his Servant (53:11; 54:17). Under each heading they are still his waiting people, for what has already been done leaves some of their needs unsatisfied. Therefore, they are called to persevere in the disciplines of 'judgement and righteousness'—the life the Lord decides and approves—until his salvation comes and his righteousness receives full expression. The Lord's true people find themselves subject to oppression and tension within a mixed community (56:6-57:21). Experience teaches them that they cannot live up to what the Lord requires (58:1-14) because of inadequacies within themselves (59:1-13). There is set before them, however, the expectation of an anointed one (59:14-63:6) whose work of salvation meets their needs, whose work of righteousness fulfils all that God requires, and whose work of vengeance deals with every opposing force. Hence they pray (63:7-64:12) and hold on to the promises (65:1-66:24), confidently expecting the eternal glory of the new creation. In a word, once more the Isaianic literature centralizes faith—the faith that persists, prays and waits in hope.[38]

Isaiah 63 anticipates a time after Israel's return from captivity in Babylon. Yet their return would leave much to be desired, as they would find themselves subject to oppression and affliction. Israel's post-exilic restoration fell short of the full restoration God had promised (cf. Hag. 2:3, 6-9). Thus, their hope was deferred as they waited upon the Lord's anointed and trusted in the fullness of his salvation. Notwithstanding the chapter's copious anthropopathic language, divine impassibility lies at the heart of the prophet's concern. *The Lord is assuring his people that in the midst of their affliction, even their sin, his saving love is without hypocrisy and entails a discipline that is without vengeance.*

Endeavoring to provide hope to an afflicted and oppressed people, the prophet promises that the day of God's vengeance is

---

[38] Motyer, *Isaiah*, 23.

coming. This hopeful expectation is established at the end of the preceding chapter:

> Indeed the LORD has proclaimed To the end of the world: "Say to the daughter of Zion, 'Surely your salvation is coming; Behold, His reward *is* with Him, And His work before Him.'" 12 And they shall call them The Holy People, The Redeemed of the LORD; And you shall be called Sought Out, A City Not Forsaken. (Isa. 62:11-12)

Whereas chapter 62 concludes with a promise of redemption from all those who afflict them, Isaiah 63:1-6 begins with a proleptic description of its fulfillment. In verse 1, a watchman (cf. 62:6) is standing guard on the city wall, and he sees a warrior approaching the city from the direction of Edom. As it is so often with Babylon, Edom here signifies all of the enemies of God's people (cf. Psalm 137:7). Edom's destruction was foretold (Isa. 34:5-6), and now the Anointed Conqueror has returned having accomplished it.

The watchman asks, "Who *is* this who comes from Edom . . . glorious in His apparel . . . Traveling in the greatness of His strength?" (Isa. 63:1). With greater certainty than the watchman, the majority of commentators understand in this place a reference to the Lord Jesus, predominantly with respect to his second coming (cf. 2 Thess. 1:10). This is confirmed both by the description and the response attributed to the warrior. He identifies himself as one who speaks the truth according to the council of God, and who is mighty to save (Isa. 63:1b). As he approaches the city covered in the blood of their enemies, he assures the watchman that there is nothing that can hinder his ability or thwart his purpose to save his people. This is no ordinary warrior. He has singlehandedly judged their enemies, trampling them in his fury like one who treads in the winepress (v. 3). He looked and there was no one among the sons of Adam capable or competent to even help him bring redemption and execute judgment; his own arm accomplished his purposes of redemption (v. 5). Therefore, their hope depended upon a single man of divine strength, the Lord (chs. 1-37) and Servant (chs. 38-55), that is, the Anointed Conqueror.

We are told that the day of vengeance was in his heart (Isa. 63:4). As John L. Mackay points out:

The warrior was not a tyrant who had lost control of his emotions and was intent on crushing all those whom he imagined to have slighted him in some way. 'Day of vengeance' repeats the term from 34:8 and 61:2 to show that this is the assertion of the sovereign rights of the King, as he vindicates himself and his rule according to the purpose that he had 'in [his] heart.' This phrase does not primarily connote divine pleasure in the process described; rather, it conveys divine resolve that punishment be carried out.[39]

The prophet's point is not to suggest that God is consumed with divine feelings of vengeance, much less a day wherein he would pour out divine feelings of fury. Herein is a day, according to God's own resolve, to pour out, not divine feelings, but divine justice. Likewise, when the warrior speaks of his own fury sustaining him in verse 5 and his anger in verse 6, he is not speaking of divine emotions, but the divine resolve that punishment be carried out upon his enemies. Elsewhere, Isaiah not only includes anger and wrath among God's external works rather than his internal emotions, but they are referred to as his "strange works" (Isa. 28:21, ESV). Similarly, the Lord assures his people in Isaiah 27:4, saying, "Fury *is* not in Me." Thus E. J. Young concludes, "This wrath is free of any malice or impurity whatsoever; it is God's just determination to punish the sinner for his sin."[40] It is not divine feelings, but God's immutable justice and holiness, his just determination to punish sin, that will sustain him in carrying out this work of anger, wrath, and fury.

Anger, wrath, and fury are not proper to God. That is, the essence of these passions is not in God. William Gouge, addressing the question, "Is anger in God?," answers:

Not properly, as in a man, a passion distinct from the essence. For God is a most simple and pure essence. He is all essence. There is nothing in him different from his essence. The things that are attributed unto him, are spoken of him

---

[39] John L. Mackay, *Isaiah*, An Evangelical Press Study Commentary (Darlington, England: EP Books, 2009), 2:549.

[40] Edward J. Young, *The Book of Isaiah*, 3 vols. (Grand Rapids: Eerdmans Publishing Company, 1972), 3:478.

only by way of resemblance, for teaching sake: to make us somewhat more distinctly conceive God's dealing with us. *Anger* in man is a *passion whereby upon apprehension of some evil done, he is stirred up to punish him that hath done it. . . .*

Anger attributed to God sets out his dislike of evil and his *resolution to punish evil doers.* When any way God manifests his dislike and his resolution to punish, he is said to be angry.[41]

Such passions are not in God properly, but rather figuratively (i.e., "by way of resemblance"). In other words, that which perfect anger, wrath, and fury *signify* is in God, though not the passions themselves. For instance, when the king of Nineveh said, "Who can tell *if* God will turn and relent, and turn away from His fierce anger, so that we may not perish?" (Jon. 3:9), *anger* signifies God's threat of judgment and resolution to punish sin (cf. v. 10). Although the passion of anger is not proper to God, that which it signifies, the resolution to punish sin, is proper to God by virtue of his immutable justice. Although God turned from his anger against the Ninevites, Isaiah informs us that on the day of God's vengeance, his fury will sustain him—not the passion itself, but the resoluteness of his immutable justice, which will no longer provide an occasion for sinners to repent. Thus, Isaiah 63:1-6 proleptically describes the climactic day of God's judgment against all of his enemies.

Moreover, in the context of God's judgment, Isaiah declares the "day of [his] redeemed" (v. 4b). The prophet speaks of the same day from different perspectives. There may be judgment without salvation, but no salvation apart from judgment. In a skillful play on words, Isaiah uses two words with the same spelling to speak of the warrior's blood *stained* (אֶגְאָלְתִּי) robes in verse 3 and the Lord's *redeemed* (גְּאוּלַי) in verse 4.[42] The prophet's intention is vividly clear. Either we will be dressed in robes covered in *his* sin-atoning, justice-satisfying, mercy-procuring blood shed on the cross (cf. Isa. 53), or

---

[41] William Gouge, "A Plaster for the Plague," in *God's Three Arrows: Plague, Famine, Sword* (London: George Miller, 1631), 67, emphasis original. Modernized language.

[42] Motyer, *Isaiah*, 511, states: "'My Redeemed' (ge'ûllāy) has the same letters as stained ('eḡ'āltî) two lines earlier; their roots (√gā'al) have the same spelling. This association must be intended; to him the defilement, to them the redemption."

else he will be covered in *our* blood as he tramples us in his just wrath. It is not he who changes; it is for sinners to repent and change because he will not change (v. 6, "My own arm brought salvation for Me; and My own fury, it sustained Me"). "We may experience his arm as the 'righteousness' of God on our behalf, or we may experience it as his wrath."[43] Isaiah's intention is to give hope to those who trust in the Anointed Conqueror alone for salvation. A day is coming when God's anointed will deliver his redeemed ones from all of their affliction and oppression.

The remainder of the chapter wrestles with the tensions that arise from living in the gap between promise and fulfillment. The hope of a blessed future is set before them, but the present reality is still one of affliction and oppression. What are they to do in the meantime? On what assistance can they count as they wait upon the Lord? In search of an answer to these questions, Isaiah, speaking on behalf of the people of God, begins to recall the days of old in verse 7:

> I will mention the lovingkindnesses of the LORD *And* the praises of the LORD, According to all that the LORD has bestowed on us, And the great goodness toward the house of Israel, Which He has bestowed on them according to His mercies, According to the multitude of His lovingkindnesses. (Isa. 63:7)

The prophet recalls the covenant faithfulness, or steadfast love, of God in the past in order to provide precedence for hope in the present.[44] They were not the first who had to live in the gap between promise and fulfillment, nor were they the first to suffer affliction. Until the day of God's vengeance, they may expect affliction, no less than those who endured affliction in the past. Moreover, they too have every reason to believe that "their Savior" (v. 8) will compassionately relieve them in their present distresses, just as he had done in the past. Because the LORD does not change,

---

[43] John N. Oswalt, *The Book of Isaiah, Chapters 40-66*, The New International Commentary on the Old Testament (Grand Rapids: Eerdmans Publishing Co., 1998), 599. Cf. Isa. 59:16 and 63:5.

[44] The covenant faithfulness of God is emphasized by placing חֶסֶד (*hesed*) as the first and last words of the verse.

what was true for the people of God in the past is true for the people of God in the present: "*In all their affliction He was afflicted, And the Angel of His Presence saved them; In His love and in His pity He redeemed them; And He bore them and carried them All the days of old*" (v. 9).[45]

Is there affliction in God?[46] What was affirmed and denied with regard to anger, wrath, and fury may be affirmed and denied with regard to affliction. Even J. A. Alexander, who opts for a different reading of the text in order to avoid a metaphorical interpretation, admits that the translation we have adopted requires "an anthropopathic explanation." He writes, "The objections to it [i.e., the translation adopted here] are, that it gratuitously renders necessary another anthropopathic explanation."[47] We agree, though we do not consider this a cause for objection. Although affliction, or co-suffering, is not in God properly, it is in God figuratively. Although all forms of suffering in God must be denied, that which co-suffering signifies may be affirmed. Isaiah is not merely comforting the true people of God by telling them that God suffers with them and literally feels their pain. Rather, their comfort comes from the declaration that God's love is without hypocrisy. He does not merely shed a tear for them and then say, "Depart in peace, be warmed and filled," and do nothing to relieve their distress (James 2:16). Having adopted his people as his own children (v. 8), he is *like* a father who is afflicted in the affliction of his child. The father's co-suffering not only signifies his love and identification with his child, but ultimately his propensity to do whatever he can to relieve his child's affliction as surely as if it were his own.[48]

---

[45] Emphasis added.

[46] With regard to the phrase in question, the MT indicates a *K^etiv-Q^ere*. The MT is *written*: בְּכָל־צָרָתָם לֹא צָר. ("In all their affliction, [he was] not afflicted"). However, the Masorah parva (i.e., the Masoretic notations in the margin) indicate that there are 15 places where לוֹ (*lo*, to him) is mistaken for לֹא (*lo*, not), and recommends it be read: בְּכָל־צָרָתָם לוֹ צָר ("in all their affliction, to him [was] affliction"). The *Q^ere* is to be preferred on account that it agrees best with the context and is supported by other texts that indicate that the Lord is not cold or callous toward his people in their affliction (Exod. 3:7; Jdg. 10:16).

[47] Joseph Addison Alexander, *Commentary on the Prophecies of Isaiah: Unabridged*, 2 vols. (1875; reprint, Grand Rapids: Zondervan, 1970) 2:418.

[48] We have here, not only encouragement, but also exhortation, for we are here told what sort of fathers we are to be toward our children, that in both correction

John Calvin shows great appreciation for this manner of speaking when he says:

> By speaking in this manner, he declares the incomparable love which God bears toward his people. In order to move us more powerfully and draw us to himself, the Lord accommodates himself to the manner of men, by attributing to himself all the affection, love, and (συμπαθεία) compassion which a father can have. And yet, in human affairs it is impossible to conceive of any sort of kindness or benevolence which he does not immeasurably surpass.[49]

God compares himself to a man who possesses all of the affection, love, and compassion that a father can possibly have for his child. When your child is suffering and afflicted, it afflicts your heart so that you are moved in compassion, if possible, to relieve his affliction. In other words, the Lord compares himself to the greatest compassion, love, and affection known among men. "And yet," as Calvin says, "in human affairs it is impossible to conceive of any sort of kindness or benevolence which he does not immeasurably surpass." The concern of verse 9 is not the ability of God to suffer, but the greatness of his love, which, *without affliction*, surpasses that of a human father who, being afflicted in the affliction of his child, seeks to relieve his affliction as surely as if it were his own.

Such was the Father's love in sending his Son into the world to save sinners, the suffering servant of Isaiah 53, the incarnate "Angel of His Presence" (Isa. 63:9),[50] who was truly afflicted in our afflictions. "Beloved! he [became] a man of sorrows, that he might be a God of succours; his heart is full of succours" in order to give aid to the seed of Abraham.[51] Commenting on Hebrews 4:15, that

---

and compassion we are to be afflicted in their affliction.

[49] Calvin, *Commentaries*, 8:346.

[50] "The Angel of His Presence" is a personalized way of speaking about God's presence in visible representation (Exod. 20:21-23; 33:2; Josh. 5:13-15); perhaps a way of speaking about Christ under the old covenant (cf. Col. 1:15).

[51] William Bridge, "Satan's Power to Tempt, and Christ's Love To, and Care of His People Under Temptation": In Five Sermons, Sermon II. Heb. II. 18., in *The Works of the Rev. William Bridge* (1657; reprint, 5 vols. in 1845; reprint, Beaver Falls, PA: Soli Deo Gloria, 1989), 1:117.

"we do not have a High Priest who cannot sympathize with [i.e., suffer with] our weaknesses," Owen says:

> In this sense of the word, συμπαθῆσαι, "to be affected with a sense," ascribes this ability in a moral and natural sense unto the Lord Christ, our high priest, as he is man, in contradistinction unto God absolutely, whose nature is incapable of the compassion intended. There are, indeed, in the Scripture assignations of such kind of affections unto God; as Isa. lxiii. 9, בְּכָל־צָרָתָם לֹא צָר. For לֹא, "not," the reading is לוֹ "to him;" and accordingly we translate it, "In all their affliction he was afflicted;" or, "there was straitening, affliction unto him," — he afflicted with their straits and afflictions. But there is an anthropopathy allowed in these expressions. These things are assigned unto God after the manner of men. And the true reason of such ascriptions, is not merely to assist our weakness and help our understandings in the things themselves, *but to show really what God doth and will do in the human nature which he hath assumed, and intended to do so from of old; on which purpose the superstructure of his dealing with us in the Scripture is founded and built.* And thus it is said of our high priest that "he is able to be affected with a sense of our infirmities," because in his human nature he is capable of such affections, and, as he is our high priest, is graciously inclined to act according to them.[52]

According to Owen, the ultimate purpose of biblical anthropopathy is not merely to accommodate our weak and finite capacity, but especially to point the people of God to what he would really do by virtue of the human nature of Jesus Christ. The Lord has not left his people to fend for themselves in the gap between promise and fulfillment.

> For we do not have a High Priest who cannot sympathize with our weaknesses, but was in all *points* tempted as *we are, yet* without sin. 16 Let us therefore come boldly to the throne

---

52 Owen, *Works*, 20:421, emphasis added.

of grace, that we may obtain mercy and find grace to help in time of need. (Heb. 4:15-16)

His love is without hypocrisy. Isaiah is pointing Israel both forward to Christ and backward to the Lord's faithfulness in the past. As in the days of old, in his love and his pity he will redeem them; he will bear them and carry them as a father would his child (Deut. 1:31).

However, Isaiah 63:10 marks a turning point in the historical review: "But they rebelled and grieved His Holy Spirit; So He turned Himself against them as an enemy, *And* He fought against them." He had chosen them for his people (v. 8a, "Surely they *are* My people") that they might also deal faithfully with him (v. 8b, "Children *who* will not lie"). Commenting on verse 8, William Day explains:

> By this God shewed what good hope he had at first of the children of Israel. And he speaks here, as a man who knoweth not secret things, and things to come, but hopeth the best. By an ἀνθρωποπάθια.[53]

The Lord was faithful, but as verse 10 reminds us, Israel frequently demonstrated hypocrisy, grieving the Holy Spirit, so that God frequently "turned Himself against them as an enemy." In highlighting the dark side of Israel's past, along with the good, it is probable that Isaiah is addressing the sort of doubt that is common among God's people this side of glory. It is much easier to accept that God will have compassion on his children when their affliction is not the result of their own sin and a potential sign of God's displeasure. Could it be that the cause of Israel's present affliction was the result of their own sin, and if so, could they count on his pity and help? Had God "turned himself against them" as he had done in the past? Were they now liable to the anger, wrath, and fury of God rather than the gracious salvation of God?

In order to understand the intent of verse 10 within the overall context, the nature of grief must first be considered. Grief, *in the context of the covenant of grace*, is notably different than anger, fury,

---

[53] William Day, *An Exposition of the Book of the Prophet Isaiah* (London: G. D and S. G., 1654), 184.

and wrath. Owen explains:

> The term of grieving, or affecting with sorrow, may be
> considered either actively, in respect of the persons grieving;
> or passively, in respect of the persons grieved. In the latter
> sense the expression is metaphorical.[54]

In other words, the term *grief* may be considered with respect to the
persons grieving, "they grieved the Spirit," or with respect to the
person being grieved, "the Spirit is grieved." Although the latter
(i.e., passive) sense of the expression is to be understood
metaphorically, the former (i.e., active) sense is not. Owen explains,
"[W]e may do those things that are proper to grieve him, though he
be not passively grieved; our sin being no less therein than if he
were grieved as we are."[55] Likewise, Thomas Boston adds that "men
are said to vex the Spirit, when they treat him so as would vex one
capable of vexation."[56]

With regard to the latter (i.e., passive) sense, Owen clarifies:

> The Spirit cannot be grieved, or affected with sorrow; which
> infers alteration, disappointment, weakness, all incompatible
> with his infinite perfections; yet men may actively do that
> which is fit and able to grieve any one that stands affected
> towards them as does the Holy Ghost. If he be not grieved, it
> is no thanks to us, but to his own unchangeable nature. . . .
> [T]he Holy Ghost is affected towards us as one that is loving,
> careful, tender, concerned in our good and well-doing; and
> therefore upon our miscarriages is said to be grieved: as a
> good friend of a kind and loving nature is apt to be on the
> miscarriage of him whom he does affect. And this is that we
> are principally to regard in this caution, as the ground and
> foundation of it, the love, kindness, and tenderness of the
> Holy Ghost unto us. Grieve him not.[57]

---

[54] Owen, *Works*, 2:265.

[55] Owen, *Works*, 2:265.

[56] Thomas Boston, *The Complete Works of The Late Rev. Thomas Boston*, ed.
Samuel M'Millan, 12 vols. (1853; reprint, Stoke-on-Trent, UK: Tentmaker
Publications, 2005), 1:541.

[57] Owen, *Works*, 2:265.

Although grief is not properly in God, it signifies his loving, careful, and tender concern in our good and well-doing, as when a good friend, on account of his love for us, is grieved by our miscarriages. Therefore, when grief is considered *in the context of the covenant of grace*, it signifies something different from anger, fury, and wrath. Righteous anger flows from violated justice, whereas grief assumes frustrated love. Moreover, anger, wrath, and fury are satisfied by vengeance, but grief is not. Because grief is rooted in love, it can only be relieved through the correction and improvement of those who are causing the grief. Although God's love cannot be frustrated, he is *like* a parent who is grieved by our sin, in the sense that his Spirit is concerned for the well-being of his children. Sin is contrary to his holiness and all that his love intends for us. Because his love is without hypocrisy, he will not sit idly by and allow us to continue in sin; rather, like one who is grieved over his children, he disciplines those whom he loves (Heb. 12:6).

That God is grieved, or *like* one who is grieved, is not cause for us to shrink back and forsake him in our affliction. It signifies no change in God, as if he had turned on us in wrath. That he is like one who is grieved by our sin assures us that *his discipline is without vengeance*. Isaiah is assuring the true people of God that even when their affliction is the consequence of their own sin, and his discipline may appear as though he has become their enemy, he has not changed. As Gouge notes, the sort of anger that is manifest in the discipline of his children is not the anger of vengeance, but the anger of mercy:

> According to the persons with whom God is angry, may his anger be distinguished: By reason of the flesh in his best saints on earth, they oft provoke his wrath, as *Moses* did, against whom *the anger of the Lord* is said to be *kindled*. This anger is as a father's compassion. Of this it is said *He will not keep it forever*. This anger ariseth from his mercy.[58]

Thus, Israel's present affliction was no time to forsake God, but to repent of their miscarriages and return to him who is unchanging in essence, being, and affection, notwithstanding their sins. "For I

---

[58] Gouge, "A Plaster for the Plague," 68.

am the LORD, I do not change; therefore you are not consumed, O sons of Jacob" (Mal. 3:6).

Despite their present affliction, and notwithstanding their sin, they call upon God's mercy (vv. 11-15) and confess, "Doubtless You *are* our Father, Though Abraham was ignorant of us, And Israel [i.e., Jacob] does not acknowledge us. You, O LORD, *are* our Father; Our Redeemer from Everlasting *is* Your name" (v. 16). Such a conclusion is "doubtless" because God does not change: "Doubtless you are our Father . . . our Redeemer from Everlasting is Your name." From this, Oswalt concludes that "God's relations with his own are deeper than the deepest we humans know, that between a parent and a child. Although an Abraham might deny his children, God cannot."[59] This is the basis of their conviction, that despite how they feel, despite what their circumstances suggest, and notwithstanding their sin, God does not change, and therefore his love cannot change.

Notwithstanding the chapter's copious anthropopathic language, as stated above, divine impassibility lies at the heart of the prophet's concern. The Lord is assuring his people that in the midst of their affliction, even their sin, his saving love is without hypocrisy and entails a discipline that is without vengeance.

Conclusion

In the modified doctrine of divine impassibility view, God is said to remain essentially immutable. As such, he has also ordained all events and decisions of history. Yet in condescending in order to relate to men, God took to himself additional properties — covenantal properties — in a fashion similar to the assumption of a human nature by the Son of God in the incarnation. It is in these so-called covenantal properties that God is said to experience genuine change: he learns, he evaluates, he is emotively moved, he grieves, and he changes his mind. While these changes are ordained eternally by God, nonetheless they are genuine responses to the contingent events and decisions of his creation. In this way, the texts of Scripture which depict change in God are taken more literally

---

[59] Oswalt, *Isaiah*, 613.

than in the classical view, in that they are not interpreted as anthropomorphisms or anthropopathisms, but rather as teaching real mutability according to God's covenantal properties.

However, there are inherent problems with this view. We have seen that the characteristics of God's covenantal properties are often contradictory to God's essential nature. For example, God is omniscient, yet in Genesis 22, God in his covenantal properties learns. God ordains the creation of man, yet in Genesis 6, God in his covenantal properties actually regrets creating man. In Deuteronomy 5:29, God in his covenantal properties wishes for something that God in his essential being has ordained will not happen. And in Jonah 3:10, God in his covenantal properties originally intends a course of action (i.e., the imminent destruction of Nineveh) which God, according to his good pleasure, had ordained would not occur at that time. God's covenantal properties, therefore, have two areas of disunion with God's essential being. First, the covenantal properties are finite and mutable. They are *distinctly different* from God's essential being. Second, there are situations in Scripture where God, in his covenantal properties, desires, wills, or intends differently from God in his essence. That is, the covenantal properties *contradict* the eternal immutable essence and attributes of God.

The classical and confessional view best explains all the Scriptures. By properly accounting for anthropomorphic and anthropopathic language in the Bible, it allows the clearer passages to interpret the figurative ones. It understands that the eternal God directly governs, guides, and relates to men through his providence. It provides the context for understanding how an unchanging God relates to his creatures, using language accommodated to those creatures. In this view, God is neither compounded, nor disunified, nor self-contradictory. Rather, he is simple, in perfect unity with himself. God is, indeed, "without . . . passions."

Chapter 6

THE NEW TESTAMENT ON
THE DOCTRINE OF DIVINE IMPASSIBILITY

(I) Texts on the Nature of God, Immutability, and Impassibility

Richard C. Barcellos and James P. Butler

The New Testament writers were men of the Book (i.e., our Old Testament). Though they wrote as those "moved by the Holy Spirit" as the authors of the Old Testament (2 Pet. 1:21; cf. 2 Tim. 3:16-17), they did so with the completed canon of the Old Testament as their revelatory-inscripturated assumption. They did not transcribe as secretaries taking dictation; rather, they wrote as those who were recording and interpreting the great redemptive-historical acts of God in Christ, by the special ministry of the Spirit (John 14:26; 15:26-27; 16:13), along with "the Law of Moses and *the* Prophets and *the* Psalms" (Luke 24:44). In other words, they were theologians, though certainly unique ones. Their text was the Old Testament, and the redemptive-historical acts of God which necessitated interpretation were the incarnation, life, ministry, sufferings, and glory (i.e., the resurrection, ascension, current session, and second coming) of the Son of God. In one sense, they were like us, standing outside the Old Testament. The difference between our understanding of the Old Testament and theirs, however, is that theirs was inspired, and therefore infallible.

It is important to remember that the New Testament authors viewed the acts of God mentioned above as fulfillments of that which Moses and the prophets had said would take place. This infuses their writings with Old Testament concepts and, due to the inspiration and infallibility of God's written Word, ensures theological continuity between their doctrine of God (and all other Old Testament doctrines) and that of the authors of the Old

Testament. What we see in the New Testament assumes and builds upon the Old Testament. The Old Testament doctrines of divine immutability and impassibility are the same ones taught by the New Testament authors. The incarnation does not alter the doctrine of God as revealed in the Old Testament.

This chapter and the next provide brief exposition of key New Testament texts used in the process of formulating the doctrine of divine impassibility, as well as discussions on the doctrines of creation and the incarnation as they relate to divine impassibility. Once this is completed, a brief conclusion will be offered.

In this chapter, texts on the *Nature of God, Immutability, and Impassibility* are discussed. Comments on apparent passibilist texts are reserved for the next chapter. These texts were selected (though there are others) because they are normally utilized in the relevant discussions in Christian theology on the subject under consideration. The order of this section is also purposeful. It is very important to understand what and who God is in order properly to interpret passages that give the appearance of change in God. The texts considered here are not fleshed out in all of their detail, but only insofar as they pertain to the doctrine under examination.

Texts on the Nature of God

John 1:18

> No one has seen God at any time. The only begotten Son, who is in the bosom of the Father, He has declared *Him*. (John 1:18)

This text clearly asserts the invisibility of God. The words "at any time" serve to emphasize this. The essence of God, that which makes him what he is, cannot be seen, and has not been "seen . . . at any time." If invisibility can be properly predicated of God, it is of his essence and is, therefore, eternally what he is. The "only begotten Son," the Word who became flesh (John 1:14), "has declared [or explained] *Him*" but this does not change the fact that divine being cannot be "seen . . . at any time."

It is of interest to note that this verse marks the end of John's prologue (John 1:1-18), which was written after our Lord ascended into heaven. This means that John's theology proper concerning God's invisibility was not altered by the incarnation of the Son of God (John 1:14). The incarnation is not the Son of God becoming, in the sense of changing into something he was not, and ceasing to be what he was as God. Human nature is just that: human, created, and not divine. The incarnation is the invisible Word, never ceasing to be the divine Son, taking on or assuming into his person a different order of being, a created order of being, a visible order of being, a not-God order of being. The invisibility of God was not compromised by the incarnation of the Son of God. Invisibility refers to the eternal divine nature; incarnation refers to the temporal human nature.

The clause at the end of the verse, "He has declared *Him*," is John's commentary on the ministry of the incarnate Son in relation to the God whom "[n]o one has seen . . . at any time." It is most likely that John had in his mind various events depicted for us in the book of Exodus as he wrote the final verses of his prologue (comp. John 1:14 with Exod. 33:7-11 and 40:34-38; and John 1:17-18 with Exod. 33:18-23 and 34:5-7).[1] If this is so, John understands some of the language Moses used as metaphorical and, in this case, anthropomorphic. It is rhetorical accommodation, depicting divine revelation in human terms or human ways of knowing.[2] For example, God does not have a literal face (Exod. 33:20, "You cannot see My face . . ."). God does not have a body; he is invisible (cf. Col. 1:15 and 1 Tim. 6:16 and the discussion below).[3] John's point is this: though Moses was greatly privileged, he did not see God and though we cannot see God, we do have something better than Moses had. We have the explanation of the God "[n]o one has seen…at any time" in and by the incarnate Son.

John 4:24

> God is spirit, and those who worship Him must worship in spirit and truth. (John 4:24, NASB)

---

[1] See the comments by Andreas J. Köstenberger in *CNTUOT*, 22-23.

[2] See the discussion in Muller, *Dictionary*, 19.

[3] It can be said that God the Son, as Mediator, has a body, but only according to his human nature.

Here we have a verse that predicates "spirit" of God. This cannot mean that only "spirit" may be predicated of God, for the Scripture says "God is love" as well (cf. 1 John 4:8 and the discussion below). Neither can it simply mean that God is invisible, immaterial, or incorporeal, for this is the case for some created things (e.g., angels). "God" here refers to the divine nature. Predicating "spirit" of the divine nature entails far more than predicating "spirit" of created beings, because all created beings derive their being from outside of themselves, and, as such, are dependent and temporal. D. A. Carson says:

> By 'God is spirit' . . . , Jesus is not suggesting that God is one spirit amongst many, nor simply that he is incorporeal in the Stoic sense, nor that 'spirit' completely defines his metaphysical properties.[4]

God is uncreated, independent, self-existent, eternal, and simple spirit (e.g., Exod. 3:14; Psalm 90:2), who gives life to others, according to his will and good pleasure. He is a one-of-a-kind "spirit." He is unique. There is none like him, and he must be worshiped as such. He does not and cannot become less "spirit" or more "spirit," for this is what he is, and what he is, he is eternally.

Acts 17:29

> Therefore, since we are the offspring of God, we ought not to think that the Divine Nature is like gold or silver or stone, something shaped by art and man's devising. (Acts 17:29)

In Acts 17:22-31, Luke records Paul's famous address to Stoic and Epicurean philosophers in Athens. The apostle Paul waited for his companions in Athens, and while there, his spirit was provoked within him "when he saw that the city was given over to idols" (Acts 17:16). The contrast between the Athenian philosophers and the apostle Paul was theological at its core; the Athenians

---

[4] D. A. Carson, *The Gospel According to John* (Grand Rapids: William B. Eerdmans Publishing Company, 1991), 225.

worshiped idols, and the apostle worshiped the true and living God. When Paul saw their altar "TO THE UNKNOWN GOD" (Acts 17:23), he used the occasion to address the Athenian idolaters with the truth about the one, true, and living God. Specifically, he presents the truth concerning the Lord Jesus Christ (Acts 17:18-19) in the broader context of God's works of creation and providence. As Greg Bahnsen notes:

> The Apostle understood his audience at Athens; they would have needed to learn of God as the Creator and of His divine retribution against sin (even as the Jews knew these things from the Old Testament) before the message of grace could have meaning.[5]

Paul sets forth the supremacy of God the Creator in Acts 17:24-26a.

> God, who made the world and everything in it, since He is Lord of heaven and earth, does not dwell in temples made with hands. 25 Nor is He worshiped with men's hands, as though He needed anything, since He gives to all life, breath, and all things. 26 And He has made from one blood every nation of men to dwell on all the face of the earth, (Acts 17:24-26a)

Far from putting down his Bible in order to reason with these philosophers, his language clearly evokes the Old Testament through and through. Verses 24-26a echo the words of Isaiah:

> Thus says God the LORD, Who created the heavens and stretched them out, Who spread forth the earth and that which comes from it, Who gives breath to the people on it, And spirit to those who walk on it. (Isa. 42:5)[6]

---

[5] Greg L. Bahnsen, *Always Ready: Directions for Defending the Faith*, ed. Robert R. Booth (Texarkana, AR: Covenant Media Press, 1996), 238.

[6] Interestingly, Isaiah 42 is the prophet's polemic against idolatry in which he, too, proclaims the supremacy of God.

Paul indicates that God is not dependent upon his creatures (Acts 17:25), that he created all things in general and the human race in particular (Acts 17:25-26), and that he is not contained in men's temples (contrary to the heathen idols) or represented by their art (Acts 17:24, 29). The Creator/creature distinction is conspicuously maintained by the apostle Paul, and for good reason. As C. J. H. Wright says:

> [T]he primal problem with idolatry is that it blurs the distinction between the Creator God and the creation. This both damages creation (including ourselves) and diminishes the glory of the Creator.[7]

Paul then declares God's absolute sovereignty in providence in Acts 17:26b-28.

> [He] has determined their preappointed times and the boundaries of their dwellings, [27] so that they should seek the Lord, in the hope that they might grope for Him and find Him, though He is not far from each one of us; [28] for in Him we live and move and have our being, as also some of your own poets have said, "For we are also His offspring." (Acts 17:26b-28)

Every step of the way, Paul makes a sharp contrast between the impotent idols of man and the omnipotent God of heaven and earth. He draws the sermon to a conclusion in Acts 17:29-31.

> Therefore, since we are the offspring of God, we ought not to think that the Divine Nature is like gold or silver or stone, something shaped by art and man's devising. [30] Truly, these times of ignorance God overlooked, but now commands all men everywhere to repent, [31] because He has appointed a day on which He will judge the world in righteousness by the Man whom He has ordained. He has given assurance of this to all by raising Him from the dead. (Acts 17:29-31)

---

[7] C. J. H. Wright, *The Mission of God* (Downers Grove, IL: InterVarsity Press, 2006), 187-88, as cited in G. K. Beale, *We Become What We Worship: A Biblical Theology of Idolatry* (Downers Grove, IL: IVP Academic, 2008), 17.

Verse 29, in particular, is important relative to our consideration of the nature of God: "Therefore, since we are the offspring of God, we ought not to think that the Divine Nature is like gold or silver or stone, something shaped by art and man's devising."

The first and obvious implication is that idolatry is sinful and condemned by God. The Athenians should repent and believe on the Lord Jesus Christ (Acts 17:30). Second, "the Divine Nature" is not like that which is created; it is of a different order of being from the creature. God is separate. God is transcendent. God is not like the creature and therefore, God is not subject to the same sort of things that affect man. Finally, the apostle draws a sharp distinction between the God of Christian theism and the deities of Greco-Roman culture. This is important to observe because some have argued that early Christianity was indebted more to the tenets of Hellenistic philosophy than to the Bible. It is clear that on Mars Hill Paul distinguishes the God of the Bible from the god(s) of the philosophers. Some have posited that the early church fathers misinterpreted Paul and sided with the Hellenists, though it has been *proven* that this, in fact, is not the case.[8]

Romans 1:20

For since the creation of the world His invisible attributes, His eternal power and divine nature, have been clearly seen, being understood through what has been made, so that they are without excuse (Rom. 1:20, NASB)

The particle "for," at the beginning of the verse, connects verses 19 and 20. Verse 20 tells us *that* and *how* God made evident to all men what is known about him. It is an explanation of the last clause of verse 19, "for God made it evident to them." That which is known about God has "been clearly seen, being understood through what has been made." Paul explains what he means by "clearly seen" by adding the clause "being understood through what has been

---

[8] For an excellent study on this subject, see Paul L. Gavrilyuk, *The Suffering of the Impassible God: The Dialectics of Patristic Thought* (Oxford: Oxford University Press, 2006), especially chapter 1, "The Case Against the Theory of Theology's Fall into Hellenistic Philosophy."

made." In other words, that which "has been made" conveys theological information to everyone. As John Murray says, ". . . what is sensuously imperceptible is nevertheless clearly apprehended in mental conception."[9] What is the theological message conveyed "through what has been made"? Paul tells us, "His invisible attributes, His eternal power and divine nature."

First, notice that "invisible attributes" are predicated of God. What does Paul mean by "attributes"?[10] These are sometimes called God's properties or perfections. *Attribute* is a term we use to describe or predicate something about God's essence or what he is. Muller defines divine attributes as follows: ". . . the conceptions or designations of the divine essence employed by the finite intellect in its declaration concerning what God is. . . ."[11] We need to be careful here, though. An attribute is not a part of God, like a piece of a pie is a part of a whole pie. God does not have parts. He is not composed of divine things. There is no part of God that is *this* divine thing and another part of God that is *that* divine thing. All of God is all that God is, ever has been, and ever shall be. Moreover, in predicating attributes of God, we are not exhausting the meaning of who and what God is. Again, attributes seek to describe an aspect of God revealed to us, not the totality of who God is. Only God knows himself exhaustively (2LCF 2.1). We can only know God in so far as he has revealed himself, and no creature knows, or even can know, God as God knows himself. God is infinite. We are finite. Since divine attributes seek to tell us something about the essence of God, they are identical with the existence of God, both eternal and unchanging. Attributes are revelations of God to us, not alterations or a refashioning of God for us.

Notice that these are called "*invisible* attributes." They cannot be seen, in themselves, but they may be, as Paul says, "clearly seen, [that is] being understood through what has been made. . . ." So Paul is saying that certain invisible attributes of God are clearly seen, understood by men and women by the effect produced (that is, by creation, or by that which has been made by God, which is everything other than God). Again, we need to be careful here. Paul

---

[9] John Murray, *Epistle to the Romans* (1959, 1965; reprint, Grand Rapids: Wm. B. Eerdmans Publishing Co., one-volume edition, 1984), 38.

[10] See the discussion in Muller, *Dictionary*, 48-50.

[11] Muller, *Dictionary*, 48.

is not saying that *everything* there is to know about God is known by that which has been made. He is not saying that if man studies creation he may know God perfectly, exhaustively, as God knows himself. As a matter of fact, since God is eternal, we cannot and will never know all there is to know about him. The finite (i.e., man) cannot comprehend the infinite (i.e., God). So Paul *is not* claiming that all that God is has been revealed through that which has been made; he *is* asserting that everyone knows something about the invisible attributes of God.

Second, notice that "eternal power" is predicated of God. God's eternal power is "clearly seen, being understood through what has been made." Power refers to divine omnipotence, exhibited to us through what God does and limited by his own nature. The adjective "eternal" refers to that which has always existed, that which is not bounded or hedged in by time or any other created entity, "without beginning or end and apart from all succession and change."[12] The things that have been made had a beginning; they are not eternal. He who brought all things into existence was not himself brought into existence. God is other than that which comes into existence. He does not become; he is (e.g., Exod. 3:14; John 1:18; 4:24; 1 John 4:8). All things which come into existence are other than him. Everything outside of the essence of God is not eternal God. All things not eternal are temporal, created. All things which come into existence are external to him who called them into existence because he is eternal and the things which have come into existence are temporal. We are not eternal. We are hedged in by time, a created reality. Our strength is limited. We grow tired. We become exhausted. Eternal power knows no exhausting. God displays power without depleting power. Paul's point is that a temporal creation (and its continued existence via divine providence) testifies to the invisible, eternal power of God. At some point, going back from your own existence there is a cause unlike that which is caused.

Third, notice that God's nature is divine. The word "nature" refers to that which constitutes the primary qualities of an object or person. It is often used as a functional equivalent of "essence."[13] In

---

[12] Muller, *Dictionary*, 28.
[13] Muller, *Dictionary*, 199.

this case, Paul is saying that the God of whom he refers is divine, true deity, the one and only true God. He alone possesses that which makes up divinity, and his divinity is "clearly seen, being understood through what has been made." That which is above the creation becomes known by creatures due to the fact and implications of creation. In other words, man knows God inescapably by that which he has made; and he knows that God is not like that which has been made. That which has been made implies the maker that is and none other; and the maker of all things is the God of the Bible, whose nature is divine, unlike ours.

It is important to note that God does not take upon himself the things predicated of him in Romans 1:20 in order to become Creator. That which had always been (i.e., God) became known (i.e., revealed) to man the creature, without ceasing to be what it always was and ever shall be.

1 Timothy 1:17

> Now to the King eternal, immortal, invisible, to God who alone is wise, *be* honor and glory forever and ever. Amen. (1 Tim. 1:17)

In 1 Timothy 1:15, Paul says that the glorious gospel of the blessed God was "committed to [his] trust." He proceeds to express his gratitude to Christ for putting him into the ministry and for having saved him by his grace. Paul expresses his thankfulness (1 Tim. 1:12) for his conversion (1 Tim. 1:13-14), and then highlights the gospel (1 Tim. 1:15-16). As is often the case in Paul's writings (cf. Rom. 11:36; 16:27; Gal. 1:5; Eph. 3:20-21; Phil. 4:20), consideration of soteriology leads Paul to doxology (1 Tim. 1:17). The apostle identifies God, the object of praise, as "the King eternal, immortal, invisible, . . . who alone is wise." In the first place, Paul acknowledges the eternity of God. This is affirmed of God in many places in Scripture as one of the attributes that are unique to him and one that differentiates him from his creatures.[14]

---

[14] Muller defines divine eternity as follows: ". . . the existence and continuance (*duratio*) of God without beginning or end and apart from all succession and change." Cf. Muller, *Dictionary*, 28.

Second, the apostle refers to God as "immortal." This too indicates something of his everlasting being and that he is incorruptible, immune from decay[15] (imperishable).[16] Being incorruptible and immune from decay certainly implies immutability: God "can neither be changed for the better (because he is the best) nor for the worse (because he would cease to be the most perfect)."[17]

Third, Paul identifies God as "invisible." The Scripture speaks of the invisibility of God relative to the fact that he is spirit (John 4:24). In Exodus 33:18-23, Moses asks to see God's glory. The God who revealed himself as "Yahweh" to Moses previously in Exodus 3:14 declares in Exodus 33:20, "You cannot see My face; for no man shall see Me, and live." That God is spirit (John 4:24) underscores, of course, the spirituality of God. Muller notes the connection between spirituality and invisibility, saying, "The spirituality of God implies his invisibility or 'insensibility, and, indeed, the reverse is also true: God's invisibility implies his spirituality."[18]

Finally, Paul praises God because he is "the only God" (NASB), a statement that underscores his independence and unity, specifically his unity of singularity. Bavinck explains:

> By the first [unity of singularity] we mean that there is but one divine being, that in virtue of the nature of that being God cannot be more than one being, and consequently, that all other beings exist only from him, through him, and to him. Hence, this attribute teaches God's absolute oneness and uniqueness, his exclusive numerical oneness, in distinction from his simplicity, which denotes his inner or qualitative oneness.[19]

For Paul, a rehearsal of soteriology leads inevitably to doxology. He rejoices in the true and living God who has sent his Son, the

---

15 J. N. D. Kelly, *A Commentary on the Pastoral Epistles* (1963; reprint, Grand Rapids: Baker Book House, 1981), 56.

16 *BDAG*, 155-56.

17 Turretin, *Institutes of Elenctic Theology*, 3.11.4 (1:205).

18 Muller, *PRRD*, 3:302.

19 Bavinck, *RD*, 2:170.

Lord Jesus Christ, to save even the chief of sinners. George W. Knight, III observes:

> When Paul considers what the King of the Ages grants to the sinner, he thinks of how wonderful it is that God who is transcendent (immortal, invisible), the only God should come into the world to save sinners in Christ and in this marvelous condescension display His eternal glory.[20]

The passage describes the nature of God. The immortality of God is specifically relevant to a discussion of impassibility as it highlights the separateness of God from his creation and underscores his incorruptibility and imperishability, both of which indicate that he is in fact immutable and, thus, impassible.

1 Timothy 6:15-16

> which He will manifest in His own time, *He who is* the blessed and only Potentate, the King of kings and Lord of lords, [16] who alone has immortality, dwelling in unapproachable light, whom no man has seen or can see, to whom *be* honor and everlasting power. Amen. (1 Tim. 6:15-16)

In 1 Timothy 6, the apostle Paul brings the first letter to Timothy to a close by reminding him of the indictment facing false teachers (1 Tim. 6:3-5), warning him against the dangers of covetousness (1 Tim. 6:6-10), and exhorting him concerning his conduct as a minister of the gospel (1 Tim 6:11-14). In concluding this hortatory section, the apostle solemnly charges Timothy that his present conduct (v. 14a) ought to be shaped by his expectation of the future coming of the Lord Jesus Christ (v. 14b). Paul's reference to "He" in verse 15 should be understood as a reference to the Father in his particular relation to the second coming of the Lord Jesus Christ (cf.

---

[20] George W. Knight, III., *The Pastoral Epistles: A Commentary on the Greek Text*, The New International Greek Text Commentary (Grand Rapids: William B. Eerdmans Publishing Company, 1992), 107.

Matt. 24:36; Acts 1:6-7; 3:20; 1 Thess. 4:14). This reference to God the Father then causes Paul to move from an exhortation to Timothy to doxology unto God. As Knight says:

> As Paul presents the epiphany of Christ and indicated that this event is to be brought about by God, he is apparently drawn to speak of God's greatness and majesty that that revelatory event will reveal.[21]

Paul then declares two descriptions of God's power: God is the "blessed and only Potentate" and he is "the King of kings and Lord of lords." The reference to "blessed and only" in the first description is expounded well in 2LCF 2.2, which states that "God, having all life, glory, goodness, blessedness, in and of Himself, is alone in and unto Himself all-sufficient, not standing in need of any creature which He has made." There is a fundamental distinction between the Creator and the creature: the Creator alone is independent; he is the unrivalled and unparalleled Potentate; he is ruler, governor, and sovereign, and he is the only one who can have "blessedness" (i.e., the fullness of divine felicity, which includes the absence of dependence upon or need for things outside himself[22]) predicated of him properly. It is also important to note that since he possesses all felicity, he does not decrease in blessedness due to grief or sorrow or other factors that affect creatures. His blessedness is complete or perfect, such that his felicity neither increases nor diminishes.

In the second description of God's power, his supremacy, dominion, and absolute lordship are highlighted and furnished as reasons for ascribing praise to him. The 2LCF 2.2 describes this accordingly: "and He hath most sovereign dominion over all creatures, to do by them, for them, and upon them, whatsoever Himself pleaseth." God is not moved by the creature; God moves the creature. God does not react to the creature; God has sovereign dominion over all creatures. The apostle Paul and the divines who composed our Confession do not speak of a god who is reactionary or subject to the whims of man, but of God who is independent and sovereign over his creation.

---

[21] Knight, *The Pastoral Epistles*, 269.
[22] Cf. Muller, *PRRD*, 3:371-73.

Paul's list of attributes that are praiseworthy in God move from a consideration of his power to his being. In the first place, Paul describes God as the One "who alone has immortality," which indicates that God is from everlasting to everlasting (Psalm 90:2), that he is incorruptible, and that he is immune from decay (or imperishable). According to Paul, God "alone" possesses this attribute. If it be objected that angels and men are also immortal, we must understand that God's being is different from that of angels and men, and therefore his immortality is not their immortality. God's immortality must be understood in relation to divine aseity: he is immortal in and of himself, whereas angels and men are immortal only insofar as God makes them such. Immortality is properly predicated of God in view of his aseity; this is not the case with angels and men. Gill explains:

> Angels are immortal, and so are the souls of men, and so will be the bodies of men after the resurrection; but then neither of these have immortality of themselves, they have it from God; who only has it, of himself, originally, essentially, and inderivatively.[23]

Second, Paul praises God as the One who is "dwelling in unapproachable light." The concepts of holiness, righteousness, and glory are involved in this description. The theological term that embodies these concepts is transcendence. Philip H. Towner has a helpful summary concerning the Old Testament background of this reference:

> [T]he light of the continually burning oil lamp symbolizes God's presence among His people (LXX Ex 27:20; 35:14; 39:16; Lev 24:2). The Sinai theophany, in which Moses was granted just a fleeting glimpse of God's 'glory,' anticipates later graphic uses of 'light' imagery to describe in tangible terms the ineffable appearance of God (Ex 33:18-23). The Psalms develop further the association of God and light, depicting Him as 'robed with light as a garment' (LXX Ps 103:2; cf. 89:15: 'whose countenance is light'). NT reflections

---

[23] Gill, *Exposition*, 9:313.

on God's glory follow suit (2 Cor 4:6), as statements such as Rev 21:23 and 22:5 declare that God's 'glory' is the 'light' of the New Jerusalem. The ultimate application of the imagery is finally made in the Johannine tradition, which not only equates God and light (1 Jn 1:5) but transfers the category to God's Son (Jn 1:4, 5, 7; 8:12; etc.). The imagery of light is then extended naturally to describe the essence of the Son's kingdom (Col 1:12-13) and of Christian existence within it (Rom 13:12; 2 Cor 6:14; Eph 5:8; 1 Th 5:5). The specification that God's light is "unapproachable" emphasizes the stark contrast between deity and humanity, and possibly intentionally calls to mind the warning that people were not to approach the mountain because of the presence of God in His glory.[24]

Towner's last statement is perceptive: there is a "stark contrast between deity and humanity." God alone is the Creator and man is the creature; there is a fundamental difference between the two, and God's immortality is given as a cause for praise ascribed to him.

Third, Paul finishes his list of praiseworthy attributes with a reference to God as the One "whom no man has seen or can see" and then gives the specific content of praise, "to whom be honor and everlasting power. Amen." As stated above, the Scripture speaks of the invisibility of God relative to the fact that he is spirit. Recall Exodus 33:18-23, where Moses asks to see God's glory. The "I AM" of Exodus 3:14 declares in Exodus 33:20, "You cannot see My face. . . ." That God is spirit (John 4:24) underscores, as stated above, the spirituality of God, which, ". . . implies his invisibility or 'insensibility, and, indeed, the reverse is also true: God's invisibility implies his spirituality."[25]

Immortality, transcendence, and invisibility are normally classed among God's incommunicable attributes. The attributes predicated of God in 1 Timothy 6 directly relate to the doctrine of divine impassibility in this way: God alone possesses immortality; he alone dwells in unapproachable light; he alone is spirit and

---

[24] Philip H. Towner, *The Letters to Timothy and Titus*, The New International Commentary on the New Testament (Grand Rapids: William B. Eerdmans Publishing Company, 2006), 421-22.

[25] Muller, *PRRD*, 3:302.

therefore invisible; thus, he alone is not subject to his creation, dependent upon his creation, nor does he react to that creation. He is the "blessed and only Potentate, the King of kings and Lord of lords" who rules all things according to "the counsel of His will" (Eph. 1:11), which is consonant with his unchanging nature.

1 John 4:8

He who does not love does not know God, for God is love. (1 John 4:8)

This text asserts that "God is love." Though love is not all that God is, it is what he *is* and not what he *becomes*. Love is not that in which God grows or shrinks. As John Murray asserts, "Love is not something adventitious; it is not something that God may choose to be or choose not to be. He *is* love, and that necessarily, inherently, and eternally. As God is spirit, as he is light, so he is love."[26] Love in God is not some latent ability to be and do good. Since God is what he is, love is "necessarily, inherently, and eternally" what he is. God's love is neither inert (i.e., having no inherent power of action) or elastic (i.e., expansive, in the sense of becoming more loving in himself). If it is what he is, then it is fully actualized and infinite. "Because God's love is unchangeably perfect and so cannot diminish, he is then the eternally living God who is unreservedly dynamic in his goodness, love, and perfection."[27] Affirming impassibility does not reduce God's love to a distant, cold, inert numbness. Instead, as Thomas Weinandy says, "it is precisely because he is all loving and good that he needs not undergo emotional changes of state depending upon temporal and historical circumstances."[28] Moreover, "God is impassible because his love is perfectly in act ('God *is* love') and no further self-constituting act

---

[26] John Murray, *Redemption Accomplished and Applied* (1955; reprint, Grand Rapids: Eerdmans Publishing Company, 1987), 10.

[27] Thomas Weinandy, "Human Suffering and the Impassibility of God," *Testamentum Imperium* Volume 2, 2009: 9. This can be found on-line at http://www.preciousheart.net/ti/2009/52-111_Weinandy_Human_Suffering_Impassibility.pdf. Accessed 9 February 2015.

[28] Weinandy, "Human Suffering and the Impassibility of God," 11.

could make him more [or less] loving."[29] If God became more or less loving, this would entail change in God, a denial of divine immutability. This means God does not and cannot fall into that which he is; God does not and cannot "fall in" love. The amazing truth is that "God just is the love . . . in virtue of which he loves."[30] It is unchanging love that moves and shapes us, but it is not moved and shaped (by God or us) in order to love us. It may be and is experienced by us in differing degrees, but it does not exist in God in differing degrees.

Texts on Immutability and Impassibility

Acts 14:15

In Acts 14, Luke reports the account of the first missionary journey of Paul and Barnabas. In Acts 14:4-8, he recounts their visit to Lystra. While there, Paul saw a crippled man who had faith to be healed (Acts 14:9), so Paul said with a loud voice, "'Stand up straight on your feet!' And he leaped and walked" (Acts 14:10). Naturally, the people of Lystra were amazed at this miracle of healing, so they responded by declaring that the "gods [had] come down to us in the likeness of men" (Acts 14:11). They identified Barnabas with Zeus and Paul with Hermes (Acts 14:12). The priest of Zeus brought oxen and garlands to the gates so that the multitude in Lystra could offer a sacrifice to these gods who had come down and dwelt in their midst (Acts 14:13). This act of worship did not succeed; Paul and Barnabas tore their clothes (Acts 14:14) and cried out to the multitude:

> Men, why are you doing these things? We also are men with the same nature as you, and preach to you that you should turn from these useless things to the living God, who made heaven, the earth, the sea, and all things that are in them. (Acts 14:15)

The words "same nature" are from the Greek word ὁμοιοπαθεῖς,

---

[29] Weinandy, "Human Suffering and the Impassibility of God," 12.
[30] Dolezal, "Still Impassible," 133.

which is literally, "pert. to experiencing similarity in feelings or circumstances, *with the same nature* τινί, *as someone* Ac 14:15; Js 5:17."[31] The missionaries set forth their solidarity with the men of Lystra; they, like the ones trying to sacrifice to them, were "frail mortal men, subject to frailty, imperfection, afflictions, troubles, diseases, and death itself; and so very improper subjects of worship."[32] Paul and Barnabas declare this truth in order to reject worship being given to man, with the obvious implication that worship is due to God alone. They further identify the God they serve as "the living God" (Acts 14:15), which is a common Old Testament designation for God, "especially when contrasting him with dead idols (Deut. 5:26; Josh. 3:10; 1 Sam. 17:26; 2 Kings 19:4, 16; Ps. 84:2; Hos. 1:10)."[33]

This particular verse is given as a proof text in the WCF 2.1, when it states that God is "without . . . passions" and therefore ought to be considered in light of the doctrine of divine impassibility. In the first place, God does not possess the same nature as man. He is of a different order of being. His being is not man's being, and in this sense may be said to be above being (*supra ens*). James Dolezal states:

> Consider, then, that God is not to be counted as existing in an ontological series with any creature. As the absolute cause of all creaturely being, God himself cannot be numbered as one of those things appearing within being in general.[34]

Bavinck writes:

> God is the real, the true being, the fullness of being, the sum total of all reality and perfection, the totality of being, from which all other being owes its existence. He is an immeasurable and unbounded ocean of being; the absolute being who alone has being in himself.[35]

---

[31] *BDAG*, 706.
[32] Gill, *Exposition*, 8:277.
[33] I. Howard Marshall, in *CNTUOT*, 588.
[34] Dolezal, *God without Parts*, 113.
[35] Bavinck, *RD*, 2:123.

Second, God is the Creator and man is the creature. Paul and Barnabas appeal to this fact in their declaration to the people of Lystra. This distinction is crucial as it reminds us of God's transcendent perfection and of the fact that he is unlike us.

Third, God is not subject to passions like man is. Our working definition of impassibility is that God does "not . . . experience inner emotional changes, whether enacted freely from within or effected by his relationship to and interaction with human beings and the created order."[36] He is not changed from without (*ad extra*) or from within (*ad intra*); he remains unchanged and unchanging. It is important to understand that the doctrine of impassibility does not take away from God. Impassibility does not mean that God is inert, static, or unrelated to his creation. Impassibility is a term that highlights the truth revealed clearly in Numbers 23:19, Malachi 3:6, and James 1:17,[37] namely, that the Lord our God does not change. Paul L. Gavrilyuk rightly explains that

> the notion of divine impassibility commonly appears in the context of other apophatic markers of the divine transcendence, such as immortality, immutability, invisibility, incorporeality, incomprehensibility, uncreatedness, and the like. This implies that *divine impassibility is primarily a metaphysical term, marking God's unlikeness to everything in the created order, not a psychological term denoting* (as modern passibilists allege) *God's emotional apathy.*[38]

Impassibility does not take from God, but reminds us of what is ever true of our immutable God.

Theologians differ on the explanation of how an unchanging God does in fact relate to a changing creation. Robert L. Dabney says with reference to God, "therefore He must feel," but explains

---

[36] Weinandy, "Impassibility of God," in *New Catholic Encyclopedia*, 2nd ed., 7:357.

[37] See the treatments of Num. 23:19 and Mal. 3:6 above and James 1:17 below.

[38] Paul L. Gavrilyuk, "God's Impassible Suffering in the Flesh: The Promise of Paradoxical Christology," in *Divine Impassibility and the Mystery of Human Suffering*, ed. James F. Keating and Thomas Joseph White (Grand Rapids; Cambridge: William B. Eerdmans Publishing Company, 2009), 139, emphasis original. It is crucial to note the distinction: impassibility is not a psychological description of God's emotions, but an apophatic marker that describes God's impassible being.

this in such a way as to continue to insist on the immutability of God by stating, "But these active principles must not be conceived of as emotions, in the sense of ebbing and flowing accesses of feeling."[39] Muller discusses the use of the words "passions," "affections," and "virtues" as applied to God and also uses the word "relatedness" to facilitate the discussion regarding God's interaction with creation.[40] Weinandy uses the word "passions" and "passionate," but carefully distinguishes what he means when applying such terms to God.[41] While good men may differ on what specific terminology to use, one thing must be clear: the God of the Bible is immutable, and thus impassible. That he is not static is clear from Scripture and the 2LCF, which describes God as "a most pure spirit . . . most holy, most wise, most free, most absolute . . . most loving, gracious, merciful, long-suffering, abundant in goodness and truth . . ." (2LCF 2.1). The doctrine of divine impassibility ensures that our unchanging God relates absolutely to his creation as the unchanging God.

On a practical level, the doctrine of divine impassibility and the 2LCF's use of "most" highlight the beauty of the doctrine. With reference to the comfort afforded to the believer by this truth, it is wonderful to remember that God cannot grow in his love for his elect because he is already "most loving" toward them in Christ! When preaching the gospel to sinners, the minister of the Word should encourage the sinner that our unchanging God, who calls men to himself, will not reject them when they come. Gavrilyuk explains:

> It is precisely because God is impassible, i.e., free of uncontrollable vengeance, that repentant sinners may approach him without despair. Far from being a barrier to divine care and loving-kindness, divine impassibility is their very foundation. Unlike that of humans who are unreliable and swayed by passions, God's love is enduring and devoid of all those weaknesses with which human love is tainted.[42]

---

[39] Robert L. Dabney, *Systematic Theology* (1871; reprint, Edinburgh; Carlisle, PA: The Banner of Truth Trust, 1996), 153.

[40] Muller, *PRRD*, 3:551-59.

[41] Cf. Weinandy, *Does God Suffer?*, 38-39.

[42] Gavrilyuk, *Suffering*, 62.

It is interesting that Luke records for us that the men of Lystra did not understand Paul's point concerning theology proper. After setting forth the transcendence and impassibility of God, the men of Lystra continued trying to sacrifice to Paul and Barnabas (Acts 14:18). May the church of Christ differ from the men of Lystra and receive with gladness the truth that God is transcendent and impassible, for these things are the truth of Scripture and the truth articulated in our Confession of Faith.

James 1:17

> Every good gift and every perfect gift is from above, and comes down from the Father of lights, with whom there is no variation or shadow of turning. (James 1:17)

This text comes in the context of the relation of the trials of believers to God (James 1:12-18). Verse 18 is James' example of a good and perfect gift God gives to us, referring to the new birth. In verse 17, James says good and perfect gifts come "down from the Father of lights." God as "the Father of lights" refers to God the Creator (and Sustainer) of lights, i.e., sun, moon, and stars.[43] Then James further amplifies "the Father of lights" with these important qualifying words, "with whom there is no variation or shadow of turning." Though that which God created may (and does) change, he who created does not change. In other words, God is essentially and, therefore, eternally immutable.

Here God is said to be not like that which he has created. Unlike that which has come into being, he who made all things is of a different order of being. Turretin says, "The succession and flow of the parts of duration (which exist successively) necessarily involve a certain species of motion (which cannot be applied to God)."[44] Here James contrasts God with an aspect of his creation. As Thomas Manton said long ago, "God, and all that is in God, is unchangeable."[45] James argues from the immutability of the divine

---

[43] Notice the allusion to antecedent revelation here. Remember, the NT authors assume the OT and its theology.

[44] Turretin, *Institutes of Elenctic Theology*, 3.10.3 (1:202).

[45] Thomas Manton, *An Exposition of the Epistle of James* (Grand Rapids:

nature (v. 17) to the immutability specifically of the divine goodness and love toward those who have been "brought . . . forth by the word of truth" (v. 18). Again, Manton says, ". . . God doth not change; there is no wrinkle upon the brow of eternity; the arm of mercy is not dried up, nor do his bowels of love waste and spend themselves."[46] God does not pass from one state of existence to another; he is what he is (Exod. 3:14; John 1:18; 4:24; 8:58; 1 John 4:8). He may communicate or reveal to us more of who he is, but that does not change who he is, though it certainly changes us. Because he is immutable, he is impassible, neither experiencing change from within or from without, unlike that which he has made.

Hebrews 6:17-18

> Thus God, determining to show more abundantly to the heirs of promise the immutability of His counsel, confirmed *it* by an oath, [18] that by two immutable things, in which it *is* impossible for God to lie, we might have strong consolation, who have fled for refuge to lay hold of the hope set before *us*. (Heb. 6:17-18)

The writer of Hebrews is seeking to promote perseverance in his hearers (Heb. 6:11). He is convinced they are those who will inherit the promises of God (Heb. 6:9). He reminds them that not only are God's promises revealed to us (cf. Heb. 6:14, citing Gen. 22:17, "Surely blessing I will bless you, and multiplying I will multiply you."), but his purpose is unchangeable and, with reference to Genesis 22:17, interposed with an oath. This is a two-fold encouragement for believers. Not only is God's purpose immutable, he has also assured us with his word that the blessing announced to Abraham will come to pass. Since "it *is* impossible for God to lie," believers may "have strong consolation." This "strong consolation" finds its ultimate ground or basis in the immutability of God. Since his purpose or counsel is eternal, it is unchangeable or immutable.

Associated Publishers and Authors, Inc., [n.d.]), 113.

[46] Manton, *James*, 114. We might add that neither do his bowels of love increase and multiply themselves.

This is a declaration of the immutability of God's purpose. As Owen says:

> But the design of God here was, not to make his counsel unchangeable, but to declare it so to be; for all the purposes of God, all the eternal acts of his will, considered in themselves, are immutable. . . . And their immutability is a necessary consequent of the immutability of the nature of God, "with whom is no variableness, neither shadow of turning," James i. 17.[47]

God's purpose is unchangeable, not merely because it is "confirmed . . . by an oath" but ultimately because the divine nature is unchangeable. However, the writer assures us that "God, determining to show more abundantly to the heirs of promise the immutability of His counsel, confirmed *it* by an oath." Though confirmation by an oath was not necessary on one level, God shows his condescending goodness, love, and care toward his children by adding the oath in order that "we might have strong consolation." Owen continues:

> . . . when God, who is truth itself, might justly have required faith of us on his single promise, yet, "ex abundanti," from a superabounding love and care, he would confirm it by his oath.[48]

Because God is immutable, his purpose is immutable, and because of his "superabounding love and care," he added an oath for our sake. These "two immutable things" are revealed to us for our "strong consolation, who have fled for refuge to lay hold of the hope set before *us*." Divine immutability ensures divine impassibility as has been proven, both of which are great inducements to our consolation.

---

[47] Owen, *Works*, 21:256.
[48] Owen, *Works*, 21:259.

Chapter 7

THE NEW TESTAMENT ON
THE DOCTRINE OF DIVINE IMPASSIBILITY
(II) Creation, the Incarnation and Sufferings of Christ, and Conclusion
Richard C. Barcellos

The New Testament texts that might give the *appearance* of passibility in God are dealt with in the theological discussions below concerning the doctrines of creation and, especially, the incarnation and sufferings of the Son of God.

The Doctrine of Creation in the New Testament and How it Relates to Divine Impassibility

Assuming the fruit of the exegetical discussions above (and the entirety of canonical revelation), this section argues that creation is a distinct order of contingent and temporal being and is to be distinguished from God, who is self-existent, necessary, eternal, and non-contingent being (i.e., *ens a se*, being from itself).[1]

As the Old Testament teaches a distinction between God and creatures (e.g., Gen. 1:1ff; Num. 23:19; Psalm 19; etc.), so does the New Testament. God and nature are distinct. Nature had a beginning and exists subsequently contingent upon divine providence (Col. 1:16-17). All things that came into existence did so without the use of previously existing materials, as Hebrews 11:3 says, "By faith we understand that the worlds were framed by the word of God, so that the things which are seen were not made of things which are visible." That the triune God created all things is

---

[1] Cf. Muller, *Dictionary*, 103.

202 | Confessing the Impassible God

both assumed and stated in the New Testament (e.g., John 1:3; Col. 1:16; Heb. 1:1-2). In fact, John 1:3 even says "nothing came into being that has come into being" (NASB) apart from God. The things that have come into being are obviously not God. God is eternal being; all things created are temporal and of a different order. This distinction between God and not-God is crucial. According to the Bible, God is uncreated, has life in and of himself eternally (John 5:26), does not lie, change, or deny himself, and cannot be added to or subtracted from. Two texts in Acts even distinguish between divine nature and human nature and other created things (cf. Acts 14:15 and 17:29 [2]). The Creator is of a different order of being from the creation. This distinction is crucial to maintain. As Weinandy says:

> As Creator, God is intimately related to and cares for his good creation, particularly his chosen people, and yet, as Creator, he is not one of the things created, and is thus completely other than all else that exists.[3]

Affirming impassibility means that God cannot change from without or from within because of what he is and what he is not. He is God, the Creator; he is not creature. He can and does reveal who he is to creatures, but he does not refashion himself or add attributes or perfections to do so. He does not become something he was not in order to reveal who he is; he simply reveals who he is.[4] He is immutable and, therefore, impassible. The relationship he has with his creation does not necessitate the creation of relational properties, though it does necessitate the use of analogical, relational language.

This is a good point in our discussion to interact briefly with the proposal of K. Scott Oliphint. He contends "that God freely determined to take on attributes, characteristics, and properties that he did not have, and would not have, without creation."[5] God does

---

[2] See the discussions of these texts in chapter 6, "The New Testament on the Doctrine of Divine Impassibility: (I) Texts on the Nature of God, Immutability, and Impassibility."

[3] Weinandy, "Human Suffering and the Impassibility of God," 1.

[4] We will discuss the incarnation below.

[5] Oliphint, *God with Us*, 110. Earlier in Oliphint's discussion, he tells us that

this in order to relate to man both prior to the incarnation and even for eternity. Oliphint asserts:

> He remains who he is, but decides to be something else as well; he decides to be the God of the covenant. It was, to be sure, a monumental decision. It changed the *mode* of God's existence for eternity; he began to exist according to relationships *ad extra*, which had not been the case before.[6]

Notice that, according to Oliphint, God changed his mode of existence "for eternity." This occurred due to creation. Because of creation (and God's desire to relate to it covenantally), God *takes on* that which he had not prior to creation. This means that these attributes, characteristics, and properties are themselves created, something Oliphint affirms.[7]

One of these attributes, characteristics, and properties God takes upon himself, according to Oliphint, "is the development of knowledge that is conducive to his interaction with his creation generally, and specifically with his people."[8] This assertion comes within a larger discussion of Genesis 22:12, where we read, "And He said, 'Do not lay your hand on the lad, or do anything to him; for now I know that you fear God, since you have not withheld your son, your only *son*, from Me.'" Later in the discussion, Oliphint says:

> So the lack of knowledge that God has, as given to us in Genesis 22:12, is a covenantal lack; it is a lack in which God's

---

"attributes," "properties," and "perfections" are used synonymously (13). It seems that he uses "characteristics" in the same vein.

[6] Oliphint, *God with Us*, 254-55, emphasis original. Note that Oliphint is claiming that "the *mode* of God's existence" changed forever. An act of God based on a decision of God changed God forever. Also, how can God remain who he is but become "something else as well" without some sort of addition in God? Oliphint's claim seems to undermine divine simplicity.

[7] Cf. Oliphint, *God with Us*, 13, n. 8, 198, 208, and 209. E.g., Oliphint says, "So, there can be little question, as one reads of the varying appearances of Yahweh throughout covenant history that, in order to appear at all, Yahweh takes on created properties and characteristics. He condescends to present himself, and in doing so he takes characteristics and attributes that belong to creation."

[8] Oliphint, *God with Us*, 194.

relationship to his people includes his real and literal interaction with us. It is a lack, which itself presupposes his essential deity and eternal decree, in which the Lord is *patient* toward us (2 Pet. 3:9). That patience surely includes his "waiting to see" how we might react in the face of trials and sufferings. And since contingency is real in God's creation, it is not until we act/react that God, as condescended to that contingency, seeks/knows what we will do (even though he always knows it, as who he is essentially).[9]

It is important to note that Oliphint is not discussing the ignorance of Christ during the days of his flesh at this point (see the discussion of Luke 2:52 below). He is talking about the pre-incarnate covenantal ignorance of God (i.e., God as covenanted or condescended), something he took upon himself and, therefore, not essential to God eternally, though according to Oliphint it "changed the *mode* of God's existence for eternity."

If we are following Oliphint correctly at this point, this means God created properties that he took on prior to the incarnation which will endure into the eternal state. If one of those properties is "the lack of knowledge . . . a covenantal lack," where God is "'waiting to see' how we might react," does it not follow that God will be lacking knowledge, be waiting to see, and be covenantally ignorant in the eternal state, since he will relate to his people via covenant in that state? Remember, according to Oliphint, deciding to be the God of the covenant "changed the *mode* of God's existence for eternity." In other words, that which God took on in time to become the covenant God is not and cannot be shed by God in the eschaton. If it could be (for sake of argument), then when and why would God shed himself of these created properties so essential for being the God of the covenant? Moreover, wouldn't this demand a different formulation for those who advocate Oliphint's view of the assumption of created properties that exist for eternity? It appears that what Oliphint himself calls "a relatively new approach to a discussion of God's character"[10] needs further thought and

---

[9] Oliphint, God with Us, 195.
[10] Oliphint, God with Us, 195.

reflection by those who advocate it.

Oliphint further claims that "God takes on covenant characteristics that are consistent with his essential character."[11] Though he attempts to balance this statement with the acknowledgement that some "covenant characteristics . . . seem to us to be inconsistent with that character"[12] (i.e., God's essential character), it is hard to fathom how a covenantal lack of knowledge can be consistent with divine omniscience, for example.

A fundamental problem with Oliphint's proposal at this point seems to be related to the Creator/creature distinction. In an effort to bring God down to us, his proposal seems to entail that God cannot be both transcendent and immanent (in the classical sense) and so must become something (prior to the incarnation of the Son) he was not (prior to the creation of all things) in order to reveal himself to or interact with us "for eternity." God condescended and God *in se* seem to be two modes of existence or orders of being—one temporal and contingent (i.e., created) and the other eternal and non-contingent (i.e., uncreated). What gets revealed to us is the condescended, covenanted mode of being, a mode of being not co-extensive with who God was prior to creation, is, and ever shall be essentially and eternally. It appears that, in an effort to protect the Creator/creature distinction, Oliphint has severely tampered with the entire doctrine of God so as to confuse categories.

Attempting to ground his proposal of voluntary condescension by God in the WCF, for example, it may be contended that he misuses that Confession. He cites WCF 7.1, which says:

> The distance between God and the creature is so great, that although reasonable creatures do owe obedience unto him as their Creator, yet they could never have any fruition of him as their blessedness and reward, but by some voluntary condescension on God's part, which he hath been pleased to express by way of covenant.

The title of chapter 7 of the WCF is "Of God's Covenant with Man." This chapter presupposes chapter 4, "Of Creation." The wording of

---

[11] Oliphint, *God with Us*, 228.
[12] Oliphint, *God with Us*, 228.

chapter 7 presupposes that creation existed prior to God's "voluntary condescension." God's "voluntary condescension" is not an act of pre-creation (i.e., the creation of the covenantal properties of God), the act of creation itself, or other subsequent acts of creating, but the *revelation* of a covenant—the covenant of works (cf. WCF 7.2). God's first covenantal act toward man was one of revelation, not the creation of properties for himself that would enable him to reveal himself or to create. Oliphint seems to confuse categories, utilizing his own Confession in a manner not intended by that Confession. According to the WCF, God did not have to condescend by taking upon himself created properties he did not have without creation in order to interact with creation. The "voluntary condescension . . . by way of covenant" in the WCF is the covenant of works, at least prior to the fall into sin.

Further, WCF 4.1 says:

> It pleased God the Father, Son, and Holy Ghost, for the manifestation of the glory of his eternal power, wisdom, and goodness, in the beginning, to create, or make of nothing, the world, and all things therein, whether visible or invisible, in the space of six days, and all very good.

Are we to believe that the framers of the WCF intended that chapter 4 include the creation of covenantal properties so that God could relate to his creation? Was there a creation of covenantal properties prior to the creation of "the world, and all things therein" in order for creation to occur? Or did the creation of covenantal properties occur subsequent to creation, since they, being created, would be part of the "all things therein" (i.e., in "the world")? If they did, who created them, the eternal or the covenanted God? It does not appear that the authors of the WCF intended to include the creation of covenantal properties in their formulation of the doctrine of creation in WCF 4.1. In fact, if one posits that God took on the covenantal property of Creator in order to create, which seems to be Oliphint's position,[13] then creation itself is not *ex nihilo* (or as the WCF asserts, "of nothing") after all; it would be creation out of the created property of Creator, a property created by God in order to create

---

[13] Oliphint, *God with Us*, 16-17.

and relate to his creation. It seems impossible to make logical, theological, and confessional sense of this proposal.

Another problem with Oliphint's proposal related to the doctrine of creation is the fact that he posits the pre-incarnate assumption of covenantal properties by God as unique to the Son. Oliphint says:

> . . . the person who took on covenantal properties, and eventually a human nature, is the same eternally as the Son of God, though from the time of creation he is different (though not essentially), and this difference obtains into eternity.[14]

> . . . the taking of covenant properties by the Logos throughout covenant history must be distinguished from that singular moment "when the fullness of time had come" and God sent forth his Son to be born (Gal. 4:4f.).[15]

If one of those covenantal properties assumed by the pre-incarnate Son is that of Creator, how can Oliphint confess WCF 4.1, where it says, "It pleased God the Father, Son, and Holy Ghost . . . to create, or make of nothing, the world, and all things therein, whether visible or invisible . . ."? Creation, according to the WCF, is an act of the triune God — Father, Son, and Holy Spirit — not only the act of the pre-incarnate Son who assumed the property of Creator as an act of covenantal condescension. God, as God, does not need to take on things outside his eternal nature to create or reveal himself as the "I AM" of Exodus 3:14 (cf. John 8:58). When the New Testament (and the Old Testament) speaks of God creating the world, he does so as he was, is, and ever shall be (i.e., Father, Son, and Holy Spirit), there being no need to refashion himself either to make or relate to that which he makes. If pre-incarnate covenantal properties are unique to the Son, and one such property is that of Creator, and creation is a divine act, then we would have the Son as God covenanted/condescended acting independent of the other

---

[14] Oliphint, *God with Us*, 205.

[15] Oliphint, *God with Us*, 206; cf. also 228, "As is the case with Christ climactically, so it is also with (the Son of) God in covenant history."

persons of the Godhead. This is not to say that Oliphint denies creation by the triune God; it is to say that his formulation necessarily leads there.

How does all of this relate to the doctrine of divine impassibility? After acknowledging that the WCF asserts that God is "without body, parts, or passions," Dr. Oliphint asks this question, "Is God truly without passions?"[16] Note that this is exactly what the WCF affirms. On the next page, he asserts that "there must be some real and fundamental sense in which God *can* have or experience passions."[17] Then he quotes Warfield approvingly, who says:

> Men tell us that God is, by very necessity of his nature, incapable of passion, incapable of being moved by inducement from without; that he dwells in holy calm and unchangeable blessedness, untouched by human sufferings or human sorrows for ever, — haunting . . .
> Let us bless our God that it is not true.[18]

Closing his initial discussion on divine impassibility, Oliphint says:

> As I will argue later, a christological hermeneutical methodology gives us at one and the same time a God who is sovereign—and also a God who suffers, and who ultimately suffers for us. So, like all of God's essential attributes, impassibility has to be understood from the perspective of the character of God *as God*, first of all, but then also from the context of the person and work of Christ himself.[19]

Later in Oliphint's discussion, he says, "So, God *does* 'authentically respond' to us, he *is* 'affected by us,' he *does* test in order to discover

---

[16] Oliphint, *God with Us*, 86.

[17] Oliphint, *God with Us*, 87, emphasis original.

[18] Benjamin Breckinridge Warfield, "Imitating the Incarnation," in *The Person and Work of Christ*, ed. Samuel G. Craig (Philadelphia: Presbyterian and Reformed, 1950), 570-71, quoted in Oliphint, *God with Us*, 87.

[19] Oliphint, *God with Us*, 88, emphasis original.

something, and he *does* change his mind."[20] All of these statements by Oliphint assume the cogency of his covenantal properties proposal but, at least on the surface, seem to cast a shadow of doubt on the formulation of the WCF on divine impassibility. It is important to remind ourselves that the WCF's statement on divine impassibility, as with the 2LCF's, occurs in chapter two, "Of God, and Of the Holy Trinity." In other words, impassibility is an essential attribute of God. According to the WCF, God is "without . . . passions" without qualification or reservation. This does not seem to be the case with Dr. Oliphint.

Now, recall the fact that Oliphint argues that the assuming of covenantal properties "changed the *mode* of God's existence for eternity." Does this apply to God being "affected by us"? Will God be affected by us in the eternal state, covenantally, even though not essentially? Does God suffer in the eternal state, since the assuming of covenantal properties "changed the *mode* of God's existence for eternity" and one of those properties is suffering? It is only fair to acknowledge that Oliphint argues that it was "Christ, the Son of God in the flesh [who] suffered [and] died . . ."[21] Just after affirming this, however, he says, "Since that is true, there must be some real and fundamental sense in which God *can* have or experience passions." Then he quotes Warfield approvingly, who appears to deny divine impassibility, saying, "Men tell us that God is, *by very necessity of his nature*, incapable of passion. . . . Let us bless our God that it is not true" (emphasis added). Warfield denies the impassibility of God "by very necessity of his nature," something Oliphint seems to affirm. It does not appear that Oliphint and Warfield are arguing for the same thing. Saying "there must be some real and fundamental sense in which God *can* have or experience passions" is, at best, a confusing way for Oliphint to affirm the sufferings of Christ, especially utilizing Warfield as he did. Christ did suffer, according to his human nature, but this is peculiar to that very nature. According to his divine nature, by "very necessity," Christ is impassible in any and all senses.

It is more orthodox to hold that God created as he existed from all eternity and when he reveals himself to us through and

---

[20] Oliphint, *God with Us*, 274, emphasis original.
[21] Oliphint, *God with Us*, 87.

subsequent to creation it is the same God revealing himself. As Bavinck says:

> [H]e is the eternal Creator, and as Creator he was the Eternal One, and as the Eternal One he created. The creation therefore brought about no change in God; it did not emanate from him and is no part of his being. He is unchangeably the same eternal God.[22]

Creation does not add a new mode of God's existence to his being. No covenantal properties are needed. God can and does remain who he is but utilizes language suitable to the creature's capacities of knowledge and experience when revealing himself to us. Dr. Oliphint's proposal seems to us to create more problems than it solves.

The Doctrine of the Incarnation and Sufferings of the Son of God and the Doctrine of Divine Impassibility

Prior to entering a formal discussion dealing with the incarnation, the *communicatio idiomatum*, and divine impassibility, it may help to discuss briefly an important text in the Gospel of Luke. Luke 2:52 says, "And Jesus kept increasing in wisdom and stature, and in favor with God and men" (NASB). Some might want to take this as inferring that God's favor is something in God that can increase and decrease. A brief response would be that the text says "Jesus kept increasing . . . in favor with God," not that God kept increasing his favor. As Christ, according to his human nature, developed, as he changed, as he "kept increasing," he conformed more and more to Heaven's never-changing standard of justice and righteousness. Christ's image-bearing capacity, according to his human nature, was a dynamic reality, not a static one. The change here is not in Christ according to his divine nature, but in the developing human nature of the incarnate Son and the revelation of the divine

---

[22] Bavinck, *RD*, 2:429. Cf. James E. Dolezal, "Eternal Creator of Time," *JIRBS* (2015): 127-58.

approbation of such development.

Luke 2:40 is related to Luke 2:52 in terms of development in the incarnate Son. It says, "The Child continued to grow and become strong, increasing in wisdom; and the grace of God was upon Him" (NASB). This "increasing in wisdom" was a constant experience of our Lord according to his human nature during the state of humiliation. He kept increasing in his ability to skillfully use the knowledge he obtained. Again, the change here is not in Christ according to his divine nature, but in the developing human nature of the incarnate Son and the revelation of the divine approbation of such development (i.e., "and the grace of God was upon Him."). The divine standard in heaven is the same throughout; the change takes place on the earth in the realm of creation. Though the incarnate Son could and did "increase . . . in favor with God," this increase changes nothing in God. God is not in the business of creating more favor to display upon those that please him on the earth. He does reveal his favor but he is not in the business of manufacturing more or becoming more favorable.

It is important at this point to mention and discuss the doctrine of the *communicatio idiomatum/communicatio proprietatum*. Muller defines it as follows: "*communication of proper qualities*; a term used in Christology to describe the way in which the properties, or *idiomata*, of each nature are communicated to or interchanged in the unity of the person."[23] To what is this referring? The Confession gives assistance at this point:

> Christ, in the work of mediation, acteth according to both natures, by each nature doing that which is proper to itself; yet by reason of the unity of the person, that which is proper to one nature is sometimes in Scripture, attributed to the person denominated by the other nature. (2LCF 8.7 [cf. WCF 8.7])

The texts cited by the Confession are John 3:13 and Acts 20:28. John 3:13 says, "And no man hath ascended up to heaven, but he that came down from heaven, *even* the Son of man which is in heaven" (KJV). Leaving some of the interpretive issues[24] and the textual issue

---

[23] Muller, *Dictionary*, 72.

[24] The title "Son of man" comes from Dan. 7:13-14 and the language of

(i.e., the final clause) aside, since the phrase "Son of man" refers to our Lord's incarnate state, how is it that he can claim that the Son of man "came down from heaven"? The answer is that sometimes the Bible attributes that which is proper to one nature to the *person* of the Son. In the case of John 3:13, the Son of man preexisted in heaven but according to his divine nature alone. The phrase at the end of John 3:13 in the KJV, "which is in heaven," assuming it is the best reading for argument's sake, refers to the divine nature, though predicated of "the Son of man."

The same way of speaking may be illustrated from Acts 20:28, which reads, "Take heed therefore unto yourselves, and to all the flock, over the which the Holy Ghost hath made you overseers, to feed the church of God, which he hath purchased with his own blood" (KJV). Assuming this translation and leaving the textual variant aside, this text illustrates the communication of idioms doctrine. Here God is said to have blood. Scripture is clear, as has been proven, on the invisibility of God and that he is a distinct order of being different from that which has been made. In other words, God, as God, does not have blood. Blood is creature; God is not. Here is another example where "that which is proper to one nature [is] . . . attributed to the person denominated by the other nature."

When considering Christ's incarnation and the union of the two natures in the person of the Son, Muller says, "the two natures are here considered as joined in the person, and the interchange of attributes is understood as taking place at the level of the person and not between the natures."[25] This is crucial to understand and is the theology which gave rise to 2LCF 8.7. This means, for example, that though the human nature of our Lord is not omniscient, it is yet true that this finite human nature is united to the divine nature in

---

ascending and descending echoes Genesis 28, alluded to in John 1:51. For discussion on the order of ascending then descending in John 3:13 see Herman Ridderbos, *The Gospel of John: A Theological Commentary* (Grand Rapids: William B. Eerdmans Publishing Company, 1997), 136.

[25] Muller, *Dictionary*, 72. Cf. Oliphint, *God with Us*, 220-22, where he applies the doctrine of the communication of idioms to the so-called pre-incarnate assumption of covenantal properties. This seems to be a novel use of this doctrine. Cf. also Oliphint, *God with Us*, 43, where he says, "This chapter [chapter 2, "I Am . . . Your God"] will begin to introduce a relatively new approach to a discussion of God's character."

the person; and it is according to the divine nature, which is essentially omniscient, that Christ, the one person, may be said to be omniscient. The human nature was "united to the [omniscient] divine [nature], in the person of the Son" (2LCF 8.3a). This means, though our Lord suffered according to his human nature (and only according to his human nature), the human nature remained united to the divine nature and was supported and sustained throughout the sufferings, for this is what God does in relation to that which has been made, which is but the truth of divine providence. The incarnate Son, according to his divine nature, upheld the incarnate Son, according to his human nature (Col. 1:17). The work of mediation is the work of both the human and divine natures of the Son. In fact, the Son's work of mediation, according to his divine nature, actually predates the incarnation itself (cf. 1 Cor. 10:4; 1 Pet. 1:10-11) and in that sense could only be the work of the divine nature.

In light of the discussion above, some relevant texts which interact briefly with the doctrine of the communication of idioms and our Lord's passion will now be considered. It will be shown that the New Testament clearly implies (even demands) the doctrine of the communication of idioms. It will also be shown that some have not been faithful to this crucial teaching, especially as it relates to the sufferings of our Lord. It will become more obvious that it is crucial to distinguish between what Christ does according to his divine nature and what he does according to his human nature, lest suffering be attributed to the divine.

First, consider John 1:14, "And the Word became flesh, and dwelt among us, and we saw His glory, glory as of the only begotten from the Father, full of grace and truth" (NASB). This is a classic text on the incarnation. It comes in an important context, so some awareness of that context is necessary. John 1:1 mentions "the Word" three times and John 1:2-3 imply it. John 1:1-3 reads:

> In the beginning was the Word, and the Word was with God, and the Word was God. 2 He was in the beginning with God. 3 All things came into being through Him, and apart from Him nothing came into being that has come into being. (NASB)

The Word is obviously a person. In fact, he is a divine person, because creative power is predicated of him (John 1:3); he is God, as John says. But it is clear also that the Word was "with God" as well as being God. In other words, the Word and God may be distinguished, yet both are of the order of divine being. These verses also echo the first verse of the Bible: "In the beginning, God [*Elohim*, plural] created [singular] the heavens and the earth" (Gen. 1:1). This is an early hint at plurality in the Godhead. The divinity of the Word is clear from John 1:1-3. When verse 14 is considered, it is the Word, who is God, who "became flesh." Due to the fact that God is eternal, unchanging, and invisible, becoming flesh cannot infer a change in the divinity of the Word. If the Word is God, then he possesses all the essential attributes of God. Any change in his deity is impossible. This is why our Confession asserts the following:

> The Son of God, the second person in the Holy Trinity, being very and eternal God, the brightness of the Father's glory, of one substance and equal with him, who made the world, who upholdeth and governeth all things he made, did, when the fullness of the time was come, take upon him man's nature . . . (2LCF 8.2a).

Though he became flesh, he never ceased being what he always was and ever shall be, "who is over all, *the* eternally blessed God. Amen" (Rom. 9:5).[26] This is the mystery and glory of the incarnation. The Word becoming flesh is not the Word ceasing to be what he always was. The incarnation wrought no change in the Word's deity. As Louis Berkhof says:

> When we are told that the Word became flesh, this does not mean that the Logos ceased to be what He was before. As to His essential being the Logos was exactly the same before and after the incarnation. . . . He acquired an additional form, without in any way changing His original nature.[27]

---

[26] Cf. Douglas J. Moo, *The Epistle to the Romans*, The New International Commentary on the New Testament (Grand Rapids: Wm. B. Eerdmans Publishing Co., 1996), 568.

[27] Louis Berkhof, *Systematic Theology* (1939; reprint, Grand Rapids: Wm. B.

When John says, "And the Word became flesh," it is understood as the person of the Son assuming the nature of man.

Another passage which speaks to the issue of the incarnation and has been the seedbed of confusion is Philippians 2:5-8.

> Have this attitude in yourselves which was also in Christ Jesus, 6 who, although He existed in the form of God, did not regard equality with God a thing to be grasped, 7 but emptied Himself, taking the form of a bond-servant, *and* being made in the likeness of men. 8 Being found in appearance as a man, He humbled Himself by becoming obedient to the point of death, even death on a cross. (NASB)

Some have taken this to mean that the Son of God emptied himself of something of the divine in order to become man or in becoming man. However, the words "emptied Himself" are immediately qualified by a participial clause which denies he became less divine or became divine in another way than he previously existed. Paul says, ". . . taking the form of a bond-servant, *and* being made in the likeness of men." Thus, emptying himself is the assumption of human nature, while existing in the form of God. The word "form" is used while describing Christ's divine and human natures in this passage (Phil. 2:6-7), which should not deter from affirming both his full deity and full humanity. Moreover, the clause "He existed in the form of God" can be translated "being in the form of God" (NKJV) which highlights the present active participial form used here, indicating a continual state of being.[28] In other words, his divine nature never ceased being just that—divine. John Owen's words are worth considering at this juncture.

> It is not said that he ceased to be in the form of God; but continuing so to be, he "took upon him the form of a servant" in our nature: he became what he was not, but he ceased not to be what he was.[29]

Eerdmans Publishing Co., 1986), 334.

[28] The Greek participle is ὑπάρχων.

[29] Owen, *Works*, 1:326.

Of special interest to this discussion is the fact that Philippians 2:5 says, "Have this attitude in yourselves which was also in Christ Jesus." "Christ Jesus" obviously refers to our incarnate Lord. Then in verse 6, Paul says, "who [i.e., Christ Jesus], being in the form of God . . ." Did the human Jesus exist in the form of God prior to his incarnation? Obviously not. Again, here is another example where "that which is proper to one nature [is] . . . attributed to the person denominated by the other nature."

Speaking of our Lord Jesus Christ, the writer of Hebrews says:

> And, "YOU, LORD, IN THE BEGINNING LAID THE FOUNDATION OF THE EARTH, AND THE HEAVENS ARE THE WORKS OF YOUR HANDS; THEY WILL PERISH, BUT YOU REMAIN; AND THEY ALL WILL BECOME OLD LIKE A GARMENT, AND LIKE A MANTLE YOU WILL ROLL THEM UP; LIKE A GARMENT THEY WILL ALSO BE CHANGED. BUT YOU ARE THE SAME, AND YOUR YEARS WILL NOT COME TO AN END" (Heb. 1:10-12, a quotation of Psalm 102:25-26, NASB).

This text is of interest because it speaks of the firstborn who was brought into the world (cf. Heb. 1:6). In Hebrews 1:10-12, the firstborn (i.e., the incarnate Son of God) is said to be the one who ". . . LAID THE FOUNDATION OF THE EARTH . . ." This obviously refers to the Son according to his divine nature, not his human nature. His human nature did not exist when the foundation of the earth was laid, nor when Psalm 102 was penned. Yet note that Hebrews 1:6 says, "And when He again brings the firstborn into the world . . ." (NASB). This refers to the incarnation, yet verses 10-12 cannot refer to acts or attributes of the Son's acquired human nature. Here is another example where "that which is proper to one nature [is] . . . attributed to the person denominated by the other nature."

Hebrews 13:8 states, "Jesus Christ *is* the same yesterday and today and forever" (NASB). In light of the discussion above, it seems obvious that this cannot refer to our Lord's human nature. It is known that "The Child continued to grow and become strong, increasing in wisdom; and the grace of God was upon Him" (Luke 2:40, NASB). In terms of our Lord's human nature, it was not "the same yesterday and today and forever." In fact, he suffered and then entered into glory (Luke 24:26, 46; Acts 26:23; 1 Pet. 1:11) and his resurrected state (i.e., glory) was an advance for his human nature (Rom. 1:1-4). The Lord's human nature was passive in the sense that it underwent change. So what does Hebrews 13:8 mean? Owen claims that "it is the person of Jesus Christ that is spoken of," and "Where the person of Christ is intended, there his divine nature is always included; for Christ is God and man in one person," and "It is from his divine person, that, in the discharge of his office, he was . . . 'the same'."[30] Once again, here is an example of "that which is proper to one nature [being] . . . attributed to the person denominated by the other nature."

One point where some disagree with divine impassibility, as classically understood, is connected to the incarnation, especially with the sufferings or passion of Christ.[31] Failing to maintain the Creator/creature distinction, among other important biblical and theological distinctions, some ascribe suffering to the divine nature of Christ and even to the Father and Holy Spirit. This is a mistake with mammoth implications. For example, in a recent book, Donald Macleod says:

> Clearly, the unity of the divine Trinity remains unbroken throughout the passion. Even while the Father is angry with the Mediator, the Son is still the beloved and still fully involved in all the external acts (the *opera ad extra*) of the Trinity. Just as it was true in his infancy he was still the eternal Logos, performing all his cosmic functions as the one in whom all things consist (Col. 1:17), so in the darkness and desolation of Golgotha he was still carrying the universe on his shoulders (Heb. 1:3). But this very fact of the trinitarian unity has profound implications for the traditional Christian doctrine of divine impassibility. If it is true at the human level that where one member of the church suffers all other members suffer with her, must the same not be true of the

---

[30] Owen, *Works*, 23:427.

[31] The passion of Christ refers to his sufferings and extends to the entire state of humiliation, during which he experienced the common infirmities of human nature, "yet without sin," as our Confession says (2LCF 8.2). More strictly, it refers to "the final trials and crucifixion" of our Lord. Cf. Muller, *Dictionary*, 219.

Trinity? The Son, we remember, is one and the same in substance (*homoousios*) with the Father. "They" are not only generically identical, but numerically one. It is the one only and eternal God who is enfleshed in Jesus, the son of Mary of Nazareth; and though the Father is not the divine person who suffers on the cross, he is one with the sufferer, and must therefore suffer with him, though in his own way.

Besides, there is the fact of the *perichoresis*.[32] Not only are God the Father and God the Son one and the same in substance and being, but they dwell in and around each other. The Father is in the Son and the Son in the Father (John 14:10; 17:21). The trinitarian persons are not three separate gods. On the contrary, where the One is, the Three are. The Three, then, are at Calvary suffering not only *from* the sin of the world, but suffering *for* it. The Son's passion cannot be external to the Father and the Holy Spirit. They are in it, as they embrace and include the Son. The pain of the cross is the pain of the triune God.[33]

The problems with this formulation are numerous. First, notice the way that Macleod argues from the creature to the Creator. He says, "If it is true at the human level that where one member of the church suffers all other members suffer with her, must the same not be true of the Trinity?" In the context of his discussion, he assumes the answer must be yes. In fact, he argues this way elsewhere. He says, "The intercourse between them [i.e., the Father and the Son at the cry of dereliction] is suspended, or at least limited to the Son's cry of lament; and it would break any father's heart. And God's, too, if we are made in his image."[34] At best, these statements reflect the fact that the Creator/creature distinction is one more of uniformity than distance.[35] Arguing from us to the divine life in this

---

[32] The coinherence of the persons of the Godhead in the divine essence and in each other. Cf. Muller, *Dictionary*, 67.

[33] Donald Macleod, *Christ Crucified: Understanding the Atonement* (Downers Grove, IL: IVP Academic, 2014), 50, italics original.

[34] Macleod, *Christ Crucified*, 52.

[35] It seems that Macleod assumes a univocal view of God and man. This would mean that whatever is predicated of man must necessarily be predicated of God. Thanks to Stefan Lindblad for sharpening the wording (and my thinking) at this and other points.

manner produces serious doctrinal difficulties. When a human father's heart is broken, it is because something from the outside came upon him and altered his state of mind. Information came to him and he was changed. That which he did not know he came to know and was affected by it. He was passive. He received something from the created realm that brought about a change in him. Also, the cry of lament was an act peculiar to the Son according to his human nature. Arguing from the solidarity of suffering on "the human level" to the solidarity of the Trinity in the sufferings of Christ is erroneous and incoherent. It lays aside the distinct mystery of the incarnation and attributes vicarious suffering (the only kind of suffering the incarnate Lord underwent) to the Trinity. It is not true that when the Son suffered the wrath of God, the Trinity suffered the wrath of God or suffered in any sense.[36] What Christ suffered, he did so according to his human nature, as punishment for human sin due to the justice of God. Deity was not guilty of deserving such punishment, though man was. Macleod's view, at worst, appears to be a form of theopassianism (i.e., God suffered) and at best a form of patripassianism (i.e., the Father suffered), both of which were amply discussed and condemned by the early church.[37]

Second, Macleod says, "The Son, we remember, is one and the same in substance (*homoousios*) with the Father. 'They' are not only generically identical, but numerically one." Then he goes on to say, "It is the one only and eternal God who is enfleshed in Jesus, the son of Mary of Nazareth . . ." What does this mean, especially in light of our discussion above? Is the triune God enfleshed in Jesus? If so, how so and why? He goes on, "and though the Father is not the divine person who suffers on the cross [which is correct], he is one with the sufferer, and must therefore suffer with him, though in his own way." The Father suffers with the Son? It seems impossible to avoid accusing Macleod of some form of patripassianism. The Father is God and the Son is God, but the Son in his sufferings suffered according to his human nature. God, as God, cannot suffer.

---

[36] See the discussion below.

[37] For detailed discussion on this see chapter four of Gavrilyuk, *Suffering*. For a very brief discussion see R. C. Sproul, "Did God Die on the Cross?" Available at http://www.ligonier.org/blog/it-accurate-say-god-died-cross/. Accessed 2 August 2014.

If he could, it would mean that the wrath of God was poured out on God, as God. God's wrath is not against God; it is against man in sin, the guilt of which was imputed to Christ (2 Cor. 5:21). Also, suffering implies the deprivation of something good or the loss of something good. Neither of these can be true of God, as God, without there being change in God, as God. There is no way for God, as God, to suffer without some change in God for the worse. But Christ can and did suffer, according to his human nature alone.

Third, Macleod seems to confuse the divine life of God, as God (*ad intra*), and the works of God *ad extra*. The earthly work of the Mediator is a work *ad extra*, the assumption of human nature by the Son, a work peculiar to the Son that does not disrupt the life of God *ad intra*. Again, Macleod says:

> The Three, then, are at Calvary suffering not only *from* the sin of the world, but suffering *for* it. The Son's passion cannot be external to the Father and the Holy Spirit. They are in it, as they embrace and include the Son. The pain of the cross is the pain of the triune God.[38]

Because God is omnipresent, we affirm the presence of the triune God at Calvary (and the work of the Father and the Spirit in relation to the incarnation and work of the Mediator [e.g., Gal. 4:4; Luke 1:35; Matt. 3:16-17]). However, we deny that "The Three, then, are at Calvary suffering not only *from* the sin of the world, but suffering *for* it." Suffering for sin is the work of Christ the Mediator, for *us* and for *our* salvation. It is not the work of the Father and the Spirit (though "willed and effected by Father, Son, and Spirit"[39]) nor is it the work of Christ according to his divine nature. Christ according to his divine nature cannot and need not suffer for sin. Deity is not guilty. Our Lord suffered and died as man, as he lived as man, for us. His sufferings were due to our sin and endured by him according to his human nature alone, though upheld by the divine nature. Remember, each "nature [does] that which is proper to itself," as our Confession asserts and, interestingly, as does

---

[38] Macleod, *Christ Crucified*, 50.

[39] These are the words of Muller which are referred to below.

Macleod's.[40] The pain of the cross is experienced by the Mediator, according to his human nature. God, as God, does not suffer the pain of the cross in any sense. If that were the case, then vicarious suffering would be an attribute of God, co-extensive with his existence and, therefore, eternal. This would mean that God is in the perpetual state of being deprived of or losing something good, an impossibility for the God of Holy Scripture, who is "infinite in being and perfection," "without . . . passions" (2LCF 2.1), and "having all . . . blessedness" (2LCF 2.2a).

Maybe Macleod would argue that it is not God *ad intra* that suffers but God *ad extra*. This appears to be the case above. If it is, it needs to be asked that if God, as God, *ad extra*, Father, Son, and Holy Spirit, in the economy of redemption, takes on the ability to suffer for sin, why the incarnation of the Son? And if the Trinity takes on the ability to suffer (i.e., possibility) *ad extra*, then this assumption is something not God *ad intra* (i.e., eternally and essentially), and that which is not God is creature (i.e., possibility is a creaturely potential). This would make the triune God both God and not God at one and the same time, though not eternally so. How can this be? Scripturally, it cannot.

Macleod utilizes the doctrine of the *perichoresis* — "the coinherence of the persons of the Trinity in the divine essence and in each other . . ."[41] — to bolster his position. He argues from this to "The three, then, are at Calvary, suffering not only *from* the sin of the world, but suffering *for* it."[42] But suffering is not the only thing Christ underwent while on the earth. He also "increased in wisdom and stature" (Luke 2:52). Can it then be said that the three, then, are with the young Jesus, increasing in wisdom and stature, even if qualified by saying, "in their own way"? Obviously not, since increasing in wisdom and stature is peculiar to creatures (and to the human nature of our incarnate Lord). The incarnate Son according to his divine nature did not and cannot increase in wisdom and

---

[40] Dr. Macleod is a retired Free Church of Scotland theologian.

[41] Muller, *Dictionary*, 67.

[42] Macleod, *Christ Crucified*, 50. In a discussion of John Frame's view of impassibility, Rob Lister says, "Where he [i.e., Frame] seems to agree with Moltmann is that on the cross the Father suffered differently, but genuinely, with the Son because of the doctrine of the mutual indwelling of the Trinitarian persons." Lister, *God is Impassible and Impassioned*, 165, n. 74.

stature, and neither can the other persons of the Trinity. The same goes for suffering; the incarnate Son according to his divine nature did not suffer and neither did the Father or the Holy Spirit. Also, if the *perichoresis* is an *ad intra* trinitarian conjunction, an ontological category, then arguing from it to the three suffering at Calvary (an economic category) does not follow because the only one who suffered the wrath of God at Calvary was the incarnate Son according to his human nature.[43] Macleod's view confuses *ad intra* and *ad extra* categories.[44]

It appears that Macleod is attempting also to uphold the doctrine of *opera Trinitatis ad extra sunt indivisa* (i.e., the external or *ad extra* works of the Trinity are undivided). This is a crucial doctrine to maintain. Muller explains that

> since the Godhead is one in essence, one in knowledge, and one in will, it would be impossible in any work *ad extra* . . . for one of the divine persons to will and to do one thing and another of the divine persons to will and do another.[45]

But does this destroy the doctrine of the incarnation as a personal work of the Son? Muller continues:

> Sometimes the Protestant scholastics will speak of the *opera ad extra* as *opera certo modo personalia,* personal works after a certain manner, because the undivided works *ad extra* do manifest one or another of the persons as their *terminus operationis,* or limit of operation. The incarnation and work of the mediator, e.g., terminate on the Son, even though they are willed and effected by Father, Son, and Spirit.[46]

The incarnation and work of the Mediator terminate on the Son, though "willed and effected" by each person of the Godhead.

Macleod fails to uphold the mystery of the hypostatic union and to distinguish between what Christ does according to his human

---

[43] Cf. Muller, *PRRD*, 4:185-86 for a brief discussion of this doctrine.

[44] From what Lister said in footnote 42 above, it appears that John Frame does the same thing.

[45] Muller, *Dictionary*, 213.

[46] Muller, *Dictionary*, 213.

nature and what he does according to his divine nature. Against this, we must confess (in good Chalcedonian fashion) that "Christ, in the work of mediation, acteth according to both natures, by each nature doing that which is proper to itself" (2LCF 8.7a).[47] Suffering is not proper to the divine nature of Christ, nor the Father, nor the Holy Spirit *ad extra* or *ad intra*. As Lister says:

> . . . we should not think that the Son (or Father or Spirit) suffers ahistorically, divinely, or ceaselessly. The Son, in other words, did not ontologically cease to be the Son for the duration of the crucifixion. Simply put, the person of the Son tasted death the only way he could — *humanly* . . .[48]

Conclusion

Brief exposition of key New Testament texts utilized in the process of formulating the doctrine of divine impassibility and contained in the discussions of the doctrine was provided. Also discussed were the doctrines of creation and the incarnation as they relate to divine impassibility. The specific texts that address the issues at stake were examined. Other texts of Scripture (Old and New Testament) were given their appropriate place in helping to understand God's intention for the texts addressed. Larger New Testament theological considerations in light of exegesis and the issue of divine impassability were discussed. There was interaction with contemporary discussions on the issue in light of exegesis and theological formulation. We think our method is sound; we trust our conclusions are as well.

---

[47] The Creed of Chalcedon says, ". . . one and the same Christ, Son, Lord, Only begotten, to be acknowledged in two natures, inconfusedly, unchangeably, indivisibly, inseparably; the distinction of natures being by no means taken away by the union, but rather the property of each nature being preserved . . ." The 2LCF follows the WCF verbatim at this point.

[48] Lister, *God is Impassible and Impassioned*, 278, emphasis original.

Chapter 8

HISTORICAL THEOLOGY SURVEY OF THE DOCTRINE OF DIVINE IMPASSIBILITY

Pre-Reformation through Seventeenth-Century England

Michael T. Renihan, James M. Renihan, and Samuel Renihan

What History Is and Is Not

Christianity is an antiquarian faith. Her source materials are thousands of years old. History is one of the most important disciplines and tools that ministers have as they teach and preach through biblical and theological themes. It is not just the chronological record of a bygone age, although it certainly includes such a record as Christianity grew in stature and in number. This record is not, however, comprehensively accessible; only a small part of the church-at-large is known through her source documents. Some men and movements are recognized solely through the writings of others, and still others are identified by name only, obscure in other ways.

Analysis is an important part of the historical disciplines. It is one thing to identify a collection of similar statements, while it is something else to evaluate them. This analysis takes into consideration the context in which a given people lived, the language they spoke, the nuances of that language, their cultural and intellectual history before the coming of Christianity, how much of their social history beyond church history is known, and a host of additional concerns that may be used in one place or another. As such, historical study must take into account these contextual factors in order to read historical texts accurately. As we read theological texts of a bygone era, in fact, we have a moral obligation to "see things their way," as Quentin Skinner put it. His words are worth quoting at length.

> [W]e need to make it one of our principal tasks to situate the texts we study within such intellectual contexts as enable us to make sense of what their authors were doing in writing them. My aspiration is not of course to enter into the thought-processes of long-dead thinkers; it is simply to use the ordinary techniques of historical enquiry to grasp their concepts, to follow their distinctions, to appreciate their beliefs, and, so far as possible, to see things their way.[1]

History is not normative. It does not give universals that are true in every particular place. Yet in the unique contexts of churches—even regionally, nationally, or denominationally considered—it casts light upon our pursuit of understanding. History is a guide. It helps us to understand the religious terrain.

Divine impassibility is one of the widely accepted tenets of the orthodox Christian faith, stated by the overwhelming majority of theologians and churchmen who are considered as safe and true guides. The doctrine of divine impassibility was derived from the careful study of the Scriptures and the scriptural ideas expressed by earlier writers. The authors who are most eloquent on the topic are the Church Fathers who were active in writing against a changing and changeable God. The issue was determined with a high degree of finality by those who were present and a part of the interactions at the Council of Chalcedon (451). The councils were called to discuss and determine what the church-at-large confessed. Nicaea (325), Constantinople (381), Ephesus (431), and Chalcedon were the most important in forming the doctrine of the holy Trinity and Christology.

Churchmen were summoned from around the known world to discuss papers and presentations made by some of the men, especially the more academically-oriented bishops. They took these times of reflection seriously, for they understood that they were fighting for truth against error. The creeds of these councils became

---

[1] Quentin Skinner, "Introduction: Seeing Things Their Way," in *Visions of Politics: Regarding Method*, vol. 1 (Cambridge: Cambridge University Press, 2002), 3.

the acknowledged catholic or universal teaching of the church. At the time of the Reformation, Renaissance scholars looked back to antiquity to find guides for their time that could be used to bring about change, that is, lasting reforms. Christian humanists like Luther and Calvin found much to use for the cause of the recovered gospel in the writings of the Fathers.

John Calvin dedicated the final edition of *The Institutes of the Christian Religion* to King Francis of France. The Reformers were being accused of innovation with their "new" doctrines. In the dedication, Calvin masterfully argues the contrary. In his own eyes, he was no innovator. Rather, he was a compiler of ancient texts which taught the same doctrines as the Reformers. In his own words, Calvin says:

> Moreover, they unjustly set the ancient fathers against us (I mean the ancient writers of a better age of the church) as if in them they had supporters of their own impiety. If the contest were to be determined by patristic authority, the tide of victory — to put it very modestly — would turn to our side. Now, these fathers have written many wise and excellent things. Still, what commonly happens to men has befallen them too, in some instances. For these so-called pious children of theirs, with all their sharpness of wit and judgment and spirit, worship only the faults and errors of the fathers. The good things that these fathers have written they either do not notice, or misrepresent or pervert. You might say that their only care is to gather dung from among the gold. Then with a frightful to-do, they overwhelm us with despisers and adversaries of the fathers! But we do not despise them: in fact, if it were to our present purpose, I could with no trouble at all prove that the greatest part of what we are saying today meets their approval. Yet, we are so versed in their writings as to remember always that all things are ours [I Cor. 3:21-22], to serve us, not to lord it over us [Luke 22:24-25], and that we all belong to the one Christ [I Cor. 3:23], whom we must obey in all things without exception [cf. Col. 3:20]. . . .[2]

---

[2] Calvin, "Prefatory Address to King Francis," in *Institutes*, vol. 1, 18-19.

We may see in this citation how Calvin, as an exemplar of the Reformers, viewed the writings of the Church Fathers. It is for this reason that we survey these writings to aid us in our understanding of the nature of the Christian doctrine of divine impassibility. This helps us to grasp the sense of the phrase "without . . . passions" in its historical context, and to note the more recent modifications to and/or deviations from this well-attested doctrine.

Divine Impassibility in the Fathers of the Church

The doctrine of divine impassibility was well-established and accepted by consensus from the earliest days of the Christian church. Scholars acknowledge that it is found in theological writings from the beginning of the post-apostolic era. Thomas Weinandy cites Jaroslav Pelikan, who states, ". . . the early Christian picture of God was controlled by the self-evident axiom, accepted by all, of the absoluteness and impassibility of the divine nature."[3] The most pressing question centers on the source of this consensus held by the early Fathers and their successors in classical theism. Did the early churchmen develop their doctrine based on Scripture, or was it the result of influences from Greek philosophy? And if from philosophy, did it import into Christian doctrine a false impersonalization or de-personalization of God?

Modern opponents of divine impassibility as understood in classical theism rely heavily on the charge of Greek philosophical influence to discredit the doctrine. The tenor of the argument seems to be something like this: the early Fathers, schooled in the tenets of Greek philosophy, unwittingly carried those tenets with them when they developed their theology, introducing foreign elements into the formulation of Christian doctrine. Adolf von Harnack was perhaps the most influential proponent of this thesis.[4] In an

---

[3] Weinandy, *Does God Suffer?*, 85. The citation is from Jaroslav Pelikan, *The Christian Tradition: A History of the Development of Doctrine — 1. The Emergence of the Catholic Tradition (100-600)* (Chicago: University Press of Chicago, 1971), 229. Weinandy calls this "Pelikan's correct assessment."

[4] Michael Allen helpfully makes this point. See his brief remarks titled "The Promise and Prospects of Retrieval: Recent Developments in the Divine Attributes," http://zondervanacademic.com/blog/common-places-the-promise-and-prospects-of-retrieval-recent-developments-in-the-divine-attributes/#citation1

important lecture series delivered at the University of Berlin in the winter term of 1899-1900, translated into English and published soon after, Harnack asserts that Greek philosophy entered the intellectual development of Christian doctrine "at about the year" A.D. 130. Once there, it "went straight to the centre of the new religion."[5] Thus began the process of the Hellenization of the church, including the development of a doctrine of divine impassibility drawn from the well of philosophy rather than Scripture. Following Harnack's lead, twentieth-century writers repeated and developed the notion so that, by the end of the century, it had become a commonplace, repeated over and over.

More recently, this idea has been challenged by a growing cadre of scholars. Michael Allen states it bluntly:

> In the last two to three decades, however, the Hellenization thesis has taken a beating and then some. First in patristic studies that sought to locate Christian intellectual work amidst the variegated world of late antiquity, and then in careful study of later theological developments that drew upon or even critiqued that early Christian period, historical theologians have reshaped the discipline such that Harnack's approach no longer carries weight. . . . 'The notion that the development of early Christian thought represented a Hellenization of Christianity has outlived its usefulness.'[6]

And yet, "the Theory of Theology's Fall into Hellenistic Philosophy"[7] continues to be promulgated by the less well-informed. The work that has been done to counter this theory is impressive. For our purposes, we will notice Paul Gavrilyuk's important *The Suffering of the Impassible God: The Dialectics of Patristic*

Accessed 20 October, 2014. Paul Gavrilyuk expresses the same argument. See Gavrilyuk, *Suffering*, 3.

[5] Adolph von Harnack, *What is Christianity?* (New York: The Knickerbocker Press, 1902), 215-16.

[6] Allen, "Promise and Prospect." In the latter part of the citation, Allen is quoting Robert Wilkin, *The Spirit of Early Christian Thought: Seeking the Face of God* (New Haven: Yale University Press, 2003), xvi.

[7] The phrase is Paul Gavrilyuk's. He helpfully employs it written in exactly this way throughout his book. See Gavrilyuk, *Suffering*, 1.

Thought. Gavrilyuk seeks to examine the factors involved in the development of classical theism arising out of the major controversies of the post-apostolic church.

We can only summarize the contents of the book. After an introduction and a survey of the basic case against the Theory of Theology's Fall into Hellenistic Philosophy (including some fascinating insights into the relationship between the Hebrew text and the Septuagint as used by the Fathers), the author proceeds to speak of the *apophatic* nature of Christian theology.[8] Gavrilyuk argues that the doctrine of divine impassibility aided the early church in distancing the God of Scripture from the deities of Greek culture. Unlike the super-human gods of the pagans who were full of passions, the Lord who was without passions was presented by Christians as the only worthy God to worship. This did not deny characteristics such as God's love, but placed them into a particular category. Apophatic theology protected the unique deity of the Christian God as over against the idols of the Greek world.

One of the early heresies afflicting the church is known as Docetism.[9] This idea denied the true humanity of our Lord Jesus Christ, asserting that he only seemed to be a man, but in reality was not. Its adherents believed that the High God could not stoop to take on human flesh and suffer in it. The Fathers rejected this notion, holding in tension the realities of the being of the impassible God and the true incarnation of Jesus Christ. Gavrilyuk says:

> The resistance to . . . Docetic tendencies led to a clearer demarcation of the function of divine impassibility. For the Docetists divine impassibility ruled out direct divine involvement in the material universe, but did not exclude the passions of the divine aeons. For the Fathers, on the

---

[8] See Gavrilyuk, *Suffering*, 47-63. Apophatic theology does theology by means of negation. For example, when we say that God is 'infinite,' we are saying that he is *not* finite; when we say that he is *incomprehensible*, we mean that we cannot comprehend him. This is an exceedingly helpful way to do theology which is grounded in Scripture itself (e.g., Num. 23:19; 1 Tim. 1:17). See the treatment of Num. 23:19 in chapter 4, "The Old Testament on the Doctrine of Divine Impassibility: (II) Texts on Immutability and Impassibility" and the discussion on the *via negationis* in chapter 1, "Analogy and the Doctrine of Divine Impassibility."

[9] Gavrilyuk, *Suffering*, 64-90.

contrary, divine impassibility was an apophatic qualifier of all divine emotions, and did not rule out God's direct contact with creation. The 'scandal' of Gnosticism lay in the contradiction between divine impassibility and far too human passions. In orthodox Christianity the scandal and paradoxical tension lay elsewhere: in the affirmation of the incarnation of the God who infinitely surpassed everything in creation.[10]

Jerome is an example of what Gavrilyuk claims of the Fathers:

> We say that a passible humanity was taken by the Son of God in such a way that the divinity remained impassible. For the Son of God suffered truly . . . all the things which Scripture attests according to that which was able to suffer, namely according to the substance that was taken. For although the person of the Son had taken a humanity that was able to suffer, yet by such indwelling it suffered nothing according to its own substance, as neither did the whole Trinity, whom we must necessarily profess to be impassible.[11]

The doctrine of divine impassibility served to protect the doctrine of the incarnation from the intrusions of Docetism.

The next controversy considered is known by the term patripassianism.[12] In this error, it was asserted that the Father suffered on the cross, dying for humanity. Though it seems to have taken subtly different forms, in essence this view argued that in some sense, the Father entered into the sufferings of the Son. In its modalistic form, it is a trinitarian heresy, denying a distinction between the persons. The orthodox response was to assert the distinction of the persons—it was the Son who died for sinners. But in an extreme form, a subordinationist strain entered into Christian thinking, paving the way for Arianism. In this error, the

---

[10] Gavrilyuk, *Suffering*, 89.

[11] Jerome, as cited by Peter Lombard, *The Sentences*, Book III, Distinction XV, Chapter 1, 12. Peter Lombard, *The Sentences: Book 3 On the Incarnation of the Word*, Medieval Sources in Translation 45, trans. Giulio Silano (Toronto: Pontifical Institute of Medieval Studies, 2008), 60.

[12] Gavrilyuk, *Suffering*, 91-100.

consubstantial deity of the Son with the Father was undermined. As part of their attack, the Arians asserted that the generation of the Son necessarily involved *pathos*.[13] The orthodox replied by stating that the generation of the Son is ultimately

> unknowable and ineffable. . . . [T]he divine impassibility commonly served as an apophatic qualifier on all analogies to the divine life drawn from human experience. This apophatic qualifier did not undermine the union of love between the divine hypostases, just as it did not exclude other God-befitting emotionally coloured characteristics. But it did purify theological discourse about the divine generation from all unseemly associations and provided an important apophatic correction to the use of analogy.[14]

In this case, the doctrine of divine impassibility was an important part of the defense of the full deity of the Son of God. In the author's words:

> It was the Arians who explained away the paradox and scandal of the incarnation by claiming that a unique creature suffered and by extricating the High God from all involvement in human history. The orthodox sustained the vital tension of the creed, just as they upheld the scandalous message of the cross.[15]

We may notice an example of this point from Athanasius. He wrote:

> . . . the divine generation must not be compared to the nature of men, nor the Son considered to be part of God, nor the generation to imply any passion whatever; God is not as man; for men beget passibly, having a transitive nature, which waits for periods by reason of its weakness. But with God this cannot be; for He is not composed of parts, but

---

[13] Gavrilyuk indicates that due to its usage, this term is very difficult to render precisely into English. One suggested rendering is 'sufferance.' See Gavrilyuk, *Suffering*, 115.

[14] Gavrilyuk, *Suffering*, 120-21.

[15] Gavrilyuk, *Suffering*, 134.

being impassible and simple, He is impassibly and indivisibly Father of the Son. This again is strongly evidenced and proved by divine Scripture. For the Word of God is His Son, and the Son is the Father's Word and Wisdom; and Word and Wisdom is neither creature nor part of Him whose Word He is, nor an offspring passibly begotten.[16]

Athanasius affirms divine impassibility with respect to the generation of the Son by the Father. If ever there were a doctrine that implied some passibility in God, it would be the Father's begetting of the Son. Yet Athanasius will not adjust the doctrines of immutability and impassibility in order to make room for any anthropomorphic notions of the Father's generation of the Son.

Commenting on Matthew 26:39, John 12:27, and other texts in the Gospels, in a moving passage written against Arianism, Athanasius states:

But they [i.e., the Arians] ought, when they hear 'I and the Father are one,' to see in Him the oneness of the Godhead and the propriety of the Father's Essence; and again when they hear, 'He wept' and the like, to say that these are proper to the body; especially since on each side they have an intelligible ground, viz. that this is written as of God and that with reference to His manhood. For in the incorporeal, the properties of body had not been, unless He had taken a body corruptible and mortal; for mortal was Holy Mary, from whom was His body. Wherefore of necessity when He was in a body suffering, and weeping, and toiling, these things which are proper to the flesh, are ascribed to Him together with the body. If then He wept and was troubled, it was not the Word, considered as the Word, who wept and was troubled, but it was proper to the flesh; and if too He besought that the cup might pass away, it was not the Godhead that was in terror, but this affection too was proper

---

[16] Athanasius, *Against the Arians*, in *NPNF*, Second Series, vol. 4, ed. Philip Schaff and Henry Wace (1891; reprint, Peabody, MA: Hendriksen Publishers, Fifth printing, 2012), I.viii.28.

to the manhood. And that the words 'Why hast Thou forsaken Me?' are His, according to the foregoing explanations (though He suffered nothing, for the Word was impassible), is notwithstanding declared by the Evangelists; since the Lord became man, and these things are done and said as from a man, that He might Himself lighten these very sufferings of the flesh, and free it from them. Whence neither can the Lord be forsaken by the Father, who is ever in the Father, both before He spoke, and when He uttered this cry. Nor is it lawful to say that the Lord was in terror, at whom the keepers of hell's gates shuddered and set open hell, and the graves did gape, and many bodies of the saints arose and appeared to their own people. Therefore be every heretic dumb, nor dare to ascribe terror to the Lord whom death, as a serpent, flees, at whom demons tremble, and the sea is in alarm; for whom the heavens are rent and all the powers are shaken. For behold when He says, 'Why hast Thou forsaken Me?' the Father shewed that He was ever and even then in Him; for the earth knowing its Lord who spoke, straightway trembled, and the vail was rent, and the sun was hidden, and the rocks were torn asunder, and the graves, as I have said, did gape, and the dead in them arose; and, what is wonderful, they who were then present and had before denied Him, then seeing these signs, confessed that 'truly He was the Son of God.'[17]

In this case, the distinction between the divine and human natures in the person of Christ is carefully maintained. Suffering must never be attributed to the divine nature, though it properly belongs to his human nature. This careful distinction protects against the inroads of Arianism which sought to deny full deity to Jesus Christ. Properly understood, the doctrine of divine impassibility was a powerful weapon against this significant heresy.

The final controversy considered by Gavrilyuk is Nestorianism.[18] Orthodox Christology asserts that the two natures, the divine and the human, are united in the one person of Christ.

---

[17] Athanasius, *Against The Arians*, III.xxix.56.
[18] Gavrilyuk, *Suffering*, 135-71..

Nestorianism, however, argues that he is in fact two *persons*, one divine and one human, due to the fact that he has two natures. It objects to the notion that there is a union of the natures in one person, thus destroying the mystery of the incarnation. In the orthodox formulation, suffering is endured by the person, Jesus Christ, in whom the two natures are united. In Gavrilyuk's terms:

> The Word who is above suffering in his own nature suffered by appropriating human nature and obtained victory over suffering. The celebration of this paradox in the creeds and hymns is the crowning achievement of a distinctly Christian account of divine involvement, an account for which no school of philosophy may take credit.[19]

The doctrine of divine impassibility was, then, an essential ingredient in the formulation of our received doctrine of God and of the person of Christ. In the words of Allen, "The doctrine of God is not just important; it is a hub to which all other doctrines relate."[20] This is directly evident in the important place that the doctrine of divine impassibility played in hammering out the received doctrines of orthodox Christianity. This scriptural and theological foundation of divine impassibility and its doctrinal relationships remained unchanged throughout the Medieval period and beyond into the Reformation era.

From our survey we are able to note some important things. In the first place, the Theory of Theology's Fall into Hellenistic Philosophy has been disproved by careful scholarship. To attribute the doctrine of divine impassibility to the influence of philosophy is to misread the history of theology and of the church. In the second place, since this theory has been soundly enervated by recent scholarship, we may also say that there is in no sense an impersonalization or de-personalization of God in classical theism. It is a serious mistake in the reading of the documents to assert that the God of Scripture and of the church lives in a detached, numb condition, far removed from the world he has created. He is an immanent God who, while impassible, is at the same time near to

---

[19] Gavrilyuk, *Suffering*, 175.
[20] Allen, "Promise and Prospect."

his creation, making himself known through general and special revelation to his creatures. Classical theism never undermines the fact that God is truly loving, merciful, compassionate, etc.; it simply seeks to define these terms in accordance with the principles of God's transcendent glory, his aseity, and the Creator/creature distinction. Classical theism refuses to speak of God univocally, always recognizing these profound distinctions.

Divine Impassibility among the Reformed

It must be asserted that the Reformed doctrine of God is the catholic doctrine. We do not mean *Roman Catholic* (though that tradition holds the orthodox view), but simply *universal*. The Reformers were under no compulsion to alter the received doctrine of God. Richard Muller helpfully comments:

> It is worth recognizing . . . that the Reformation altered comparatively few of the major loci of theology: the doctrines of justification, the sacraments, and the church received the greatest emphasis, while the doctrines of God, the trinity, creation, providence, predestination, and the last things were taken over by the magisterial Reformation virtually without alteration.[21]

A survey of impassibility in the theology of the Reformers demonstrates a great degree of self-conscious continuity with the theology of the church preceding the time of the Reformation (1523-1565). In the post-Reformation periods of Early Orthodoxy (1565-1640) and High Orthodoxy (1640-1725), the same is true. But whereas the Reformation stands on the shoulders of the Fathers (especially Augustine) and some of the medieval theologians, the post-Reformation periods add to this the writings of the Reformers themselves. All in all, there is a direct line of self-conscious continuity on the doctrine of God, with a united voice raised contra deviations from the boundaries of orthodoxy.[22]

---

[21] Richard A. Muller, *The Unaccomodated Calvin* (Oxford: Oxford University Press, 2001), 39.

[22] The boundaries of this orthodoxy are delineated negatively in treatises

The Reformed doctrine of impassibility is constructed upon a very specific and interwoven understanding of the Creator/creature distinction, which is itself drawn from Scripture. Based on this doctrinal distinction, the fundamental assertion of the Reformed with regard to what we call impassibility is that God is all that he is; he is pure essence. Thus, Scripture's attribution of affections and passions to God communicates the actions of God's will or his essential perfections, but *nothing* creaturely such as mutability, succession, composition, or finitude. This is argued *exegetically* and *systematically*. Four authors will suffice to represent the Reformation and post-Reformation arguments on these two fronts: Heinrich Bullinger (1504-1575), John Calvin (1509-1564), Wolfgang Musculus (1497-1563), and Peter Martyr Vermigli (1499-1562).

Exegetically, several texts are used to argue the pure essence of God. Yet perhaps the single most pertinent example is the divine name, "I AM WHO I AM," in Exodus 3:14. Throughout their writings, the Reformers and their followers argued that this is God's self-revelation of the fact that he is all that he is.[23] Nothing can be added to him, subtracted from him, or changed about him. God is pure essence, pure actuality, and pure simplicity.[24] An extremely common assertion that derives from this name is, "Whatsoever is in God is God."[25]

---

where certain heretics (e.g., Anthropomorphites) are repeatedly mentioned by various authors as a testimony to the church's opposition to heresy throughout the ages. In a complementary fashion, these boundaries are delineated positively, on the one hand, through a united testimony of what the Scriptures teach in theological treatises, exegetical commentaries, and sermons, and on the other hand, through successive confessions of faith built one upon the other.

[23] Heinrich Bullinger, *Fiftie Godlie and Learned Sermons, Divided Into Five Decades, Containing The chiefe and principall points of Christian Religion, written in three seuerall Tomes or Sections*, trans. H. I., student in divinity (London: Imprinted by Ralph Newberie, 1587), 608. Bullinger explains the divine name as meaning, ". . . I am God that will be, and he hath sent me, who is himself Being, or Essence, and GOD everlasting." Later, he considers other divine names and adds, "Now these words also are derived of being, and do teach us that God is always like him self, an essence which is of it self eternally, and which giveth to be unto all things that are." Bullinger, *Fiftie Godlie and Learned Sermons*, 609.

[24] A complementary exegetical resting place for the doctrine of God's unity, simplicity, and pure actuality is Jesus' statement to the Samaritan woman in John 4:24 that God is spirit.

[25] It is often stated in Latin, "Quicquid est in Deo, Deus est."

From this exegetical foundation, systematic theology builds an impregnable fortress on the pure essence of God. Wolfgang Musculus said:

> First therefore of the essence of God it is most truly said, that it is one alone setting before us one God: now let us look what else may be conveniently said thereof. Surely there is many other things, but for this present we think good to rehearse but a few, as, that it is not made of any other thing but simple and pure. With simplicity it agreeth that he is a spirit: with the pureness, that he is called a light in which there is no darkness. It is also without body, occupying no place, incomprehensible, immutable, indivisible, impassible, incorruptible, immortal, unspeakable perfect & everlasting: which all appertaineth to the consideration of the quality of God's essence or being.[26]

Musculus is drawing inferences that interconnect with each other. He begins with God's essence, and then speaks about "what else may be conveniently said thereof," in other words, the things which go with it or belong to it. He then draws forth an impressive list of those things which pertain to God's pure essence, while saying that there are "many other things" that could be added to it. His list is concluded by restating that everything named "appertaineth" to or is necessarily contained in the nature of God's essence or being.

Within Musculus' list is impassibility. Because God is all that he is, in and of himself, he cannot undergo experiences or be acted upon by external objects. Within creation (i.e., time and space), God is at all times accomplishing his singular and immutable decree, unobstructed and unimpeded. He cannot suffer. He cannot change. He cannot be added to. He cannot diminish. For that reason he cannot have passions or affections properly predicated of him, which by definition include the ideas of sensory experience, change, temporality, and passivity.

This leads to an important part of understanding impassibility,

---

[26] Wolfgang Musculus, *Common Places of Christian Religion*, trans. John Man (London: Imprinted by Henry Bynnerman, 1578), 11. The spelling has been updated for ease of reading.

defining passions and affections. There are overlaps and nuances in the ways writers use these words. Most commonly, affections and passions are treated synonymously. When distinguished, passions are treated as a subset of the affections.

To understand passions and affections, however, they must be placed in their natural context, the human nature. Writers in the sixteenth and seventeenth centuries considered man to be comprised of *parts* and *faculties*. Man's *parts* are body and soul. Man's *faculties*, seated in the *parts* of human nature, are the mind, will, and affections.

Edward Leigh defines the affections as "certain powers of the soul by which it worketh and moveth it self with the body to good and from evil."[27] William Bridge offers a similar definition, "Affections in the general are these movings of the rational soul, whereby the heart is sensibly carried out upon good or evil; so as to embrace the one, or refuse the other."[28] Both definitions combine the parts and faculties of man. The affections are the actions of the whole man (parts and faculties) relative to an external object which it perceives as good or bad.

William Fenner provides an example of defining passions synonymously with affections:

> The affections are the passions of the Soule. When the heart is affected with a thing, it lets in that thing, and it suffers a change by that thing; when a man is affected with anger at a wrong or injury, we say he is in a passion; that is, he lets in the wrong, and there does his heart bite upon the wrong, and chase at it; thus he is passionate, when a man is affected with love to a pleasure, hee lets in the pleasure, and suffers it to prevaile on the heart.[29]

---

[27] Edward Leigh, *A Systeme or Body of Divinity* (London: Printed by A. M. for William Lee, 1662), 758.

[28] William Bridge, *Bridge's Remains, Being VIII Sermons* (London: Printed by John Hancock, 1673), 26.

[29] William Fenner, *A Treatise of the Affections* (London: Printed by R.H., 1642), 12. Cf. John Weemes, *The Portraitvre of the Image of God in Man* (London: Printed by T.C., 1636), 139, "*Passion, is a motion of the sensitive appetite, stirred up by the apprehension, either of good or evill in the imagination, which worketh some outward change in the body.*"

Later he says, "This is one reason why the affections are called passions, for they make the soule to suffer, and the body to suffer."[30] Fenner says that the words "affections" and "passions" are sometimes used synonymously because they both indicate that one thing has been changed by something else. One thing has been affected by another thing or has suffered (i.e., "been passive" or "undergone") something. It is very common to see the two words used in this synonymous fashion.

How are they distinguished, then? Passions are treated as a subset of the affections in the context of intensity and irrationality or corporeal change. Nicholas Moseley demonstrates this approach. While beginning with the common definition of affections as motions based on reactions to good or evil, he goes on to say:

Affections as long as they be but rightly, ordinate, and subject, nor may, nor can be expelled being natural and good, but when they grow heady, sensual, fleshy, & terrene, set upon the lusts and pleasures of this stage-play world, are vitious and hurtful, which a wise man & a virtuous will keep under, and not suffer to range and rule; for these are they which are properly called Passions.[31]

For example, to love is an affection, but to lust is a passion, to be angry is an affection, but to rage is a passion, and to be sad is an affection, but to be overwhelmed by sorrow is a passion. The intensity of the affection makes it a passion and presupposes an irrationality or loss of control on the part of the individual. A man in lust, rage, or heartbrokenness is not in control of himself. Anthony Burgess said, "These passions have several names, sometimes they are called perturbations, but that is most properly, when they have cast off the dominion of reason."[32]

Passions, as distinguished from affections, violate the boundaries of reason and nature. They are inordinate affections.

---

[30] Fenner, A Treatise of the Affections, 7.

[31] Nicholas Mosely, Psychosophia: Or, Natural & Divine Contemplations of the Passions & Faculties of the Soul of Man (London: Printed for Humphrey Mosley, 1653), 9-10.

[32] Anthony Burgess, A Treatise of Original Sin. The First Part (London: n.p., 1658), 327.

Passions trouble the mind and cause violent reactions based on external stimuli.

When understood in the context of human nature, it is clear that whether one considers affections and passions to be synonymous or whether one distinguishes passions as a subset of the affections, neither can be predicated properly of a purely essential, actual, and spiritual God. Though affections and passions are not necessarily *sinful*, they are *creaturely*. God is not composed of parts and faculties. His understanding is omniscient and eternal. His will is immutable, unobstructed, and eternal. Nothing can cause God to violate his nature, to be troubled in his mind, or to act in any way that contradicts his self-sufficient and all-sufficient perfection.

With these definitions in mind, the Reformed wrestled with various passages of Scripture that attribute passions and affections to God. Here their exegesis and systematics united in comparing Scripture with Scripture in order to shed greater light on those passages that would *seem* to attribute affections and passions to God. For example, John Calvin explains in what sense God repented and was grieved in Genesis 6:5-6. He says:

> The repentance which is here attributed unto God, doth not properly belong unto him, but is referred to our sense and capacity. For because we cannot comprehend him as he is, it is necessary that he transfigure himself after a sort for our sake. That God cannot repent him, it doth evidently appear by this one thing, because nothing happeneth unto him unlooked for, or not foreseen. The like consideration is to be had of that which followeth, how that God was sorry. God verily is not grieved or sorry, who always remaineth one and like him selfe in his heavenly and blessed rest. But because we can not otherwise understand how much God hateth sin, therefore the holy Ghost frameth himself to our capacity. . . . The learned have called this figure *Anthropopathia*, so often as God taketh to himself, which is proper to human nature.[33]

---

[33] John Calvin, *A Commentarie of John Calvine, upon the first booke of Moses called Genesis*, trans. Thomas Tymme (London: Printed by John Harison and George Bishop, 1578), 178. Spelling has been updated for ease of comprehension.

Calvin makes it clear that repentance is not *properly* attributed to God, that is, it does not belong to his nature. But rather it is attributed by *anthropopathy*, wherein God is described in the language of human passions and affections.

Vermigli concurs. He says:

> So, when it is said, that God waxed angry, it is not to be understood, as though God were troubled with affects; for that belongs unto men: but according to the common and received exposition of these places, we understand it, that God behaved himself like unto men that be angry. After the selfsame manner it is sometimes written, that he repented him: wherefore God, either to repent, or to be angry, is nothing else, but that he does those things, which men repenting, or being angry, are wont to do. For the one sort do either alter or undo all that ever they had done before; and the other revenge themselves of such wrongs as have been done unto them. Ambrose in his book of Noah and the ark, the fourth chapter, speaks otherwise of the anger of God. For neither (says he) doth God think as men do, as though he should be of any new mind; neither is he angry, as though he were mutable.

He adds:

> But yet peradventure some man will doubt, whether God, when he repented him, were in any respect changed. All the godly in a manner with one mouth confess, that God cannot be changed one iota, because that would be a certain sign, both of imperfection, and also of inconstancy.[34]

What other language can Scripture speak than our language? God speaks to us in terms that align with our experience and knowledge, yet he is not contained in that language. He remains incomprehensible and ineffable.

Why is it, then, that these writers will make arguments that *seem*

---

[34] Peter Martyr Vermigli, *The Common Places of the most famous and renowned Diuine Doctor Peter Martyr*, trans. Anthonie Marten (n.p., 1583), 109-10.

to contradict the plain sense of such passages? Their systematic conclusions were based on exegetical foundations. The Scriptures themselves deny such affections and passions in God. Vermigli says:

> For God says; I am God, and am not changed. And in the first of Samuel; The triumpher of Israel is not changed. And Balaam in the book of Numbers says; God is not as a man, that he should be changed: neither as the son of man that he should be a liar. Yet in Genesis he says; It repents me that I have made man. Forsomuch as these places seem to be repugnant, they must be accorded together.[35]

Vermigli goes on to explain that in these passages the change brought about is always in the creature, and not in the Creator.

In what sense, then, does God have love, mercy, anger, and such attributes? And why does Scripture use passions and affections to describe God if he does not have them? The Reformed maintained a careful balance here. Approaching God through the *via eminentiae* and the *via negationis*, they removed from God anything creaturely or imperfect which in turn caused God's perfections to shine forth. Musculus demonstrates this balance:

> As touching men's affections which do go with the love of man, it is not meet that we should refer them unto the nature of God in that sort as they be found in men. In the nature of man, love doth believe all things, doth trust all things, doth weep with them which do weep, and is weak with them which be weak, is it convenient, that the like be referred unto the love of God? The Scripture doth attribute many things unto God by figure and similitude of man's affections, which do not so agree unto the nature of God, as they do unto our nature. And yet for all that, it is not without reason, that it doth speak unto men in this wise of God, to apply it self unto our capacity.[36]

---

[35] Vermigli, *The Common Places*, 206.
[36] Musculus, *Common Places*, 958-59. Spelling updated.

We must be careful not to draw a one-to-one correlation between the language God uses to describe himself and God as he is in himself. We must consider what is fitting to his nature, and what is not.

Musculus explains that God's love is not like our love. He says:

> In the nature of man, love doth believe all things, doth trust all things, doth weep with them which do weep, and is weak with them which be weak, is it convenient, that the like be referred unto the love of God?[37]

God's love is not a passion or an affection, rather it is a perfection described in the language of human passion and affections.

The same is said of God's mercy. Musculus begins by using the common definition of mercy, that of feeling the misery of another and acting kindly towards them, and says that such a definition cannot be true of God because God cannot be moved by feeling another's suffering, or having "heart misery" with another. But he goes on to define mercy as *a regard toward the helpless* and concludes:

> This we may truly, and uprightly consider in the definition of mercy. But as touching the nature and operation thereof which it practiceth in the heart of man, where it stirreth up sometimes sorrow and compassion, that is not to be applied unto God. Like as all affections and operations of love which hath place in the heart of man, do not straight way frame unto God, and yet for all that, love is attributed unto him, that he is reported to be very love it self.[38]

The result of this careful distinction between God's mercy and the mercy of humanity (as of God's love and humanity's love) maintains that balance which befits the Creator/creature distinction. In denying human mercy to be in God, the Reformers did not remove true mercy from God. Quite to the contrary, they argued that his mercy *transcends* everything we know. Musculus adds:

---

[37] Musculus, *Common Places*, 958-59.
[38] Musculus, *Common Places*, 981.

Therefore it remaineth, that the greater the mercy is in God, than it is in the hearts of men, and the less that the causes of men's compassion do take place in him, the more manifest it is, that he hath no other cause of his mercy, but his incomparable goodness of nature, unto which we did also refer his lovingness towards man in the place before.[39]

Musculus makes the same argument regarding God's anger and other actions of his will that we would call "affections."[40]

In conclusion, the Reformed doctrine of impassibility is constructed upon a very specific and interwoven understanding of the Creator/creature distinction, drawn from Scripture. Based on this doctrinal distinction, the fundamental assertion of the Reformed with regard to what we call impassibility is that because God is all that he is, pure essence, Scripture's attribution of affections and passions to God communicates the actions of God's will or his essential perfections, but *nothing* creaturely such as mutability, succession, composition, or finitude. Thus what we call affections in God are perfections that transcend our knowledge of love, mercy, anger, etc. This is argued *exegetically* from the divine names and passages of Scripture that deny passions in God, and *systematically* from the nature of God.

Divine Impassibility in Seventeenth-Century England

Tracing the doctrine of impassibility in seventeenth-century England is not difficult. Already in the time of the Reformation, the Church of England had declared in 1552 and 1563 in its 42 and 39 Articles that, "There is but one living, and true God, and he is everlasting with out body, parts, or passions, of infinite power, wisdom, and goodness, the maker, and preserver of all things both visible, and invisible." The Irish Articles of 1615 followed suit, saying, "There is but one living and true God everlasting, without body, parts, or passions, of infinite power, wisdom, and goodness, the maker and preserver of all things, both visible and invisible." These confessional documents establish a tradition of the doctrine of

---

[39] Musculus, *Common Places*, 983.
[40] See Musculus, *Common Places*, 981-82.

God which specifically includes the doctrine of divine impassibility.

When the Westminster Assembly of Divines was called to its work by both houses of Parliament, their inaugural task, assigned at their first sitting on July 5, 1643, was to take "into their consideration the ten first Articles of the 39 Articles of the Church of England, to free and vindicate the doctrine of them from all aspersions and false interpretations."[41] The church needed reforming. The good should be vindicated, the unclear explained, and the bad removed. What was it that made it through their scrutiny? In Article 1, the Assembly "vindicated," or found no error in the statement that, "There is but one living and true God, everlasting, without body, parts, or passions; of infinite power, wisdom, and goodnesse."

When the time came for the Assembly to draft their own confession of faith, they saw no reason to depart from these words. They declared:

> There is but one only, living, and true God who is infinite in Being and Perfection, a most pure Spirit, invisible, without body, parts, or passions, immutable, immense, eternall, incomprehensible, almighty, most wise, most holy, most absolute . . . (WCF 2.1)

The Savoy Declaration, published in 1658, copied these words precisely, extending the chain of confessing the truth that God is without passions.

In 1677, the Baptists, drawing from a rich history in their previous Confession and the Reformed Confessions of the English churches before them, confessed:

> The Lord our God is but one only living, and true God; whose subsistence is in and of himself, infinite in being, and perfection, whose Essence cannot be comprehended by any but himself; a most pure spirit, invisible, without body, parts, or passions, who only hath immortality, dwelling in

---

[41] Adoniram Byfield, Charles Herle, and Henry Robrough, *The Proceedings of the Assembly of Divines upon the Thirty nine Articles of the Church of England* (n.p., 1643), 1.

light, which no man can approach unto, who is immutable, immense, eternal, incomprehensible, Almighty, every way infinite, most holy, most wise, most free, most absolute, working all things according to the counsel of his own immutable, and most righteous will . . . (2LCF 2.1)

The theology behind the Second London Baptist Confession, the Savoy Declaration, the Westminster Confession, the Irish Articles, and the 39 Articles of the Church of England demonstrates that seventeenth-century England reflects a confessionally united consensus, and from a variety of ecclesiastical flavors, on the doctrine of impassibility — the same doctrine as expressed by the Reformers articulated in the section above.

The united voice of these Confessions rose in unison not only to proclaim the truth but also to combat the rising prevalence of Socinianism. The Socinians' arguments tended to level the distance between the Creator and the creature by using language univocally of both. For example, they denied the Trinity because human persons are distinct and divided from other human persons. God was one, they said, and a trinity of persons contradicted this truth. So also, when it came to God's anger, love, mercy, and other passions and affections, they treated these in such a way that as such affections are in mankind, so they are in God.

John Owen wrote against the Socinians, raising and answering this very issue. Owen said:

> Quest. *Are there not according to the perpetuall tenor of the Scriptures, affections and passions in God, as Anger, Fury, Zeale, Wrath, Love, Hatred, Mercy, Grace, Jealousy, Repentance, Grief, Ioy, Feare?* Concerning which he [Owen's Socinian opponent, John Biddle] labours to make the Scriptures determine in the affirmative . . .
>
> To the whole I aske, whither these things are in the *Scripture* ascribed *properly* unto God, denoting such *affections* & *passions* in him as those in us are, which are so termed, or whither they are assigned to Him, & spoken of him *Metaphorically*, only in reference to his outward workes and dispensations, correspondent and answering to the actings of men, in whom such affections are, and under the power

whereof they are in those actings. If the latter be affirmed, then as such an attribution of them unto God, is eminently consistent with All his infinite Perfections, and Blessednesse, so there can be no difference about this Question, and the answers given thereunto; all men readily acknowledge, that in this sence the Scripture doth ascribe all the affections mentioned unto God.[42]

Notice that Owen denies that such things are in God *properly*, but rather they are *metaphorical*. This is what Calvin called anthropopathy, and this is the method Musculus demonstrated by distinguishing between God's love, mercy, and anger, and ours. It is not that God does not love, but that God's love is distinct from ours. His is a perfection, an act of the divine will. Ours is a passion or an affection. Over and over, the same argument rises in the writings of the seventeenth-century English theologians.

Examples of the theology behind the Confessions are far too numerous to include in this section. A few, offered below, will have to suffice. Thomas Adams says:

Though hands bee heere attributed to God, yet it is but by way of metaphore; not literally, and in a true proprietie of speech. To conceive GOD to bee as man, with human dimensions, was the heresie of the *Anthropomorphites*: and hee that thus grossely thinkes of God, saith Ierome, makes an Idoll of God in his heart. But herein God stoopes to the qualitie of our understandings, ascribing to himself anger and displeasure, as it were passions to the impassible: whereas *Nec Deus affectu capitur, Nec tangitur ira*: they are not passions, but perfections.[43]

Anthony Burgess says:

As affections do denote any passions, or imperfections

---

[42] John Owen, *Vindiciae Evangelicae Or, The Mystery of the Gospell Vindicated, and Socinianisme Examined* (Oxford: Printed by Leon. Lichfield, 1655), 73. This page is incorrectly numbered 65 in the original. The spelling is original.

[43] Thomas Adams, *The Workes of Tho: Adams* (London: Printed by Tho. Harper, 1629), 875.

intermixed with them, so they cannot be attributed to him, who is the fountain of perfection, yet because the Scripture doth generally attribute these affections unto God, he is said to love, to grieve, to hope, to be angry: Hence it is that Divines do in their Theological Tractates, besides the attributes of God, handle also of those things, which are (as some expresse it) analogical affections in him; They treat of his love, his mercy, his anger, which are not so properly Attributes in God, as analogical affections; As when the Scripture saith, God hath eyes and hands, these are expressions to our capacity, and we must conceive of God by those words according to supream excellency that is in him: Thus it is also in affections; There is an *anthropomorphia*, in the former, and an *anthropopatheia* in the later.[44]

He adds:

Yea some *Socinians* . . . doe positively maintain affections to be properly in God; And although to mollifie their opinion, they sometimes have fair explications of themselves, yet they grant the things themselves to be in God, which we call affections; Hence they call them often, The commotions of Gods will, which are sometimes more, sometimes lesse; Yea they are so impudent, as to say the denial of such affections in God, is to overthrow all Religion: But this opinion is contrary to the pure simplicity and immutability of Gods Nature, as also to his perfect blessednesse.[45]

Thomas Hodges says:

How doe we change in all we are and have? From child-hood to youth, from youth to mans estate, from thence to age, we never stand at a stay till dust returns to dust. . . . Though heaven and earth threaten to come together, though the waves roare, and waters lift up their voice; though the thunder rattles and lightnings flye abroad; though men

---

[44] Burgess, *A Treatise of Original Sin*, 338.
[45] Burgess, *A Treatise of Original Sin*, 339.

perish and creatures be cut off as in the flood; yet as the sunne, being above the place of stormes and tempests, goes on its course, and is not checkt by these; so it is far above the spheare of change, to make the least mutation in this God. And therefore if you read that he repents, doe not mistake the phrase: 'tis true; 'tis over man; but not as man, he doth it. In man it intimates a turbation of minde, a displicencie[46] of the fact, a mutation of counsel, but in God 'tis not a change of counsel, but of fact; of things which are made by him, not of his prescience; nor is it an alteration of his nature, but a suspension of his wrath, power, or some other attribute: he is a free agent, and whether he works or no, it alters not himself.[47] So if you read that he is angry, jealous, or the like, then know, the Scripture being ordained for men, speakes in their dialect; and as the nurse in talking with her young one brings down her language to the childs conception, so God doth his; hence comes such low expressions in holy writ, because in spirituall things we are very dull, but yet we must not thinke that passions, or such things are really in God; but it is because his workes are such as mens when passions doe possesse their minds; as to destroy, consume, confound, the worke he hath wrought, yet perturbations have no place in him.[48]

These examples are just a tiny taste of the united voice of the English theologians of the seventeenth century on the doctrine of divine impassibility.[49]

We can conclude this section by approaching the issue from a different angle: the doctrine of Christ. The Socinian errors were systemic, corrupting the doctrine of Christ's deity. As the Reformed writers defended orthodox doctrine, they carefully distinguished between the divine and human natures of Christ. Nehemiah Coxe faced a similar opponent as he wrote against Thomas Collier, who

---

[46] The fact or condition of being displeased or dissatisfied.

[47] A note in the text at this point refers to a marginal note that reads "Passions attributed to God doe not prove him mutable."

[48] Thomas Hodges, *A Glimpse of Gods Glory* (London: Printed for Iohn Bartlet, 1642), 37-39.

[49] See Renihan, ed., *God without Passions: A Reader*.

maintained views akin to the Socinians. In his refutation of Collier, Coxe stated:

> They [the Scriptures] say indeed, That the Prince of Life was killed, and the Lord of Glory was Crucified: So the Scripture saith also, that God purchased his Church by his blood; and laid down his life for us: The person that died was very God, the Prince of Life and Lord of Glory, but it was in the Humane nature, and not in his Divine that he suffered, although both made but one person; and to reject this, and say with Mr. *Collier*, that as God *&c.* his Bloud was shed, he was crucified and died, *i.e.* that all these things befell the Divine as well as the Humane nature; is impious to that degree, as may make a tender heart bleed, and the ears of a godly man to tingle.[50]

Coxe adds, "The common faith of Christians about this matter is, That the same Jesus who suffered made satisfaction to Divine Justice for their sins; but that his sufferings were in his Humane nature only."[51]

Serious doctrinal connections were at stake in these issues, and Coxe made it clear that denying impassibility by attributing exclusively creaturely actions to the Creator was a grievous sin contrary to the collective common faith of Christians. Given the consensus of the Confessions quoted above, and given the continuity of doctrine on this point throughout the ages in general and the Reformed and post-Reformation eras in particular, it is not difficult to see why Coxe would make such a claim. The doctrine of divine impassibility was alive and well, confessed by the collected Christian church, expressed in their writings, and defended against any and all opposition, Socinian or otherwise.

---

[50] Nehemiah Coxe, *Vindiciae Veritatis, Or a Confutation of the Heresies and Gross Errors of Thomas Collier* (London: Nath. Ponder, 1677), 17.

[51] Coxe, *Vindiciae Veritatis*, 18.

Chapter 9

HISTORICAL THEOLOGY SURVEY OF
THE DOCTRINE OF DIVINE IMPASSIBILITY
The Modern Era
Brandon F. Smith and James M. Renihan

As the preceding survey of the history of theology demonstrates, the doctrine of divine impassibility has been confessed as the teaching of the Bible by orthodox Christian theologians and churches for centuries. More specifically, it is affirmed to be a necessary article of faith by the Reformed symbols of the confessional era, including the 2LCF. As with many doctrines, however, the modern era has increasingly regarded divine impassibility with disinterest and outright disdain. For the better part of the last two centuries the orthodox consensus has been slowly eroding, to the point that, as it stands today, this particular doctrine is a byword for archaic and mistaken theology in both academic and ecclesiastical circles. In this chapter, we seek to survey the landscape of the modern era since 1700.

What follows is not an extensive discussion of the fate of the doctrine of divine impassibility in the modern era. Neither are we able to demonstrate at length how various cultural, philosophical, and theological trends contributed to the widespread rejection of the classical doctrine. Rather, we suggest some basic causative factors and review the history of acceptance, modification and rejection of the doctrine of divine impassibility. Our goal is modest—simply to point the reader to various theologians and their published conclusions.

The eighteenth century was an era of continuity with the past as well as theological retrenchment for European Christians. Faced with massive desertions to Unitarianism and Socinianism, orthodox English theologians circled the proverbial wagons. The

Enlightenment, with all of its rationalism and anti-supernaturalism, introduced a new philosophical paradigm into Christian theology.[1] Tending to decry the theological systems of the past, the views of many evangelicals may be summarized in Charles Simeon's simplistic dictum: "Be Bible Christians, not system Christians."[2] While the result of such a dictum may have been unwitting, it nevertheless provoked reassessment and revision of many classical Christian doctrines in the nineteenth century.

The Eighteenth Century

An important bridge between centuries may be found in the English Baptist theologian John Gill (1697-1771). Richard Muller writes:

> The eminent Particular Baptist . . . John Gill . . . stands as powerful proof, if any were needed, that the thought of English nonconformity and, within that category, English Baptist theology, is in large part an intellectual and spiritual descendant of the thought of those Reformers, Protestant orthodox writers, and Puritans who belonged to the Reformed confessional tradition.[3]

As one might expect, Gill's writings confirm his commitment to classical theism, and particularly to its enunciation of divine

---

[1] David Bebbington, *Evangelicalism in Modern Britain: A History from the 1730s to the 1980s* (Grand Rapids: Baker, 1989), 57ff. In a book intended to challenge some of Bebbington's conclusions, Michael Haykin largely supports Bebbington's analysis of the impact of the Enlightenment on English evangelicals. See Michael A. G. Haykin, "Evangelicalism and the Enlightenment: a Reassessment" in *The Advent of Evangelicalism: Exploring Historical Continuities*, ed. Michael A. G. Haykin and Kenneth J. Stewart (Nashville: B&H Academic, 2008), 39-48. Haykin says, ". . . there are close ties between eighteenth-century evangelicalism and the Enlightenment. . . . [T]here is clear evidence of positive cross-fertilization and interaction between our eighteenth-century forebears and their culture." *Advent*, 48.

[2] Bebbington, *Evangelicalism*, 58.

[3] Richard A. Muller, "John Gill and the Reformed Tradition: A Study in the Reception of Protestant Orthodoxy in the Eighteenth Century," in *The Life and Thought of John Gill (1697-1771): A Tercentennial Appreciation*, ed. Michael A. G. Haykin (Leiden: Brill, 1997), 51. We have supplied birth/death years for selected individuals born prior to 1900.

impassibility. Approaching God's immutability from the familiar categories of apophatic theology, the *via negationis* and the *via eminentiae*, Gill grounds his doctrine in the fact of divine simplicity, and argues against change postulated in God due to his creative activity or to the incarnation. He states that there was no

> change made in the divine nature by the sufferings of Christ: the divine nature is impassible, and is one reason why Christ assumed the human nature, that he might be capable of suffering and dying in the room and stead of his people; and though the Lord of life and glory was crucified, and God purchased the church with his own blood, and the blood of Christ is called the blood of the Son of God; yet he was crucified in the human nature only, and his blood was shed in that, to which the divine person gave virtue and efficacy, through its union to it; but received no change by all this.

A few paragraphs later he notes, "God is unchangeable in his love and affections to his people."[4] The entire section reflects the classical doctrine.

Gill's colonial American contemporary, the Presbyterian Gilbert Tennent (1703-64), expresses the same doctrine as he considers the incarnation:

> This Guilt, the Judge and Legislator, because of his natural Holiness, his governing Wisdom, Truth and Justice, cannot pass by without an equal Satisfaction.
>
> But this the Sinner cannot perform, because he is finite, and therefore either he must suffer eternally, or a Surety undertake for him, and do and suffer in his Room and Place, what he was and is uncapable of.
>
> Now the Person that so interposes must be Man, that he might be capable of suffering, for the Deity is impassible; and it is but just and reasonable that the Nature that sinn'd shou'd suffer, that the Sin of Man should be punish'd in Man.

---

[4] John Gill, *A Complete Body of Doctrinal and Practical Divinity* (Reprint, Paris, AR: Baptist Standard Bearer, 1995), 59. Gill does not employ the Latin phrases, *via negativa* and *via eminentiae*, though he clearly articulates the principles they express.

And indeed it is as necessary, that the Person interposing be God, that so the human Nature shou'd be Supported under its Sufferings, which being equal to the Demerit of Sin, and consequently infinite, would otherways destroy it. It is also necessary, that the Mediator should be God, that so an infinite Dignity might be put upon the Sufferings and Obedience of his human Nature by its Union to the Divine, that so the Satisfaction made might be Equivalent to the Debt contracted.[5]

The early American theologian Jonathan Edwards (1703-58) advocated the classical doctrine of impassibility.

Our Lord Jesus Christ, in his original nature, was infinitely above all suffering, for he was "God over all, blessed for evermore;" but when he became man, he was not only capable of suffering, but partook of that nature that is remarkably feeble and exposed to suffering.[6]

In a compilation volume entitled *Our Great and Glorious God*, Edwards' teaching about divine impassibility is collected as a subset under the larger heading "The Nature of God." Asserting that "there is no such thing truly as any pain, grief, or trouble in God," he proceeds to demonstrate that any such things would necessitate that God is less than he is—neither omniscient nor immutable.[7]

---

[5] Gilbert Tennent, *Discourses, on Several Important Subjects*. By Gilbert Tennent, A.M. Minister of the Gospel in Philadelphia (Philadelphia: W. Bradford at the Bible in Second-Street, 1745), 40–42.

[6] Jonathan Edwards, "Sermon VI," in *The Works of Jonathan Edwards* (Reprint, Edinburgh: The Banner of Truth, 1976), II:866. See also Edwards' sermon "God Never Changes His mind," in *The Puritan Pulpit: Jonathan Edwards*, ed. Don Kistler (Morgan, PA: Soli Deo Gloria, 2004), 1-13. A transcription of the original sermon notes may be consulted at the website for the Jonathan Edwards Center at Yale University, *Sermons, Series II, 1729 (WJE Online Vol. 44)*, http://edwards.yale.edu/archive?path=aHR0cDovL2Vkd2FyZHMueWFsZS5lZH UvY2dpLWJpbi9uZXdwaGlsby9nZXRvYmplY3QucGw/Yy40Mjo3LndqZW8=. Accessed 26 March 2015.

[7] Jonathan Edwards, *Our Great and Glorious God*, compiled by Don Kistler (Morgan, PA: Soli Deo Gloria, 2003), 17ff. Sadly, the book does not provide any specific indications for the source of the material beyond the statement on the title page "taken from the sermons and miscellanies."

Edwards clearly articulates the classical doctrine.

These examples serve to demonstrate the continuity present between the doctrine as expressed in the Reformed Confessions and some eighteenth-century Reformed thinkers. How may we account for the consistency of these scholars in the face of the powerful encroachments of the Enlightenment? It has been perceptively suggested that the continued adherence to classical doctrines was based on the "'hard, bitter rind of Calvinism' which . . . covered Baptist faith from the solvent acids of rationalism."[8] There is no reason to limit this notion to the Baptists—it applies equally to Tennent and Edwards as well. In fact, each of these theologians understood the dangers of Socinianism and its seemingly kindly and moderate daughter Unitarianism. They recognized that the classical doctrine of God was like Christ's robe—a seamless garment. It was necessary to defend the doctrine *in toto*, without modification.

The Nineteenth Century

As we come to the next century, we notice that the river of orthodoxy flowing from the peaks of Reformation and post-Reformation thought diverges into multiple streams when it reaches the basin and borderlands of modern thought. Reformed and evangelical theologians struggled to follow the main channel and stay the course. Some succeeded; others were swept into marshes, bogs, fens, and quagmires, with doleful consequences, especially for their heirs in the twentieth and twenty-first centuries.

Jonathan Edwards' transatlantic disciple Andrew Fuller (1754-1815) serves as an example of a steady hand on the rudder near the beginning of the nineteenth century. In a 1796 sermon "Preached before the Baptist Association at St. Albans," Fuller argues for the importance of systematic divinity. Always derived from Scripture,

---

[8] Olin C. Robison, "The Legacy of John Gill," *The Baptist Quarterly* 24 (July, 1971): 122. The phrase "hard bitter rind of Calvinism" and the idea expressed are from Bernard Manning, *Essays in Orthodox Dissent* (London: Independent Press, 1953), 191-93. We strongly dispute the negative caricature, but agree with the point. Careful adherence to the Reformed system of theology is a preventative against error. Manning's thrust is that Calvinism was actually a blessing to the churches since it provided theological protection from Enlightenment thinking.

believers ought to strive to know both the "first principles" of faith as well as the "deep things of God." These may only be known as they are organized into a consistent and coherent system. He lamented that "Systematic divinity, or the studying of truth in a Systematic form, has been of late years decried."[9]

In his work *Apparent Contradictions*, Fuller addresses the problem of the attribution of repentance to God in Genesis 6:6 and the denial of such in 1 Samuel 15:29. He says:

> The seeming contradiction in these passages arises from the same term being used in the one metaphorically, and in the other literally. It is literally true that repentance is not predicable of the Divine nature, inasmuch as it implies mutability and imperfection in knowledge and wisdom, neither of which can be applied to the infinitely blessed God. But, in order to address himself impressively to us, he frequently personates a creature, or speaks to us after the manner of men. . . . Notice the amazing displeasure of God against sin. 'It repented the Lord that he had made man on the earth, and it grieved him at his heart!' — Was ever such language uttered! What words besides them, could convey to us such an idea of the evil of sin? It is true we are not to understand them literally; but they convey to us an idea that the sin of man is so heinous, and so mischievous, as to mar all the works of God, and to render them worse than if there were none.[10]

It would seem that Fuller's use of "frequently personates a creature" is a circumlocution for the more familiar *anthropomorphism* and *anthropopathism*. Without question, Fuller expresses himself in the familiar terms of orthodoxy. Some things, such as repentance, may

---

[9] Andrew Fuller, "The Nature and Importance of an Intimate Knowledge of Divine Truth," in *The Complete Works of the Rev. Andrew Fuller*, 3 vols., ed. J. Belcher (1845; reprint, Harrisonburg, VA: Sprinkle, 1988), 1:160-74. We owe the citation to Haykin, *Advent*, 42. Dr. Haykin points out that though Fuller here argues for the importance and legitimacy of systematic theology, he never produced a formal theology. It should be noted, however, that he did begin to develop such a work. See "Letters on Systematic Divinity," in *Works*, 1:684-711.

[10] Andrew Fuller, "Apparent Contradictions," in *Works*, 1:669-71.

not be predicated "of the Divine nature" since proper predication would produce an inherent contradiction in the received doctrine of God. He is "infinitely blessed." He is impassible.

In America, the challenge of foreign missions was suddenly thrust upon the Baptists when Adoniram Judson and Luther Rice, missionaries sent to India by New England Congregationalists, adopted Baptist principles *en route*. With great fervor, the Baptists of the young republic took up the challenge, forming in 1814 the *General Missionary Convention of the Baptist Denomination in the United States of America for Foreign Missions*, or perhaps more simply, the Triennial Convention.[11] In Boston, pastors quickly rallied in support of the cause, issuing the *American Baptist Magazine and Missionary Intelligencer*, a revised and expanded version of an earlier and more locally oriented periodical. In the first issue of their new paper, they included, as the second article (following an editorial and a memoir of Roger Williams), a piece entitled "On the Immutability of God." The author says:

> It will not be difficult to perceive how we are to explain those passages of scripture where God is represented as repenting of certain deeds, as the creation of man, and the crowning of Saul. We have only to recollect that these are among the multitude of instances, not only in the poetical parts of the Old testament, but also in the historical, where, in condescension to the conceptions of men, God is described in the *language* of men. *When men repent, they change their conduct. Now, by an easy and natural figure, God, when he changes his conduct, is said to repent.* This simple solution, it is believed, will, upon examination, be found supported by the context in every instance in which repentance is ascribed to God.[12]

---

[11] Robert G. Torbet, *Venture of Faith: The Story of the American Baptist Foreign Mission Society and the Woman's American Baptist Mission Society 1814-1954* (Philadelphia: Judson Press, 1955), 20ff.

[12] "On the Immutability of God," *The American Baptist Magazine and Missionary Intelligencer*, New Series, Vol. 1 (1817): 15, emphasis original. The author of the article is given as "*Hospes.*" It is difficult to identity this person specifically. Hospes is the Latin term for both 'host' and 'guest.' If 'host' is intended, perhaps the editor, Boston pastor Thomas Baldwin, contributed this piece.

This truth is then applied to both the unconverted and believers. For those without faith, God's immutability is a matter of great concern, as he will send judgment upon them for their impenitence. For believers, however, it is a source of great comfort. In any case, divine impassibility was considered to be an important element in the missionary endeavor.

As the decades pass, however, we find adumbrations of adjustments and modifications to the classical doctrine in the writings of important theologians. The prominent New York preacher Henry Ward Beecher (1813-1887)[13] softened the blow of his father's Calvinism by directing people toward issues of the heart rather than rigid doctrine.[14] Among the Reformed, men such as Charles Hodge (1797-1878) and Benjamin B. Warfield (1851-1921) expressed new perspectives on the classical formulation.

Princeton Theological Seminary stood in its day as a bulwark against the onslaught of multi-faceted parties of humanistic thinking. It represented and defended Old School Presbyterianism through the writings of men such as Charles Hodge, A. A. Hodge, and B. B. Warfield. These Old School Presbyterians took a strong stance for historic Calvinism, proclaiming it as the purest form of religion.[15] Charles Hodge sought to resist the downgrade among

---

[13] Henry Ward Beecher rejected the doctrine of divine impassibility. A contributor to a volume published in Beecher's honor, Newell Dwight Hillis, in describing Beecher's theology says of him, "The first ruling idea is his conception of the suffering God. . . . The very heart of his message is that God neither slumbers nor sleeps, by reason of the emotions of love that suffer and make him the burden-bearer of all his children. . . . From the old pagan notion that was still taught when I was in the seminary, that God was not susceptible to pain, that God dwells at a far remove from this earth, impassive and with marble heart, that God is eternally young and eternally happy, lifted up above all possibility of tears, or anxiety, or solicitude—from all these Grecian and heathen and former ultra-Presbyterian and medieval conceptions he utterly revolted." Newell Dwight Hillis, "The Ruling Ideas of Henry Ward Beecher's Sermons," in *Henry Ward Beecher as His Friends Saw Him* (New York: The Pilgrim Press, 1904), 28. This book has no author or editor listed, though a J. H. Tewksbury is given as the copyright holder.

[14] George M. Marsden, "The Era of Crisis: From Christendom to Pluralism," in *Eerdmans' Handbook To Christianity In America*, ed. Mark Noll (Grand Rapids: Eerdmans, 1983), 290. The same might be said of E. Y. Mullins, from 1899 President of The Southern Baptist Theological Seminary in Louisville, KY. See his *The Christian Religion in Its Doctrinal Expression* (Philadelphia: Roger Williams Press, 1917).

[15] Mark A. Noll, *Reformed Theology In America: A History Of The Modern*

Presbyterians, laboring to recapitulate the historical doctrine of the Old School. He confronted Nathaniel Taylor on the doctrine of the imputation of sin from Adam, but advanced a personal formulation itself not directly in conformity with historic confessionalism.[16] David Wells writes:

> It is not difficult to see Hodge's weaknesses. He was not a great historian; only when he was stiffly debated about his claims to historic Calvinism did he grudgingly allow that he believed many things that Calvin never taught. He did not recognize as matters for serious theological reflection what was going on in the culture. . . . He also imbibed the interests of Common Sense realism, which was, after all, an Enlightenment philosophy.[17]

Although Hodge was a stalwart against the decline of his time, his flaws are important. A staunch Calvinist, he was at the same time a cultural sentimentalist, believing, as did Charles Finney, that the gospel was making significant progress in the young republic.[18] He desired to defend adherence to the WCF, but refused to support a policy of strong subscription within his church.[19]

The history of the American Presbyterian Church in the nineteenth and twentieth centuries is an account of progress and decline. The conclusion of the process may be found in the reorganization of the board of Princeton Seminary in 1929 and the formation of Westminster Theological Seminary and the Orthodox Presbyterian Church. These events are well-known and cannot be rehearsed here. Recent studies have suggested that the seeds of this process and its conclusion had been unwittingly planted at Princeton long before. The 2013 book *Process and Providence: The Evolution Question at Princeton, 1845-1929* by Bradley J. Gundlach

---

Movement, ed. David F. Wells (Grand Rapids: Baker, 1997), 18.

[16] Wells, *Reformed Theology In America*, 49-55. Wells directly makes these points on page 50 and in the conclusion of the chapter.

[17] Wells, *Reformed Theology In America,* 58.

[18] John Woodbridge, Mark Noll, and Nathan Hatch, *The Gospel In America* (Grand Rapids: Zondervan, 1979), 45.

[19] See the Excursus at the end of this chapter.

provides strong evidence for this fact.[20] Gundlach asserts that while Hodge, Warfield, and others opposed Darwinian naturalistic evolution, they were willing to consider the validity of a divinely directed process of evolution, despite their confessional commitments.

It is also well-known that Hodge and Warfield dissented from the classic doctrine of God at points. Even in his own day, Hodge did not escape the censure of orthodox theologians for his alteration of divine simplicity and immutability.[21] For our purposes, we note their modifications of the classical doctrine of divine impassibility. Hodge briefly addressed the matter in his *Systematic Theology*.[22] Arguing against contemporary philosophical speculation[23] from the human experience of love, he asserts:

> We must believe that God is love in the sense in which that word comes home to every human heart. . . . The word love has the same sense throughout this passage. God is love; and love in Him is, in all that is essential to its nature, what love is in us.[24]

Hodge rightly critiques the contemporary views expressed by Bruch and Schleiermacher, necessarily emphasizing the reality of the love of God. In doing so, however, he opens a door to a definition of impassibility based on univocity with human experience.

---

[20] Bradley J. Gundlach, *Process and Providence: The Evolution Question at Princeton, 1845-1929* (Grand Rapids: Eerdmans, 2013). See the review of this work in *JIRBS* (2015): 173-77.

[21] Bavinck brings Hodge under strong criticism for his deviations from the classic doctrine of God. See Bavinck, *RD*, 2:119.

[22] Charles Hodge, *Systematic Theology* (New York: Charles Scribners, 1871), 1:428-30.

[23] Though Hodge mentions the "schoolmen," his argument proceeds against contemporary European philosopher-theologians Johann Friedrich Bruch and Friedrich Schleiermacher. It is unclear who Hodge intends by "schoolmen." In J. Ligon Duncan's essay "Divine Passibility and Impassibility in Nineteenth-Century American Confessional Presbyterian Theologians," *The Scottish Bulletin of Evangelical Theology* 8 (1990): 5, Duncan attributes the phrase "God cannot be subject to passivity in any form" (cited in Hodge) to "scholastic theologians." In fact, it is a citation from Johann Bruch. The characterization may be misleading if the reader concludes that it refers to earlier writers.

[24] Hodge, *Systematic Theology*, 1:429.

It is difficult to understand his language as anything other than univocal in this citation. Hodge fails to recognize the crucial difference between divine and human modes of being, conflating them into one. Stephen R. Holmes affirms that Hodge's univocal affirmations were intentional and inconsistent with the Reformed tradition from which he wrote. Holmes thinks Hodge may not have realized the "full ramifications" of his denial of analogy.[25] Hodge's legacy leaves us with gratitude for his positive contributions, while recognizing that he was subject to the winds of contemporary philosophical culture and at times failed to support historic Reformed doctrine.

Following in the footsteps of Charles Hodge, Benjamin B. Warfield expressed thoughts on impassibility that were profoundly influenced by contemporary philosophy. He wrote:

> Men tell us that God is, by the very necessity of His nature, incapable of passion, incapable of being moved by inducements from without; that he dwells in holy calm and unchangeable blessedness, untouched by human sufferings or human sorrows for ever. . . . Let us bless our God that it is not true. God can feel; God does love. . . . We decline once for all to subject our whole conception of God to the category of the Absolute. . . . As has been set forth renewedly by Andrew Seth, "we should be unfaithful to the fundamental principle of the theory of knowledge" "if we did not interpret by means of the highest category within our reach." "We should be false to ourselves if we denied in God what we recognize as the source of dignity and worth in ourselves." In order to escape an anthropomorphic God, we must not throw ourselves at the feet of a zoomorphic or an amorphic one.[26]

---

[25] Stephen R. Holmes, "Divine Attributes," in *Mapping Modern Theology: A Thematic and Historical Introduction*, ed. Kelly M. Kapic and Bruce L. McCormack (Grand Rapids: Baker Academic, 2012), 47-66.

[26] Benjamin B. Warfield, "Imitating the Incarnation," in *The Person and Work of Christ* (Philadelphia: Presbyterian & Reformed, 1950), 570-71. In the midst of this quotation, Warfield cites six lines from Tennyson's poem *Lucretius* which curiously describes pagan deities who are, in the poem itself, passionate! Warfield takes a great deal of poetic license to use these lines to make his point. This citation may be found in Paul Helm, "B. B. Warfield On Divine Passion," *WTJ* 69:1 (Spring 2007):

Warfield seems to deny the language of his own WCF 2.1. He praised Andrew Seth Pringle-Pattison's[27] (1856-1931) stance on theism and argued against an aloof God as asserted by the then popular proponents of Absolute Idealism, a philosophy which denied personhood to God.[28] Yet, Warfield still wrote that God is capable of being moved by inducements from without. Warfield's linguistic verbiage contains troubling reformulations about the passions of God in spite of his fight against Absolute Idealism.

Late in the nineteenth century and into the twentieth, several conservative Protestants held the classical doctrine of impassibility with thoughtful commitment, even while it began to lose traction with other theologians. Baptist theologian (and Princeton graduate) James P. Boyce (1827-1888) asserted the importance of divine impassibility in his writing on God's immutability.

> It is again objected, that the Scriptures represent change in God, when they speak of him as "repenting" of the acts which he had done. . . .
>
> In reply to this objection, it may be stated that these are merely anthropopathic expressions, intended simply to impress upon men his great anger at sin, and his warm approval of the repentance of those who had sinned against him. The change of conduct, in men, not in God, had

---

96-97. The unusual use of quotation marks is in Warfield's original text. Helm's article delves into connections and interpretations in the language of Warfield in light of statements in several of his articles and sermons on the emotions of God. Helm seeks to formulate a better understanding of Warfield's language about our incarnate Lord in his emotions and impassibility in the Godhead. Warfield stated, "The embarrassment in studying the emotional life of Jesus arising from this cause, however, is more theoretical than practical. Some of the emotions attributed to him in the Evangelical narrative are, in one way or another, expressly assigned to his human soul. Some of them by their very nature assign themselves to his human soul. With reference to the remainder, just because they might equally well be assigned to the one nature or the other, it may be taken for granted that they belong to the human soul, if not exclusively, yet along with the divine Spirit; and they may therefore very properly be used to fill out the picture" (96). Warfield's statement assigns the emotional aspects of Christ to the human nature, but he leaves the door open for further speculation as to its effects on the divine nature.

[27] Andrew Seth changed his name to Andrew Seth Pringle-Pattison near the end of the nineteenth century.

[28] Helm, "B. B. Warfield On Divine Passion," 99-100.

changed the relation between them and God.[29]

The Dutch Reformed writer Herman Bavinck (1854-1921), seeking to describe the importance of the doctrine of divine impassibility, defended the classical view by identifying anthropopathic language as a subset of anthropomorphic speech.[30] Later, in explaining the necessity of the immutability of God, Bavinck acknowledged anthropomorphic language in proper context.

> Scripture . . . however anthropomorphic its language, at the same time prohibits us from positing any change in God himself. There is change around, about and outside of him, and there is change in people's relations to him, but there is no change in God himself.[31]

In his section on "Accommodation and Anthropomorphism," Bavinck further concluded, "God is as immutable in his knowing, willing, and decreeing as he is in his being. . . . Neither creation, nor revelation, nor incarnation (affects, etc.) brought about any change in God."[32]

Along similar lines, in the twentieth century, American theologian Louis Berkhof (1873-1957) asserted in his *Systematic Theology*:

> And if Scripture speaks of His repenting, changing His intention, and altering His relation to sinners when they repent, we should remember this is only an anthropopathic way of speaking. In reality the change is not in God, but in man and in man's relations to God.[33]

These men addressed divine impassibility in greater or lesser detail from the perspective and importance of the immutability of

---

[29] James P. Boyce, *Abstract Of Systematic Theology* (1887; reprint, Hanford, CA: den Dulk Christian Foundation, n.d.), 76.

[30] Bavinck, *RD*, 2:99-107.

[31] Bavinck, *RD*, 2:158.

[32] Bavinck, *RD*, 2:154.

[33] Louis Berkhof, *Systematic Theology* (Edinburgh; Carlisle, PA: Banner of Truth Trust, 2003), 59.

God. They recognized that Scripture's teaching about the being of God must serve as a foundation prior to drawing implications from anthropomorphic or anthropopathic language.

The Twentieth and Twenty-First Centuries: Does God Sovereignly Manage His Emotions?

The emergent humanism of nineteenth-century philosophers cast profound doubt on the doctrine of divine impassibility.[34] In fact, modifications of this doctrine may be traced directly to nineteenth- and twentieth-century philosophical movements. In 1893, A. M. Fairbairn (1838-1912) called divine impassibility the most untrue concept of God.[35] Although James Ward (1843-1925) and William James (1842-1910) do not describe in detail a passible God, their philosophical constructs led to open-theistic concepts of God and eventually to pluralism.[36] One of Ward's greatest quests was to

---

[34] An interesting statement of this may be found in James Lindsay, *Recent Advances in Theistic Philosophy of Religion* (Edinburgh: Blackwood, 1897), 478. Lindsay places the following in quotation marks, but provides no citation information: "It has even been said that 'theology has no falser idea than that of the impassibility of God. If He is capable of sorrow, He is capable of suffering; and were He without the capacity for either, He would be without any feeling of the evil of sin or the misery of man. The very truth that came by Jesus Christ may be said to be summed up in the passibility of God.'" The citation seems to be from A. M. Fairbairn, see Andrew Greenleaf, "The Problem of Pain," *The Church: A Journal of American Churchmanship*, VI:3 (November, 1898): 39. It is enlightening to note that the modern movement to reject the classical doctrine is rooted in the emerging philosophies of the later nineteenth and early twentieth centuries! And yet many assert that the doctrine of divine impassibility is the product of (to use the previously cited phrase of Paul Gavrilyuk) "Theology's Fall into Hellenistic Philosophy." Careful study turns the tables.

[35] Weinandy, *Does God Suffer?*, 1. Cf. A. M. Fairbairn, *The Place of Christ in Modern Theology* (New York: Charles Scribner's Sons, 1893), 483.

[36] J. K. Mozley, *The Impassibility Of God: A Survey Of Christian Thought* (Reprint, Cambridge, UK: Cambridge University Press, 2014), 132-36. As a young man, James Ward desired to enter the ministry in the United Kingdom, but struggled with major tenets of the faith. He left the ministry behind and became one of the most recognized philosophers spanning the last quarter of the nineteenth century into the first quarter of the twentieth. One of his most well-known students was Bertrand Russell. *Stanford Encyclopedia Of Philosophy*, "James Ward," http://plato.stanford.edu/entries/james-ward/. Accessed 30 March 2015. Bertrand Russell would later devalue the place of God and eventually eliminate

achieve an understanding of the freedom of man.[37] He wished to define God by first defining man and his will, subsequently fabricating God from this humanistic perspective. Ward had already walked away from the truth of God's revelation, with the result that his philosophical musings required that God be defined by the rationalistic understanding of man. Ward's work opened the door for his students, particularly Bertrand Russell (1872-1970). Similarly, Andrew Seth Pringle-Pattison expressed influentially progressive ideas into the twentieth century, proposing a passible God unlike the God of his predecessors. Pringle-Pattison declared, "if we are to reach any credible theory of the relations of God and man the traditional idea of God must be profoundly transformed."[38] Pringle-Pattison considered the historic formulation of the doctrine of God to produce a distant deity. He devalued New Testament Christianity, as it was a product of the same detached God. The views of these philosophers profoundly influenced theologians, so that their rejection of classical theism demanded a revision in theology proper and the stream of liberal theology moved further toward the passible God of Jürgen Moltmann.[39]

Some theologians promoted the idea of change and passibility in God based in his essential sovereignty. A. J. Mason (1851-1928) espoused this interpretation in his 1875 work *The Faith of the Gospel*. He wrote:

> If words mean anything God is capable of grief and joy, of anger and gratification; though there is nothing which can

---

him altogether. Russell's mentor James Ward valued God, but valued him from a humanistic perspective. Russell built upon the thinking of his professor and took his thinking to a new arena. Cf. Bertrand Russell, *Is There A God?* www.personal.kent.edu/~muhamma/Philosophy/RBwritings/isThereGod.htm. Accessed 30 March 2015.

[37] *Stanford Encyclopedia Of Philosophy*, "James Ward," http://plato.stanford.edu/entries/james-ward/. Accessed 30 March 2015.

[38] A. Seth Pringle-Pattison, *The Idea Of God In The Light Of Recent Philosophy* (New York: Oxford University Press, 1920), 407.

[39] Pringle-Pattison, *The Idea Of God In The Light Of Recent Philosophy*, 399-417. Pringle-Pattison works out his theodicy in these pages. He grapples with a monotheistic view of God and the reality of evil. Ultimately this presses him to construct a passible God in order to maintain monotheism or to accept pluralism instead of trinitarianism.

force such states of feeling upon Him without His being willing to undergo them. It would be a defect in Him, not a perfection, were it otherwise.[40]

The idea of God willing emotional change controlled by his sovereignty causes damage to the doctrine of God; based in a voluntaristic philosophy, it makes his sovereignty the starting point for his attributes, creates potential for becoming in God, and calls into question how genuine such emotive activity would be in his existence. If someone sovereignly determined to cry tomorrow at 3:00 p.m., isn't there something intrinsically disingenuous about this type of emotivity?

Several prominent late twentieth-century evangelical theologians have followed this philosophical trail, offering perspectives of God's suffering based on his sovereign will. Their views promote an important change in the classical and confessional doctrine of God. Robert Reymond proposes what he calls "decretal immutability":

> [God] is not static in his immutability; he is dynamic in his immutability. But his dynamic immutability in no way affects his essential nature as God (that is, his "Godness"); to the contrary, he would cease to be the God of Scripture if he did not will and act in ways the Bible ascribes to him. But he always wills and acts, as Isaiah declared, in faithfulness to his decrees: "In perfect faithfulness you have done marvelous things, things planned long ago" (Isa. 25:1). . . .
>
> . . . Whenever divine impassibility is interpreted to mean that God is impervious to human pain or incapable of empathizing with human grief it must be roundly denounced and rejected. When the Confession of Faith declares that God is "without . . . passions" it should be understood to mean that God has no bodily passions such as hunger or the human drive for sexual fulfillment. As A. A. Hodge writes: "we deny that the properties of matter, such as bodily parts and passions, belong to him."

---

[40] A. J. Mason, *The Faith of the Gospel: A Manual of Christian Doctrine* (New York: Dutton, 1891, revised edition), 32-33.

We do, however, affirm that the creature cannot *inflict* suffering, pain, or any sort of distress upon him *against* his will. In this sense God *is* impassible.[41]

Reymond then proposes further understanding of his position as he quotes J. I. Packer extensively. He agrees with Packer's concept of God having experiences by his own volition.[42]

Bruce Ware asserts that God does not undergo intrinsic change *per se*, but only changes as he relates to his creatures.[43] Ware begins with a "reformulation" of God in time and in the classical understanding of his immutability, extending the concept further into "relational mutability."[44]

> God's disposition toward us in our unforgiven sin is one of judgment, wrath, and condemnation; but in Christ his disposition is one of peace, acceptance, and fatherly love.
>
> This is just an example of what might be called the "relational mutability" of God, a change not of his essential nature . . . but of his attitude and disposition toward his moral creatures in ways that are commensurate to changes that happen in them. So, when we change, say, from rebellion to repentance, God changes commensurately . . .[45]

Ware assesses that changes in God are "commensurate to changes" in the creature. This type of univocal language denigrates the importance of the Creator/creature distinction. When he addresses the matter of divine impassibility, he says:

> God may *experience internally* and *express outwardly* appropriate moral responses to these changed situations

---

[41] Robert L. Reymond, *A New Systematic Theology of the Christian Faith* (Nashville: Thomas Nelson, Inc., 1998), 178-79, emphasis original.

[42] Reymond, *A New Systematic Theology*, 179. The citations are referenced as "Packer, "Theism for our Time," ed. Peter T. O'Brien and David G. Peterson, *God Who is Rich in Mercy* (Grand Rapids: Baker, 1986) 7, 16-17."

[43] James Dolezal, "Still Impassible," 143-44. This is a critical article for our discussion. It is essential reading.

[44] Bruce A. Ware, *Perspectives on the Doctrine of God: Four Views*, ed. Bruce A. Ware (Nashville: Broadman & Holman, 2008), 85.

[45] Ware, *Perspectives*, 91.

when they occur in history. That is, he may literally change in emotional disposition. . . .[46]

When Ware's student, Rob Lister, published his work on divine impassibility, he combined the idea of God's voluntary, willful change in experiences with Ware's idea of relational mutability.[47] Lister's viewpoint attempts to adopt Barthian categories within classical theological constructs concerning God's sovereignty.[48]

From the stand point of divine passion . . . as surely as God's in-time volitional response to a newly redeemed sinner shifts from a posture of judgment to one of forgiveness, God's in-time emotive response to a newly redeemed sinner shifts from a posture of wrath to a posture of loving acceptance.[49]

Now, alongside God's possessing dominion over all his creation, he possesses dominion over himself, that is, a dominion in which he is able to shift from one emotional posture to another.[50] Lister's perspective creates consequential concerns in relation to divine immutability and eternality. He propounds an intrinsic change in God. Dolezal adduces, "God acquires being that he did not eternally possess in his essence."[51]

Other theologians, some with a Reformed background, modify impassibility in the modern era. Kevin Vanhoozer estimates God has authorial sovereignty over his experiences. Vanhoozer interprets God as telling Moses, in Exodus 3:14, that "'I am my own author' or 'I author therefore I am.'"[52] "It is difficult to see," says

---

[46] Ware, *God's Lesser Glory*, 92, emphasis original.

[47] Dolezal, "Still Impassible," 144-46.

[48] Rob Lister, *God Is Impassible and Impassioned*, 179. We have not mentioned the profound influence of Barthian voluntarism in this discussion. Lister cites him approvingly (though not completely uncritically): "As Karl Barth puts it, 'God is not dependent on anything that is not himself; on anything outside Himself. He is not limited by anything outside Himself. On the contrary, everything that exists depends on His will."

[49] Lister, *God Is Impassible and Impassioned*, 179.

[50] Dolezal, "Still Impassible," 145-46.

[51] Dolezal, "Still Impassible," 146.

[52] Kevin J. Vanhoozer, *Remythologizing Theology: Divine Action, Passion, and*

Dolezal, "how this does not make the perfection of God's inner being the consequence of the act of his will and thus something that is . . . created in God."[53]

John Feinberg presents a modern evangelical attempt to find a supposed middle way between classical impassibility and the twentieth-century passibilism of Open Theism and Process Theology. He portrays the classical model as heavily influenced by Greek philosophy resulting in an "impersonal, distant God."[54] Additionally, Feinberg abandons the analogical language category when speaking of God, opting rather for a system advocated by philosopher William Alston that seems to be built on the univocal nature of divine and human psychology.[55] He further rejects classical theism's doctrine of immutability, again positing a *via media* between process and classical theism as he understands them.[56] "God has no choice," writes Feinberg, "but to change from anger to forgiveness when a sinner repents."[57] There is much accommodation to Open Theism's and Process Theism's critique of classical theism in Feinberg's doctrine of God and rejection of classical impassibility.

John Frame presents a plethora of Scriptures on immutability and impassibility in an attempt to maintain solidity among biblical tensions. Frame contends that

> . . . in Amos 7:1-7 God engages in a conversation with a man. . . . In my view this is more than just anthropomorphic description. . . . God is not merely an agent in time; he really is in time, changing as others change.[58]

Authorship (Cambridge: Cambridge University Press, 2010), 446. Cited in Dolezal, "Still Impassible," 142.

[53] Dolezal, "Still Impassible," 142.

[54] John S. Feinberg, *No One Like Him: The Doctrine of God* (Wheaton, IL: Crossway Books, 2001), 62-67. See our previous chapters for a demonstration that this is a false charge.

[55] Feinberg, *No One Like Him,* 78-80. The argument from Alston is cited as William Alston, "Functionalism and Theological Language," in *Readings in the Philosophy of Religion: An Analytic Approach,* ed. [Baruch] Brody (Englewood Cliffs, NJ: Prentice-Hall, 1992).

[56] Feinberg, *No One Like Him,* 264-67.

[57] Feinberg, *No One Like Him,* 272.

[58] John M. Frame, *The Doctrine of God: A Theology of Lordship* (Phillipsburg, NJ:

Frame addresses impassibility under two headings, "Does God Have Feelings" and "Can God Suffer."[59] He reformulates classical theism based in part upon the conclusion that older views demanded a God with no emotions. He assumes that classical theism was too much affected by Greek metaphysical speculation, a point challenged by Weinandy and even Lister. Ultimately Frame concedes, "I agree with Moltmann that Christ's sufferings are the sufferings of God. . . . His experiences as a man are truly his experiences, the experiences of God."[60]

Another contemporary theologian, K. Scott Oliphint, introduces his perspective of God by distinguishing between essential and covenantal attributes in God.[61] Essential attributes are "those attributes that are associated with *God as God*, that is, those attributes that God has apart from creation," while covenantal attributes are not necessarily in God. As an example, he points to the fact of God's creatorship. Creation was not a necessary act of God, hence being Creator is not an essential property of God.[62] As his argument develops, Oliphint affirms a form of passibility in God, acquired from the covenantal attribute received in the incarnation of the second person of the Trinity:

> Second, we should remember that the second person of the Trinity underwent what has been called in the orthodox tradition "the passion." This will be central and paramount in our discussions as we proceed. Christ, the Son of God in the flesh, suffered; he died, and he did that as God-man, the quintessential covenant person. Since that is true, there must be some real and fundamental sense in which God *can* have or experience passions.[63]

Even more recently, in a lecture entitled "Theological Principles from Van Til's Common Grace and the Gospel" delivered to the 2014 Reformed Forum Theology Conference in Gray's Lake, IL,

---

P&R Publishing, 2002), 571.

[59] Frame, *The Doctrine of God*, 608-16.

[60] Frame, *The Doctrine of God*, 613.

[61] Oliphint, *God with Us*, 40. See Appendix 2 for a detailed review of this book.

[62] Oliphint, *God with Us*, 16.

[63] Oliphint, *God with Us*, 87, emphasis original.

Oliphint expressed that several "brilliant" theologians, viz., Augustine, Aquinas, Stephen Charnock, Paul Helm, and Herman Bavinck failed to be "fearlessly anthropomorphic" in their formulation of the doctrine of God. Though they (and many others) correctly assert divine aseity, eternity, and immutability, they have imposed faulty conclusions on these doctrines based on philosophical deduction rather than being "fearlessly anthropomorphic." For Oliphint, this idea does not seem to be a recognition of anthropomorphism in Scripture, but rather that God must be viewed through these anthropomorphisms, and they must shape our theological conclusions. As a result, "much of systematic theology that is done, especially in theology proper, needs a complete revision and rewrite."[64] This is a stunning evaluation and a breathtaking proposal. Have Christians, for nearly two millennia, unknowingly worshiped an idol?

We must state that these evangelical theologians desire to promote a high view of God, but their language introduces confusion into discussions of theology proper. They hope to reach humanity with a sympathizing God for the turbulent storms of life. While we understand their motivation, we suggest that their solution fails to account for other foundational theological facts.[65] They tweak the biblical-theological forms to plow a middle way between impassibility and passibility, but invent new theological categories while straining long-accepted definitions of classical doctrines.

Paul Helm dealt with many of these issues in a paper presented in 1989 to the "Third Edinburgh Conference in Christian Dogmatics." Toward the end he states:

> But could there be *timelessly eternal* affects in God? It is hard to see that there could be. For any change, from wrath to love, from self-sufficiency to self-giving, appears to pre-

---

[64] K. Scott Oliphint, "Theological Principles from Van Til's Common Grace and the Gospel," Lecture delivered at the 2014 Reformed Forum Theology Conference, Gray's Lake, IL, October 2014. http://reformedforum.org/rf14_08/. Accessed 30 March 2015. This is strangely reminiscent of the words written nearly a century earlier by Andrew Seth Pringle-Pattison. See the discussion above.

[65] Do not the Scriptures point us to the incarnate Jesus Christ, our great High Priest, as the one able to sympathize with us in our weakness (Heb. 2: 14-18, 4:14-16)?

suppose or to imply a corresponding change in belief or knowledge. For it is the change in belief which gives to the emotional affect its distinctive character. . . .

If so, then a God who has (undergoes?) emotional changes (whether timelessly eternal or not) also has changes in belief or knowledge, and either was not or is not omniscient.[66]

Helm argues for the proper recognition and interpretation of anthropomorphic and anthropopathic language in Scripture.[67] He notes the importance of the doctrine's link to immutability.[68] Helm argues also against false notions of the doctrine's Greek and metaphysical foundations.[69] He has faithfully defended the biblical, classical, and confessional position on impassibility for more than twenty-five years. Helm encourages other men to look back to the orthodox position of divine impassibility.[70]

In this brief survey, we have noticed alterations and development in the expression of the doctrine of divine impassibility. Throughout the periods under consideration, we noticed many examples of theologians who affirmed their views in continuity with the ancient doctrine received by the church. We observed also that others developed the doctrine, framing it in new and sometimes unexpected ways. As differing philosophical views developed, so also did expressions of the doctrine of God. The end result, at least for evangelical and even Reformed theology, is a broadening acceptance of views that are unknown among orthodox theologians of the earlier period. There can be no question that the various modern proposals are not envisioned in the Reformed Confessions.

---

[66] Paul Helm, "The Impossibility of Divine Passibility," in *The Power and Weakness of God*, ed. Nigel M. de S. Cameron (Edinburgh, Scotland: Rutherford House Books, 1990), 137.

[67] Helm, "The Impossibility of Divine Passibility," 127-34.

[68] Helm, "The Impossibility of Divine Passibility," 128-30.

[69] Helm, "The Impossibility of Divine Passibility," 136.

[70] In more recent times other men have put forth more writing and evidence for the classical position. Paul Helm continues to write on the subject. James Dolezal, Peter Sanlon, and Samuel Renihan have also produced valuable material on the subject.

Excursus:
Hodge and Warfield on Confessional Subscription

In the debate over confessional subscription and the doctrine of divine impassibility, some have suggested that Charles Hodge and B. B. Warfield stand as examples of men who subscribed and defended their Confession (the WCF), but who modified the understanding of the language and intention of chapter 2.1 when it asserts that God is "without body, parts, or passions." In this way, modified views of the doctrine are asserted to be acceptable in subscribing churches. We would suggest that this must be evaluated and understood very carefully. While Hodge and Warfield did largely defend the doctrines of the WCF, their views of confessional subscription must be considered. They explicitly denied any form of strict or full subscription, instead maintaining a much looser view.[71] For churches holding a strict or full view, they should not serve as models.

First, we notice Charles Hodge and a series of incidents related to his views of confessional subscription. In a July 1858 article in *The Biblical Repertory and Princeton Review*, Hodge reports that at the General Assembly of the Presbyterian Church meeting earlier that year, Dr. R. J. Breckinridge proposed that the General Assembly direct the Board of Publication to prepare a commentary on the entire Bible in accordance with the Westminster Standards. It was intended for use in the homes and churches of Presbyterians everywhere. After citing the resolution verbatim, Hodge comments:

> It is evident, from the very nature of this proposal, as well as from the arguments of its advocates, that it contemplates an exposition of the whole Scripture, to which shall be given the sanction of church authority. If the mere suggestion of such an idea does not strike a man dumb with awe, he must be impervious to all argument. It is a fearful thing to give church authority even to articles of faith gathered from the general sense of Scripture. How large a part of the church

---

[71] For a brief statement defining "Full Subscription" see Appendix #1 of the Constitution of the Association of Reformed Baptist Churches of America. http://www.arbca.com/arbca-constitution. Accessed 31 March 2015.

universal, or even of the church of England, can conscientiously adopt the Thirty Nine Articles in their true sense? How do we get along with our more extended Confession? We could not hold together a week, if we made the adoption of all its propositions a condition of ministerial communion. . . . If it is not only difficult but impossible to frame a creed as extended as the Westminster Confession, which can be adopted in all its details by the ministry of any large body of Christians, what shall we say to giving the sanction of the church to a given interpretation of every passage of Scripture?[72]

Hodge's comments apparently elicited strong replies. In the October 1858 issue of the same journal, Hodge published a long article entitled, "Adoption of the Confession of Faith." In that piece, he mentions that a "passing remark in the last number of this journal" brought forth "almost universal condemnation from the Old-school press." Much of the rest of the article provides Hodge's understanding of and defense of his views of confessional subscription. He states:

The proposition, that the adoption of the Confession of Faith does not imply the adoption of every proposition contained in that Confession, might mean much or little. It might be adopted by the most conservative, and is all that the most radical need claim. Still the proposition is undeniably correct.[73]

Hodge proceeds to state that while this is not the whole rule of subscription, it is nevertheless an essential rule. He then describes at great length his own view of subscription to the system of doctrine contained in the Confession. In a later article from 1867,

---

[72] Charles Hodge, "The General Assembly," *The Biblical Repertory and Princeton Review* (July 1858): 561. The relevant section was reprinted in Charles Hodge, *The Church and its Polity* (London: Thomas Nelson, 1879), 380-84.

[73] Charles Hodge, "Adoption of the Confession of Faith," *The Biblical Repertory and Princeton Review* (October 1858): 669. The relevant section was reprinted in Hodge, *The Church and its Polity*, 317-35. Hodge says that he expressed this position so far back as October 1831 (669).

commenting on how Presbyterians adopt the Westminster Confession and Catechisms, he further explains how different churchmen have understood the terms of their subscription: "some understand them to mean that every proposition in the Confession of Faith is included in the profession made at ordination." Hodge does not approve of this position, stating that it "can never be practically carried out." He says, "we do not expect that our ministers should adopt every proposition contained in our standards. This they are not required to do. But they are to adopt the system,"[74] which is then followed by an enumeration of the doctrines he believes compose that system. This is a straightforward denial of the principle of full or strict subscription.

B. B. Warfield held the same view as Hodge. Writing in 1889, he notes that the "Presbyterian world" had recently witnessed "widespread agitation regarding the relation of the churches to the Westminster Standards."[75] The first cause of this unrest was "over strictness . . . in the formula of subscription which is required of office-bearers."[76] So far as Warfield was concerned, a strict view of subscription was unsustainable and led to significant problems. He cites approvingly Charles Hodge's article noted above.[77] In Warfield's estimation, what is called full subscription was one of an assortment of issues fomenting unrest among Presbyterians. He urges what he calls a "liberal formula" of subscription.[78] Among the other reasons for this "restlessness" he notes that some view the Confession as too narrow, restricting fellowship with other professing believers, it is too long and detailed, too scholastic, and it fails to place the gospel and the free offer at the forefront of its

---

[74] Hodge, *The Church and its Polity*, 338.

[75] Benjamin B. Warfield, "The Presbyterian Churches and the Westminster Confession," *The Presbyterian Review* 10:40 (1889): 646.

[76] Warfield, "Presbyterian Churches," 648.

[77] Warfield, "Presbyterian Churches," 649.

[78] Warfield, "Presbyterian Churches," 650. Lest this be misunderstood, Warfield still argues that subscription to the standards must be *quia* subscription, i.e., subscription *because* a Confession accords "with the Word." He proceeds to state that a change to *quatenus* subscription, i.e., subscription *in so far as* a confession accords "with the Word" is "fatal." On this point we agree completely. Warfield, "Presbyterian Churches," 650. Warfield seems to advocate *quia* subscription, not to every proposition in the Confession, but to those that construct the system of the Reformed faith.

statements. Warfield rightly rubbishes these notions. He clearly, however, rejected full or strict confessional subscription.

Little did Charles Hodge know how prescient his remark that the principle "the adoption of the Confession of Faith does not imply the adoption of every proposition contained in that Confession . . . might be adopted by the most conservative, and is all that the most radical need claim" would be. We may notice this in two ways. On the one hand, it allowed Hodge, Warfield, and others to explore new and different formulations of doctrine which they perceived to be outside of the essentials of the system of doctrine. Their willingness to entertain certain forms of evolutionary theory, as well as their rejection of the classic doctrine of divine impassibility, evidence this fact. They were not in any sense being dishonest with their Confession; it was their rejection of full subscription that allowed them to explore new ideas.

On the other hand, the "most radical" of the Presbyterians also had a means by which to undermine and eventually change the faith and practice of the Presbyterian church. The lax views of subscription permitted them to move the boundaries. The seeds Hodge allowed to be sown in 1831 finally brought forth poisoned fruit in 1929. It may have taken long for them to germinate, but they did, to disastrous consequences.

Charles Hodge and B. B. Warfield, rather than serving as witnesses for confessional latitude on divine impassibility actually testify against this idea. They were not committed to the principle of full subscription, and for this reason alone do not satisfy the profile of robustly confessional proponents of a modified view. But perhaps more ominously, their view of subscription allowed men of more liberal theological views eventually to take over the Presbyterian church, leading to the death of orthodoxy in its churches and ministers.

When churches loosen their theological commitments, the inevitable result is decline. It may take two or three generations, but the result cannot be avoided. We must learn this lesson, or the same will happen to our sons and grandsons.

Chapter 10

A Theology of

the Doctrine of Divine Impassibility

(I) Impassibility and the Essence and Attributes of God

Charles J. Rennie

Why does the doctrine of divine impassibility matter? For many Christians, this doctrine is at best obscure and unfamiliar, which may give the impression that it is impractical and unimportant. It should be kept in mind, however, that its contemporary obscurity is a relatively new phenomenon. The doctrine of impassibility was the orthodox consensus for the last two millennia, and most notably included in several Reformed Confessions.[1] As confessional Reformed Christians neither truth nor confessional integrity will permit us to be indifferent or sentimental with respect to this doctrine. All truth is important, but some truths are more important than others. The relation of impassibility to the doctrine of God should, above all else, indicate to us that this is a profoundly significant doctrine which cannot be modified or rejected without extensive theological consequences.

The burden of this chapter is to clarify and defend the orthodox and confessional understanding of the doctrine of impassibility. It will be considered in relation to the essence and attributes of God in this chapter and the divine affections and Christology in the next two chapters, in order to explain what it is and why it is important. Herman Bavinck succinctly summarizes our conclusion:

---

[1] The exact phrase "without body, parts, or passions" appears in the Forty-Two Articles composed by Thomas Cranmer for the Church of England (1552), and appears subsequently in the Thirty-Nine Articles of the Church of England (1563), the Irish Articles (1615), the Westminster Confession of Faith (1647), the Savoy Declaration (1658), and the Second London Confession of Faith (1677/89).

Those who predicate any change whatsoever of God, whether with respect to his essence, knowledge, or will, diminish all his attributes: independence, simplicity, eternity, omniscience, and omnipotence. This robs God of his divine nature, and religion of its firm foundation and assured comfort.[2]

The doctrine of impassibility, classically and confessionally understood, states that God does not "experience inner emotional changes of state, whether enacted freely from within or effected by his relationship to and interaction with human beings and the created order."[3] This definition has recently been subject to revision among evangelical theologians who would otherwise purport to maintain a classical view of God. Some have outright rejected the doctrine,[4] while others have unwittingly done nothing less by way of redefinition.[5]

It should be observed, however, that the doctrine of impassibility does not stand or fall alone. Calling attention to what seems to have escaped the notice of many evangelical critics of the classical understanding of impassibility, Nicholas Wolterstorff, himself a proponent of rejecting the classical doctrine, says:

Over the years in working in this area, it became clear to me that though nowadays the traditional understanding of God is often presented as if it were an assortment of distinct and separate "attributes," in fact, it is as far from being an assortment as anything could possibly be. The attributes were traditionally understood as hanging together in an extraordinarily tight and profound manner; pull out one, and most of the others come along with it. The picture that comes to my mind is of those sweaters knit in such a way

---

[2] Bavinck, *RD*, 2:158.

[3] Weinandy, "Impassibility of God," in *New Catholic Encyclopedia*, 2nd ed., 7:357.

[4] See, e.g., Wayne A. Grudem, *Systematic Theology: An Introduction to Biblical Doctrine* (Grand Rapids: Zondervan, 1994), 166.

[5] Vanhoozer, *First Theology*, 93, "It may come as something of a surprise that a position that gives pride of place to such 'communal' notions as communication and communion would nevertheless wish to affirm the concept of divine impassibility, but such indeed is the case. *Everything hinges on what divine impassibility means, however.*" Emphasis added.

that when you pull on one thread, the whole thing unravels before your eyes. Impassibility is one component in that tightly integrated traditional way of understanding God. . . . Once you pull on the thread of impassibility, a lot of other threads come along. Aseity, for example. . . . One also has to give up immutability (changelessness) and eternity. If God really responds, then God is not metaphysically immutable, and if not metaphysically immutable, then not eternal.[6]

The attributes of God cannot be denied or affirmed in isolation; God cannot be divided. The doctrine of impassibility cannot be modified or rejected without a proportionate alteration to the entire doctrine of the essence and attributes of God. Yet most evangelicals who have proposed revisions and critiques of impassibility have sought to do so while simultaneously affirming the other attributes. Clark Pinnock, a proponent of Open Theism, has indicted the entire evangelical enterprise for its half-heartedness and inconsistency:

Impassibility is undoubtedly the Achilles heel of conventional thinking. It was as self-evident to our ancestors as it is out of question to us, but as soon as one tinkers with it the edifice trembles. . . . Most evangelical theists, however, either do not acknowledge a problem or, if they do, respond to it with half measures. Like Arminius himself, they know modifications have to be made but draw back from making them — at least, coherently. Typically, Calvinists reject impassibility and, therefore, modify immutability but hold onto timelessness, all controlling sovereignty and exhaustive foreknowledge . . . but why would God grieve if he were meticulously sovereign? . . . (A theologian is not obliged to be logically consistent but there is a price to pay for exempting oneself from the laws of rationality, it is intelligibility.). . . . If you retain one, you might as well retain them all. . . . The conventional package of attributes is tightly woven. You cannot deny one, such as impassibility, without casting doubt . . . on others, like immutability. It's like pulling on a thread and unraveling a sweater. A little

---

[6] Wolterstorff, "Does God Suffer?," 45, 47, emphasis original.

boldness is required; tentative changes will not do.[7]

Impassibility is the Achilles heel of classical theism, in that if it is modified or rejected, *everything* must be modified or rejected, which is precisely the path Open Theism has trod. Pinnock's theology is not itself a thing to admire, but, given his rejection of impassibility, we can admire the logical (not biblical!) consistency of his theological conclusions.

Impassibility and the Pattern of Sound Doctrine

We may rejoice that most evangelical revisions of impassibility are not nearly as consistent as Pinnock, or even Wolterstorff, but their inconsistency still comes at a cost. The price is not only intelligibility, as Pinnock pointed out, but is even more serious. Bavinck notes that "[t]hose who predicate any change whatsoever of God . . . diminish all his attributes" and rob "God of his divine nature."[8] Those who are committed to more than a generic Calvinism must be committed to more than God's sovereignty. Impassibility is inseparably related to all of the other attributes of God, perhaps most significantly divine infinity, simplicity, immutability, and omnipotence.

Infinity

Regarding divine infinity, James Dolezal explains, "Divine infinity is often articulated negatively as the opposite of finitude and positively as God's plentitude of being and nature."[9] Divine infinity implies that there is no limit to God's being and perfections (cf. Job 11:7; Psalm 145:3; 1 Kings 8:27; Isa. 40:13; Matt. 5:48). That which is most pertinent to the purpose at hand is the realization that the classical doctrine of impassibility does not rob God of affections, but rather affirms that his affections are infinite with respect to time (i.e., eternal) and perfection. It is of the essence of God *to be* (Exod.

---

[7] Pinnock, *Most Moved Mover*, 76-77.

[8] Bavinck, *RD*, 2:158.

[9] Dolezal, *God without Parts*, 77.

3:14), not to *become*, and therefore he has no beginning or end. He subsists eternally in the fullness and perfection of his own being. He is in "every way infinite" and therefore "*most* holy, *most* wise, . . . *most* loving" (2LCF 2.1, emphasis added).

If it is maintained that God's affections or so-called emotions change, his infinity must also be denied. In this respect, Dolezal argues that God's infinity and immutability stand or fall together.

> God's immutability seems to be an entailment of his infinity. Anything actually infinite in being and perfection can neither lose a perfection it already possesses and remain infinite nor receive any additional act of being since it lacks no actuality; thus it cannot undergo change either by augmentation or diminution.[10]

If God were to undergo an emotional change, or acquire a new emotional experience, that change would be either for the better or for the worse. If for the better, then he must not have been infinite in perfection prior to the change, and therefore was not God. If for the worse, then he would no longer be infinite in perfection after the change, and therefore no longer God.[11]

Moreover, if God subsists in the plentitude of his infinite perfection, *why* would he undergo change? If God were to self-will his own emotional or relational mutability, unto what end would he do so? What greater affection, and what greater perfection, could he attain that he does not already eternally have in himself? Why would he rob himself of any of his infinite perfections through change? And why should he? For an infinite being, "[t]o be immutably good is no point of imperfection, but the height of perfection."[12] Charnock writes:

> Immutability considered in itself, without relation to other things, is not a perfection. It is the greatest misery and imperfection of the evil angels, that they are immutable in malice against God; but as God is infinite in essence,

---

[10] Dolezal, *God without Parts*, 81.
[11] Charnock, *Existence and Attributes*, 1:331.
[12] Charnock, *Existence and Attributes*, 1:328.

infinitely good, wise, holy; so it is a perfection necessary to his nature, that he should be immutably all this, all excellency, goodness, wisdom, immutably all that he is; without this he would be an imperfect Being.[13]

He is most loving because he is infinite love in himself. It may sound comforting to insist that God undergoes emotional changes of state as he relates to his creatures, but in reality it presupposes that God is less, not more, loving. Weinandy expresses the same conclusion in a positive manner.

> . . . *only* an impassible God, and not a passible God, is truly and fully personal, absolutely and utterly loving, and thoroughly capable of interacting with human persons in time and history.[14]

Simplicity

Writing on the confessional doctrine of divine simplicity, that God is "without . . . parts" (2LCF 2.1), Dolezal offers the following explanation.

> The classical doctrine of simplicity . . . famously holds forth the maxim that there is nothing in God that is not God. If there were, that is, if God were not ontologically identical with all that is in him, then something other than God himself would be needed to account for his existence, essence, and attributes. But nothing that is not God can sufficiently account for God. He exists in all his perfection entirely in and through himself.[15]

God is his existence, essence, and attributes. It is God's essence to exist; unlike every other being (i.e., creatures), he cannot not exist as he is, and therefore is unchangeable by nature or essence. A man's existence is distinct from his essence. Though God could have

---

13 Charnock, *Existence and Attributes*, 1:317-18.
14 Weinandy, *Does God Suffer?*, 37-38.
15 Dolezal, *God without Parts*, xvii.

preserved Adam's life forever, by his very nature the first man was capable of *not* existing. It is not of the essence of a man to exist *necessarily*, and therefore man is capable of changing in the manner in which he exists. But God is his essence and existence, and therefore cannot but exist as he always is.[16] In order to maintain that something in God undergoes change, emotions or affections included, God's aseity (i.e., necessary and independent existence) and simplicity must either be explicitly denied or implicitly rejected by way of redefinition.

Furthermore, God is his essence. This cannot be said of any individual created being. For instance, the essence of a particular man is his humanity, but Bill (an individual man) is not identical to the essence of humanity, which equally denotes others within the same species. Bill has other qualities, *accidental* properties, *in addition* to his essence which distinguish him from other men. In other words, we cannot say all that may be predicated of Bill *is identical with the essence* of Bill. We cannot say, "Bill is humanity," but only "Bill is *this* human." God, however, is his essence, so that all that may be predicated of God is identical with the essence of God. *All* that is *in* God *is* God. Therefore, in order to maintain that something in God, such as emotions, undergoes change, God's *essence* must be capable of change, which is impossible.

In defense of divine impassibility against the avalanche of criticism and rejection within conservative Reformed and evangelical circles, Michael Horton proposes that it could be beneficial to shift the discussion of divine passions to the *persons of the Trinity, rather than God's essence*. He writes:

> . . . *it is crucial to bear in mind that impassibility refers to God's essence rather than to the particular persons who share it*. It is the *persons* of the Trinity who are affected by creatures, not the divine *essence* itself. This is true even of human beings. Even in life-altering experiences of delight or despair, one's humanity is not altered; rather, the person is changed. Essences (or natures) cannot feel, will, or act. Only persons can love, be disappointed or delighted, angry or pleased, disturbed or satisfied. God's essence is not a person. It is

---

[16] Charnock, *Existence and Attributes*, 1:187.

only the persons who share this essence who can be affected.[17]

This particular proposal, though well-intended, provides more confusion than clarification. As argued above, Horton is correct to insist upon the distinction between the human essence and a particular human person; individual humans are not identical with their essence. So, a man may delight or despair, just as he may get a sunburn, without any essential change in his human-ness. His attempt to posit similarly of God, however, is incoherent, since God is his essence and the essence is not "shared" in a generic sense, but is numerically and indivisibly one. The persons of the Trinity not only each have the whole undivided divine essence, but they have no subsistence outside of or apart from the divine essence. The divine essence is not a fourth "thing" that the divine persons "share." The divine essence is undivided and common to all three persons of the Trinity.[18]

Articulating orthodox trinitarian theology, the Athanasian Creed confesses this very point.

> For there is one person of the Father, another of the Son, and another of the Holy Ghost. But the Godhead of the Father, of the Son, and of the Holy Ghost, is all one. . . . [T]he Father is Almighty, the Son Almighty, and the Holy Ghost Almighty; and yet they are not three Almighties, but one Almighty.

For the purpose of our present discussion, it may be added that the Father is love, the Son is love, and the Holy Ghost is love, yet they are not three loves, but one love. Although love, joy, and the like may be predicated of the *persons*, they are all nonetheless "*ad extra* relations of the [one] divine essence or nature."[19] To maintain that the persons experience shifting emotions, therefore, would be to

---

[17] Horton, *The Christian Faith*, 249, emphasis original.

[18] Muller, *PRRD*, 3:566, says, "Following the fundamental rule of trinitarian orthodoxy that all of the work of God *ad extra* is the undivided work of the divine persons, orthodox discussion of the *amor voluntarius* [i.e., voluntary love] belongs properly to the doctrine of the essence and attributes, which the persons have in common."

[19] Muller, *PRRD*, 3:569.

suggest that God's essence also undergoes change.

Finally, God is his attributes. There is nothing in God that is not God. Unlike Bill, who is a mixture of essence and accidents, there are no accidents in God. An accident is a non-essential quality or property that exists in something else, such as Bill's height, hair color, and so forth. For instance, Bill may undergo shifting emotions without becoming more or less human. In such a case, Bill would undergo an accidental change, rather than a substantial change, but Bill changes nonetheless. He changes from one manner of existing (e.g., joy) to another manner of existing (e.g., sadness). Conversely, there are no accidental properties, qualities, or attributes in God; all that is predicated *of* God *is* God. For example, God does not merely *have* love as an *accidental property*, such that it can grow and diminish without undergoing *substantial* change. Instead, God *is* love (1 John 4:8). His love, therefore, is as unchanging as his essence and existence. In order to predicate an emotional change in God, the classical and confessional understanding of divine simplicity and aseity must either be explicitly denied or implicitly rejected by way of redefinition.

Immutability

Without equivocation, divine immutability refers to God's inability to undergo any change whatsoever (Mal. 3:6; James 1:17), whether it be considered absolutely (with respect to his essence and attributes), relatively (with respect to space, time, and creation), or ethically (with respect to the constancy of his character). While impassibility more narrowly concerns the affections of God, immutability is the glory of every divine attribute and perfection, and therefore cannot be modified, as we have seen, without consequence. Likewise, because the doctrine of impassibility is a subset of immutability, any revision of the former necessitates a corresponding revision of the latter.

The way this has most commonly been done among contemporary evangelicals is by minimizing the ontological aspects of divine immutability (i.e., the immutability of God's essence). Emotional mutability is advocated within the sole framework of God's ethical immutability, or the constancy of his character, so that God may be said to undergo emotional change while remaining ethically immutable. Dolezal is correct, however, to point out that "the classical understanding of immutability argues that God's ethical immutability requires his ontological immutability as its foundation."[20] Muller agrees:

> If God can become something that he was not, then the constancy of the promises and, indeed, the laws made prior to the change cannot be guaranteed either in or subsequent to the change. Only a God who remains eternally and essentially the same can have a counsel that stands for ever (Isa 46:10) and a covenant that is everlasting (Isa 53:3; Jer 32:40; Heb 13:20).[21]

In other words, God is either immutable in every way, his affections included, or not at all (cf. Heb. 6:18). One cannot minimize God's ontological immutability without logically undermining his ethical immutability. The same thread unravels the whole garment.

Omnipotence

The omnipotence (i.e., all-potency) of God is also intimately tied to divine infinity, simplicity, and immutability (and thus impassibility as well). It is important to understand that there are two ways theologians have spoken about *potency*: active and passive. In relation to divine simplicity, classical theism has always maintained that there is no passive potency in God, who is pure actuality. A passive potency is a potentiality in the strictest sense, and refers to the ability or capacity for something to be affected. On the other hand, an active potency is a power or ability to bring about an effect, or actualize the potential of something else. Active potency "is a kind of act relative to the substance possessing it, though a kind of potency relative to the action it grounds."[22] In the creature, active potency is always mixed with passive potency. For example,

---

[20] Dolezal, "Still Impassible," 129-30.
[21] Richard A. Muller, "Incarnation, Immutability, and the Case for Classical Theism," *WTJ* 45 (1983): 30.
[22] Feser, *Scholastic Metaphysics*, 39.

a husband has both the active potency (i.e., power) to make his wife feel loved, effecting an emotional change within her, and the passive potency (i.e., potentiality) to realize his capability to do so. He has the power to effect change and the potential to undergo change in the process.

In view of the doctrine of divine simplicity, that there is no passive potency in God to be other than he eternally is, classical theists have maintained that only "active potency" can be attributed to God, yet with an important qualification. In the example of the husband, when he exercises his active potency or power to love his wife, he undergoes a change from "being capable of," to having that capability "realized." "Yet God's active might is from-eternity-active might."[23] Unlike creatures, in the exercise of his power, God is not seeking greater fulfillment or perfection in his own being. "Pure active potency or power unmixed with any passive potency or potentiality is just pure actuality," that is, God.[24] To maintain that God is pure actuality is not to close God in a cold, dark box and deny him the ability to act. Rather, it is to confess that he is *pure act*, — an all-potent, ever-living, always-active agent capable of effecting change outside of himself (i.e., in his works *ad extra*), without, however, himself undergoing any change whatsoever. Thus, a proper understanding of omnipotence denies God the active potency to effect his own change. To say that God is sovereign over his own emotional changes would require that he have power to bring about his own passive potency. Indeed, it would require that there be in God a mixture of active and passive potency, which necessarily entails a rejection of divine simplicity, immutability, and a loss of the Creator/creature distinction.

Moreover, to speak of a change in God's emotional state would inevitably undermine omnipotence itself, if for no other reason than the necessary relationship between his omnipotence and his infinity. He is "all-potent" because his power is as infinite and perfect as his being. His power is in need of no further perfection, either from an internal or an external principle. Any change whatsoever in God has to be explained either in terms of greater perfection or lesser perfection. The former would imply that God

---

[23] Hoogland, *God, Passion and Power*, 154.
[24] Feser, *Scholastic Metaphysics*, 39.

was not yet infinite, while the latter would imply that God is no longer infinite. If God is not infinite, then God's power cannot be infinite. "If he be made better, he was not almighty before; something of power was wanting to him."[25] If God possesses passive potency, then he cannot possess an infinite active potency, in which case he would be unable to actualize any of what Scripture terms his "mighty works" (Deut. 3:24; Psalm 145:4; Matt. 11:20-21). The omnipotence (i.e., all-potency) of God is intimately tied to divine infinity, simplicity, and immutability (and thus impassibility as well). To pull the thread of divine impassibility is to unravel the whole truth of God's existence, essence, and attributes.

Impassibility and Contemporary Calvinism

Nonetheless, as Pinnock has pointed out, Calvinistic evangelicals have been willing to throw immutability under the bus in order to redefine impassibility, and have most commonly done so by shifting the focus exclusively to divine sovereignty.[26]

God's Sovereignty over His own Relational Mutability

In an attempt to circumvent an Open Theist understanding of God as a passive and impotent victim, D. A. Carson avers that God is sovereign over his own emotional mutability. Carson says:

If God loves, it is because he chooses to love; if he suffers, it

---

[25] Charnock, *Existence and Attributes*, 1:334.

[26] This trend has greater affinity with neo-orthodox theology of the early- to mid-twentieth century than it does with confessional Reformed orthodoxy. Karl Barth, reducing everything to his own peculiar understanding of divine freedom, proposed something very similar: "[T]he personal God has a heart. He can feel and be affected. He is not impassible. He cannot be moved from outside by an extraneous power. But this does not mean that He is not capable of moving Himself. No, God is moved and stirred, yet not like ourselves in powerlessness, but in His own free power, in His innermost being: moved and touched by Himself, i.e., open, ready, inclined (*propensus*) to compassion with another's suffering." *Church Dogmatics*, vol. II/1, ed. G. W. Bromiley and T. F. Torrance and trans. T. H. L. Parker, W. B. Johnston, Harold Knight, and J. L. M. Haire (1957; reprint, Peabody, MA: Hendrickson Publishers, 2010), 370.

is because he chooses to suffer. God is impassible in the sense that he sustains no "passion," or emotion, that makes him vulnerable from the outside, over which he has no control, or which he has not foreseen.[27]

Rob Lister adopts the same voluntarist approach. He says:

> I take it that God is impassible in the sense that he cannot be manipulated, overwhelmed, or surprised into an emotional interaction that he does not desire to have or allow to happen. But this is not at all the same thing as saying that God is devoid of emotion, nor is it the equivalent of saying that he is not affected by his creatures. To the contrary, God is *impassioned* (i.e., *perfectly* vibrant in his affections), and he may be affected by his creatures, but as God, he is so in ways that accord rather than conflict with his will to be so affected by those whom, in love, he has made.[28]

According to such argumentation, among the "whatsoever comes to pass" that God has freely ordained are his own inner emotional responses to the in-time actions and circumstances of his people. In an attempt to protect God's essential and eternal immutability, Lister proposes a duality in God: God-in-eternity and God-in-time. In order for God-in-eternity to relate and respond to his creatures in time, he "takes on" temporal properties. K. Scott Oliphint similarly distinguishes these properties from God's essential character, while very clearly affirming that they nonetheless effect a real change *in God*. He writes:

> This is covenant condescension, and God takes on new properties in executing it; . . . It was, to be sure, a monumental decision. It changed the *mode* of God's existence for eternity; he began to exist according to relationships *ad extra*, which had not been the case before. But it in no way changed his essential character.[29]

---

[27] Carson, *The Difficult Doctrine*, 60.
[28] Lister, *God is Impassible and Impassioned*, 36.
[29] Oliphint, *God with Us*, 254-55.

In other words, these contingent emotional experiences and properties are not essential properties of God, but they are nonetheless *in God* so as to change "the *mode* of God's existence for eternity." So what are they? They are contingent accidental properties in God,[30] "certain dispositions of passion that God takes

---

[30] Accidental properties and essential attributes are distinguished in the manner of their existence. An essential attribute is inherent and necessary to the essence or what-ness of a thing which exists independently *in itself* and not in another. An accidental property refers to a quality or characteristic that exists *in another* and is not necessary to the essence of the thing in which it inheres. According to the voluntaristic proposal, these temporal-covenantal properties exist *in God,* yet they are distinguished from the essence of God and, therefore, may be defined as accidental properties, qualities, or characteristics.

In *God with Us*, Oliphint states, "I will be arguing below that there are essential properties relative to God (i.e., the Son of God) and other contingent (accidental?) properties that God takes on" (154). Given Oliphint's particular proposal, that the incarnation is the paradigm for these so-called covenantal properties (i.e., that God takes on covenantal properties throughout redemptive history in the same manner the Son of God assumed human flesh without any change in his essential divinity), he asks, "Would that imply that the uniting of a human nature to the Logos was an accidental union?" (154). The question is an important one, because the plausibility of his particular proposal depends upon a particular, namely accidental, understanding of the incarnation. He quotes Thomas Aquinas and John Owen who clearly reject an accidental union in the incarnation and then, without interacting with their argument (which sets forth a classical creedal Christology), Oliphint dismisses not only their terminology but also the entire question as an unnecessary consequence of Thomistic substance metaphysics (*God with Us*, 153-56).

Addressing all of Oliphint's metaphysical assumptions would take us too far afield, but the question still needs to be answered: What is the nature of the relationship between the human nature and the person of Christ? In order for his proposal to work, the incarnation would have to entail an accidental union; either the divine nature or the person of the Son would have had to unite to itself certain nonessential, contingent, accidental human properties. Yet, this cannot be affirmed of the incarnation and thus the proposal fails.

The human nature was not united to the Son, much less the divine nature, as accidental nonessential properties. Rather, the *person* of the Son "did when the fullness of time was come take upon him man's nature, with all the essential properties . . . so that two whole, perfect, and distinct natures, were inseparably joined together in one person: without conversion, composition, or confusion" (2LCF 7.2); he did not assume accidental created properties, but a whole *essential* human nature, that is, a reasonable soul and true body. There was not an absolute necessity that the Son become a man, but having freely decreed to do so, it was a consequent necessity that he assume *all* that is inherent and necessary to the essence or what-ness of a man.

Likewise, the union of the human nature with the person of the Son was not an

on in respect to his creation."[31] Thus, while he self-wills his own "relational mutability" in time, this voluntarist approach maintains that God is able to remain essentially immutable.[32]

As Dolezal explains, it is absolutely critical to emphasize that, according to the voluntarist approach to impassibility, these emotions are real changes *in God*, and not merely in the external works or revelation of God. He asserts:

> [F]or Lister, immutability does not mean that God cannot be internally changed in any sense. God voluntarily wills changes in his affections. Furthermore, Lister is clear that God's responsiveness to his creatures involves "a transition that occurs *in God*." In other words, emotive change is intrinsic to God, an *ad intra* operation, not merely in his *ad*

---

accidental union, but substantial. "Human nature" is that by which a human is what it is, while a "person" is the individual subject of a rational nature (i.e., *this* human), "by which nature becomes self-existent *and is not an accident of another entity*" (Bavinck, *RD*, 3:306, emphasis added). The relationship between person and nature is, therefore, essential and inseparable. Ordinarily, a person does not exist apart from its nature, nor the individual nature apart from its person. As Bavinck notes:

> For though it [i.e., the human nature of Christ] did not complete itself with a personality and selfhood of its own, it was nevertheless from the start personal in the Logos, who as subject lived, thought, willed, acted, suffered, died, and so on in and through it with all its constituents, capacities, and energies" (Bavinck, *RD*, 3:307).

The human nature is that by which the person of Christ is what he is, a true man; the divine nature is that by which the person of Christ is what he is, true God. The relationship between person and nature is substantial, not accidental. Although the two natures of Christ do not exist as independent entities apart from his person, neither does the human nature of Christ accidentally exist *in another* any more than the divine nature exists *in another*. It is always the one person, the same subject, that lives, thinks, and acts according to the two natures respectively.

Oliphint states, "The christology we have been delineating here is nothing new" (156). Not only is it new, it is incoherent. It is erroneous to speak of an accidental union in the incarnation, and it would be equally problematic to speak of a hypostatic/substantial union of two essential natures in the Son prior to the virgin birth, much less in the Godhead. Cf. Bavinck, *RD*, 3:304-08.

[31] Lister, *God is Impassible and Impassioned*, 225.

[32] Lister, *God is Impassible and Impassioned*, 210-11. Cf. Ware, "An Evangelical Reformulation of the Doctrine of the Immutability of God," 431-46.

extra works of unfolding revelation. It follows that the fullness of God's inner actuality is variously altered by these (accidental) changes.[33]

An Appraisal and Response

The voluntarist approach, and Lister's proposal in particular, may be the most thoughtful attempt at a revision of the doctrine of divine impassibility that intends to maintain a biblical distinction between Creator and creature. Nonetheless, such an approach runs afoul of God's infinity, simplicity, immutability, and as will be argued, even divine sovereignty itself, and therefore unwittingly robs God of his divine nature. It demonstrates once again that you cannot pull on one thread without undermining the integrity of the entire classical and confessional garment. In light of what has already been said with respect to the tightly woven garment of classical theism, consider the following brief observations.

First, voluntarism robs God of his *infinite sovereignty*. It may seem strange that a view which exalts God's sovereignty, to the detriment of God's immutability and impassibility, would undermine the very truth it purports to protect. By predicating change or emotional and existential newness of God, however, God is robbed of his infinite perfections. Any kind of change *in God*, regardless of how it is explained, must either be for the better or for the worse. For instance, someone might argue that it would be an imperfection in God if he did not sovereignly will to undergo emotional suffering when confronted with the suffering of his people (which seems to be the assumption of the voluntarist approach). On these grounds, it might be concluded that such suffering in God would be "for the better." This conclusion would imply that God was not yet infinite in his perfections, but had potential for new modes of perfection. Not only would this give a necessary and positive role to evil and suffering in the perfecting of God's love, but it also serves to undermine the infinity of God's perfections.[34] Again, we must conclude with Charnock, "If he be

---

[33] Dolezal, "Still Impassible," 145. Cf. Lister, *God is Impassible and Impassioned*, 179.

[34] This argument is developed in greater detail by David Bentley Hart in "No

made better, he was not almighty before; something of power was wanting to him."[35] If God possesses passive potency, then he cannot possess an infinite active potency.

Dolezal helpfully clarifies the relationship between divine impassibility and sovereignty as follows:

> The connection between impassibility and divine sovereignty is an important one. If God were to be emotionally changed by the actions of his creatures it might imply some sort of dominance of the creature over God and so flout God's absolute sovereignty over creation. Impassibility, then, is an indispensable condition for the traditional account of God's sovereignty. But this does not mean that it is a proper *function* of God's sovereignty. God is not impassible *because* he is sovereign. In fact, quite the opposite is true—he is perfectly sovereign over all creation because he is impassible and so cannot be subject to change on account of creatures.[36]

If it is maintained that impassibility is a function of God's sovereignty, so that he exercises control over his own emotional changes, God is unwittingly robbed of his omnipotence. Only by confessing that God is "without . . . passions" can the biblical doctrine of divine sovereignty be preserved.

Second, self-causation robs God of his *aseity* (i.e., absolute independence). Not only does the voluntarist approach undermine the infinite sovereignty of God, it also rests upon dubious philosophical assumptions that, if maintained, rob God of his aseity. In order for God to be sovereign over his own emotional mutability, it must be assumed that it is possible for something to be the cause of its own actuality. However, potency can only be actualized by *something else* that is already actual. That which is potential cannot be the cause of its own actuality precisely because it is merely potential rather than actual. If it is maintained that God self-wills, in time, new emotional changes of state and new existential properties,

---

Shadow of Turning: On Divine Impassibility," *Pro Ecclesia* 11.2 (2002): 191.

[35] Charnock, *Existence and Attributes*, 1:334.

[36] Dolezal, "Still Impassible," 141.

these properties must be considered either divine or created. In either case, God would be robbed of his aseity.

If it is maintained that these newly-acquired ways of existing are divine, the proposal would necessarily entail that God be the cause of his own actuality — self-causing a new manner of existing. Yet such a proposal (i.e., that something be its own cause) is logically impossible and theologically undesirable (i.e., that God has a cause). As Charnock points out, although God is the first cause of all things, he is not caused by anything, not even by himself. He says:

> Who hath not being from another, cannot but be always what he is: God is the first Being, an independent Being; he was not produced of himself, or of any other, but by nature always hath been, and, therefore, *cannot by himself, or by any other, be changed from what he is in his own nature.*[37]

Neither God's essence nor existence have a cause, and therefore it is impossible that he be his own cause. God is his essence *and* existence; it is God's nature to exist. He is not the cause of his own existence, for it is his essence simply *to be* (Exod. 3:14), and therefore he cannot but be always what he is. God cannot not exist. If God cannot not exist, and it is of his essence to exist, then he cannot acquire new modes of existing, but must always be what he is.[38] Charnock captures the idea well, saying, "As he hath a necessary existence, so he hath a necessary unchangeableness."[39] If God were capable of self-willing newly acquired modes of existing, he would no longer have a necessary existence; such a god is nothing more than a metaphysical myth.

Lister's revision of impassibility and immutability, in favor of divine sovereignty, rests upon dubious philosophical assumptions which undermine God's aseity. Under the umbrella of omnipotence, Lister has ironically attributed to God the very thing that God does

---

[37] Charnock, *Existence and Attributes*, 1:319, emphasis added.

[38] Contra Oliphint, *God with Us*, 254-55, where he says, "He remains who he is, but decides to be something else as well; he decides to be the God of the covenant. It was, to be sure, a monumental decision. It changed the *mode* of God's existence for eternity; he began to exist according to relationships *ad extra*, which had not been the case before."

[39] Charnock, *Existence and Attributes*, 1:187.

not have the power to do—change. Charnock explains:

> Mutability is absolutely inconsistent with simplicity, whether the change come from an internal or external principle. . . . God being infinitely simple, hath nothing in himself which is not himself, *and therefore cannot will any change in himself,* he being his own essence and existence.[40]

God cannot decree his own mutability, neither can he be his own cause, for it is of the essence of God to be without a cause.

If it is maintained that these newly acquired ways of existing are *created* properties *in God,* it would no less undermine the aseity of God.[41] Dolezal explains:

> Regarding God's pure actuality and perfection, the voluntarist version of impassibility implies that God brings about aspects of his being as effects of his will. God is not perfect (i.e., complete) in being if he is in fact acquiring new states of actuality, emotive or otherwise. Furthermore, that which is the consequent of God's efficacious will is a reality that is produced, or caused, and is therefore a created reality. *But if God is self-caused, even partiality [sic], then he is in fact a creature and is not now the God he has been from all eternity.*[42]

Oliphint is surely correct; if God were to self-will created properties *within himself,* he would be changed in "the mode of his existences for eternity." But at what cost? As Dolezal points out, his new mode of existence would necessarily be that of a creature and no longer the God he has been from all eternity.

Third, whether they be conceived of as divine or created, to predicate accidental properties of God would rob him of his *simplicity.* The voluntarist approach proposes that God "takes on" temporal emotional properties which are "in God," though distinct

---

[40] Charnock, *Existence and Attributes,* 1:332-33, emphasis added.

[41] K. Scott Oliphint, in fact, asserts that God has taken on temporal or created properties. See Oliphint, *God with Us,* 13, n. 8, 198, 208, and 209.

[42] Dolezal, "Still Impassible," 150, emphasis added. "Partiality" should be "partially."

from his essence, that enable God to be affected by his creation. By all accounts, these alleged properties would be *accidental*, rather than essential, qualities in God. Yet it is foundational to the doctrine of divine simplicity that there be no accidental property in God. All that is in God is God, so that God is his essence, existence, and attributes. In order to make room within classical theism for a God who is capable of emotional change, therefore, divine simplicity must first be compromised. As Dolezal points out below, the compromise is too great.

> [T]he voluntarist account of impassibility runs afoul of the doctrine of God's simplicity by implying that God is composed of essence and accidents. Lister dubs this God's "duality." The relations and emotive states that God chooses for himself, and which accrue to him over time, are genuine existential features of his being, and yet are not identical with his divine nature. This means that God's fullness of life and being must be explained in virtue of something other than his own divinity. Not all that is in God is God. This also means that God depends on that which is not God—the acquired relations which are consequents of his efficacious will—in order to possess the fullness of being that presently belongs to him. This strikes at the very heart of God's self-sufficiency and absoluteness.[43]

Fourth, relational mutability robs God of his *immutability*. It is no solution, as some have supposed, to advocate a God that is impassible in his transcendence and passible in his immanence, or immutable in his essence and mutable in his relationality. This has the appearance of moving the discussion away from the essence and attributes of God, but in reality does much more. Although Carson is sympathetic to a revision of the doctrine of impassibility, he is not in favor of divorcing the God who *is* from the God who is *with us*.

Nor is it adequate to suggest a solution that insists that the immanent Trinity (which refers to God as he is in himself,

---

[43] Dolezal, "Still Impassible," 150. He cites Lister, *God is Impassible and Impassioned*, 226.

transcendent from creation and focusing on his internal acts) is utterly impassible, while the economic Trinity (which refers to God as he is immanent in his creation, focusing solely on God's deeds outside of himself and in relation to his creation) does indeed suffer, including the suffering of love. I worry over such a great divorce between God as he is in himself and God as he interacts with the created order. Such distinctions have heuristic usefulness now and then, but the resulting synthesis in this case is so far removed from what the Bible actually says that I fear we are being led down a blind alley.[44]

Not only does such a shift in the discussion lead us down a blind alley, it dangerously presupposes two mutually exclusive Gods: the one who is (transcendent, impassible, immutable, and so on) and the other who is with us (immanent, passible, mutable, and so on). It is ironic, therefore, that the very proposal that seeks to affirm God's ability to relate genuinely with his creation culminates in a relationship with a God who, in significant ways, is different from the one who *is*.

Too much of the contemporary discussion tends to treat God's transcendence as an ontological problem that needs to be overcome. It is assumed that God must be affected by his creation in order to be truly relatable. How can God create, govern, redeem, and be affected by his creation, it is asked, without jeopardizing his transcendent immutability? Contemporary Calvinists have tended to solve this "problem" by proposing that God freely and sovereignly takes on temporal, relational, relative, and covenantal properties (i.e., accidental properties) that are capable of being affected by creation without affecting God's essential being. Utilizing the example of the property of God *as Creator*, Oliphint clearly lays out their concern. He asserts:

[I]s the property "Creator" of the essence of God? One way to answer that question is to ask whether it was *necessary* for God to create. Did God create the universe because *he had to*? . . . [To say that the property "Creator" is of the essence of

---

[44] Carson, *The Difficult Doctrine*, 59.

God] would mean that God was in need of [creation] in order to be who he essentially is. So "being Creator" is not an essential property that God has. It would seem, then, that God has properties that are essential to him and others that are not essential to him.[45]

The name "Creator," like the name Lord, is a name predicated of God relative to creation. Oliphint's presupposition is that creation must bring about a new relation *in God*, that of Creator, and therefore if "Creator" is an essential property of God, creation would be essential to what God is. In an attempt to preserve God's transcendence and independence, therefore, Oliphint concludes that there must be non-essential properties that God takes on in order to relate to the created order.

The argument is built upon two assumptions. First, that God's transcendence, indeed essence, hinders his works *ad extra*. The second provides the reason for the first, namely, that God's works *ad extra* affect a change, a new relationship, in God. It is proposed, therefore, that God sovereignly overcomes this problem by taking on mutable, relational, non-essential properties so that he may be affected without essential change.

The inadequacy of the proposed solution must be pointed out. Change is change, and any change *in God* would undermine his immutability. As Dolezal writes:

All change, whether of essence or accidents, causes the one changed to exist in a way that one previously did not. . . . It matters not whether the change is essential or accidental; all real change introduces existential newness and is repugnant to a God who is being and not becoming.[46]

Whether the change is essential or accidental, it is such that it brings about *in God* a new manner of existing. Assuming it were possible for God to have such properties by which he undergoes change, it would still be *God* who is changed.

Moreover, Oliphint's argument assumes what it fails to prove,

---

45 Oliphint, *God with Us*, 16-17.
46 Dolezal, "Still Impassible," 150.

that the so-called relative attributes of classical theism are called such because they signify properties that are relative *in God*. Both the novelty and the category error of this assumption need to be pointed out. Zanchi is representative of classical theism, when he writes:

> [H]e cannot be changed . . . by any passive potency which is in himself. For he is a most simple and perfect act; and therefore cannot be in potency to anything, be it essential, or accidental. All other things may be changed by his power, by which they are, and upon which they depend.[47]

As was argued above, God possesses an uncreated active potency, that is, a power to create which belongs only to a Creator, whether he chose to create or not. God's power is a from-eternity-active power. In other words, God is pure *act,* all-potent, an ever-living, always active agent with the active potency to effect change outside of himself, without any passive potency whatsoever to undergo change within himself. Thus, Zanchi concludes:

> Those names which argue a relative respect betwixt God and his creatures, and the names Creator, Lord, Redeemer, &c. are indeed in time given to him, and not from eternity, yet so as that no new thing is added to him, neither is there any change in him.[48]

The name Creator signifies an absolute *reality* essential to God from eternity. Yet, it is a *name* which is given to him, insofar as it signifies a new relation established *in the creature* relative to the ever-existing immutable Creator. It is a name given to God that signifies to us, not a new reality in God, but what it means for us to be a creature; a creature is one who is dependent upon, and owes obedience to, the one in whom it lives, moves, and has its being (i.e., the Creator). Therefore, it is a category error to equate these newly-proposed temporal-covenantal properties with the relative properties of classical theism. Unlike the latter, these newly-

---

47 Zanchi, *Life Everlasting*, 73.
48 Zanchi, *Life Everlasting*, 20.

proposed temporal-covenantal properties are non-essential (i.e., accidental), ontologically relative, created realities in God that are assumed to be necessary, not only for God to be able to create, but also for him to be capable of relating to his creation.

Contrary to the voluntarist's assumptions, God possesses active potency, or a power to create which belongs only to a "Creator," whether he chose to create or not. But the fact of the matter remains that God did, by a single and eternal act of his will, choose to create. As Michael Dodds writes:

> In this way, it is possible for God, without changing his will, to will that certain things be changed. Without change of will, even we can will that one thing be done first and another afterward, as I might decide to go to the movies not now but later this evening. Without changing his will, God may will that the world exist not eternally, but "after" not existing. The fact that God eternally wills the existence of the world does not require God will the world to exist eternally. Similarly, the fact that God wills that the world have a beginning does not imply a beginning in God's will to will the beginning of the world.[49]

In a single from-eternity-act of his will, God decreed to create at a certain "time," and to establish a new relation within creation itself. The name "Creator" signifies the nature of that relationship: creation itself is given a new relation to the ever-existing immutable Creator. The *ad extra* work of creation brought about a real change in the creature, but not in God (cf. Psalm 102:26-28). Dodds clarifies:

> When we say God has no real relation to creatures, we do not imply that he is remote or that there is no relationship at all between him and creatures. We rather designate the special kind of relation that exists between God and creatures, which allows both for God's complete distinction from creation and for the utter intimacy of his presence to each creature as the source of its very to-be (*esse*). . . . *There is a relation between God and creature, and it is precisely the sort of*

---

[49] Dodds, *Unchanging God of Love*, 181.

relation proper to beings that are not of the same order. We may call it a 'mixed relation.' It is the sort of relation that exists whenever two things are related to each other in such a way that one depends upon the other, but the other does not depend upon it.[50]

Our relation as creatures depends upon God as our Creator, but God is Creator with or without a creation.[51] Thus, the very relationship which is established is "precisely the sort of relation proper to beings that are not of the same order." In other words, God does not need us to provide him with properties that enable him to be immanent; neither must he be capable of being emotionally affected in order to be relatable. He does not need to overcome his transcendence. It is precisely as the one who transcends the created order that he relates the creature to himself.[52] To argue otherwise would inevitably rob God of his immutability, indeed, of his divine nature.

Conclusion

Pinnock appears to be close to the mark, when he writes, "Many are taking advantage of the rhetoric of the open view of God, which Bible readers find compelling, and are trying to work it into their own language."[53] With the voluntarist approach in mind, Dolezal observes that "their proposal would be better characterized as self-controlled passibilism rather than as a version of impassibility."[54] Much of the discussion over the doctrine of impassibility tends to reveal that the contemporary theological agenda has more or less to do with a desire to affirm the God of Open Theism without a total abandonment of the God of classical theism. However, once the

---

[50] Dodds, *Unchanging God of Love*, 168, emphasis added.

[51] This argument is developed in greater detail by Aquinas in *The Power of God*, 222-25.

[52] This argument is developed in greater detail by Richard A. Muller, "God: Absolute & Relative, Necessary, Free, & Contingent," in R. Scott Clark and Joel E. Kim, eds., *Always Reformed: Essays in Honor of W. Robert Godfrey* (Escondido, CA: Westminster Seminary California, 2010), 58-59.

[53] Pinnock, *Most Moved Mover*, 75.

[54] Dolezal, "Still Impassible," 151.

thread of immutability, and impassibility in particular, is pulled, the integrity of the entire garment becomes compromised. As Charnock observes:

> In our notion and conception of the Divine perfections, his perfections are different: the wisdom of God is not his power, nor his power his holiness, but immutability is the centre wherein they all unite. There is not one perfection but may be said to be and truly is, immutable; none of them will appear so glorious without this beam, this sun of immutability, which renders them highly excellent without the least shadow of imperfection. How cloudy would his blessedness be if it were changeable! How dim his wisdom, if it might be obscured! How feeble his power, if it were capable to be sickly and languished! How would mercy lose much of its lustre, if it could change into wrath; and justice much of its dread, if it could be turned into mercy, while the object of justice remains unfit for mercy, and one that hath need of mercy continues only fit for the Divine fury! But unchangeableness is a thread that runs through the whole web.[55]

---

[55] Charnock, *Existence and Attributes*, 1:318.

Chapter 11

A Theology of the Doctrine of Divine Impassibility

(II) Impassibility and the Divine Affections

Charles J. Rennie

We have argued that because God is infinite, simple, immutable, and omnipotent in his being, it is necessary to affirm divine impassibility. Bavinck has perceptively noted:

> Those who predicate any change whatsoever of God, whether with respect to his essence, knowledge, or will, diminish all his attributes: independence, simplicity, eternity, omniscience, and omnipotence. This robs God of his divine nature, and religion of its firm foundation and assured comfort.[1]

In other words, to predicate of God emotional changes of state will inevitably undermine the very attributes that distinguish the Creator from the creature.

While such a conclusion is exegetically, theologically, and rationally necessary, it raises certain questions concerning the nature of the divine affections in general and the love of God in particular. Because change is inseparably annexed to how creatures experience love, joy, etc., the foregoing conclusion raises issues concerning the way love may be predicated of an infinite, simple, immutable, and omnipotent God, who in no way undergoes change. If God's love is in every way simple, infinite, and immutable, moreover, how is it that God's affections do not extend to all things equally (e.g., the elect and reprobate)? These and related questions will be the focus of what follows.

---

[1] Bavinck, *RD*, 2:158.

Impassibility and the Divine Love

Classical theism has always affirmed that love may be properly predicated of God in a manner consistent with his unique mode of being and immutable perfections, *essentially* (or, absolutely) with regard to the love by which he loves himself (*ad intra*), and *relatively* with regard to the affection by which he loves his creatures with respect to himself (*ad extra*). Furthermore, while the inequality among the objects of God's love denotes a real distinction in the creature, and the degree to which each individual experiences his love, it cannot thereby imply a change or variation in God whose love is as immutable as his being. In order to flesh this out and account for both the nature of God's unchangeable love and the creatures' varying experience of it, it is necessary, in the first place, to identify the objects of God's love, and in the second place, to identify the nature of divine love according to its mode of being.

The Objects of God's Love

Although our immediate interest may be with regard to God's affections toward his creation, and especially his love for the elect, the discussion most properly belongs to the essence and attributes of God, in particular the intra-trinitarian, or natural, love of God. This is confirmed when we bear in mind that the divine "affections are all *ad extra* relations of the divine essence or nature."[2] In other words, God's love, considered as a divine affection, has its source in the essence and being of God (*ad intra*) and terminates upon certain objects outside of God (*ad extra*).[3] Or, to put it yet another way,

---

[2] Muller, *PRRD*, 3:569. This is especially true with regard to the love of God, which may be treated both *naturally* as an essential attribute of God (*ad intra*), as well as *affectively or voluntarily* as a divine affection (*ad extra*).

[3] Muller, *PRRD*, 3:554. As it is noted elsewhere, there is a qualified sense in which there are no "affections" in God. Love, for instance, does not exist in God in the same way that it exists in the creature. What we call an affection in the creature is more properly called a perfection in God, for it formally exists in God in an infinitely more eminent way, with all distinctively creaturely characteristics removed (i.e., much of what we, as creatures, associate with affections). Nonetheless, the so-called divine affections signify God's several perfections, not as they are considered in themselves (perfections *ad intra*), but the perfections of God relative to objects outside of himself (*ad extra*). Therefore, as a perfection, God's

God's love *toward us* has its source and foundation in God's love *in and for himself*, wherein he most perfectly, unchangeably, and absolutely loves himself. Therefore, God's love *toward us* must be understood in relation to God's love *in himself*, his own goodness being the primary object of his love, and therefore the proper place to begin. Such a starting point will result in the conclusion that God's love toward his creation, particularly his love for the elect, is as immutable, fixed, and constant as God's love for himself, however varied our experience of its effects may be.

That our inquiry into the love of God must begin with God's intra-trinitarian love for himself, the attribute of love considered in itself apart from the existence of any creature, is further confirmed when a basic definition of love is taken into consideration. Generally, love is a fixed disposition of the will which seeks union with that which it deems good and "having obtained it to rest in the same . . . whereby one doth entirely adjoin himself to an other, and wholly doth both rest and delight himself in him."[4] Christian theologians have always located the *summum bonum*, the highest good, in God alone, for he alone is goodness (Matt. 19:17). He alone, therefore, is the proper object of his own love, eternally resting and delighting in his own infinite goodness.

The Love of God Proper

This natural love which characterizes the divine life has been made

---

love is infinite and immutable, but as an affection, it may be said to vary insofar as God does not will to communicate his infinite and immutable love to all creatures alike.

[4] Zanchi, *Life Everlasting*, 357. Cf. Owen, *Works*, 2:24, "Generally, love is an affection of union and nearness, with complacency therein." Augustine, *De Trinitate*, in *NPNF*, First Series, vol. 3, ed. Philip Schaff and trans. Arthur West Haddan (1887; reprint, Peabody MA: Hendrickson Publishers, 2012), VIII.x.14, "But what is love or charity, which divine Scripture so greatly praises and proclaims, except the love of good? . . . [S]o let it suffice to have said thus much, that we may have, as it were, the hinge of some starting-point, whence to weave the rest of our discourse." So also Gouge, *Hebrews*, 1:228, sec. 63, "*Love* unites the heart to the thing loved. *Joy* enlargeth the heart with a pleasing content in that which it apprehendeth to be good. Thus it is said of the church, that in regard of the confluence of people, her 'heart should be enlarged,' Isa. Ix. 5, that is, she should rejoice. Joy is contrary to grief. Now grief contracteth and straiteneth the heart, and consumeth it, Ps. xxxi. 9, 10. But joy enlargeth and reviveth it, Gen. xlv. 27." Cf. Zeph. 3:17 (KJV).

known to us in the revelation of Jesus Christ. The Gospel of John is replete with references to the Father's unparalleled love for the Son, and to the Son's uncompromising love for the Father (John 1:18; 3:34-35; 5:20; 14:31; 15:9; 17:24; cf. Prov. 8:27, 30; Matt. 11:27; Col. 1:13). Owen observes:

> No small part of the eternal blessedness of the holy God consisteth in the mutual love of the Father and the Son, by the Spirit. As he is the only-begotten of the Father, he is the first, necessary, adequate, complete object of the whole love of the Father. . . . In him was the ineffable, eternal, unchangeable delight and complacency of the Father, as the full object of his love. . . . [H]erein doth the principal part (if we may so speak) of the blessedness of the holy God consist, so is it the only fountain and prototype of all that is truly called love;—a blessing and glory which the creation had never been made partaker of, but only to express, according to the capacity of their several natures, this infinite and eternal love of God! For God's love of himself—which is natural and necessary unto the Divine Being—consists in the mutual complacency of the Father and the Son by the Spirit. And it was to express himself, that God made any thing without himself.[5]

The life of God is one of infinite delight, rest, and satisfaction in his own perfection. The Father infinitely delights in the express image of his nature in the Son, and the Son reciprocally in the Father, both in and by the Holy Spirit that proceeds from them both. In short, God is pure actuality; his love needs no object outside himself for his own eternal complacency and joy. He is "*most* loving" in himself (2LCF 2.1, emphasis added), so as to admit no increase, for then it would imply some potential perfection in God yet to be actualized, and no decrease, for then he would no longer be most loving. Rather than a cold and stoic deity, "God is the fullness of an infinitely completed, and yet infinitely dynamic, life of love, in which there is regard, knowledge, and felicity."[6]

---

[5] Owen, *Works*, 1:144-45. Cf. Musculus, *Common Places*, 959-60.
[6] Hart, "No Shadow of Turning," 197.

The Love of God by Participation

Although this undisturbed celestial and happy repose may seem to undermine any reasonable motive for the *ad extra* divine affections, it in fact provides the basis for them. Love, as we know it, frequently involves the lover seeking out greater fulfillment through union with the beloved, but not so with the triune God whose act of creation is purely gratuitous. His most absolute and perfect love for himself is the fixed, yet over-flowing, fountain of all of his works *ad extra*. Bavinck agrees:

> He is "pure form," "utterly pure act." He does not have to become anything, but is what he is eternally. He has no goal outside himself but is self-sufficient, all-sufficient (Ps. 50:8ff.; Isa. 40:28ff.; Hab. 2:20). He receives nothing, but only gives. All things need him; he needs nothing or nobody. He always aims at himself because he cannot rest in anything other than himself. Inasmuch as he himself is the absolutely good and perfect one, he may not love anything else except with a view to himself.[7]

If God's love toward his creation, and in particular his people, rested upon anything within them, he would have ceased to love them long ago. Creation in no way adds anything to God, alters him, fulfills any longing, or brings about a new relation in him. He alone is free *from* creation so that he may be free *for* creation. He is goodness and all-sufficient in himself, and therefore he has the sole ability to be the all-sufficient "overflowing source of all good."[8]

---

[7] Bavinck, *RD*, 2:211.

[8] Belgic Confession, Art. 1. Cf. Owen, *Works*, 2:90: "God's all-sufficiency in himself is his absolute and universal perfection, whereby nothing is wanting in him, nothing to him: No accession can be made to his fullness, no decrease or wasting can happen thereunto. There is also in him an all-sufficiency for others; which is his power to impart and communicate his goodness and himself so to them as to satisfy and fill them, in their utmost capacity, with whatever is good and desirable to them. For the first of these,—his all-sufficiency for the communication of his goodness, that is, in the outward effect of it,—God abundantly manifested in the creation, in that he made all things good, all things perfect; that is, to whom nothing was wanting in their own kind;—he put a stamp of his own goodness upon them all." Cf. 1 Cor. 4:7.

Dodds is surely correct that "God is in no way seeking to enhance or augment his goodness through his creative activity. He wills only to share his goodness with creatures according to their capacities of nature and grace."[9] By participation, creation manifests the goodness of God, especially man who "is the image and glory of God" (1 Cor. 11:7); he creates with a view to himself and therefore also loves that which he creates with a view to himself. In other words, when God's love is predicated of anything outside himself, it must always be understood with a view to himself. God's love *toward us* (*ad extra*), the divine affections, must be understood in relation to God's natural love *in himself* (*ad intra*), for "when he loves others, he loves himself in them: his own virtues, works, and gifts."[10] In this way, Paul's doxology is no mere flourish of rhetoric, "For of Him and through Him and to Him *are* all things, to whom be glory forever. Amen" (Rom. 11:36).

God's love *toward us* has its source and foundation in God's love *in and for himself*, wherein he most perfectly, unchangeably, and absolutely loves himself. It is from this perspective, with a view to himself, that we may begin to understand the various degrees to which God's love may be secondarily predicated of objects outside himself. The most blessed God rests and delights in himself, and in others with a view to himself as something of himself (i.e., in his own goodness variously communicated to his creatures according to their capacities of nature and grace), and in return commands each accordingly to find their rest and delight in the same—to love most what he loves most, himself.[11]

The Lord does not will to communicate his goodness, or the enjoyment of it, however, to all alike, and therefore he is not said to love all with an equal love. Addressing this issue, Zanchi notes both the unchangeableness and the so-called inequality of God's love, but in different respects. He observes

> that God loveth not only himself, but also every thing that he hath made: although he love not all things with an equal love. For he loveth the better things better than those things

---

[9] Dodds, *Unchanging God of Love*, 210.

[10] Bavinck, *RD*, 2:211.

[11] All of creation is called to join the doxology of praise (Psalm 148), but especially man (Deut. 6:4-5). Cf. WSC 1.

that are less good: the godly than the ungodly.[12]

The Scripture speaks of God's love as though its intensity varies relative to its external object. The Lord loves all the works of his hands (Psalm 104:31),[13] but especially man whom he created in his own image (Matt. 6:26b).[14] Furthermore, his love for mankind is not without distinction, for he has most discriminately set his love upon the elect alone (Rom. 5:8; Deut. 7:7-8).[15]

Notwithstanding these distinctions, Zanchi continues, "the love of God is free, infinite, constant, and everlasting."[16] Such distinctions are not to be understood as varying degrees of emotion within the divine life,[17] but rather denote the varying degrees to

---

[12] Zanchi, *Life Everlasting*, 356.

[13] Musculus, *Common Places*, 960, argues that God's love for his creation rests ultimately not upon anything with creation itself, but upon the foundation of God's immutable nature: "This is the love wherein God as Creator loveth all his creatures, in as much he created them all very good at the beginning, according unto that: And God saw all things that he had made, and they were very good. Both these should be far from the nature of God, if he should either make evil things, and love them after they were made: either make good things, and not love them when they were made: neither is it to be imagined, that he loved his works at the time when he first made them, and that afterwards this love decayed by the process of so many hundred years, and fell to be a loathsomeness. God forbid. For the love of God is as immutable, as his very nature and goodness is immutable. Neither doth it hinder this love at all, that the creature is subject unto vanity and bondage of corruption. For whatsoever it is, it is his work, for he made it subject unto vanity, by his most wise and unsearchable purpose unto us."

[14] God's general love for all people (i.e., love of benevolence) must be both affirmed and distinguished from his special love for the elect (i.e., love of beneficence). His love is not communicated to the reprobate in a saving way and their participation in it is only in accord with the capacity of their sinful nature. Yet, his general love is nonetheless consistently made evident by the common grace he providentially communicates to the just and the unjust alike (Matt. 5:45-46; cf. Acts 14:15-17; Rom. 2:4-5). Moreover, his love for even a fallen human race is evident in the Son's willingness to assume a human nature and come in the likeness of sinful flesh (Rom. 8:3; John 3:16; Heb. 2:16), as well as the willingness of the Father to extend the free and sincere offer of the gospel to all men (Acts 2:21; 1 John 2:2; cf. Psalm 86:5). Cf. Musculus, *Common Places*, 961-63.

[15] For a standard treatment of these distinctions, see Musculus, *Common Places*, 959.

[16] Zanchi, *Life Everlasting*, 356. Cf. Musculus, *Common Places*, 959.

[17] Musculus, *Common Places*, 959, "As there is not in God a divers and sundry goodness, so there is not in him a divers and sundry love: but as there is in him one simple and self same goodness, so there is also in him one simple and self same

which God wills each creature respectively to participate in the divine goodness, or more precisely, its effects.[18] Zanchi explains:

> In some [men] God is said there to love more or less, where his benefits appear to be more; and therefore to love more, because he communicateth more good: therefore the more of God's benefits a man feeleth in himself, the more let him acknowledge himself to be loved of God, than many are which want these benefits.[19]

Thus, such distinctions refer to a real difference in the creature, the nature of the covenant to which they are adjoined, and their experience of, and participation in, the unchanging love of God, but not a difference within the divine life itself. Although *our* relation to the love of God may vary according to the will of God, his love does not. Such variation in our experience of the effects of God's unchanging love is not the result of any change in his affections; he has not, nor could he, will such a change in himself. Without willing any change in his own perfect and impassible affections, God wills change in our experience of his love, resulting only in a changed relation on our part to his infinite, eternal, immutable, impassible love. Bavinck says:

> In him there is no higher and lower, no greater and smaller. Still [i.e., notwithstanding what our experience may suggest], love is most certainly identical with God's being. It is independent, eternal, and unchangeable, like God himself.[20]

This is most profoundly evident with regard to the love which God communicates to the elect according to the covenant of grace, to whom he grants the highest participation in that communion

---

love."

[18] Bavinck, *RD*, 2:212, "In him alone is everything creatures seek and need. He is the supreme good for all creatures, though in varying degrees, depending on the extent to which each creature shares in the divine goodness and is able to enjoy him."

[19] Zanchi, *Life Everlasting*, 366.

[20] Bavinck, *RD*, 2:216.

which he has in himself. Jesus, in his High Priestly Prayer, thus said to the Father:

> I do not pray for these alone, but also for those who will believe in Me through their word; 21 that they all may be one, as You, Father, *are* in Me, and I in You; that they also may be one in Us, that the world may believe that You sent Me. 22 And the glory which You gave Me I have given them, that they may be one just as We are one: 23 I in them, and You in Me; that they may be made perfect in one, and that the world may know that You have sent Me, and have loved them as You have loved Me. 24 Father, I desire that they also whom You gave Me may be with Me where I am, that they may behold My glory which You have given Me; for You loved Me before the foundation of the world. (John 17:20-24)

With regard to the elect, God gratuitously wills more than a general participation and experience of his goodness, and promises as much in the new covenant (Jer. 31:33-35).

Three distinctive characteristics of God's love toward his elect emerge. In the first place, it is a *saving* love (cf. Rom. 9:13; Gal. 2:20; Eph. 1:4b-5; Titus 3:4-8; 1 John 3:1; 4:10). As Creator, he loves his creation with a general love according to the nature of the covenant of creation (Gen. 9:9-11; Jer. 33:25); as Savior, he loves his elect people with a saving love, effectually unto the end that they would be adjoined with their Savior in glory, according to the nature of the new covenant.

Accordingly, it is in the second place a *mediated* love grounded in the person and work of the Lord Jesus Christ, the Mediator of the covenant. As was stated before, the ground of this love cannot be found in man, not even the elect who are themselves equally deserving of God's revenging justice (Rom. 5:8; Deut. 7:7-8), but only in Christ who is himself *beloved* of God (Matt. 3:17).[21] Owen

---

[21] Edward Leigh, *A Treatise of Divinity Consisting of Three Books* (London: John Downham, 1647), II.viii., 71, "God's love to Christ is the foundation of his love to us, Matt. 3:17; Ephes. 1:6. God loves all creatures with a general love, Matt. 5:44, 45, as they are the work of his hands; but he doth delight in some especially, whom he hath chosen in his Son, John 3:16; Ephes. 1:6." Otherwise, the personal and pastoral implications would be devastating. If 1 John 4:10 were to be inverted, "In this is

remarks well:

> In the pouring out of his love, there is not one drop falls
> besides [i.e., apart from] the Lord Christ. The holy anointing
> oil was all poured on the head of Aaron, Ps. cxxxiii. 2; and
> thence went down to the skirts of his clothing. Love is first
> poured out on Christ; and from him it drops as the dew of
> Hermon upon the souls of his saints. . . . So that though the
> saints may, nay, do, see an infinite ocean of love unto them
> in the bosom of the Father, yet they are not to look for one
> drop from him but what comes through Christ. He is the
> only means of communication.[22]

Indeed, it could be no other way, for there was no other way for
God to love sinners with a saving love without injury to his honor,
justice, or holiness. With vivid anthropopathic language, Hosea
describes God reasoning in himself over his wayward people, the
way a father might reason over his wayward son, saying:

> My people are bent on backsliding from Me. Though they
> call to the Most High, None at all exalt *Him*. [8] How can I give
> you up, Ephraim? *How* can I hand you over, Israel? How can
> I make you like Admah? *How* can I set you like Zeboiim? My
> heart churns within Me; My sympathy is stirred. (Hos. 11:7-
> 8)

On the one hand, his justice demands that a proper satisfaction be
made for their sins, and yet his love also pleads its case, saying,
"How can I?" In this way, God personifies a father in whom justice
and love are reasoning together with respect to his wayward child.
In equally vivid and anthropopathic language, Burroughs writes:

> We little think what reasonings there are many times
> between mercy and justice about our lives, about our souls;
> could we but hear them as they debate in heaven regarding

---

love, not that God loved us, but that we loved him," God would be passible
indeed, and all men would be without hope.

[22] Owen, *Works*, 2:27.

us, it would go to our hearts. The great salvation that comes by Christ was not determined without many reasonings between mercy and justice; there was presented to God whatsoever justice could say, and whatever mercy could say: What! (saith God,) must my son be under my wrath, and be made a curse, for the satisfying of justice? yet this must be; justice requires satisfaction; how can it be done without the Son of God being made a curse for man's sin?[23]

Wisdom found a way of communicating God's love to us in Christ without injury to the honor of his justice. "In this is love, not that we loved God, but that He loved us and sent His Son *to be* the propitiation for our sins" (1 John 4:10; cf. Rom. 3:25-26). God's love for the elect is a mediated love, grounded in his eternal and unchanging love of the elect *in Christ*, or with respect to Christ. He does not love us for our own sakes, but for Christ's sake. "He chose us in Him [i.e., Christ] before the foundation of the world . . . by which He has made us accepted in the Beloved" (Eph. 1:4, 6). Manton adds:

> The ground of all that love God beareth to us is for Christ's sake. There is indeed an antecedent love showed in giving us to Christ, and Christ to us: John 3:16, "For God so loved the world. . . ." The first cause of Christ's love to us was obedience to the Father; the Son loved us, because the Father required it; though afterwards God loved us because Christ merited it. All consequent benefits are procured by the merit of Christ. . . . God could not love us with honour to himself, if his wisdom had not found out this way of loving us in Christ.[24]

The love of God, understood in the context of the covenant of redemption (*pactum salutis*), is the antecedent love of God. In love, the Father gave an elect humanity to the Son (John 17:6), and in love the Son redeemed those whom the Father had given to him (John

---

[23] Jeremiah Burroughs, *An Exposition of the Prophesy of Hosea* (1863; reprint, Grand Rapids: Reformation Heritage Books, 2006), 494.

[24] Thomas Manton, *Sermons upon John XVII*, in *The Works of Thomas Manton*, 22 vols. (Birmingham, AL: Solid Ground Books, 2008), 11:77.

6:39). The primary object of the Father's love was his Son, and the first cause of Christ's love was not something within the elect, but purely because the Father's love-gift required it. All consequent benefits of God's love that flow down to the elect through the covenant of grace are procured by the merit and mediation of Christ.[25]

In the third place, God's love for the elect involves the highest *participation*, in that he makes them participants in that eternal, infinite, and unchangeable communion between the Father and the Son. "And I have declared to them Your name, and will declare *it*, that the love with which You loved Me may be in them, and I in them" (John 17:26). On account of creation, all mankind are by nature capable of communion with God, but are by sin rendered morally incapable. Only through the grace of God in Christ, by virtue of the new covenant in his blood, are the elect alone given a renewed nature capable of participating in the fullness of his love. Distinctively with regard to the elect, the lover is most fully united with the beloved, through his *beloved* Son, Jesus Christ, so that they too may behold, rest, and delight in his love. "Whose love is it?" Owen asks. He answers as follows:

> It is the love of him who is in himself all sufficient, infinitely satiated with himself and his own glorious excellencies and perfections; who has no need to go forth with his love unto others, nor to seek an object of it without himself. There might he rest with delight and complacency to eternity. He is sufficient unto his own love. He had his Son, also, his eternal Wisdom, to rejoice and delight himself in from all eternity, Prov. viii. 30. This might take up and satiate the whole delight of the Father; but he will love his saints also. And it is such a love, as wherein he seeks not his own satisfaction only, but our good therein also.[26]

In this way, it may be affirmed that God loves the elect more than the rest of mankind, not for anything in themselves, nor as a

---

[25] Manton, *Works*, 11:74, "He loveth Christ as God, and as mediator, as God-man. As God; so he is *primum amabile*, the first object of his love, as his own express image, that represents his attributes exactly."

[26] Owen, *Works*, 2:32-33.

heightened or differentiated emotion within the divine life itself, but by his gratuitous will to grant to the elect, to the utmost of their re-created capacity, a participation in his infinite and unchanging love. He has loved his elect with the same all-sufficient, infinite, eternal, perfect, and unchangeable love with which he has loved his only begotten Son, the Lord Jesus Christ. Therefore, if God's love for the elect is savingly grounded in his love for Christ, and is a participation in the same, it cannot be otherwise concluded but that it is as eternal and unchangeable as his love for himself in Christ.

Two implications necessarily follow, both of which affirm that God's love *toward us* is as immutable, fixed, and constant as that love whereby he loves *himself*, however varied our experience of its effects may be. In the first place, if the Father has loved his people with the same love whereby he has loved Christ (John 15:9; 17:23, 26), then it must be affirmed that the divine affections toward the elect are likewise *eternal,* and in the second place, *immutable.* Regarding the eternality of God's love, the apostle Paul informs us that God has saved us, "not according to our works, but according to His own purpose and grace which was given to us in Christ Jesus before time began" (2 Tim. 1:9); and again, "for *the children* not yet being born, nor having done any good or evil, that the purpose of God according to election might stand, not of works but of Him who calls . . . As it is written, 'Jacob I have loved, but Esau I have hated'" (Rom. 9:11-13).

It might be objected at this point that Paul also states elsewhere that the elect, prior to their effectual calling, justification, etc., were "by nature children of wrath, just as the others" (Eph. 2:3; cf. Col. 1:21-22). Therefore, it might be concluded that God's affection for his elect changes upon their coming to faith in Christ in due time, and that to argue otherwise would reduce his wrath to an empty concept.[27] With such objections in mind, however, Manton, crediting Zanchi, makes a distinction between God's love *toward us* and God's love *in us*. God's love *toward us* is from all eternity, in his eternal purpose and decree (he loved us from "before the foundation of the world"; cf. John 17:22; Eph. 1:4). God's love *in us*

---

[27] E.g., Carson, *The Difficult Doctrine*, 67, "Wrath, like love, includes emotions as a necessary component. Here again, if impassibility is defined in terms of the complete absence of all 'passions,' not only will you fly in the face of the biblical evidence, but you tumble into fresh errors that touch the very holiness of God."

refers to his external works in the execution of his eternal decree, such as when the elect are actually called and receive the effects of his love. "But God, who is rich in mercy, because of His great love with which He loved us, even when we were dead in trespasses, made us alive together with Christ" (Eph. 2:4-5).[28] With this distinction in mind, Manton adds:

> Some are not called as soon as others, but all are loved as soon as others, even from eternity. God's love is as ancient as himself, there was no time when God did not think of us, and love us . . . not only before we were lovely, but before we were at all.[29]

Prior to conversion (i.e., God's love *in us*), there is a sense in which the wrath and anger of God still abides on the elect. Several distinctions, however, must be kept in mind. First, although the elect are not justified from eternity, they do not become the elect, and therefore loved, when they are justified in time. Rather, they are such who have been chosen in Christ before the foundation of the world, and thus unchangeably loved of God according to his eternal purpose and decree. The elect are justified in time because God has loved them from eternity (Jer. 31:3), otherwise there would have been no moving cause for him to do so.

Second, our hell-deserving sin no more stirs up an emotional change in God than our conversion wins over his love. And yet, this is precisely the implication if we were to say that wrath is proper to God, for wrath is a relative response to sin. While God is love, even apart from the existence of any creature, wrath presupposes the presence of sin. Where there is no sin, there is no wrath. Are we to presume that, of all things, the creature's sin has the ability to bring about a change in God? Elihu addressed this very presupposition which appears to lie behind much of Job's complaint, saying:

> [Y]ou ask, 'What advantage have I? How am I better off than if I had sinned?' 4 I will answer you and your friends with you. 5 Look at the heavens, and see; and behold the clouds,

---

28 Manton, *Works*, 11:84.
29 Manton, *Works*, 11:80.

which are higher than you. 6 If you have sinned, what do you accomplish against him? And if your transgressions are multiplied, what do you do to him? (Job 35:3-6, ESV)

Job's complaint all along was that he was righteous and did nothing to deserve his suffering, and yet he was suffering as though he had sinned. Therefore, he said, "What difference does it make whether I sin or not?" Elihu is quick to point out that while his sin would effect no change in God, emotionally or otherwise, it would effect a most terrible change upon Job. Thus Elihu's conclusion in verse 8, "Your wickedness affects a man such as you."

Although the language of wrath and anger would seem to imply an emotional and dispositional change in God, this is not necessarily the case. Someone may say, "Last year I was taller than my son, but this year I am shorter than he is." Although the expression seems to imply that the father's height had changed, it is possible that, while the father's height remained the same, his son outgrew him. In that case, it would be the son who has changed relative to his father; he has a different relation to his father than he had before.[30] In the same way, when God's anger is said to be kindled, it ultimately points to a change that has taken place in the sinner relative to God; it is the sinner who bears a different relation to God than he had before. Calvin is surely correct when, in response to this objection, he concludes, "Expressions of this sort have been accommodated to our capacity that we may better understand how miserable and ruinous *our condition* is apart from Christ."[31]

Third, as Calvin has just pointed out, the wrath of God needs to be understood anthropopathically, or after the manner of men. Defining anger as "a certain commotion or perturbation," Zanchi is representative of classical theism in general and the Reformed tradition in particular when he concludes that "[God] cannot be moved, but is inalterable and immutable."[32] His conclusion is not arbitrary; rather, he avers that God cannot be so moved on the basis of the analogy of faith, with a firm commitment to what Scripture

---

[30] This is called a Cambridge change.

[31] Calvin, *Institutes*, II.xvi.2., emphasis added.

[32] Zanchi, *Life Everlasting*, 426.

teaches about the immutability of God. "Yet," he continues,

> . . . it is necessary we attribute anger to God . . . in that sense in which the scriptures attribute it to him. . . . I say in the same sense in which the scriptures attribute it to God, because the scriptures useth many kinds of speeches of God, which properly agree not: but according to man's capacity, and improperly.[33]

How then does the Scripture attribute anger to God? If not *formally* and *properly*, anger must be in God *figuratively* and *improperly*. Zanchi mentions three things that anger and wrath signify in the Scripture. First, "it signified a certain, and with all a most just will of God, to revenge or punish injuries done to himself or to his Church," citing John 3:36 and Romans 1:18. Second, "it signifieth the threatening of punishments," citing Psalm 6:1, etc. Lastly, "the word anger, signifieth the effects thereof, or the punishments and revengements of injuries," citing Romans 2:5.[34]

We may take notice of two things. In the first place, wrath is not attributed to God in the same way love and justice are attributed to God. Wrath is not attributed to God properly or formally, but improperly, or figuratively. There is no *form* of emotion in God which corresponds to the *form* of human anger or wrath. In the second place, the foregoing conclusion in no way empties divine wrath of its meaning, but rather explains it in a way that is consistent with what the Scripture reveals about his immutability, love, simplicity, etc. While the *form* of wrath and anger are not in God, that which wrath and anger *figuratively signify* must be attributed to him. As Gouge points out:

> His justice, power, prudence, truth, and other like attributes,

---

[33] Zanchi, *Life Everlasting*, 426.

[34] Zanchi, *Life Everlasting*, 426-27. Cf. Edward Leigh, *A Treatise of Divinity*, II.ix., (74), "Anger is given God, *Non secundum turbationis affectuum, sed secundum ultionis effectuum* [Not in the sense of disordered affections, but in the sense of punishments executed], say the Schoolmen. God's wrath is his revenging justice; which justice of God, as it simply burns against sin, the Scripture calls his *anger*; when it doth most fiercely sparkle out, it is called his *wrath*; the same justice when it pronounceth sentence is called his *judgment*; when it is brought into execution, it is called his *vengeance*."

stir him up thus to maintain the glory of them. Otherwise his wrath, his grief, and other like passions (to speak of God, ἀνθρωποπαθῶς, after the manner of man) would be little regarded, nay, altogether [slighted].[35]

His wrath is not something to be regarded lightly as an empty concept, for although it does not tell us what God *is*, it does tell us what he is *like* in his works *ad extra*, when he executes his revenging justice. It signifies his inscrutable and unchanging justice and power that, as it were, so terribly cause him "thus to maintain" the love of his own honor.

This is of no small consequence to his creatures. As Elihu said to Job, our sin produces no change in God, but it most certainly affects us and the nature of our relationship to his immutable justice. The lack of emotional perturbation in God in no way diminishes the fearful reality of his judgments for those who *experience* them or diminishes the intention of such texts, which is to warn and to persuade. When the *effects* or *execution* of God's revenging justice are described from the standpoint of the creatures who *experience* them, he describes himself as though he were a man of war pouring out the fury of his wrath, only much worse.

What then of God's love towards his elect while they are still children of wrath, prior to their conversion? In addition to making a distinction between God's love *toward us* and God's love *in us*, there is a sense in which we must also affirm that God's wrath abides on the elect (John 3:36), both before the cross and before conversion. Prior to the cross, his just and immutable will to revenge and punish their sins had not yet been historically accomplished for them, and prior to conversion, the work of Christ's propitiation still needs to be personally applied to them. In either case, there is a sense in which the justice of God was still pleading its case against them, although he had decreed from eternity to uphold the honor of his justice toward them at the cross by means of the surety (Heb. 7:22). God's love toward the elect is as eternal as his love for Christ, though they may neither know nor feel it as of yet.

The same must be said of the elect, after their conversion, even

---

[35] Gouge, *Hebrews*, 1:286, sec. 168. The reprint reads "regarded." The facsimile reads "slighted."

when they sin. God loves his people in their sinning, as well as in their obedience. Owen's remarks are worth quoting at length.

> The love of God in itself is the eternal purpose and act of his will. This is no more changeable than God himself: if it were, no flesh could be saved; but it changeth not, and we are not consumed [Mal. 3:6]. What then? loves he his people in their sinning? Yes; his people,—not their sinning. Alters not his love towards them? Not the *purpose* of his will, but the *dispensations* of his grace. He *rebukes* them, he *chastens* them, he *hides* his face from them, he *smites* them, he *fills* them with a sense of [his] indignation; but woe, woe would it be to us, should he change in his love, or take away his kindness from us! Those very things which seem to be demonstrations of the change of his affection towards his, do as clearly proceed from love as those which seem to be the most genuine issues thereof. "But will not this encourage to sin?" He never tasted of the love of God that can seriously make this objection. The *doctrine* of grace may be turned into wantonness; the *principle* cannot.[36]

Again:

> Our Father will not always chide, lest we be cast down; he doth not always *smile*, lest we be full and neglect him: but yet, still his love in itself is the same. When for a little moment he hides his face, yet he gathers us with everlasting kindness.[37]

Woe it would be to us, sinners, if God should change in his love.

The second implication of Jesus' statement in John 17, that the Father has loved his people with the same love whereby he has loved Christ, is that the divine affections toward the elect must be as *immutable* as his love for Christ. This is an inevitable conclusion, given what has already been observed, namely, that God's love is in no way grounded upon something within the elect, but solely in

---

[36] Owen, *Works*, 2:30-31.
[37] Owen, *Works*, 2:30.

Christ. Our sense and assurance of his love *in us* may change, but his love *toward us* remains the same. Manton observes:

> The foundation of God still standeth sure: "The Lord knoweth those that are his," 2 Tim. ii.19. He knoweth his own, when some of them know not they are his own; he seeth his mark upon his sheep, when they see it not themselves. God doubteth not of his interest in thee, though thou doubtest of thy interest in him; and you are held faster in the arms of his love than by the power of your own faith; as the child is surer in the mother's arms than by its holding the mother.[38]

Likewise, the sanctifying fruits and effects of his love *in us* may vary. Experience proves that the Christian does not always enjoy the same measure of the sanctifying fruits of God's love. Sometimes there is great spiritual strength, light, and faith, while at other times God is pleased in his manifold wisdom to restrain the fruits of his love, so as one might feel an acute sense of one's weakness and unbelief. Yet even such occasions are a sign of his unchanging love *toward us*, "that they may be humbled; and to raise them to a more close and constant dependence for their support, upon himself" (2LCF 5.5).

Although God's love is immutable, our sense and enjoyment of it is not. Therefore, the Scripture exhorts us to keep ourselves in his love (Jude 21; Eph. 3:17-19), that is, in our sense and assurance of his love, as well as the sanctifying fruit that is bestowed upon us in the context of Christian discipleship (John 15:9-10). Musculus reminds us that God not only loves the elect with respect to himself, but he also, in a secondary sense, loves the goodness and virtue that he graciously works within them: "The love of God is to be considered of us the second way, in respect that he loveth the good, just, faithful and obedient person unto him, etc."[39] God not only loves his people by communicating his goodness to them, but also in "delighting in what he hath bestowed. . . . The more grace we have, and the more we act it, the more like God, and so more delightful

---

[38] Manton, *Works*, 11:86.
[39] Musculus, *Common Places*, 965.

and lovely in his sight."[40] God is said to love more when he communicates more good. "For to everyone who has, more will be given, and he will have abundance . . ." (Matt. 25:29).

> This consideration shall work thus in us, that we shall well employ the grace of God's love once received, and become the more studious in all kind of goodness, godliness & justice, knowing that it is specially required of us, that the more benefits we do receive of God, not deserving any, yea rather deserving evil, & that we receive . . . by his only love, we may so much the more study to be thankful towards him, and to make us the meeter to receive his love towards the good.[41]

This consideration, that our sense and assurance of his love, as well as the fruits of sanctification, are inextricably tied to Christian discipleship, should compel us by the love of Christ to abide in his love. Let us, therefore, not presume upon the immutability of his love; such unconditional love does not encourage sin, but compels us otherwise (2 Cor. 5:14). "This is love," concludes Owen, "that God loves us first, and then we love him again."[42]

The profundity of Bavinck's conclusion ought to be clear, that "Those who predicate any change whatsoever of God, . . . [rob] God of his divine nature, and religion of its firm foundation and assured comfort."[43] The burden of this section has been to demonstrate that God's love *toward us* is grounded in God's love *in himself*, and particularly *in Christ*. His love toward us, therefore, must be as immutable and eternal as his love for himself, and in particular, Jesus Christ. The doctrine of divine impassibility is inextricably wrapped up with the doctrine of salvation; to undermine the impassibility and immutability of God's love not only robs God of his divine nature, but robs the gospel of its "firm foundation" and his people of their "assured comfort."

---

[40] Manton, *Works*, 21:352.
[41] Musculus, *Common Places*, 965.
[42] Owen, *Works*, 2:24.
[43] Bavinck, *RD*, 2:158.

Love and its Mode of Being

It should be clear by now that whatever is meant by "the love of God," it must be eternal and unchangeable. With this conviction in mind, we may return to a question posed earlier: since change is inseparably annexed to how we experience love, how can love be predicated of a simple, infinite, and omnipotent God who in no way undergoes change? Our answer to this question will necessarily recall what has already been said with regard to analogy and mode of being. God's love stands in relation to the divine nature in a mode proportionately similar to the way human love stands in relation to human nature. Recalling the *via negationis* and *via eminentiae*, we should expect that the perfection of God's love will be, in some significant ways, differentiated from human love, given the difference between God's nature and human nature. We must avoid the mistake of assuming that every perfection of love in the creature must have a corresponding perfection in God. For instance, viciousness may be considered a perfection in a guard dog, but an imperfection in a man. Similarly, it will be argued here that sympathy, insofar as it implies suffering and a loss of joy, would be an imperfection in God, though it could be considered a perfection in man.

Failure to give adequate consideration to the different ways in which love stands in relation to the divine and human natures respectively has the unintended consequence of placing the Creator and the creature in the same order of being. The most common way this occurs among contemporary Reformed and evangelical theologians is by emphasizing the *via eminentiae* without *adequate* regard to the *via negationis*. It is frequently assumed that every perfection in man has a more eminent perfection in God, so that God's love is portrayed as a more perfect version of our own.

For instance, in *Lord and Servant,* Horton cautions his readers of the potential pitfalls of the *via negationis*. He writes, "There is an appropriateness to analogies that must not be given short shrift in order to save God from his own revelation." In other words, if the Scripture says that God pities, or sympathetically suffers with his people, we must not attempt to "save God from his own revelation" by explaining away the passage by way of negation. "And yet," turning to the analogical proviso, he adds, "analogies are not an exact fit between sign and reference."[44] He explains:

> Similarly, while God participates in the joy and sorrow of his
> people, without which the moral attributes of God would be
> empty . . . God is never overwhelmed with distress because
> God is more unlike than like us.[45]

Thus, the *via eminentiae* accounts for significant qualitative
differences, but taken alone it unwittingly leaves the door open to a
univocal gradation of hierarchal steps between God and man. An
analogical proviso that does not also give *adequate* regard to the *via
negationis* will necessarily fail to account consistently for the
quiddative (i.e., essential) differences inherent within the analogies
that arise from fundamentally different modes of being. The
problem here is not the omission of an analogical proviso, but that,
for all practical purposes, without *adequate* regard to the *via
negationis* it can have the unintended effect of becoming an
analogical-until-it's-not proviso. Such is the case in this particular
instance.

Without adequate regard to the *via negationis*, Horton, following
Kevin Vanhoozer, argues that the difference between divine and
human suffering merely lies in God's inability to be "overwhelmed
with distress." Vanhoozer explains as follows:

> Though certain feelings may *befall* God, he will not be *subject*
> to them. In this strict sense, then, it is no contradiction to say
> that God experiences human sorrow yet is nevertheless
> apathetic (because this experience does not compromise his
> reason, will or wisdom).[46]

Regrettably, such an argument necessarily reduces divine
immutability to what might be referred to as divine perseverance or
constancy. Accordingly, God is said really and truly to experience
pity in a manner analogous to our experience; although he suffers
like us, his suffering is qualitatively unlike ours insofar as he is

---

[44] Michael S. Horton, *Lord and Servant: A Covenant Christology* (Louisville: Westminster John Knox Press, 2005), 46.

[45] Horton, *Lord and Servant*, 48.

[46] Vanhoozer, *First Theology*, 93.

never overwhelmed with despair, or rage, or impatience. His, therefore, is merely an eminently more perfect suffering than our own—man writ large. "Beyond this," Horton concludes:

> we could speculate perhaps on what is "worthy" or "appropriate" of God's nature, by appealing to one metaphysical scheme or another, but to that extent we lose our connection with the God of Israel who confronts us as a stranger—and, in fact, a judge, apart from Christ. Idolatry is what happens when we project our own ideals of perfection onto the metaphysical map.[47]

We share Horton's concern to avoid idolatrous apophatic (i.e., negative) speculation about the nature of God beyond what he has revealed. But we would also do well to remember that this warning cuts both ways. Not only must the analogies God has revealed not be given short shrift, but they must also be interpreted in light of all that God has revealed about himself. God cannot contradict himself and he knows all of the necessary consequences of his word, so that Scripture itself provides us with a metaphysical map that determines for us what is "worthy" or "appropriate" of God's nature. Understanding God's so-called pity in light of his immutability helps us to see, not only what it *does* mean, but also what it *cannot* mean. Idolatry is what happens when we speculate beyond what God has revealed, *as much as when we fail to account for all that he has revealed*. In either case, we may be guilty of projecting "our own ideas of perfection onto the metaphysical map." As Dodds has observed:

> Without the *via negationis*, which underlines the radical difference between God and creatures, the God affirmed in the *via eminentiae* would become nothing more than a beneficent creature "writ large."[48]

The implied assumption is that love could not be properly predicated of God if he did not truly co-suffer with his people.

---

[47] Horton, *Lord and Servant*, 51-52.
[48] Dodds, *Unchanging God of Love*, 137.

Donald Macleod makes this assumption clear, when he states:

> . . . the idea that God is unaffected by occurrences outside himself is inconsistent with the divine pity. Pity means by definition that one is stirred by the spectacle of human misery, temporal and spiritual. God cannot pity and yet remain unmoved. Indeed, for God to remain unmoved would raise serious questions as to his morality. *The pain and grief which we feel when confronted with inhumanity, deprivation and squalor must have its counterpart (and indeed its source) in the God whose image we bear.*[49]

It is assumed that if sympathetic suffering is a perfection in us, it must also be a perfection in God. In this way, God's love, co-suffering and all, becomes a more perfect and eminent version of our own.

Since change, even suffering, is inseparably annexed to how we experience love, how can love be predicated of a simple, infinite, and omnipotent God who in no way undergoes change? In particular, can love be predicated of a God who cannot sympathetically suffer with his people? How we define the necessary attributes of love will determine how we respond to these questions. As we seek an answer, we must also fully account for the *via negationis*, resisting the temptation to project our own experience of love upon God. Our conclusion is that neither change nor sympathetic suffering are necessary components of love *qua* love (i.e., love considered in and of itself). When love is predicated of God, the emotional change and suffering that is so often associated with our experience must necessarily be figurative.

Love and Emotional Mutability

When we think of the mechanics of love, we naturally begin with our own experience, that is, love as it stands in relation to human nature. Dodds points out:

> Human   love   is   often   associated   with   motion—the

---

[49] Macleod, *From Glory to Golgotha*, 106, emphasis added.

restlessness of desire, the impulse of passion, the steady unfolding of affection and commitment. If we tend to associate love with movement, how is it possible for us to attribute love to a Being in whom there is no movement or change?[50]

How should love be defined? Is emotional mutability, though inseparably fixed to our experience of love, essential for love to be what it is?

In reply, Dodds observes that human love is both mutable and relatively immutable. Emotional mutability and arousal are inseparable from our experience of love because of what we are, but there is no reason to insist that it is inseparable from love itself. Our love is certainly aroused and thus mutable, but once it is aroused, its affection fixes itself upon its object, and it is this *fixed* position, not the arousal *per se*, that we call love. Human love is like human nature; it is mutable insofar as it increases and decreases and relatively immutable insofar as it fixes upon its object. God's love stands in relation to God's nature, and therefore is like God himself, absolutely and immutably fixed without need or capability of emotional arousal. Acknowledging these differing modes of being, Owen writes:

> They differ in this also: — *The love of God is like himself, — equal, constant, not capable of augmentation or diminution; our love is like ourselves, — unequal, increasing, waning, growing, declining.* His, like the *sun*, always the same in its light, though a cloud may sometimes interpose; ours, as the *moon*, hath its enlargements and straightenings.[51]

This in no way implies that God's love is cold and detached, but that he does not undergo "inner emotional changes of state, either of comfort or discomfort, whether freely from within or by being acted upon from without."[52] As Dodds observes, moreover, "Unlike

---

[50] Dodds, *Unchanging God of Love*, 204.

[51] Owen, *Works*, 2:29-30.

[52] Weinandy, *Does God Suffer?*, 39. It is important to bear in mind that the term rendered "passions" in English has not simply the narrow meaning "to suffer," but a broader meaning "to undergo." Cf. Dolezal, "Still Impassible," 127-29.

our love, which is awakened by the goodness perceived in the beloved, God's love is not caused by the goodness of its object."[53] This is never truer than with respect to unholy and sinful creatures. There is nothing in his people that could arouse God's love. The Lord set his love upon Israel simply because he loved them (Deut. 7:7-8). Pointing forward to the day of redemption, the prophet Zephaniah comforts the people of God, not by telling them that God's love will be aroused, but that "he will be quiet [over you] in his love" (Zeph. 3:17).[54] Owen explains:

> Both these things are here assigned unto God in his love,— REST and DELIGHT. The words are, יַחֲרִישׁ בְּאַהֲבָתוֹ,—"He shall be silent because of his love." To rest with contentment is expressed by being silent; that is, without repining, without complaint. This God doth upon the account of his own love, so full, so every way complete and absolute, that it will not allow him to complain of any thing in them whom he loves, but he is silent on the account thereof. Or, "Rest in his love;" that is, he will not remove it,—he will not seek farther for another object. It shall make its abode upon the soul where it is once fixed, for ever.[55]

Owen, therefore, concludes that

> on whom he fixes his love, it is immutable; it doth not grow to eternity, it is not diminished at any time. It is an eternal love, that had no beginning, that shall have no ending; that cannot be heightened by any act of ours, that cannot be lessened by any thing in us. I say, in itself it is thus.[56]

---

[53] Dodds, *Unchanging God of Love*, 207.

[54] O. Palmer Robertson, *The Books of Nahum, Habakkuk, and Zephaniah*, New International Commentary on the Old Testament (Grand Rapids: Eerdmans Publishing Company, 1990), 340, "The Hebrew verb *ḥāraš*, 'to be quiet,' is intransitive in meaning, with the possible exception of Job 11:3. It describes the inward condition of the subject of the verb rather than depicting a quietness which is conveyed to another. Here God is the subject of the verb, and he is said to *be quiet in his love*." This is further supported by the parallelism of the surrounding phrases which add (*'alayik*) "over you." Thus, "he will be quiet [over you] in his love."

[55] Owen, *Works*, 2:25.

[56] Owen, *Works*, 2:30.

In God, there is no arousal of love because his love is infinitely and immutably fixed upon his own infinite and immutable goodness and the creature's unmerited participation in it. And, therefore, it is especially this fixed position that we call love. It is a fixed disposition of the will that takes delight and rest in union with the beloved.

Placing the emphasis upon the fixed disposition of love in no way implies that God is unable to act or relate. It is from this fixed position, not the arousal *per se*, that love gives rise to all sorts of actions aimed at union with the beloved. With respect to God's works *ad extra*, his love is the infinite, dynamic, fixed fountain of all of his works of creation, providence, and redemption (cf. John 3:16). God's love remains the *fixed* fountain of all motion (i.e., the external operations of God).

Love and Sympathetic Suffering

Since change is inseparably annexed to how we experience love, how can love be predicated of a simple, infinite, and omnipotent God who in no way undergoes change? It has been argued thus far that change, or emotional mutability, is not a necessary component of love *qua* love. God's love is the fixed and immutable fountain of all motion outside of himself (*ad extra*). As such, few would be willing to say that God's love is a fixed fountain of pity. Yet it can be difficult for us to conceive of love apart from God's ability to be affected emotionally by the affliction of his people. In what follows, it will be argued that as with change in general, sympathetic suffering is not a necessary ingredient of love *qua* love.

Any difficulty we may have with this conclusion is owing to our difficulty to conceive of love in any other way than how we experience it. This is particularly the case because, according to our own experience, sympathetic suffering is an inseparable component of compassion. "Such we learn by experience [what] love is in us," but must it necessarily be so in God? Zanchi replies:

> But love in God is not such as it is in us, no more than that being which he hath imparted unto us is like to that which he is in himself. It is therefore to be noted that love was first in God before it was in us or in any creature. . . . And it is in

God most perfect (for there is nothing imperfect in him) but in us imperfect and joined with passion and impure affection and weakness of the mind. Wherefore although we be drawn through the consideration of that love which is in us, to consider what manner of love that of God is, yet are not all things to be transferred to God's love which we do find in our own: but only those things which signify perfections, and are most beseeming the nature of God.[57]

Although we necessarily begin with an understanding of love based upon our own experience, we are thereby drawn to a consideration of love in God. In doing so, we must remember that not every perfection in man has a corresponding perfection in God because his being is not like ours.

Wherefore that rule which we have used elsewhere, is to be held, that whatsoever imperfection we find in our affections, we are first to take that away, and then the same affections, love, and mercy, being purged as it were from all imperfection, is to be attributed to God.[58]

As we move from an understanding of love as it stands in relation to human nature to that love which stands in relation to the divine nature, we must do so according to the *via negationis*. Divine and human love are as different in kind as God's being and man's being are different in kind. This means that we must not only take away "whatsoever imperfection we find in our affections," but also any perfections in us that would imply an imperfection when considered in relation to the nature of God revealed in Scripture. Therefore, as Musculus reminds us, we must discern wisely, not merely the letter of such expressions, but their true intent. He says:

The Scripture doth attribute many things unto God by figure and similitude of man's affections, which do not so agree unto the nature of God, as they do unto our nature. And yet for all that, it is not without reason, that it doth speak unto

---

[57] Zanchi, *Life Everlasting*, 358.
[58] Zanchi, *Life Everlasting*, 358.

men in this wise of God, to apply it self unto our capacity. The discrete and godly person must wisely make this difference betwixt those things which do agree unto the nature of God, and those which can not agree there withal, & in the speeches of the holy scripture, not to wrest the words, but reverently to embrace those things, which he set forth to be understanded after the meaning of the spirit.[59]

At the same time, as Dodds perceptively points out, it is especially difficult to decide how sympathetic suffering should be interpreted. "Because human sympathetic suffering has both good and evil aspects, it is difficult to decide whether and how such suffering should be attributed to God." He explains:

> Since sadness and suffering are evils in themselves, they cannot properly be predicated of God. . . . The sadness that characterizes sympathetic suffering, however, though it must be recognized as an evil insofar as it is itself a form of suffering, may also be seen as good insofar as it is a loving response to the suffering of another. . . . Indeed, when something saddening is presupposed, it would be an evil for a human being *not* to feel some sort of pain or sorrow. . . . Human sympathetic suffering is at once an evil (insofar as it is itself a form of suffering) and a good (insofar as it is a laudable response to the suffering of another).[60]

Insofar as the lack of sympathetic suffering would imply indifference, as it could in humans, it cannot "be denied of God without detriment to his perfection in love. But to the extent that such suffering in itself entails imperfection, it cannot be applied to God without detriment to his perfection in being."[61] The solution to this difficulty lies in the acknowledgment that while the two perspectives are inseparable in humans, this is not the case with God. Contrary to human experience, God is able to love with sincere and perfect compassion without co-suffering.

---

[59] Musculus, *Common Places*, 959.
[60] Dodds, *Unchanging God of Love*, 220.
[61] Dodds, *Unchanging God of Love*, 221.

Suffering for another, or in response to the suffering of another, is not what makes compassion praiseworthy. What is praiseworthy is the love that is revealed through the sympathetic suffering. While humans cannot separate the two, they may be distinguished. Dodds provides an analogy as follows:

> A mother who wiped away [her child's] tears without becoming visibly saddened herself, however, might well be considered loving and compassionate. . . . It is not the degree of suffering as such we admire in the compassionate person, but the degree of love that suffering manifests. When Jesus wept at the death of Lazarus, the crowd did not say, "See how he suffers," but "See how he loved him" (Jn 11:35-36). . . . But again, we may ask the question whether it is compassionate suffering itself that consoles the beloved, or whether it is not rather the love that shines through such suffering. If it were my friend's compassionate suffering itself that brought me consolation, then I would be in the peculiar situation of reacting in quite the opposite way to my friend's suffering from the way he reacts to mine. For I would be taking some sort of joy in his suffering while he reacts with sadness at my own.[62]

The last illustration profoundly demonstrates the moral inconsistency of locating our comfort in the notion that God is suffering with us in our distress, rather than finding our comfort in his impassible compassion that, because he does not suffer, is fully able to overcome the suffering of his people. Sympathetic suffering, though inseparable in human experience, is not of the essence of love *qua* love; it is not what makes love praiseworthy. If a mother wept bitterly with her children but did not pick them up, wipe away the tears, and bandage the wounds when it was within her ability to do so, we would not look upon her tears as compassion. God *is* impassible and infinite love, and from that dynamic fixed fountain overflows compassionate relief, yet without suffering.

While a lack of co-suffering on the part of a man may indicate an indifference toward his fellow man, this is not so with God.

---

[62] Dodds, *Unchanging God of Love*, 224.

Loving his creation, and especially the elect, with respect to himself, he freely identifies himself with his people. Apart from co-suffering, he empathetically identifies with them in their suffering as though it were his own (Prov. 14:31; 17:4; 19:17; Isa. 63:9). That which united them is not a mutual experience of suffering, but love. Love has the ability to unite the person loving and the beloved as if to form one person. God's love unites his people to himself, in participation of his goodness, as if to see them as something of himself.

> Just as we, seeing those whom we love most deeply "as something of ourselves," are identified with them in their suffering, so God, seeing us "as something of himself," makes us one with him in love and so calls our suffering his own.[63]

This provides tremendous insight into the spirit and intent of those passages that speak of God as though he were afflicted in our affliction. The point is not that he suffers with us, but that he identifies with his people in their affliction *like* a father or mother would with their children.

> As a friend regards the sufferings of the beloved as his own, so God is said to look upon our distress as his own in dispelling it. . . . It is for this reason that we make our stammering assertion: "the God of love is not a God who suffers, but a God who, in his tender unceasing care for his people, casts out and triumphs over suffering."[64]

Like a father, he seeks to provide compassionate relief to his children as if their suffering were his own (Deut. 1:31). He so identifies with his people that he loves them as though they were part of himself.

Sympathetic suffering, though inseparable from love in human experience, is not of the essence or perfection of love *qua* love. It is not sympathetic suffering itself that consoles the beloved, but the love that is signified through it. Therefore, when Scripture attributes

---

[63] Dodds, *Unchanging God of Love*, 228.
[64] Dodds, *Unchanging God of Love*, 229, 232.

such suffering to God *as God*, it speaks figuratively and thereby signifies the love with which God identifies with his people in their affliction so as to relieve them *as though* it were his own. Love, in that mode of being which stands in relation to the divine nature, is not only not overwhelmed by suffering, but incapable of it, and therefore is fully able to overcome it—a conclusion profoundly affirmed in the person and work of Christ, to which we turn in our next chapter.

Chapter 12

A Theology of
the Doctrine of Divine Impassibility
(III) Impassibility and Christology
Charles J. Rennie and Stefan T. Lindblad

Divine impassibility refers to that attribute which says that God cannot undergo any emotional or affectional change whatsoever, whether it be caused freely from within or from without. Much confusion may be avoided when we understand that impassibility refers to an attribute of God and therefore properly belongs to theology proper, rather than Christology. In other words, its intent is not to deny the real emotions and sufferings of Jesus Christ. Neither, however, can the emotions and sufferings of Christ, the God-man, be marshaled against divine impassibility. Orthodox Christology upholds the truth that God, *as God*, cannot and does not suffer, emotionally or otherwise, nor is there any need for him to do so. We are not in need of a God who suffers *as God*, but rather an impassible God who, by suffering *as a man*, is able to overcome suffering on behalf of man.

Suffering and the *Communicatio Idiomatum*

If there were ever an occasion for God to undergo emotional change and suffer passions, it would have been the birth, life, and death of Jesus Christ. After all, he is truly God and truly man, the "fullness of the Godhead bodily" (Col. 2:9) and the "express image of His person" (Heb. 1:3). On the grounds of the incarnation of the Son and the union of the two natures in his person, it might be objected that since it was the Son of God who became a man and suffered, therefore God, *as God*, must be capable of suffering.

In response to such ill-fated logic, orthodoxy has always

affirmed that a proper understanding of the *communicatio idiomatum* (i.e., communication of properties) precludes the predication of suffering to the deity of Christ. The doctrine of the communication of properties presupposes the careful and precise Christology of the Formula of Chalcedon (451), which asserts:

> We, then, following the holy Fathers, all with one consent, teach men to confess . . . one and the same Christ, Son, Lord, Only-begotten, to be acknowledged in two natures, inconfusedly, unchangeably, indivisibly, inseparably. The distinction of the natures being by no means taken away by the union, but rather the property of each nature being preserved, and concurring in one Person . . .

The biblical distinction between Creator and creature is maintained as the divine and human natures of Christ are distinguished, but not separated. The two natures cannot be separated, because the incarnation is not a union of two persons, one human and one divine (the Nestorian heresy). Likewise, they cannot be confused into some kind of hybrid, for neither does one nature assume the other so as to engulf it (the Eutychian or Monophysite heresy). Rather, the second person of the Trinity assumed a Spirit-created human nature without undergoing any change in his divine nature. Watson observes, "If the divine nature had been converted into the human, or the human into the divine, [then] there [would have] been a change, but they were not so."[1]

The divine nature of the Son did not become human and the human nature did not become divine. The eternal Son of God became what he once was not (true man), without ceasing to be what he always is (true God). As Charnock explains:

> There was no change in the Divine nature of the Son, when he assumed human nature. There was an union of the two natures, but no change of the Deity into the humanity, or of the humanity into the Divinity: both preserved their peculiar properties. The humanity was changed by a communication

---

[1] Thomas Watson, *A Body of Divinity* (Reprint, Edinburgh: Banner of Truth, 1957), 47.

of excellent gifts from the divine nature, not by being brought into an equality with it, for that was impossible that a creature should become equal to the Creator.[2]

Herein lies the mystery and wonder of the incarnation, that the divine Son assumed a passible human nature, without any alteration or subjugation of his impassible divine nature. Being united in the person of the Son, both natures preserve their peculiar properties, such that "the incarnate Son of God was not limited to fleshly, human existence but continued to exist *extiam extra carnem* (even beyond the flesh)."[3]

Rightly understood, the doctrine of the *communicatio idiomatum* is an effect of the hypostatic union. Briefly stated, this doctrine maintains that "the two natures are here considered as joined in the person, and the interchange of attributes is understood as taking place at the level of the person and not between the natures."[4] That is, the hypostatic union, according to the strictures of Chalcedon, does not permit a communication of properties in the abstract, such that the properties of the human nature are predicated of the divine nature, or *vice versa*. Rather, the communication of properties is concrete; the properties of the human nature are predicated of Christ, the person, as are the properties of the divine nature. Perkins helpfully articulates the Reformed doctrine of the communication of properties in the following words:

> Of those things which are spoken or attributed to Christ, some are only understood of his divine nature. (John 8:58) *"Jesus said unto them, verily, verily, I say to you, Before Abraham was, I am."* (Colossians 1:15) *"Who is the image of the invisible God, the firstborn of every creature."* Some again agree only to his humanity, as born, suffered, dead, buried. (Luke 2:52) *"And Jesus increased in wisdom and stature, and in favour with God and man."* Lastly, other things are understood only of

---

[2] Charnock, *Existence and Attributes*, 1:339.

[3] Andrew M. McGinnis, *The Son of God Beyond the Flesh: A Historical and Theological Study of the* extra Calvinisticum, T & T Clark Studies in Systematic Theology, vol. 29, ed. John Webster, Ian A. McFarland, and Ivor Davidson (London: Bloomsbury, 2014), 1.

[4] Muller, *Dictionary*, 72.

both natures united together. (Matthew 17:5) *"This is my beloved Son, in whom I am well pleased; hear ye him."* (Ephesians 1:22) *"And he put all things under his feet, and gave him to be the head over all things to the church."*[5]

The peculiar properties of one nature are not attributed to the other nature so as to confuse the two. It is not human nature to be of itself (*a se*) any more than it is proper to the divine nature to be born, suffer, or die. Yet, according to the *communicatio idiomatum*, the attributes of both may be predicated of the one *person*. The distinction of natures aside, the acts of Christ, the Mediator, are always attributed to the whole person, the Son of God incarnate, albeit not to the whole of the person (i.e., both natures considered in the abstract).

> So it is that all the acts and sufferings of Christ are rightly referred to his whole person as the one responsible, though some go with one nature, some with the other, depending on their sources and forms.[6]

Thus, the Scriptures may speak of "the church of God which He purchased with His own blood" (Acts 20:28), or the crucifixion of "the Lord of glory" (1 Cor. 2:8), by which we understand the Son of God *according to his human nature.*

Bavinck notes well that at the time of the Reformation, Reformed and Lutheran theologians always "asserted that Christ was a mediator in both natures," whereas Roman Catholic scholars "maintained that Christ was only a mediator in his human nature."[7] Notwithstanding this difference, Protestant and Roman Catholic alike denied that Christ suffered according to his divine nature.

---

[5] William Perkins, *A Golden Chain or the Description of Theology*, ed. Greg Fox (1597; reprint, Puritan Reprints, 2010), 38.

[6] Ames, *The Marrow of Theology*, XVIII.xxii.

[7] Bavinck, *RD*, 3:364. Cf. Peter Martyr Vermigli, *Life, Letters, and Sermons*, The Peter Martyr Library vol. 5, ed. and trans. John Patrick Donnelly (Kirksville, MO: Thomas Jefferson University Press, 1999), 152. As Vermigli's writings demonstrate, the Reformed polemic on this theological topic was not only directed against Roman Catholic teaching, but more pointedly against the teaching of Stancarus, a Polish theologian, who, like Rome, insisted that Christ was a mediator only according to his human nature.

Thus Ursinus is representative of both traditions, indeed orthodoxy itself, when he concludes that

> Christ suffered, not according to both natures, nor according to the Divinity, but according to the human nature only, both in body and soul; for the divine nature is immutable, impassible, immortal, and life itself, and so cannot die. But he suffered in such a manner, according to his humanity, that by his passion and death, he satisfied for the sins of men.[8]

Therefore, in the words of Gregory of Nazianzen, Jesus Christ was "passible in His Flesh, Impassible in His Godhead."[9]

It needs to be stressed that even if the Son of God *according to his deity* were capable of suffering, it would not have produced any benefit for sinners. Indeed, it was not necessary that he suffer according to his divine nature, for "since by man came death, by

---

[8] Zacharias Ursinus, *Commentary of Dr. Zacharias Ursinus on the Heidelberg Catechism*, trans. G. W. Williard (1852; reprint, Phillipsburg, NJ: P&R Publishing, 1985), 215-16. Vermigli, *Life, Letters, and Sermons*, 151-52, concurs: "I strongly deny that Christ suffered in his divine nature. I would grant that God was born, suffered, and died and was crucified because Christ as one person is indivisible; he thus has the two natures conjoined in himself, but not confused or mixed. Hence this Christ, who is truly God and man, is believed to have suffered, been crucified, and to have died. But if it is asked: by virtue and reason of both natures? The response will be by virtue of the human nature; since when Paul says the Lord of glory was crucified he attributes to the whole Christ what applies to him because of the condition of one part. Thus a person is called lame when he is affected by the defect of lameness because of his leg or foot. So too Christ is said to have been born and made; because this should be understood relative to his human nature, therefore in the Scriptures the phrase 'according to the flesh' is added. How without a mutation of itself could the nature of God suffer and die? The Scriptures testify as clearly as possible that God cannot change. But if God in his nature was able to suffer, there would have been no need to become man. Paul says in Romans, 'God sent his own Son in the likeness of sinful flesh and for sin, he condemned sin in the flesh,' because if Christ had suffered according to his divinity, sin in the divine nature, not in the flesh, would have been condemned, and God proposed Christ as propitiator through his blood; finally when the divine letters recount the Lord's passion and our redemption through his passion, they constantly make mention of the body, flesh, and blood (but never of the divine nature) which suffered for us."

[9] Gregory of Nazianzen, *To Cledonius the Priest against Apollinarius*, in *NPNF*, Second Series, 7:439.

Man also came the resurrection of the dead" (1 Cor. 15:21). The Lord Jesus did not suffer for himself, much less for God, but on behalf of sinful man, as a man, according to his human nature (1 Tim. 2:5). Nevertheless, as Ursinus also points out, it was also necessary that he was God, insofar as "[t]he divine nature sustained the humanity, in the sorrows and pains which were endured, and raised it when dead unto life."[10] The Son of God did not "become incarnate in order to overcome . . . divine impassibility," as Rob Lister poorly expresses.[11] Rather, his divine impassibility enabled him to overcome human suffering. Satisfaction for our sins had to be made by the God-man because only God can make satisfaction and only man owed satisfaction. Insofar as the Mediator is truly man, he was capable of suffering for man, and insofar as he is also the impassible God, he was fully capable of *overcoming* suffering on behalf of his people.[12]

According to the doctrine of the *communicatio idiomatum*, orthodoxy has always confessed that the person of the Son of God suffered and died, not, however, according to his deity, but according to his humanity, the former incapable of suffering, the latter fully capable of suffering. Nevertheless, the deity of Christ was in no way quiescent in this act, or any act for that matter, of Christ's mediation. Witsius carefully distinguishes, writing:

> To impart this infinite worth to his sufferings, it was not necessary that the Divine nature itself, or that Christ *as God* should suffer. It was sufficient that he *who is God*, should suffer. All the actions and sufferings are the actions and sufferings of the person, and receive their value and denomination from the dignity of the person.[13]

---

[10] Ursinus, *Heidelberg Catechism*, 216.

[11] Lister, *God is Impassible and Impassioned*, 37.

[12] St. Gregory Thaumaturgus, *To Theopompus, on the Impassibility and Passibility of God*, in *The Fathers of the Church: St Gregory Thaumaturgus Life and Works*, trans. Michael Slusser (Washington, D.C.: The Catholic University of America Press, 1998), 172-73, "He came therefore, O happy one, Jesus came, who is king over all things, that he might heal the difficult passions of human beings, being the most blessed and generous one. But yet he remained what he is, and the passions were destroyed by his impassibility, as darkness is destroyed by light."

[13] Herman Witsius, *Sacred Dissertations on the Apostles' Creed*, vol. 2, trans. Donald Fraser (1823; reprint, Phillipsburg, NJ: P&R, 1993), XV.vi. (40).

It is profoundly appropriate, therefore, to confess that the Son of God emotionally and physically suffered, or that the impassible suffered. Yet, it is profoundly unorthodox to conclude from this that God, *as God*, is therefore capable of emotional suffering. As Weinandy explains:

> Who is it who truly experiences the authentic, genuine, and undiminished reality of human suffering? None other than the divine Son of God! He who is one in being with the Father. What is the manner in which he experiences the whole reality of human suffering? As man! It is actually the Son of God who lives a comprehensive human life, and so it is the Son who, as man, experiences all facets of this human life, including suffering and death.[14]

Analogy and the Revelation of God in Christ

With a two-natures distinction in mind, it may help to ask, in what manner does Jesus Christ reveal the Father (John 1:18)? It is not uncommon for those who otherwise maintain a two-natures Christology to use the inner life of Jesus as a paradigm for understanding the inner emotional life of God. It is presupposed that because Jesus Christ is truly God, and "the express image of His person" (Heb. 1:3), he must therefore provide a univocal core through which we may locate parallel kinds of experiences within the Godhead.[15] Against this approach, we maintain that even in the incarnation God reveals himself analogically, so that a direct line cannot be drawn between God revealed in the flesh and God as he is in himself. To suggest otherwise would inevitably confuse the two natures of Christ and obscure the distinction between Creator and creature.

Such confusion is evident in Vanhoozer's *First Theology*, where

---

[14] Weinandy, *Does God Suffer?*, 201.

[15] Such an argument may be more influenced by Barth than it would like to acknowledge. "Who God is and what it means to be divine is something we have to learn where God has revealed Himself and His nature, the essence of the divine. And if He has revealed Himself in Jesus Christ as the God who does this, it is not for us to be wiser than He and to say that it is in contradiction with the divine essence." Barth, *Church Dogmatics*, IV/1, 186.

he argues that the narratives of the gospel of Jesus Christ must discipline theological thought. He writes, "The metaphor of love adequately describes God's being, but only when biblical narrative — that is, the storied history of Jesus Christ — is allowed to regulate the use of the term love."[16] Thus, we must allow Christology to regulate theology proper, and biblical theology to regulate systematic theology. Whereas the early Christological debates demonstrate a tendency to allow divine impassibility to regulate how we understand the incarnation, the hypostatic union, and the sufferings of Christ, Vanhoozer proposes the opposite. This is precisely what he does when he turns to Christ in order to provide the paradigm for understanding divine impassibility.

> Jesus, the author of Hebrews tells us, was truly tempted as we are (Heb 2:18) though he remained sinless (Heb 4:15). There is no contradiction between Jesus' being "open" to temptation and it being certain that he would not sin. Though some have said that Jesus must not have felt the force of temptation, others contend that it is precisely the person who resists temptation who feels its full force. . . . Something similar, I believe, may be said for divine impassibility.[17]

In other words, just as Jesus felt the full force of temptation, yet without being overwhelmed and surrendering to sin, "God feels the force of the human experience without suffering change in his being, will or knowledge," or without being "*overcome* or *overwhelmed* by passion."[18]

How God, *as God*, can internally and emotionally suffer the full force of human affliction without suffering change in his being is not a question Vanhoozer addresses. Presumably, it is in the same way that Christ felt the weight of temptation, yet without sin. Yet one of the weaknesses of Vanhoozer's proposal lies in his failure to take into account the two natures of Christ in relation to his temptation. As part of his public ministry and antitypical trial as the

---

[16] Vanhoozer, *First Theology*, 95.
[17] Vanhoozer, *First Theology*, 93.
[18] Vanhoozer, *First Theology*, 93.

second Adam, we may confidently say that he underwent temptation according to his human nature, since God cannot be tempted (James 1:13). As Mediator, he felt the full force of temptation *as a man*, by virtue of his human nature, on behalf of man. Though he is God, he did not undergo temptation *as God*, and therefore the analogy, which is predicated upon the presupposition of a parallel divine experience, immediately breaks down.

The weakness of this proposal is further demonstrated when we inquire how it was that Jesus underwent such temptation *without sinning*. Either his impassible divine nature preserved his humanity, or else the Spirit of God, who not only rested upon him from his conception and birth but with whom he was also anointed, strengthened and sustained him. It is difficult, even impossible, however, to see how either answer provides an explanation for how God can emotionally and internally suffer in our suffering without any change in his being. According to this proposal, God's being is preserved in the midst of emotional affliction in a manner similar to how Christ's moral perfection was preserved in the midst of strong temptation—either by virtue of his divine nature or by the work of the Holy Spirit. If it were by virtue of the former, then it would be God's own nature that sustains him in the midst of his co-suffering, though (maintaining the parallelism) we must also conclude that his divinity itself no more suffers than it underwent temptation in Christ. This makes no sense outside of the incarnation, for God has no other nature by which to endure emotional affliction. If it were by virtue of the latter, then it would become the peculiar work of the Spirit to sustain, strengthen, and preserve the Father and the Son from becoming overwhelmed in their suffering, in which case all manner of questions are raised concerning the doctrine of the Trinity.

Moreover, we are still left with the question of how an immutable God can suffer the full emotional force of sympathetic suffering for his people *without change* in his being, will, or knowledge. Assuming that any one of the foregoing explanations is remotely plausible, we have merely explained how it is that God is not *overcome* by suffering, but not how he remains *unchanged* by it. In such a case, it may be said that God emotionally perseveres and overall remains constant in his covenant purposes, but not that he is immutable. When scrutinized, we come to see that Vanhoozer's argument is based upon a superficial similarity between Jesus' impeccability and God's impassibility. This is unquestionably a category mistake. By allowing Christology to regulate theology, biblical theology is permitted to run roughshod over systematic theology, so that to a greater or lesser extent all theology becomes Christology, or at least some version of Christology.

Vanhoozer's argument fails to account for a two-natures Christology, as if God were merely acting as God *in a man* who was tempted. In so doing, he unwittingly presupposes a univocal core between God-in-himself and God-in-Christ, and therefore draws a direct line from the manner in which God-in-Christ felt temptation to the manner in which God-in-himself feels our grief. Conversely, we must maintain that the Son of God felt the full force of his temptation in a manner peculiar *to his human nature*, albeit holy and undefiled by sin, and not according to his deity. Therefore, it cannot simply be assumed that, because Jesus is God, he provides a univocal window into the inner life of God's very being.

Speaking of Christ the Mediator, Owen maintained that in all of the actions of his "rational faculties and powers of his soul, his understanding, will, and *affections* . . . he acted grace *as a man*."[19] All that he experienced in the flesh, as a representative of his people, he experienced as a man. Weinandy expressed the same concern, which is the acknowledgement of the full humanity of the Mediator in his work.

> Within the Incarnation the Son of God never does anything as God. If he did, he would be acting as God in a man. This the Incarnation will never permit. All that Jesus did as the Son of God was done as a man—whether it was eating carrots or raising someone from the dead. He may have raised Lazarus from the dead by his divine power or better, by the power of the Holy Spirit, but it was, nonetheless, as man that he did so. Similarly, the Son of God did not suffer as God in a man, for to do so would mean that he was not a man. The Son of God suffered as a man.[20]

---

[19] Owen, *Works*, 3:169, emphasis added.
[20] Weinandy, *Does God Suffer?*, 205.

All that the Son of God did in the flesh, he did, not merely as God within a man, but as a man. Hence, in the incarnation, God is not merely revealed in a man, but as a man.

"No one has seen God at any time. The only begotten Son, who is in the bosom of the Father, He has declared *Him*" (John 1:18), but we must not forget that it is as a man that he has done so. "And the Word became flesh and dwelt among us, and we beheld His glory, the glory as of the only begotten of the Father . . ." (John 1:14). In this way, God has condescended in the revelation of himself in the person of Jesus. He is the express image of God, the image of the invisible God, who has declared the Father whom no one has seen, and is the fullest and final revelation of God, and indeed is God. Nonetheless, he is God *in the flesh*, and as such preeminently reveals God to us analogically, according to his creaturely mode of being. Although Jesus is God, he reveals God to us as a man, *via causalitatis* (by way of causality).[21]

This means love cannot be predicated of God-in-himself and God-in-the-flesh univocally, but only analogically. In other words, the love which he reveals to us in his own person is most certainly the love of God, but it is God's love clothed over in flesh. "'God is love,' as John says, and Christ is love covered over with flesh, yea, our flesh."[22] That is, Christ reveals God's love to us in a different manner from what it is in God himself — as a glorified perfection in man, rather than its infinite mode of being in God himself. In the flesh, God's incomprehensible divine love is most fully and perfectly communicated to his people *in a human manner*, accommodated to our capacity.

The Love of God and a Truly Christ-centered Hermeneutic

It may be safe to assume that much of the contemporary evangelical propensity to modify or reject divine impassibility is motivated by a legitimate desire. It is, perhaps, the desire to know that there is a

---

[21] See chapter 1, "Analogy and the Doctrine of Divine Impassibility."

[22] Thomas Goodwin, *The Heart of Christ in Heaven Towards Sinners on Earth*, in *The Works of Thomas Goodwin*, vol. 4, ed. Thomas Smith (Edinburgh: James Nichol, 1862), 116.

God who sympathizes with our weaknesses, knows what it is like to be tempted as a man, and especially knows how to help in time of need, as one man to another. It is a good desire and a legitimate need, but we dishonor God and the unique design of his condescension in the incarnation when we look for the remedy anywhere but in Christ, the Mediator.

It is important to remember that these needs arise because of something lacking in us, not in God. We need a sympathizing Savior on account of our sin and misery, and, as it has been shown, it is no imperfection in God, *as God*, to be incapable of such things. Therefore, the Son of God did not assume a human nature in order to overcome a problem within the Godhead, but freely and graciously to provide the remedy for sinners. Thus, in Christ the Mediator, we discover that what cannot be properly said of God, *as God*, may now be said of God, *as man*, on behalf of man.

When the glory of God in Christ and his work as Mediator are understood as the scope of Scripture (2LCF 1:5), we are able to apply a truly Christ-centered hermeneutic to the Old Testament.[23] That which was improperly and figuratively predicated of God, after the manner of men, in the Old Testament finds its proper and formal fulfillment in the person and office of Jesus Christ.[24] For

---

[23] For discussions on the scope of Scripture see James M. Renihan, "Theology on Target: The Scope of the Whole (which is to give all glory to God)," *RBTR* II:2 (July 2005): 36-52 and Richard C. Barcellos, "*Scopus Scripturae*: John Owen, Nehemiah Coxe, our Lord Jesus Christ, and a Few Early Disciples on Christ as the Scope of Scripture," *JIRBS* (2015): 5-24.

[24] A crucial distinction must be maintained between OT theophanies/Christophanies and the incarnation of the Son of God. When God, even the Son, revealed himself in the OT, he did not assume the nature of a man, or an angel, or so-called covenantal properties so as to unite them to himself in a unity of person, which is proper to the incarnation alone. In an editorial comment in the translation of Augustine's *On the Trinity*, W. G. T. Shedd concludes:

A theophany, though a harbinger of the incarnation, differs from it, by not effecting a hypostatical or personal union between God and the creature. When the Holy Spirit appeared in the form of a dove, he did not unite himself with it. The dove did not constitute an integral part of the divine person who employed it. Nor did the illuminated vapor in the theophany of the Shekinah. But when the Logos appeared in the form of a man, he united himself with it, so that it became a constituent part of his person. A theophany, as Augustin

instance, in Isaiah 63:9, God is described figuratively and
improperly, after the manner of men.

> In all their affliction He was afflicted, And the Angel of His
> Presence saved them; In His love and in His pity He
> redeemed them; And He bore them and carried them All the
> days of old.

God did not undergo grief, but he was *like* a father to Israel who
was afflicted in the affliction of his children. He not only identified
with them in their affliction, but in compassion, he relieved them of
their distress as surely as if it were his own.

Isaiah was reminding Israel that although the people of God
could expect suffering and affliction, they may also expect God to
be their deliverer, even as he was in the past. God is assuring those
who trust in him that nothing can separate them from his love; "the
Angel of His Presence" will save and deliver them. Yet Isaiah has
already revealed to them that their deliverer, in the ultimate sense,
will endure a brutal participation in their affliction (Isa. 52:13-53:12).
In this way, the Lord was proleptically speaking of, and pointing his
people to, the Son of God incarnate. In the greatness of God's love,
he has not only freely identified himself with his children in their
misery, but he has acted in unspeakable compassion to relieve their
affliction as surely as if it were his own. Indeed, in the person of
Christ, God assumed our misery as his own.

> In this the love of God was manifested toward us, that God
> has sent His only begotten Son into the world, that we might
> live through Him. [10] In this is love, not that we loved God,

---

notices, is temporary and transient. The incarnation is perpetual. Cf.
Augustine, *On the Trinity*, in *NPNF*, First Series, II.vi, 11 [n. 6] (3:43, n.
6).

As argued above, the distinction between Christophany and incarnation is no
less than the distinction between *God in a man*, albeit temporarily and transiently,
and *God as a man*. Augustine, *On the Trinity*, II.vi.11, notes, "For the word in the
flesh is one thing, and the Word made flesh is another; *i.e.* the word in man is one
thing, the Word that is man is another." The incarnation is not the consummation
of an incarnational process begun in the OT, but the fullness-of-time-fulfillment of
that which was proleptically revealed and figuratively foreshadowed in the OT.

but that He loved us and sent His Son *to be* the propitiation for our sins. (1 John 4:9-10)

In all our affliction, the Son of God was properly and formally afflicted, *as a man*. As Goodwin says:

> And so, that what before was but improperly spoken, and by way of metaphor and similitude, in the Old Testament . . . might now be truly attributed unto him in the reality [in Christ]. . . . And thus by this happy union of both natures, the language of the Old Testament, uttered only in a figure, becomes verified and fulfilled in the truth of it, as in all other things that shadows of it were in Christ fulfilled.[25]

In Christ, it may be said properly that *God* was afflicted in the affliction of his people, *as a man*.

The author of the epistle to the Hebrews labors to show the consequent necessity of the incarnation.

> Therefore, in all things He had to be made like *His* brethren, that He might be a merciful and faithful High Priest in things *pertaining* to God, to make propitiation for the sins of the people. [18] For in that He Himself has suffered, being tempted, He is able to aid those who are tempted. (Heb. 2:17-18)

It was necessary that God become a man, not only that he might make propitiation as a man, but also that he might be a sympathizing High Priest on behalf of man. In a sermon on Hebrews 4:15, Goodwin wrestled with the implications of the author's argument, saying:

> I confess I have often wondered at that expression there used, 'He took the seed of Abraham, that he might be made a merciful high priest,' Heb. ii., which at the first reading sounded as if God had been made more merciful by taking our nature. But this solved the wonder, that this assumption added a new way of God's being merciful, by means of

---

[25] Goodwin, *The Heart of Christ in Heaven*, 4:139.

which it may now be said, for the comfort and relief of our faith, that God is truly and really merciful, as a man. . . . Hence, therefore, amongst other ends of assuming man's nature, this fell in before God as one, that God might thereby become loving and merciful unto men, as one man is to another . . . that God might be for ever said to be compassionate as a man, and to be touched with a feeling of our infirmities as a man.[26]

It should be recalled that while sympathetic suffering is a perfection in relation to human nature, it entails an imperfection, insofar as it implies suffering, in relation to the divine nature. Although God lacks no divine perfection of love or mercy, apart from the incarnation he is incapable of human sympathy. It was necessary that God become a man, that he might be tempted and suffer as a man, so that he might be able to sympathize with weak and sinful man. God loves in a unique way in the person of Christ, i.e., in a human way. Goodwin elaborates:

That is, merciful in such a way as otherwise God of himself had never been; namely, even as a man. . . . Christ's manhood had all his largeness of mercy from the Deity. So that, had he not had the mercies of God to enlarge his heart toward us, he could never have held out to have for ever been merciful to us. But then, this human nature assumed, that adds a new way of being merciful. It assimilates all these mercies, and makes them the mercies of a man; it makes them human mercies, and so gives a naturalness and kindness unto them to our capacities. So that God doth now in as kindly and as natural a way pity us, who are flesh of his flesh, and bone of his bone, as a man pities a man, thereby to encourage us to come to him, and to be familiar with God, and treat with him for grace and mercy, as a man would do with a man; as knowing that in that man Christ Jesus (whom we believe upon) God dwells, and his mercies work in and through his heart in a human way.[27]

---

26 Goodwin, *The Heart of Christ in Heaven*, 4:139.
27 Goodwin, *The Heart of Christ in Heaven*, 4:136.

Conclusion

In addition to Bavinck's conclusion that "[t]hose who predicate any change whatsoever of God . . . [rob] God of his divine nature, and religion of its firm foundation and assured comfort,"[28] we may add an additional observation. Those who predicate sympathetic suffering of God, as God, rob the Son of God of the unique and gracious design of his coming in the flesh. It may be that the contemporary propensity to reject and redefine the doctrine of impassibility is motivated by legitimate felt-needs. However, the tendency to redefine the nature and character of God in search of a remedy actually robs the people of God of that very remedy. God's people are not crying out to hear that God knows their suffering in a divine way, but that there is one such as themselves who is seated upon the throne of grace on their behalf, who knows their suffering and weaknesses in a human way. As man, he is fully able to sympathize with our weaknesses; as God, he is fully able to help in time of need. As Weinandy observes:

> This is what humankind is crying out to hear, not that God experiences, in a divine manner, our anguish and suffering in the midst of a sinful and depraved world, but that he actually experienced and knew first hand, as one of us — as a man — human anguish and suffering within a sinful and depraved world.[29]

---

[28] Bavinck, *RD*, 2:158.
[29] Weinandy, *Does God Suffer?*, 206.

Chapter 13

CONFESSIONAL THEOLOGY AND
THE DOCTRINE OF DIVINE IMPASSIBILITY

James M. Renihan

By way of introduction, two things must be stated. First, our fathers in the faith understood that when confessing the doctrine of God, we must do so with the greatest reverence. Our holy God is not a specimen to be dissected and examined, but a majestic Creator to be worshiped. Our study of the doctrine of God must always be placed in a context of reverence and humility. We receive what he says about himself, and prostrate ourselves before him. Second, it is essential to remember the Creator/creature distinction. Only God may know what it means to be deity. He is unique and belongs to his own order of being. For this reason, we may only know him by way of analogy. If we keep these things in mind, we will do well.

Chapter 2 in the Structure of the Confession

Our Confession is carefully structured according to a well-established pattern. The first chapter, "Of the Holy Scriptures," provides for us the *principium cognoscendi* or principle of knowing. Richard A. Muller says:

> [T]he *principium cognoscendi,* the principle of knowing or cognitive foundation, is a term applied to Scripture as the noetic or epistemological *principium theologiae,* without which there could be no true knowledge of God and therefore no theological system . . .[1]

---

[1] Muller, *Dictionary*, 246.

The second chapter, "Of God and of the Holy Trinity," supplies us with the *principium essendi*.

> The *principium essendi*, the principle of being or essential foundation, is a term applied to God considered as the objective ground of theology without whom there could be neither revelation nor theology.[2]

Together, these two chapters provide the foundation for everything contained in the Confession. Our fathers first provide us with a statement identifying the raw material for doing theology, the Scriptures, then present to us the nature and character of the one who reveals himself in Scripture, and whose being is the basis for all true theology, the Lord our God. His being and essence, in fact, is the foundation for the existence of Scripture itself. Apart from God, there is no revelation. The nature of infallible and inerrant Scripture rests on the eternal, immutable God. Whatever follows in the Confession is molded and shaped by these two foundational principles. They are the unalterable pillars of Reformed theology. The succeeding chapters build on the doctrine contained in these two opening chapters. This is true in general, but it is also true specifically with reference to the statement that God is "without body, parts, or passions."

Immediately following the chapter on God, we encounter teaching about his decree and how it is executed in the works of creation and providence. As sovereign Lord, he purposes and brings his intention to historical fruition in his works *ad extra*. This is followed by a chapter describing the fall of man (chapter 6 elaborates on the doctrine found in 5:4), and then a lengthy section (chapters 7-20) describing God's saving purpose, granted to his elect, in and through Jesus Christ. As such, upon the foundation of Scripture and God, the Confession unfolds an understanding of God's works *ad extra*: creation, providence, and redemption.

This leads to a section on the liberty he gives to his people and finally to two chapters describing his eschatological purpose. As a whole, the Confession is a tightly woven garment — a system of theology based on scriptural exegesis, foundational principles, and mutual dependence.

---

[2] Muller, *Dictionary*, 246.

A Summary of 2LCF Chapter 2

The doctrine of chapter 2 is presented in three paragraphs. The first might be called "The One True God," the second "God's External Relations," and the third "God's Internal Relations." This is the standard order of treatment of theology proper. Muller states:

> It is . . . the typical pattern of the confessions to move from a declaration of the unity of God in his essence and attributes to the presentation of the doctrine of the Trinity. This pattern is found in the Gallican Confession, the Belgic Confession, the Scots Confession, the Thirty-nine Articles, the Second Helvetic Confession, the Irish Articles, and the Westminster Confession. All of these confessions, including . . . the Westminster Confession, refrain from developing speculative statements concerning the divine essence and attributes, but several, notably the Gallican, the Belgic and the Westminster Confessions, do present lists of the divine . . . . attributes, without elaboration, for consideration by the faithful. This pattern of doctrinal declaration reflects the Reformed view that presentation of attributes like the unity, simplicity, omnipotence, omnipresence, and eternity of God is a profoundly scriptural exercise and not at all the result of philosophical argumentation or natural theology, neither of which have any place in confessions of the church. Indeed, that most elaborate of confessions, the Westminster Confession of Faith, in its virtually exhaustive list of divine attributes, provides a clear scriptural reference for each in what may be the closest scriptural argumentation in the entire confession.[3]

A comparison of the supporting Scripture texts in the WCF and 2LCF demonstrates that the Baptists shared this conviction and commitment. Though the texts are not always the same, and the WCF's list is slightly more extensive, it is clear that our fathers would agree with Muller's characterization. The Baptists were men concerned not with philosophical speculation, but with a

---

[3] Muller, *PRRD*, 3:93.

demonstration of the teaching of Scripture.

The movement from general to specific is important to note. All that is stated in paragraphs 1 and 2 applies to the Godhead in unity; the third paragraph details the doctrine of the Trinity in classic Nicene language. In all three paragraphs, historic catholic theology is stated. Orthodox believers through the ages of the church would be able to recognize and affirm the doctrine expressed in this chapter. It is a classic articulation of the doctrine of God, based in Scripture and the reflection on Scripture found in the best theologians since the apostolic era. For this reason alone, we should be highly cautious of modifying its doctrine or terminology.

Paragraph 1 as a Whole

The first paragraph of chapter 2 of the 2LCF states:

1. The Lord our God is but (*a*) one only living, and true God; whose (*b*) subsistence is in and of himself, (*c*) infinite in being, and perfection, whose Essence cannot be comprehended by any but himself; (*d*) a most pure spirit, (*e*) invisible, without body, parts, or passions, who only hath immortality, dwelling in the light, which no man can approach unto, who is (*f*) immutable, (*g*) immense, (*h*) eternal, incomprehensible, (*i*) Almighty, every way infinite, (*k*) most holy, most wise, most free, most absolute, (*l*) working all things according to the counsel of his own immutable, and most righteous will, (*m*) for his own glory, most loving, gracious, merciful, long-suffering, abundant in goodness and truth, forgiving iniquity, transgression and sin, (*n*) the rewarder of them that diligently seek him, and withal most just, (*o*) and terrible in his judgments, (*p*) hating all sin, and who will by no means clear the (*q*) guilty.
a 1 Cor. 8. 4, 6. Deut. 6. 4. *b* Jer 10. 10. Isaiah 48. 12. *c* Exod 3. 14. *d* Joh. 4. 24. *e* 1 Tim. 1. 17. Deut. 4. 15, 16. *f* Mal. 3. 6. *g* 1 King. 8. 27. Jer. 23. 23. *h* Ps. 90. 2. *i* Gen. 17. 1. *k* Isa. 6. 3. *l* Ps. 115. 3. Isa. 46. 10. *m* Pro. 16. 4. Rom. 11. 36. *n* Exod. 34. 6, 7. Hebr. 11. 6. *o* Neh. 9. 32, 33. *p* Ps. 5. 5, 6. *q* Exod. 34. 7. Nahum 1, 2, 3.

Paragraph 1 deals with the identity of the one true God. God's self-existence and self-knowledge are presented; God exists in and of himself, he alone knows himself thoroughly and completely. He has a perfect knowledge of himself, and can alone and uniquely know what it means to be God.

The Baptists include some interesting changes to the text of the WCF. Where the Presbyterians wrote, "There is but one only, living and true God . . .," the 2LCF beautifully personalizes the statement, making it more intimate, stating, "The Lord our God is but one only living, and true God." This alteration of terminology does not change the doctrine of the WCF but brings it much closer to the believer and the church. It is language most fitting a *confession of faith*. From the outset of the chapter, God is presented as the one true and living God in his relation to his people. The editors of the 2LCF are keenly aware that the God who is infinite in perfection and being does not need to become other than what he is in order to relate to humans; he relates to us *as* the one true living God. This is a significant observation, since it sets a climate for the following phrases. When, for example, the paragraph states that God is "without . . . passions," the sense of this phrase must be understood in reference to the preceding, "The Lord our God." Though opponents of the confessional doctrine of divine impassibility seek to characterize it negatively, for our fathers it was in no sense at odds with a genuinely personal God. Unless the paragraph is self-contradictory, this is vitally important to recognize. Likewise, we must notice that our God is said to be infinite in perfection. God lacks nothing, and his perfection knows no bounds. There can be no sense of any kind in which God comes short of this perfection. He is incapable of further perfection, just as he is incapable of diminished perfection. He is perfection to the fullest sense that word is able to convey.

Divine perfection is foundational to all of the statements in this paragraph, each one being built on the preceding truths and connected to those that follow. For example, God's oneness or unity is a perfection. If there are two gods, then each relies upon some former cause outside of itself for its existence. If, however, God is the one true God, then he is truly perfect. This is asserted in God's aseity. His subsistence, or manner of existence, is of himself. This perfect independence makes God "a most pure spirit." Because he is one, caused by nothing, there is no multiplicity in him. There are no causes or effects in God. He is all that he is, simply, infinitely, and perfectly. God's unity, simplicity, actuality, and spirituality necessarily contain further truths. As infinite, God cannot be comprehended or seen. A purely actual, spiritual, perfect, infinite being cannot have passions. A self-existent eternal being is the only truly immortal being.

Wolfgang Musculus offers a helpful illustration of the logical connections in the development of the doctrine of God.

> First therefore of the essence of God it is most truly said, that it is one alone setting before us one God: now let us look what else may be conveniently said thereof. Surely there is [sic] many other things, but for this present we think good to rehearse but a few, as, that it is not made of any other thing but simple and pure. With simplicity it agreeth that he is a spirit: with the pureness, that he is called a light in which there is no darkness. It is also without body, occupying no place, incomprehensible, immutable, indivisible, impassible, incorruptible, immortal, unspeakable perfect & everlasting: which all appertaineth to the consideration of the quality of God's essence or being.[4]

Paragraph 1 of 2LCF reflects the very same interconnected development in the doctrine of God, all of which begins with a strong foundation of divine perfection. It is important to understand the interwoven character of these statements so that we can place the phrase "without . . . passions" carefully within its context.

We may summarize the design of the paragraph simply. As noted above, here we have a straightforward delineation of many of the attributes of God. The attributes of God outlined in this paragraph are intended to highlight that God is, in his very existence, complete and perfect unto himself, or, as stated simply by the Confession, "every way infinite." Even the attributes modified by the superlative "most" teach that God is utterly infinite and

---

[4] Musculus, *Common Places*, 11. The spelling has been updated for ease of reading.

independent as the holy, wise, free, and absolute God.[5] We are taught, moreover, that God is "working all things according to the counsel of His own immutable and most righteous will, for His own glory." His glory consists in and is expressed by the fact that he is "most loving, gracious, merciful, long-suffering," etc. The phrase "without . . . passions," therefore, does not contradict or diminish the fact of God's love, graciousness, mercy, and long-suffering. The concluding statements of the paragraph express the fact that God saves sinners and punishes his enemies. He "hates" all sin and will not "clear the guilty."

Taken as a whole, this first paragraph of chapter 2 is a wonderfully balanced, carefully nuanced doctrine of God. He is unlike any of his creatures and glorious in his being. He is loving, gracious, merciful, and long-suffering, he hates sin, and is a pure spirit who has no body, parts, or passions.

The Relevant Section of Paragraph 1

The phrase "without body, parts, or passions" is found in a carefully-constructed section of the first paragraph. It is preceded

---

[5] Cf. Zanchius, *Life Everlasting*, 10-11. "We affirm and teach that many names are properly given to God. Such are they which signify those things which are in God, but far more perfect, and in a more perfect manner than in the creatures: such are the names of *Goodness, Justice*, and such like, which signify some perfection in God, and which we call properties. . . . But this distinction which follows will give no small light to this question. Although almost all the names of God in the word, are taken from creatures, yet in those names must we consider two things. First the things, or the perfections signified by those names; secondly the manner how these names signify this perfection. As for the things and perfections signified by these names, as they were first, and are in God, and that in a more perfect manner than in the creatures, and by this means proper to God: so also the names themselves, in as much as these perfections are signified by them, are more properly attributed to God than to the creatures; yea do agree and are affirmed of him before any creature. . . . If then we regard the manner of signifying, they do not so properly belong to God as to us; because that which they signify is after an imperfect manner: therefore we shall make them more properly to belong to God, if we add some such words as doth increase the signification of these names, and so distinguish betwixt God and the creatures; as if that we call God *most just, most wise, most mighty*: for by this shall we put a difference betwixt the imperfect justice of man, & the perfect and essential justice of God." The spelling has been updated for ease of reading.

by another important addition, the clause, "whose Essence cannot be comprehended by any but himself." This is notable in that it emphasizes the Creator/creature distinction. Muller tells us the term "essence" refers to the "whatness or *quiddity* of a being, which makes the being precisely what it is . . . the essence of God is deity or divinity."[6] Thus, only God is able to comprehend his "whatness," or to state this differently, man cannot comprehend God in his essence. This clause is immediately followed by a series of phrases that presuppose God's incomprehensibility. God is incomprehensible because, unlike the creature, he is "a most pure spirit" who is "invisible" and "without body, parts, or passions" and the added clause influences the sense of these terms. God's infinite and perfect being, which may not be comprehended by us, cannot and does not consist of these qualities in analogous fashion in any of his creatures, including humans.

Lest the point be missed, the Baptists inserted an epexegetical statement immediately after the words "without body, parts, or passions." It reads "who only hath immortality, dwelling in the light, which no man can approach unto." Once more, emphasis is placed on the uniqueness of God. Unlike his creatures, he alone is immortal by nature. Both of these additional statements are taken from the first paragraph of the First London Confession of 1646, where they were drawn from William Ames' *The Marrow of Sacred Divinity*, Book 1, Chapter 4, Division 2. Here is how Ames expresses the doctrine in this chapter, which is titled "Of God, and his Essence":

2. God as he is in himself cannot be apprehended[7] of any, but himself 1 Tim. 6.16. Dwelling in that inaccessible light, whom never man saw, nor can see.

3. As he hath revealed himself unto us, he is conceived as it were, by the back parts, not by the Face. *Exod.* 33.23. Thou shalt see my back-parts, but my Face cannot be seen, and

---

[6] Muller, *Dictionary*, 105-06. Cf. the seventeenth-century Particular Baptist Thomas Whinnell, "An Appendix: Or, A Brief Answer to Mr. Marlow's Notion of the Essence of Singing," in Joseph Wright, *Folly Detected* (London: John Harris, 1691), 79. Whinnell says, "The term *Essence* . . . properly denotes the *Quiddity*, the Nature and Being of a Thing."

[7] I.e., "comprehended."

darkly, not clearly, that is, after an human manner, and measure, 1 Cor. 13.12. Through a glass: darkly, after a sort.

4. Because those things that pertain to God are necessarily explained after an human manner: hence is that manner of speaking frequent in these matters which is called ἀνθρωποπάθεια I.E. figure that attributes those things to God which be proper to men, as in human affections senses or members.

5. Because also they are explained after our measure, to man's capacity, hence many things are spoken of God according to the way of our conceiving, rather than from his Nature.[8]

This information is highly significant. Ames, reflecting the classical understanding of the uniqueness of God, places anthropopathisms into the very context expressed by the expanded (as over against WCF) confessional statement of the Particular Baptists. In fact, it is highly significant that the Baptists, following Ames, placed these words immediately prior to the description of God as "immutable." In Ames' exposition, we read, "hence it is that he is void of that power which is called passive, hence he is unchangeable . . . "[9] There is an intimate connection between God's essence and his immutability.

The additions to the 2LCF strengthen the sense of "without . . . passions" and elucidate its meaning. The framers of the 2LCF clarify the sense of "without . . . passions" by setting it in the context of God's incomprehensibility and ontological dissimilarity. Since God is perfect in his being, those things confessionally attributed to him must also be perfect, applicable only to God. In the case of "passions" attributed to God, they cannot and must not be understood as though God were a being like our own; the being of God, unlike the being of the creature, is "without . . . passions."

---

[8] William Ames, *The Marrow of Sacred Divinity, Drawne out of the holy Scriptures, and the Interpreters thereof, and brought into Method* (London: Edward Griffin, 1642), 10. I have modernized the spelling in this citation.

[9] Ames, *The Marrow of Sacred Divinity*, 12. This is a direct reference to and rejection of the concept of "passive potency."

The Phrase "without Body, Parts, or Passions"

This phrase is intended to serve further as part of the description of God as a "most pure spirit." He is invisible (1 Tim. 1:17), and does not possess the physical characteristics of his creatures. He is incorporeal; he is not a composite being, and he has no passions. All of these are aspects of the doctrine of divine simplicity.[10] While most Christians acknowledge that the many texts in Scripture that describe God having physical characteristics (i.e., eyes, hands, heart, etc.) are metaphorical,[11] and are willing to affirm that God is not a composite being,[12] the sense of "passions" as intended by the historic doctrine is frequently misunderstood or rejected.

There is really no doubt as to how the word "passions" is to be understood.[13] Muller helpfully defines the term:

> An affection is usually favorable or positive, whereas passion is usually negative. . . . A passion, most strictly, is a form of suffering and would not have the connotation of a permanent disposition . . . . Passions . . . indicate a declension from an original or natural condition that is at variance with the fundamental inclination of the individual — and therefore, a loss of power or self-control.
>
> . . . Since a passion has its foundation *ad extra* and its terminus *ad intra*, it cannot be predicated of God, and, in fact, fails to correspond in its dynamic with the way that God knows. An affection or virtue, by way of contrast, has its foundation or source *ad intra* and terminates *ad extra*, corresponding with the pattern of operation of the divine

---

[10] See Dolezal, *God without Parts*.

[11] Though there is a growing movement toward accepting these as having some literal sense.

[12] Though perhaps without a clear comprehension of the implications of the teaching.

[13] Contra Robert Letham, who makes the incredible claim that "the meaning of 'passions' is not entirely clear" in *The Westminster Assembly: Reading its Theology in Historical Context* (Phillipsburg, NJ: P&R Publishing, 2009), 160. In fact, the meaning of passions is well-established in the literature from the sixteenth century onward. See Muller, *PRRD*, 3:551ff., as well as Renihan, ed., *God without Passions: A Reader*. One wonders how such a scholar could write such a howler. Is it possible that his distaste for the classical doctrine has influenced him at this point?

communicable attributes and, in particular, with the manner of divine knowing.[14]

"Most strictly" passions are "usually negative," insofar as they usually "indicate a declension" or "a loss of power or self-control." It is easy to see how rage, for instance, could be considered a negative passion or "a form of suffering." Moreover, a passion may refer to any internal emotional change, positive or negative, that has its cause in something external to itself. More generally, the term passion may refer to any change that has its terminus *ad intra*. The issue is neither merely whether the change is negative or positive, nor whether it is caused from without or within, but whether or not God is in any way capable of *inner* changes of emotional state.

Edward Reynolds, a member of the Westminster Assembly, defined passions in this way:

> Passions are nothing else, but those naturall perfective and unstrained motions of the Creatures unto that advancement of their Natures, which they are by the Wisdom, Power, and Providence of their Creator, in their own severall Spheres, and according to the proportion of their capacities, ordained to receive, by a regular inclination to those objects, whose goodness beareth a naturall conveniencie or vertue of satisfaction unto them; or by an antipathie and aversion from those, which bearing a contrarietie to the good they desire, must needs be noxious and destructive, and by consequent, odious to their natures. This being the propertie of all unconstrained self-motions it followeth, that the root and ground of all Passions, is principally the good; and secondarily, or by consequent, the evill of things: as one beareth with it *rationem convenientiae*, a quieting and satisfactory; the other, *rationem disconvenientiae* a disturbing and destroying nature.[15]

---

[14] Muller, *PRRD*, 3:553-54. Please note that Muller carefully employs the word "usually." In the vast post-Reformation literature on the topic, it is not difficult to find examples of theologians who use the term "passions" positively. See for example the citation from Reynolds below.

[15] Edward Reynolds, *A Treatise of the Passions and Faculties of the Soul of Man* (London: Printed for Robert Bostock, 1656), 31-32.

This is a helpful definition, in that it demonstrates that passions are possessed by creatures, and are to be understood in terms of response to external stimuli and movement toward perfection. Creatures experience passions as a response to new external stimuli, but, as Muller points out, God neither acquires new information nor responds to external stimuli. Likewise, creatures may experience passions in a positive sense, as when someone's joy is perfected. Something is lacking in the creature, and it seeks to complete itself. Passions may be righteous or evil. Yet God lacks no perfection. If we remember that the statement "without body, parts, or passions" is found in the midst of a discussion of the uniqueness of God, we may see the vital importance of the doctrine. God does not need perfecting and he does not respond to external stimuli. He knows all things and cannot be caught off guard by any action in the universe he created and rules. Moreover, because of what he is, he is imperfectible. Passions may be ascribed to creatures in their finitude, but cannot be predicated of the infinite God. This is not to deny genuine love, mercy, wrath, etc. in God. It is simply to say these things must be understood in a sense proper to God, and not univocally to humans. To quote the man most likely to have served as one of the editors of our Confession, Nehemiah Coxe, "we must always remember, that those things that are spoken of God *anthropopathos* after the manner of men, must be interpreted *theoprepos* in a sense becoming God."[16]

Other Relevant Expressions in the Confession

Chapter 2, paragraph 1 is not the only relevant place in the Confession to address this issue. We have already noted that in this paragraph itself we find statements about *our* God's love, grace, mercy, long-suffering, and goodness. Though the term wrath is not used,[17] it is clearly implied at the end of the paragraph. We must not be guilty of the word-concept fallacy which assumes that a specific term must be present in order for a topic to be under consideration. In fact, there is much else in the Confession relevant to the phrase

---

[16] Nehemiah Coxe, *Vindiciae Veritatis*, 2.

[17] It appears at 6:3 and 21:1.

"without . . . passions." In the second paragraph of chapter 2, we read:

2. God having all (r) life, (s) glory, (t) goodness, blessedness, in and of himself: is alone in, and unto himself all-sufficient, not (u) standing in need of any Creature which he hath made, nor deriving any glory from them, but only manifesting his own glory in, by, unto, and upon them, he is the alone fountain of all Being, (x) of whom, through whom, and to whom are all things, and he hath most sovereign (y) dominion over all creatures, to do by them, for them, or upon them, whatsoever himself pleaseth; in his sight (z) all things are open and manifest, his knowledge is (a) infinite, infallible, and independent upon the Creature, so as nothing is to him contingent, or uncertain; he is most holy in all his Counsels, in (b) all his Works, and in all his Commands; to him is due (c) from Angels and men, whatsoever worship, service, or obedience as Creatures they owe unto the Creator, and whatever he is further pleased to require of them.
r Joh. 5.26. s Ps. 148.13. t Ps. 119.68. u Job, 22.2,3. x Rom. 11.34.35,36. y Dan. 4.25. and v.34,35. z Heb. 4.13. a Ezek. 11.5 Act. 15.18. b Ps. 145.17. c Rev. 5.12,13,14.

In this section, which describes God's relations to the world he has created, we learn that God possesses all that is necessary to be God. He needs nothing and takes nothing from his creatures, but only gives to them. At the beginning of the statement, we read that God has "all life, glory, goodness, blessedness, in and of himself." His life, glory, goodness, and blessedness are imperfectible—they cannot increase to a greater level of perfection. Blessedness here must be understood as happiness. God exists eternally in perfect bliss. He has always and will always enjoy this personal delight. His joy cannot decrease, nor will it increase—it is perfect. He has all blessedness.

When we think of the grace of God in salvation, we must think in terms of God's virtues, his love being prominent among them all. God is love, and our Confession reflects the rich recognition of this fact in the Reformed writers. It does so in direct relation to the phrase "without . . . passions." For example, in chapter 3, "Of God's Decree," we read:

> 5. Those of mankind (*l*) that are predestinated to life, God before the foundation of the world was laid, according to his eternal and immutable purpose, and the secret Counsel and good pleasure of his will, hath chosen in Christ unto everlasting glory, out of his mere free grace and love; (*m*) without any other thing in the creature as a condition or cause moving him thereunto.
> *l* Eph. 1.4.9.11. Rom. 8.30. 2 Tim. 1.9. 1 Thes. 5.9. *m* Rom. 9.13.16. Eph. 1.6.12.

The salvation of the elect is dependent on an eternal love which has no regard to anything in the creature but is only a manifestation of God's own "secret Counsel and good pleasure." He sets his love upon them from eternity. This same idea is carried throughout the Confession. In chapter 17, "Of the Perseverance of the Saints," we read that God accepts the elect "in the beloved." This is Christ. God's love for his people is based in his eternal love for his own Son. Later in the chapter, speaking of how the perseverance of the saints is effected, we read:

> 2. This perseverance of the Saints depends not upon their own free will; but upon the immutability of the decree of (*d*) Election flowing from the free and unchangeable love of God the Father; upon the efficacy of the merit and intercession of Jesus Christ (*e*) and Union with him, the (*f*) oath of God, the abiding of his Spirit & the (*g*) seed of God within them, and the nature of the (*h*) Covenant of Grace from all which ariseth also the certainty and infallibility thereof.
> *d* Rom. 8.30. ch. 9.11.16. *e* Rom. 5.9,10. John 14.19. *f* Heb. 6.17,18. *g* 1 Joh. 3.9. *h* Jer. 32.40.

Here we find perseverance grounded in the immutability of the decree of God, which is itself founded on the unchangeable love of God. These statements ought to bring the mind of the reader back to chapters 2 and 3 and their carefully stated doctrine of God. The decree is eternal because God is eternal, and it is immutable because God is immutable. Notice carefully that perseverance finds its source in the "unchangeable love of God." This is a source of immense blessing for God's people. His love for them is eternal and unchangeable, just as he is. It does not and cannot fluctuate—it is not passionate—it is unchangeable, i.e., impassible.

Chapter 23, paragraph 3 also provides a relevant piece of the picture. Chapter 2 established a methodology for theology proper. It taught that we must exercise caution in the way that we speak of God. We must not violate the perfection of his nature. Given, then, that the Confession is clear in denying passions to God, one might be surprised to see it speak of God being "provoked." In 2LCF 23.3, when guarding the ways and occasions in which lawful oaths may be taken, the oath-taker is exhorted to

> consider the weightiness of so solemn an act; and therein to avouch nothing, but what he knoweth to be the truth; for that by rash, false, and vain *Oaths* the Lord is provoked, and for them this Land mournes.

Can God be provoked? What we need to do is to apply the methodology of chapter 2 to chapter 23. There is no sin or error in speaking as the Scriptures do. God is provoked by sinful vows that invoke his name. It would be an error, however, to understand this concept univocally of God and man. If we apply the methodology of chapter 2 to chapter 23, then we understand that provoking God simply means that God has stated that he punishes oath-breakers and those who take his name in vain, on the basis of his immutable justice. This in turn takes us back to chapters 3 and 19 where we understand the distinction between God's decree concerning what he will do, which cannot change or be changed, and the will of God for mankind (2LCF 19.6). If God has commanded us not to make rash vows, and more so not to break them, and if God has decreed to punish oath-breakers, not absolutely but generally, then we have a scripturally balanced way of understanding God being "provoked" by the infidelity of oath-breakers.

Implications for Succeeding Chapters and Doctrines

To modify the doctrine of divine impassibility has serious consequences. It would be a serious mistake to conclude that these words are somehow disconnected from the body of the Confession as a whole, or that they may be modified without adjusting other theological statements in the Confession. For example, the next chapter of the Confession, "Of God's Decree," begins with these words:

> 1. God hath (*a*) *Decreed* in himself from all Eternity, by the most wise and holy Counsel of his own will, freely and unchangeably, all things whatsoever comes to pass; yet so as thereby is God neither the author of sin, (*b*) nor hath fellowship with any therein, nor is violence offered to the will of the Creature, nor yet is the liberty, or contingency of second causes taken away, but rather (*c*) established, in which appears his wisdom in disposing all things, and power, and faithfulness (*d*) in accomplishing his *Decree*.
> *a* Is. 46.10. Eph. 1.11. Heb. 6.17. Rom. 9.15,18. *b* Jam. 1.15,17. 1 Joh. 1.5. *c* Act 4.27,28. Joh. 19.11. *d* Numb. 23.19. Eph. 1.3,4,5.

One must ask, if God has decreed all things in himself, infallibly knowing them and bringing them to pass, how is it possible for him to react to the events he foreordains? His decree, as an *ad intra* divine work, is consistent with his very being, and cannot be otherwise than perfectly just, gracious, etc. If God is in any sense passible, however, then so also is his knowledge and will, and so also then his decree. This relationship is at the very root of objections raised by Arminians, Semi-Pelagians, Pelagians, and Open Theists.

Perhaps most significant are the implications for Christology and the incarnation of our Lord Jesus Christ. In chapter 8, "Of Christ the Mediator," we find a description of the person and work of Christ, the eternal Son of God who took upon himself our humanity so we might be redeemed. The doctrine taught there rightly conforms, in paragraph 2, to the Chalcedonian definition of the incarnation and hypostatic union, instructing us that Jesus Christ is two natures in the one person. These two natures are "inseparably joined together in one person, without conversion, composition, or confusion." This is an ancient distinction, made to avoid several heresies present in the early church. These heresies arose because people could not hold in tension doctrinal propositions that seemed to be contradictory. How could God become man? Arianism, in its various forms, denied that Christ was fully God; Docetism denied his true humanity; Nestorianism divided or separated the divine and human natures; Eutychianism confused the two natures. Orthodox Christology refuted these errors by holding in tension the fact that our Savior is at the same time truly God and truly man, yet only one person. Theopaschism and Patripassianism argued, in various forms, that the Godhead entered into suffering. Orthodox Christology avoided this error by asserting that Christ, *according to his human nature*, suffered, and that this cannot then be read back into the Godhead. In paragraph 4, we read about his office of Mediator:

> 4. This office the *Lord Jesus* did most (s) willingly undertake, which that he might discharge he was made under the Law, (t) and did perfectly fulfill it, and underwent the (u) punishment due to us, which we should have born and suffered, being made (x) *Sin* and a *Curse* for us: enduring most grievous sorrows (y) in his Soul; and most painful sufferings in his body; was crucified, and died, and remained in the state of the dead; yet saw no (z) *corruption*: on the (a) third day he arose from the dead, with the same (b) body in which he suffered; with which he also (c) ascended into heaven: and there sitteth at the right hand of *his Father*, (d) making intercession; and shall (e) return to judge *Men* and *Angels*, at the end of the World.
> s Ps. 40.7,8. Heb. 10.5-11. Joh. 10.18. t Gal. 4.4. Mat. 3.15. u Gal. 3.13. Isa. 53.6. 1 Pet. 3.18. x 2 Cor. 5.21. y Mat. 26.37,38. Luk. 22.44. Mat. 27.46. z Act. 13.37. a 1 Cor. 15.3,4. b Joh. 20.25.27. c Mark 16.19. Act. 1.9,10,11. d Rom. 8.34. Heb. 9.24 e Act. 10.42. Rom. 14.9,10. Act. 1.10.

The seventh paragraph states:

> 7. Christ in the work of *Mediation* acteth according to both natures, by each nature doing that which is proper to itself; yet by reason of the Unity of the Person, that which is proper to one nature, is sometimes in *Scripture* attributed to the Person (k) denominated by the other nature.
> k Joh. 3.13. Act. 20.28.

This is the doctrine of the *communicatio idiomatum*, or communication of idioms (i.e., respective properties). It explains to us the careful distinction that is necessary in this case. For example, though Scripture may speak of God's blood in Acts 20:28, we know this is only stated in this fashion because it is the blood of the one person, who is both God and man, which is spilled. God does not have blood, but the God-man, according to his human nature, does have blood, and he spills his blood for his people.[18]

The doctrine of the *communicatio idiomatum* is based on the carefully-worded declaration of the Council of Chalcedon from A.D. 451. In English translation, it states:

> We, then, following the holy Fathers, all with one consent, teach men to confess . . . one and the same Christ, Son, Lord, Only-begotten, to be acknowledged in two natures, inconfusedly, unchangeably, indivisibly, inseparably. The distinction of the natures being by no means taken away by the union, but rather the property of each nature being preserved, and concurring in one Person . . .[19]

Notice how our Confession employs this language in Chapter 8.2:

> 2. The *Son* of *God*, the second Person in the *Holy Trinity*, being very and eternal *God*, the brightness of the Fathers glory, of one substance and equal with *him*: who made the World, who upholdeth and governeth all things he hath made: did when the fullness of time was come take unto him (*f*) mans nature, with all the Essential properties, and common infirmities thereof, (*g*) yet without sin: being conceived by the *Holy Spirit* in the *Womb* of the *Virgin Mary*, the *Holy Spirit* coming down upon her, and the power of the

---

[18] Cf. Coxe, *Vindiciae Veritatis*, 17. "They [the Scriptures] say indeed, That the Prince of Life was killed, and the Lord of Glory was Crucified: So the Scripture saith also, that God purchased his Church by his blood; and laid down his life for us: The person that died was very God, the Prince of Life and Lord of Glory, but it was in the Humane nature, and not in his Divine that he suffered, although both made but one person; and to reject this, and say with Mr. *Collier*, that as God *&c.* his Bloud was shed, he was crucified and died, *i.e.* that all these things befell the Divine as well as the Humane nature; is impious to that degree, as may make a tender heart bleed, and the ears of a godly man to tingle."

[19] Creed of Chalcedon (A.D. 451).

most *High* overshadowing her, (*h*) and so was made of a *Woman*, of the Tribe of *Judah*, of the Seed of *Abraham*, and *David* according to the *Scriptures*: So that two whole, perfect, and distinct natures, were inseparably joined together in one *Person*: without *conversion*, *composition*, or *confusion*: which *Person* is very *God*, and very *Man*; yet one (*i*) *Christ*, the only *Mediator* between *God* and *Man*.
f Joh. 1.1.14. Gal. 4.4. *g* Rom. 8.3. Heb. 2.14.16,17. ch. 4.15. *h* Luk. 1.27,31.35. *i* Rom. 9.5. 1 Tim. 2.5.

There is a carefully woven doctrine here. In agreement with Chalcedon's strictures regarding each nature retaining its particular properties, the Confession necessarily insists that we speak carefully of Christ as a Mediator according to both natures. All the acts of the Mediator are acts of the undivided person; and yet Christ Jesus accomplishes each mediatorial act according to each nature, divine and human, doing that which is proper to itself.

We must maintain this distinction. The term "passion" properly applies only to Christ as our Mediator according to his human nature, and must not flow back into Christ as our Mediator according to his divine nature and thus to the eternal Trinity.[20] In fact, this emphasis is exactly what we find in the New Testament. The apostles do not point us to a passionate God, but rather to a compassionate Savior who has taken our nature and is able to sympathize with us in our time of weakness (Heb. 4:14-16). When we modify the confessional doctrine of divine impassibility, we undermine the source of greatest comfort and blessing available to us — our understanding of the person and work of our great high priest, Jesus Christ.

Summary

The phrase "without . . . passions," found in chapter 2, paragraph 1 of the 2LCF, is an important and foundational doctrine in the

---

[20] Cf. Coxe, *Vindiciae Veritatis*, 18. "The common faith of Christians about this matter is, That the same Jesus who suffered made satisfaction to Divine Justice for their sins; but that his sufferings were in his Humane nature only."

system of the Confession. It functions as part of the doctrine that the immutable God is unique, self-existent, and perfect in every way. It teaches us that he does not have emotions univocal to human emotions, yet it never denies, even by implication, the perfections of love, grace, mercy, justice, etc. in the true and living God. In the 2LCF, divine impassibility is founded in the eternal nature of God, and has significant implications for the topics of theology found in the rest of the Confession.

Chapter 14

PRACTICAL THEOLOGY AND
THE DOCTRINE OF DIVINE IMPASSIBILITY

James P. Butler

Confessional Reformed Christians believe theology is practical for the church. We rightly resist the trend to moralize the text of Scripture; rather, we exegete it to determine its meaning and then draw implications or applications from the text or the specific doctrine under consideration. Moreover, we believe the doctrine of God itself (theology proper) is particularly practical for the believer. We are in good company. For instance, the Lord Jesus identifies the sum and substance of eternal life (which is a present possession of the believer) as the knowledge of God and of Christ (John 17:3). John Calvin begins his famous *Institutes of the Christian Religion*[1] with a discussion of "The Knowledge of God the Creator" which serves as the foundation for the entirety of his systematic presentation of the Christian faith, including those things particularly labeled practical. The 2LCF also highlights the practicality of the doctrine of God in the same paragraph in which it is articulated. After a rehearsal of God in his essential glory, the Confession then describes God in a most heartwarming manner as follows:

> [God is] most loving, gracious, merciful, long-suffering, abundant in goodness and truth, forgiving iniquity, transgression and sin; the rewarder of them that diligently seek him, and withal most just and terrible in his judgments. (2LCF 2.1)

In this chapter, we seek to present some of the practical

---

[1] Calvin, *Institutes*, I.

implications of the doctrine of divine impassibility. Among them will be its relationship to the saving knowledge of God, the Christian life, and the worship we offer to God. Finally, it will consider the important consequences of the doctrine of divine impassibility for the pastor who labors in the Word and in doctrine.

The Saving Knowledge of God

The apostle Paul declares the universal guilt of all mankind in the sight of God in Romans 1:18-3:20. In chapter 1, he deals specifically with those who were outside of the covenant community. He speaks of general revelation and indicates that men by nature know God (Rom. 1:19), but because of sin, they do "not glorify God, nor [are] they thankful" to him (Rom. 1:21). After highlighting the Gentile defection from God in the remainder of chapter 1, Paul demonstrates the guilt of the Jews in chapter 2 and then concludes his argument in 3:1-20 by stating unequivocally that all men, everywhere, are justly liable to punishment from God because of their depravity. Thankfully, our gracious God did not leave all mankind in this state: he purposed to save his elect by Jesus Christ. According to his immutable plan, he sent his Son into the world to save his people from their sins (Matt. 1:21). Christ secured redemption through his life, death, and resurrection.

Paul continues, in Romans 3:21ff, to demonstrate how men, by God's grace, are moved from wrath to life; it is by grace alone through faith alone in Christ alone.[2] The Bible identifies this message as the gospel, or good news. Scripture clearly teaches that this gospel is to be freely and indiscriminately preached to every creature (Mark 16:15).[3] The doctrine of divine impassibility ensures that when the gospel is preached, it ought to be preached with the absolute conviction that the God who is proclaimed does not waver; he does not fluctuate; he does not change on a whim. Gavrilyuk rightly comments:

---

[2] As argued in the systematic theology section, it is not God who changes in relation to man, but it is man, who, by God's grace, is changed in relation to God.

[3] The doctrine of divine impassibility does not negate the free offer of the gospel, but rather secures it.

It is precisely because God is impassible, i.e., free of uncontrollable vengeance, that repentant sinners may approach him without despair. Far from being a barrier to divine care and loving-kindness, divine impassibility is their very foundation. Unlike that of humans who are unreliable and swayed by passions, God's love is enduring and devoid of all those weaknesses with which human love is tainted.[4]

The saving knowledge of God does not change. What was true concerning Abraham and his justification by faith (Gen. 15:16; Rom 4:3; Gal. 3:6) is true of men today. The believer who possesses the saving knowledge of God has a sure foundation, an unchangeable foundation for his acceptance with God.

This knowledge is also foundational for everything that follows from man's acceptance with God. John Gill writes:

Since the knowledge of God and of divine things is a part and branch of true godliness, or of experimental religion, and a very essential one too, it is first to be considered; for without it there can be no good disposition in the mind towards God; for *ignoti nulla cupido,* there are no affections for, nor desires after an unknown object.[5]

Since impassibility is properly predicated of God, then a denial of this truth will have damaging consequences for the believer. However, as the previous chapters make clear, the classical doctrine of divine impassibility is biblical. Therefore, it is crucial that the believer who has been given this saving knowledge of God understand it, affirm it, and respond accordingly in light of it, because as Gill says, "the knowledge of God and of divine things is a part and branch of true godliness."

The immutable God executes his eternal plan by revealing himself to his elect through the gospel. Once justified by the grace of God through faith in the Lord Jesus, the child of God lives the life of an adopted son under the gracious care and infinite wisdom of his Father in heaven.

---

4 Gavrilyuk, *Suffering,* 62.
5 Gill, *Body of Divinity,* 705.

The Christian Life

The Christian life is a life lived unto the God who is set forth in the Scriptures. The Bible teaches that "God is love" (1 John 4:8). The 2LCF 2.1 asserts that God is "most loving." Critics of the classical doctrine of divine impassibility fear that to affirm this doctrine would reduce God to a static, inert, and unfeeling being. We wholeheartedly assert that nothing could be further from the truth! Impassibility secures the absolute love of God for his people; he does not increase in his love for them, since he is "most loving." Neither does his love for them decrease, because he is "most loving." The love that God has for his people is the love that God has for his Son; it is a love that is utterly and completely absolute. This love is unchanging and unchanged, even though his children do not always respond to him as they ought. John Owen comments:

> The love of God in itself is the eternal purpose and act of his will. This is no more changeable than God himself: if it were, no flesh could be saved; but it changeth not, and we are not consumed [Mal. 3:6]. What then? loves he his people in their sinning? Yes; his people, — not their sinning. Alters not his love towards them? Not the *purpose* of his will, but the *dispensations* of his grace. He *rebukes* them, he *chastens* them, he *hides* his face from them, he *smites* them, he *fills* them with a sense of [his] indignation; but woe, woe would it be to us, should he change in his love, or take away his kindness from us! Those very things which seem to be demonstrations of the change of his affection towards his, do as clearly proceed from love as those which seem to be the most genuine issues thereof. "But will not this encourage to sin?" He never tasted of the love of God that can seriously make this objection. The *doctrine* of grace may be turned into wantonness; the *principle* cannot.[6]

The believer not only derives much comfort from the love of God, but he also gains immeasurable comfort from the doctrine of divine providence. The doctrine of divine impassibility affords

---

[6] Owen, *Works*, 2:30-31.

immeasurable comfort with reference to divine providence. Chapter 5 in the 2LCF treats "Of Divine Providence" which is one of the means by which God executes his decree.[7] The chapter deals with the absolute sovereignty of God over all that takes place in this world and clearly states that these things come from "God the good Creator of all things" (2LCF 5.1). This means the difficulties that come to the believer come from the hand of a good God, a God who is working out his purpose for his children. When Job lost his children to death, he did not lose his refuge in God. It was his understanding of who God is that led him to worship and declare in the midst of terrible tragedy, "Naked I came from my mother's womb, and naked shall I return there. The LORD gave, and the LORD has taken away; blessed be the name of the LORD" (Job 1:21). Job acknowledges God's hand of providence in provision and deprivation and his response is consistent because in both instances God remains unchanged, and as a result, he remains worthy of worship. Matthew Henry comments:

> He adores God in both. When all was gone, he fell down and worshipped. Note, Afflictions must not divert us from, but quicken us to, the exercises of religion. Weeping must not hinder sowing, nor hinder worshipping. He eyed not only the hand of God, but the name of God, in his afflictions, and gave glory to that: *Blessed be the name of the Lord.* He has still the same great and good thoughts of God that ever he had, and is as forward as ever to speak them forth to his praise; and can find in his heart to bless God even when he takes away as well as when he gives.[8]

In addition to these seasons, there are also difficult providences that occur on a corporate level. In such circumstances, the immutability of God provides stability for the people of God. Psalm 46 is an excellent example of this type of frowning providence. The psalmist does not minimize the difficulties facing the people of God, but he does counsel the saints on the way to deal with such

---

[7] The WSC 8 says, "How doth God execute his decrees? God executeth his decrees in the works of creation and providence." This ties together chapters 3-5 in the 2LCF.

[8] Henry, *Commentary on the Holy Bible,* 3:7.

difficulties: they are to seek help in God and it is because he is immutable and impassible that he is "our refuge and strength, a very present help in trouble" (Psalm 46:1). It is because God is immutable and impassible that the psalmist can exhort the people of God: "Be still and know that I am God" (Psalm 46:10). The believer may be still because his God is still; that is, he is in absolute control of all things and remains unchanged and unchanging. This is true in even the most severe seasons of distress.

The 2LCF 5.5 states, "The most wise, righteous, and gracious God doth oftentimes leave for a season his own children to manifold temptations and the corruptions of their own hearts . . ."[9] Even in those seasons when it appears to the believer that his God has left him, impassibility, in concert with divine providence, ensures the believer that such is not the case. For instance, the Lord chastens his children during various times of their Christian life. This is not the result of an emotional conflict in God, but is the means by which he sanctifies his children. These periods of chastening are not a forfeiture of God's goodness for a time; rather they are a means by which God executes his eternal decree. In the book of Hebrews, the author acknowledges the presence of trials in the believer's life. In Hebrews 12:7, the author states, "If you endure chastening, God deals with you as with sons." The author does not declare that God has altered his goodness and love for a period of time; rather he instructs the believer that the God who executes his immutable decree has a remedial purpose for his children. "Now no chastening seems to be joyful for the present, but painful; nevertheless, afterward it yields the peaceable fruit of righteousness to those who have been trained by it" (Heb. 12:11). As Owen (quoted above) says:

> He *rebukes* them, he *chastens* them, he *hides* his face from them, he *smites* them, he *fills* them with a sense of [his] indignation; but woe, woe would it be to us, should he change in his love, or take away his kindness from us! Those very things which seem to be demonstrations of the change

---

[9] The attentive reader should recognize the same sort of description here of God as is found in 2LCF 2.1. A denial of the truth of 2.1 affects the entirety of the Confession.

of his affection towards his, do as clearly proceed from love as those which seem to be the most genuine issues thereof.[10]

The doctrine of divine impassibility assures us that God remains perfectly good, infinitely wise, absolutely righteous, and unalterably gracious, even during those seasons of difficulty endured by his children. In light of this, the believer not only confesses such glorious truth in his doctrinal affirmation, but sings this truth in the midst of trial and difficulty: "Judge not the Lord by feeble sense, but trust him for his grace; behind a frowning providence he hides a smiling face."[11] It is feeble sense which posits change in God; it is biblical truth that steels the soul in the midst of affliction.

The doctrine of divine impassibility is the backdrop for God's covenantal dealings with his people. The 2LCF 7.3 traces this reality: the covenant of grace is revealed in the context of the broken covenant of works, it is communicated to Adam in "the promise of salvation by the seed of the woman," and it is "founded in that eternal covenant transaction that was between the Father and the Son about the redemption of the elect."[12] While it is good to reflect upon the salvation of individual sinners, it is also helpful to view the macrocosmic plan of God. The totality of God's elect come to eternal salvation because of the plan of an unchanging and unchanged God who purposed from before time began to save his people. The means by which he carries out his plan is through covenant. If God is swayed by circumstances or fluctuates, the believer has no certain foundation for the covenantal relationship that God initiates with him. Impassibility ensures that those promised to Christ in the eternal transaction agreed upon by the Father and the Son will most assuredly reap every spiritual blessing in the heavenly places in Christ (Eph. 1:3).

The doctrine of divine impassibility ensures the application of redemptive benefits to all those whom the Father gave to Christ. Chapters 10-18 of the 2LCF give a detailed explanation of the order

---

[10] Owen, *Works*, 2:30-31.

[11] William Cowper, "God Moves in a Mysterious Way," in *Trinity Hymnal* (Philadelphia: Great Commission Publications, 1961), 21.

[12] This "eternal covenant transaction" is also called the covenant of redemption.

of salvation (*ordo salutis*). Chapters 10-13 specifically highlight God's blessings for his elect.[13] As far as God's acts are concerned, his effectual call comes to those "whom God hath predestinated unto life" (10.1); justification is an act of his free grace toward those "whom God effectually calleth" (11.1); adoption is the blessed result for "those that are justified, [whom] God vouchsafed, in and for the sake of his only Son Jesus Christ, to make partakers of the grace of adoption" (12.1); and sanctification is the possession of those "who are united to Christ, effectually called, and regenerated" (13.1). Chapters 14-18 describe the covenant graces and indicate man's response to the proffered grace of God: saving faith "is the work of the Spirit of Christ in their hearts" (14.1); repentance is a gift given by God "in their effectual calling" (15.1); good works "are the fruits and evidences of a true and lively faith" (16.1); perseverance is confirmed because "those whom God hath accepted in the beloved, effectually called and sanctified by his Spirit, and given the precious faith of his elect unto, can neither totally nor finally fall from the state of grace" (17.1); and therefore it follows that assurance of grace and salvation is available to the elect (18.1). Viewed in this light, it ought to be obvious that if God were mutable or passible, the believer could have no certain confidence that his God is in fact committed to the salvation of his people. That God is immutable and impassible means that all of the redemptive benefits secured by Christ for his people will most certainly be applied to his people in accordance with his unchanging plan to do his people good through the Lord Jesus Christ.

Because some believers struggle with assurance, it will be helpful to see how impassibility affords a cordial for the soul under such difficulty. Again, the 2LCF is helpful here, as our Particular Baptist forefathers were aware of the troubles faced by the people of God. The 2LCF 18.4 treats the struggle specifically, but the foundation of the believer's assurance is described in paragraph 2:

> This certainty is not a bare conjectural and probable persuasion grounded upon a fallible hope, but an infallible assurance of faith founded on the blood and righteousness

---

[13] The outline adopted here is from Dr. James M. Renihan's course on Symbolics.

of Christ revealed in the Gospel; and also upon the inward evidence of those graces of the Spirit unto which promises are made, and on the testimony of the Spirit of adoption, witnessing with our spirits that we are the children of God; and, as a fruit thereof, keeping the heart both humble and holy.

The Confession does not ground the believer's assurance in the believer's faith or conduct; rather, the emphasis in the paragraph is upon the "infallible assurance of faith founded on the blood and righteousness of Christ revealed in the Gospel." It is because the gospel is true; it is because God cannot lie; it is because God has purposed to accomplish his work of salvation that the believer can have assurance. The believer can sing with the people of God, "My hope is built on nothing less than Jesus' blood and righteousness; I dare not trust the sweetest frame, but wholly lean on Jesus' name."[14] While sweet frames are certainly desirable in the Christian life, it is the blood of Christ, according to the unchanging plan of God, which ultimately fortifies the soul when doubts arise. The hymn continues, "His oath, his covenant, his blood support me in the whelming flood; when all around my soul gives way, he then is all my hope and stay." Christ is the believer's hope and stay because of the immutability and impassibility of our gracious God.

The doctrine of divine impassibility affords immeasurable comfort for the people of God at the throne of grace. The worshipers of Baal sought to manipulate their faux deity for their own ends. The worshipers of God bow before One "with whom there is no variation or shadow of turning" (James 1:17), the One who sustains his people during times of trial (James 1:2-8), and the One who initially brought them forth unto salvation of his own will by his word of truth (James 1:18). God has promised his presence and his blessing to his people. At the throne of grace, the believer comes armed with those promises to entreat God's favor according to his own unchanging plan to do good to his people.

When a sailing party is run adrift and they locate a rock upon which to cast their anchor, their hope is not to pull the rock to them; rather, they trust that the rock will remain stationary to provide the

---

[14] Edward Mote, "My Hope is Built on Nothing Less," in *Trinity Hymnal*, 582.

stability necessary to provide relief from storm and waves. The believer, likewise, goes to the throne of grace, not to try to manipulate God, but to draw near to the One who changes not and who has promised his presence and power as their situation demands, and as he sees fit to remedy that situation (Heb. 4:16).

Though the specific context in Hebrews 6 deals with the believer and assurance, it should be evident that a primary means by which the believer seeks assurance is through prayer. The praying saint does not offer arguments concerning his faith or his faithfulness, but he casts his anchor upon the Rock which is God. The writer to the Hebrews makes this connection in Hebrews 6:17-19, which says:

> Thus God, determining to show more abundantly to the heirs of promise the immutability of His counsel, confirmed *it* by an oath, [18] that by two immutable things, in which it *is* impossible for God to lie, we might have strong consolation, who have fled for refuge to lay hold of the hope set before *us*. [19] This *hope* we have as an anchor of the soul, both sure and steadfast, and which enters the *Presence* behind the veil.

The anchor for the Christian soul is a hope grounded in the immutability of the counsel of God and the impossibility for God to lie. Philip E. Hughes comments:

> The metaphor of an anchor in itself effectively portrays the concept of fixity, for the function of an anchor is to provide security in the face of changing tides and rising storms. Human anchors cannot hold man's life secure in stresses and troubles that assail it; but the anchor of Christian hope is unfailingly sure and steadfast.[15]

The last thing the believer wants at the throne of grace is for God to move, fluctuate, or change. The believer desperately needs the God of the Bible and of our Confession, the God who is

---

[15] Philip Edgcumbe Hughes, *A Commentary on the Epistle to the Hebrews* (1977; reprint, Grand Rapids: Wm. B. Eerdmans Publishing Co., 1993), 235. Hughes also notes that "the anchor was adopted as the symbol of Christian hope and security" in the early church. He cites C. Spicq who remarked that there were 66 representations of the anchor found in the catacomb of Priscilla.

"without . . . passions." At the throne of grace, the believer can say with Henry F. Lyte, "Change and decay in all around I see; O thou who changest not, abide with me."[16] This alone brings stability in life's storms.

The doctrine of divine impassibility provides stability, security, and assurance for the child of God. The doctrine also governs the worship of God, which is the chief component of the Christian life.

The Worship of God

The doctrine of divine impassibility informs the believer concerning the nature of God, which certainly affects the disposition of the worshiper of God. Properly understood, impassibility (along with the other incommunicable attributes) ought to remind the believer of the great distance between God and man. The God of heaven and earth is not like man; he is transcendent; he is far above us; he is worthy to be feared and honored and glorified. The psalmist declares, "For the LORD is great and greatly to be praised; He is to be feared above all gods" (Psalm 96:4). Calvin notes this connection, writing that "our knowledge [of God] should serve first to teach us fear and reverence."[17] God himself highlights this connection in Malachi 1:14. In his indictment of Israel for their heartless worship, God links his glory with what should have been Israel's response: "A son honors his father, and a servant his master. If then I am the Father, where is My honor? And if I am a Master, where is My reverence? Says the LORD of hosts to you priests who despise My name." This "great King" (Mal. 1:14), who does not change (Mal. 3:6) is worthy to be feared by his people. Additionally, our Confession says:

> there is a God, who hath lordship and sovereignty over all; is just, good, and doth good unto all; and is therefore to be feared, loved, praised, called upon, trusted in, and served, with all the heart and all the soul, and with all the might. (2LCF 22.1)

---

[16] Henry Francis Lyte, "Abide with Me," in *Trinity Hymnal*, 335.

[17] Calvin, *Institutes*, I.ii.2.

Theology proper informs the creature concerning the God with whom we have to do and, as a result, this knowledge ought to produce fear and reverence on the part of the worshiper. Fear and reverence are not only the proper response to our great God, but these also lead to joy in the presence of God. The idea that the fear of God excludes the joy of the Lord is patently unbiblical. David entreats kings and judges in the nations surrounding Israel to "Serve the LORD with fear, and rejoice with trembling" (Psalm 2:11). Luke describes the condition of the churches throughout Judea, Galilee, and Samaria by saying they "had peace and were edified" (Acts 9:33). He goes on to say, "And walking in the fear of the Lord and in the comfort of the Holy Spirit, they were multiplied." Fear and joy, as well as fear and comfort, are friends in the believer's soul. Sound theology proper promotes the fear that is due his name, and it is this fear which inevitably leads to the joy and comfort that exist in the believer's communion with God.

The doctrine of divine impassibility is also helpful with reference to our corporate worship. The public worship in the old covenant differed from the new covenant in the forms utilized. The consistency between the covenants, however, lies in the fact that God alone is the lawful object of worship and that he alone defines "acceptable worship" (Heb. 12:28), which indicates there is no substantial difference between Deuteronomy 12:32 and Hebrews 12:28. The mandate in both texts is clear: the unchanging God alone has the authority to command the manner by which his people approach him. In both covenants, "good" worship was not a matter of personal preference, personal experience, or personal satisfaction, but obedience to the Word of God. The 2LCF 22.1 states:

> But the acceptable way of worshipping the true God, is instituted by himself, and so limited by his own revealed will, that he may not be worshipped according to the imagination and devices of men, nor the suggestions of Satan, under any visible representations, or any other way not prescribed in the Holy Scriptures.

The doctrine of divine impassibility also stands behind the day specified by God for his worship. While all believers would readily acknowledge a difference between Saturday and Sunday, they should also acknowledge the unchanging nature of God as the basis for the day set aside for his worship. The foundation for the Christian Sabbath is the unchanging moral law of God. While there are positive elements attached to the day of worship according to the covenant in which the command is couched, the moral law that undergirds the command remains unchanged because it is God's law. The 2LCF 22.7 is helpful here:

> As it is the law of nature, that in general a proportion of time, by God's appointment, be set apart for the worship of God, so by his Word, in a positive-moral, and perpetual commandment, binding all men, in all ages, he hath particularly appointed one day in seven for a sabbath to be kept holy unto him, which from the beginning of the world to the resurrection of Christ was the last day of the week, and from the resurrection of Christ was changed into the first day of the week, which is called the Lord's day: and is to be continued to the end of the world as the Christian Sabbath, the observation of the last day of the week being abolished.

The doctrine of divine impassibility does not fail to take into consideration positive law. It does, however, secure what is essential to God, namely, that by "perpetual commandment" his people are to come to him on the day specified to bow before him in public worship.

As noted above, the doctrine of divine impassibility (along with the other incommunicable attributes), highlights the great distance between God and man. The Lord our God is not like man; he is transcendent; he is far above us; he is worthy to be feared and honored and glorified. As will be seen in the next section, this immutable and impassible God uses men to declare his glorious truth to other men.

The Pastoral Ministry

The doctrine of divine impassibility provides a helpful boon to the minister of the gospel. Chapter 3 of the 2LCF is entitled "Of God's

Decree." The soteriological implications of the doctrine of God's decree are spelled out in 2LCF 3.2-7. Relevant to our purpose is paragraph 6:

> As God hath appointed the elect unto glory, so he hath, by the eternal and most free purpose of his will, foreordained all the means thereunto; wherefore they who are elected, being fallen in Adam, are redeemed by Christ, are effectually called unto faith in Christ, by his Spirit working in due season, are justified, adopted, sanctified, and kept by his power through faith unto salvation; neither are any other redeemed by Christ, or effectually called, justified, adopted, sanctified, and saved, but the elect only.

That Christ is the Redeemer who brings the eternal decree to pass in the salvation of the elect, no one will deny. John Gill writes:

> The means fixed in the decree of election, for the execution of it, or in order to bring about the end intended . . . are, the principal of them, the mediation of Christ, and redemption by him, the sanctification of the Spirit, and belief of the truth.[18]

In order for the elect to come to "belief of the truth," it is crucial to note that the means by which Christ operates is primarily the Holy Spirit working by and through the Word. Romans 10:17 is clear: "Faith comes by hearing and hearing by the word of God." The Word of God applied by the Spirit of God is the primary means by which he carries out his purpose to save. Therefore, none of the components involved in the *ordo salutis* come to pass apart from the Word. The Word of God functions as the bridge between the eternal decree and the application of God's grace to his elect.

In light of this, it should be apparent how the pastoral ministry is one of the "means thereunto" established by the immutable God for the execution of his plan to save his elect. By way of comparison, in the opening greetings in several of his letters (1 Cor. 1:1; 2 Cor. 1:1; Eph. 1:1; Col. 1:1; 1 Tim. 1:1; and 2 Tim. 1:1) Paul states that he is

---

[18] Gill, *Body of Divinity*, 188.

an "apostle of Jesus Christ by the will of God." Philip H. Towner notes concerning the use in 2 Timothy:

> Paul defines his apostleship in relation to Christ Jesus and identified its origin in the will ("command," 1 Tim 1:1) of God. In each case, too, the meaning of Paul's apostleship is expanded as the allusion to the mind of God develops into a reference to the salvation he himself provides in Christ. Thus Paul's ministry is linked to the plan of salvation.[19]

To be sure, the modern pastor is not an apostle according to the will of God as Paul was. However, insofar as the pastor preaches and teaches the truth of God's Word like Paul did, his ministry is also linked to the plan of salvation, "the outworking of God's redemptive plan."

Practically, we observe that the pastor's primary function is the ministry of the Word. The pastoral ministry is not limited to his preaching on the Lord's Day, but everything that he does is to be with a conscious desire of making known the truth of God's Word. If God's Word is the bridge between the eternal decree and the application of God's grace to his elect, the pastoral ministry is a bridge which serves to facilitate the application of redemptive benefits to specific local churches. Of course, the pastor cannot facilitate this blessed transaction apart from the power of the Holy Spirit; but God has purposed "all the means thereunto" and to bypass this vital link is to betray the unchanging God who has decreed to save. While we certainly should not overemphasize a pastor's importance (God did speak through Balaam's ass and is also able to raise up children to Abraham from stones, Num. 22:28; Matt. 3:9), neither should we minimize his importance. As Paul writes in 1 Corinthians 1:21, "For since, in the wisdom of God, the world through wisdom did not know God, it pleased God through the foolishness of the message preached to save those who believe." While the accent certainly falls on the message, it is, nevertheless, the message preached.[20]

The doctrine of divine impassibility also provides a solid

---

[19] Towner, *The Letters to Timothy and Titus*, 439.

[20] I gained this insight through a sermon preached by Pastor Tom Lyon of Providence Reformed Baptist Church, Tacoma, WA.

foundation for the under-shepherds of God's sheep. The minister of the gospel will be called upon to offer counsel to the people of God, more often than not, in times of severe distress. God's people are not immune from trials, illnesses, and distresses. The minister is not called upon to offer good advice, but to declare the good news of Christ's salvation for his people. This gospel (as was noted above) is set in the larger context of theology proper. The God who is unchanged and unchanging has purposed to save his people from their sins. The faithful pastor will bring to bear upon the consciences of his brethren the promises of God, promises that are rock solid because the Promiser is rock solid. Also, the faithful pastor will not overemphasize one truth to the exclusion of other truths. Relative to divine impassibility, the doctrine should never be understood in a manner that would remove human responsibility. Specifically, a commitment to the classical doctrine of impassibility does not yield a practical hyper-Calvinism. One biblical example should illustrate this. On the heels of the great declaration of James concerning God, "with whom there is no variation or shadow of turning" (James 1:17), the people of God are exhorted to be "swift to hear, slow to speak, slow to wrath" (James 1:19). The swiftness to hear is, of course, a swiftness to hear the Word of God. James continues his exhortation by declaring, "But be doers of the word, and not hearers only, deceiving yourselves" (James 1:22). The doctrine of divine impassibility not only provides the stability of divine government to the believer, it also grounds the responsibility of the believer to respond properly to that government.

Another fruit of this doctrine is that it provides a global context for the pastor to consider in his ministry. Local church pastors do not work in isolation; they are part of something greater, namely God's eternal decree by which he has purposed the salvation of a "great multitude which no one could number, of all nations, tribes, peoples, and tongues" (Rev. 7:9). There is an echo in this text of the promise made to Abraham in Genesis 22:17-18:

> blessing I will bless you, and multiplying I will multiply your descendants as the stars of the heaven and as the sand which *is* on the seashore; and your descendants shall possess the gate of their enemies. 18 In your seed all the nations of the earth shall be blessed, because you have obeyed My voice.

The promise made to Abraham is fulfilled in Christ who is Abraham's seed (Matt. 1:1; Gal. 3:16). It is in this sense that Abraham became the "heir of the world" (Rom. 4:13), a promise which obviously includes both Jews and Gentiles. Because God is immutable, it necessarily follows that his promise is immutable. Therefore, the pastor who labors in the Word and doctrine does so in light of the massive plan by God to redeem men from every tribe, tongue, people, and nation (Rev. 5:9). As a result, the local church pastor ought to take seriously the cause of God and truth in both local church planting and foreign missions. The doctrine of divine impassibility does not diminish the pastor's hope for the advancement of Christ's kingdom, but empowers it. The pastor prays with the psalmist with a heartfelt expectation, "Oh let the nations be glad and sing for joy! For You shall judge the people righteously, and govern the nations of the earth" (Psalm 67:4).

The pastor not only has the promise made to Abraham, the purpose of God explained in Revelation 7:9, and the paradigmatic prayer of the psalmist, he also has the Commission of the Lord Jesus Christ in Matthew 28:18-20. Christ is the Mediator of the covenant of grace, that covenant that is fully discovered in the New Testament (2LCF 7.3). In the covenant of grace, the Lord God almighty "freely offereth unto sinners life and salvation by Jesus Christ" (2LCF 7.2) and it is the pastor's great privilege to engage in this blessed task and hence comply with the Great Commission given by Christ to his church. The Commission is great in at least three ways. First, it is great because of the Christ who gave it. He has all authority in heaven and on earth (Matt. 28:18) and is the One alone who saves men from every tribe, tongue, people, and nation. Second, the Commission concerns the salvation of sinners and the edification of saints. Christ commanded, "make disciples of all the nations" (Matt. 28:19), which is carried out by the proclamation of the free offer of the gospel to every sinner in every corner of the earth. The pastor is charged with teaching those newly made disciples "all things that [Christ has] commanded" (Matt. 28:20), which speaks to the ongoing pulpit ministry conducted in local churches. Third, the Commission is grounded in the eternal decree of the immutable and impassible God who has foreordained whatsoever comes to pass for his glory. The doctrine of divine impassibility does not hinder the pastor in his proclamation of the free offer of the gospel to all sinners; rather, the doctrine ensures that the God who has purposed to save through the means of preaching (1 Cor. 1:21; Titus 1:1-3) will accomplish his plan. In sum, the doctrine of divine impassibility provides a firm foundation for the Commission, energizing its fulfillment.

Conclusion

The previous chapters of this book have established the truth summarized in our Confession, namely, that God is "without . . . passions." This chapter has demonstrated some of the practical implications which flow from the doctrine. It should be remembered that theology is practical, and as we have sought to demonstrate, theology proper is properly practical. It is hoped that those who confess the Christian faith in accordance with the 2LCF and other creedal statements will find an increased unity in light of this study. May our prayer ever be as follows:

> Sovereign God, Thy cause, not my own, engages my heart, and I appeal to thee with greatest freedom to set up thy kingdom in every place where Satan reigns; glorify thyself and I shall rejoice, for to bring honor to thy name is my sole desire. I adore thee that thou art God, and long that others should know it, feel it, and rejoice in it. O that all men might love and praise thee, that thou mightest have all glory from the intelligent world![21]

---

[21] "God's Cause," in *The Valley of Vision: A Collection of Puritan Prayers and Devotions,* ed. Arthur Bennett (1975; reprint, Edinburgh; Carlisle, PA: The Banner of Truth Trust, 1989), 177.

Chapter 15

CLOSING COMMENTS AND
AFFIRMATIONS AND DENIALS

Ronald S. Baines and Charles J. Rennie

The twentieth and twenty-first centuries have seen significant attempts to refashion the doctrine of God as articulated in the classical tradition. The array of alternatives vying for prominence is at times almost dizzying. On the one hand, there are a number of Constructivist theologies which claim in Kantian fashion an almost unknowable God.[1] The pluralism that flows out of these reformulations of God not only rejects the very idea of authoritative infallible revelation but run directly counter to the exclusivist claims of God as understood in historic classical and confessional Christian history. On the other hand, Developmental theologies such as Process Theology are less agnostic about God's knowability and somewhat more open to the exclusivist demands of historic Christianity but are equally certain with Constructivists that the God of classical theism must go.[2] This is true of much of Open

---

[1] According to Johnson and Huffman, "Constructivism is a skeptical theological stance that questions the human ability to know much about God with any confidence. Rather than being primarily a theological position per se (concerned with God as an object of understanding), it is actually more an epistemological position (concerned with the human subject and its ability to know, an orientation that has significant implications for theology). Flowing fairly directly out of the Enlightenment skepticism of Immanuel Kant, Constructivism regards the theological enterprise as intrinsically compromised by humanity's inability to grasp things as they are in themselves, particularly things that lie beyond the empirical universe, which the natural sciences can describe." Eric L. Johnson and Douglas S. Huffman, "Should the God of Historic Christianity Be Replaced?," in *God Under Fire: Modern Scholarship Reinvents God*, ed. Douglas S. Huffman and Eric L. Johnson (Grand Rapids: Zondervan, 2002), 13-14.

[2] "Developmentalist theologians are more willing to make assertions about the nature of God and thus are generally less skeptical about our ability to know God. Nevertheless, Developmentalists also wish to jettison the historic Christian

Theism as well. Often unwilling to go as far as Process theologians, Open Theism nonetheless has little room for the doctrine of God as understood in the classical and confessional traditions of the historic and catholic church. The theological landscape of today is both diverse and divided.

Thankfully much work has been done within evangelical theological circles to counter the inadequate and false claims of both Constructivist and Developmental theologies. Our task has not been to add our voices to theirs in any truly substantive way. However, what has emerged within conservative critiques of Enlightenment and modernist/post-modernist theological reformulations has been a willingness to tinker with the classical formulations of the doctrine of God in a number of ways. Johnson and Huffman claim that "historic Christian theism" at present has bifurcated the doctrine of God. Rallying around a core set of beliefs has enabled evangelicals to speak in unison against Constructivist and Developmental theologies alike. But it has also given rise to the acceptance of a second tier of divine attributes that are open for outright rejection or substantive reformulation. Evidence for this is available among evangelical authors, according to Johnson and Huffman, regarding divine simplicity, immutability, eternity, and impassibility. They insist:

> We recognize too that certain features of the God of classical theism have been questioned by contemporary members of the historic Christian tradition (e.g., his immutability and simplicity . . .). Nonetheless, the authors of this book maintain that there is far more overall continuity among those who adhere to historic Christian views of God, including those who subscribe wholly to the theology, say, of Thomas, than discontinuity, so that questions about such things as simplicity can legitimately be seen as "in-house."[3]

---

understanding of God because, contrary to historic Christianity, they believe that God is undergoing constant development as he interacts with humans and reacts to human actions, creativity, and cultural progress." Johnson and Huffman, "Should the God of Historic Christianity Be Replaced?," in *God Under Fire*, 19.

[3] Johnson and Huffman, "Should the God of Historic Christianity Be Replaced?," in *God Under Fire*, 30. Impassibility and eternity are referenced on page 38.

We remain unconvinced that this evangelical bifurcation is either helpful or warranted. We believe that classical theism is too often modified because the authors have either bought into the mischaracterizations of classical theism by those outside the tradition (this would be especially true of the claim of Hellenization leveled against the early Christian tradition) or they have not adequately represented or understood the classical tradition. This is especially true of the doctrine of divine impassibility. Some of the authors that Johnson and Huffman acknowledge as "in-house" have come under examination in these pages. We are firmly convinced that many of the arguments encountered in present-day theological debate are not all that new. We are also firmly convinced that the well-constructed and tightly-articulated doctrine of God in the Reformed tradition confessed in the Westminster/Savoy/Second London Confessions both accurately represents the God of Scripture and sufficiently counters modernist and post-modernist unbiblical alternatives.

While we appreciate the work that has been done to counter the Constructivist and Developmental deconstruction of classical theology by many whom we critique in these pages, we are convinced the task is unfinished. Countering the aberrations of our day is a necessary task, but guarding the deposit of truth handed down to us is equally necessary. Pulling on threads which some like Johnson and Huffman consider secondary, we are convinced, incrementally and at times almost imperceptibly, begins the process of unraveling the whole fabric of the classical and confessional doctrine of God. Indeed, several have acknowledged this reality.

Furthermore, who is the arbiter of what doctrine classifies as secondary? How is one to be assessed if what starts as a supposed "in-house" deviation becomes a real and substantive reformulation under the guise of an incremental shift? It appears that the evangelicalism of the early twenty-first century is ill-equipped to govern its own theological boundaries. It is at this point that we believe defending an historic confessional declaration of God is both valuable and warranted.

Before one relegates doctrines such as divine impassibility to the rank of a secondary attribute of God one must defend the premise that such bifurcation is both necessary and valid. We see it as neither. Hoping to remove the confusion of some and the prejudice of others against this doctrine, we believe we have expressed the confessional doctrine of God's impassibility which is at once biblically sound, historically anchored in the classical tradition, theologically necessary, and personally rich. We do not believe our theological forefathers deemed the doctrine of divine impassibility to be of a secondary nature and we join our voices with theirs.

We believe that the affirmations and denials which follow clarify the points where confusion has entered the discussion and we hope they will serve to remove the prejudices often attached to the classical doctrine of divine impassibility by its critics. It is not a doctrinal relic of classical theism we quietly confess hoping no one notices. It is a biblical doctrine which we believe robustly enabled the church to counter the errors endangering the faith in ages past and robustly counters the errors we find lurking in the theological shadows of our own day.

To be sure, we do not consider what we have written to be the final word on this important doctrine. But we hope that it will give our brethren within the classical and confessional tradition cause to rethink the need for rejection or reformulation of this significant attribute of God and to see that it is fundamental to the whole. We hope also that it will give to those who subscribe to the confessional declaration that God is "without . . . passions" a helpful biblical, historical, theological, confessional, and practical delineation and defense of the doctrine of divine impassibility.

Affirmations and Denials

The discussion above enables us to make the following affirmations and denials concerning the doctrine of divine impassibility.

1. **We affirm** the unity and analogy of Scripture, which states that unclear, difficult, or ambiguous passages are to be interpreted with clear and unambiguous passages that touch upon the same teaching or event (2LCF 1.9). **We deny** that the purported meaning of any text may be pressed in isolation or contradiction to other passages of Scripture.
2. **We affirm** the unity of Scripture and the analogy of faith, which states, "the true and full sense of any Scripture" (2LCF 1.9) must

be interpreted in a manner consistent with the system of doctrine "necessarily contained" (2LCF 1.6) in the whole of Scripture. **We deny** that the purported meaning of any text may be pressed in isolation or contradiction to systematic theological considerations and that which is necessarily contained in the whole of Scripture.

3. **We affirm** that passages which speak of God's being and essence must be given interpretive priority, not only because they are the less difficult and ambiguous, but also because what God is precedes what he is like toward us. The latter must be interpreted in a manner consistent with the former. **We deny** that passages which posit divine passions (i.e., what he is like toward us) take priority over passages which speak of God's being and essence (i.e., what he is).

4. **We affirm** that the foundation for language about God is the reality of creation *ex nihilo*. This principle grounds the way of causality, which states that we may know something about the cause (i.e., God) from the effect (i.e., creation). **We deny** that scriptural language about God is equivocal, that is, for example, that love is predicated of God and man in a completely unrelated sense.

5. **We affirm**, in all scriptural language about God, both the way of negation, which states that he is that being who is infinitely unlike all other beings, and the way of eminence, which states that he is infinitely greater than the language and analogies used to reveal him, so that divine love is as different from human love as God is from man. **We deny** that scriptural language about God is univocal, that is, for example, that love stands in relation to God in the same way it does to man, albeit more perfect.

6. **We affirm** that all scriptural language about God is analogical, which states that divine love stands in relation to the divine nature in a mode proportionately similar (and proportionately different) to the way human love stands in relation to human nature. **We deny** that scriptural language about God must be either univocal or equivocal.

7. **We affirm** that *some* scriptural analogies with respect to the affections of God are anthropopathisms, wherein the thing attributed to God exists in him figuratively. **We deny** that *every*

scriptural analogy with respect to the affections of God refers to something *proper* to God, wherein the thing attributed exists in both the Creator and the creature formally.

8. **We affirm** that biblical anthropopathisms signify that which is in God truly but figuratively. Anthropopathisms signify something that is in God, not according to the letter, but according to the design of the analogy, and in a manner consistent with the whole of Scripture and suitable to the divine perfections. **We deny** that anthropopathisms empty the scriptural analogies of meaning or fail to reveal something about the God who is.

9. **We affirm** that God is pure *being* without *becoming*. **We deny** that there is any *becoming* in God.

10. **We affirm** that, given *what God actually is*, infinite, simple, and immutable in perfection, we must also confess that God *is* infinite, simple, and immutable love. **We deny** that God has the potential to be other than infinite, simple, and immutable love.

11. **We affirm** that God is his essence *and* existence, and therefore cannot but exist as he eternally and essentially is. **We deny** emotional change in God, for that would involve a new manner of God's existing, which would compromise God's aseity (i.e., his necessary and independent existence).

12. **We affirm** that love (and all other affections proper to God) is not an accidental or relational property that God has, but what he is. Therefore, an emotional change in God of any kind would necessarily entail a change in the essence and existence of God. **We deny** that God has any accidental or relational properties, that is, properties that are distinct from his essence.

13. **We affirm** that only an impassible God is truly and fully "most loving" (2LCF 2.1). **We deny** that the confessional understanding of divine impassibility leads to a view of God that is cold and impersonal.

14. **We affirm** that God is impassible without qualification. **We deny** that God can, in any sense, undergo inner emotional changes of state, and that God is without passions merely in the sense that he is incapable of suffering, surprise, or being overwhelmed.

15. **We affirm** that God, who is his essence and existence, has no cause; his existence is necessary and therefore unchangeable.

We deny that God can be his own cause, and that he is capable of sovereignly affecting his own emotional change of state.

16. **We affirm** that passages which speak of the arousal or pacification of God's affections imply a change only in God's external (*ad extra*) works. **We deny** that passages which speak of the arousal or pacification of God's affections imply an internal (*ad intra*) change in God.

17. **We affirm** that all of God's affections are infinite in perfection. Therefore, if God were to undergo an emotional change, that change would be either for the better or the worse. If for the better, then he must not have been infinite in perfection prior to the change, and therefore was not God. If for the worse, then he would no longer be infinite in perfection after the change, and therefore no longer God. **We deny** that it is an imperfection in God to be incapable of emotional change.

18. **We affirm** that God loves his creation, particularly his elect (John 17:23-24), with a view to himself (Rom. 11:36). His affection is therefore as immutable, fixed, and constant as his love for himself, however varied our experience of its effects may be. **We deny** that the triune God's infinite delight in his own infinite perfection (i.e., his blessedness) undermines his ability genuinely to love his creation.

19. **We affirm** a real distinction among creatures, and the degree to which each is made to experience God's love and participate in his goodness. **We deny** that the inequality among the external objects of God's love (i.e., creation, humanity, the elect) implies a change or variation in God whose love is as immutable as his being.

20. **We affirm** that the confessional doctrine of divine impassibility supports and necessitates the free offer of the gospel and Christian missions (2LCF 7.2). **We deny** that the confessional doctrine of divine impassibility in any way hinders the free offer of the gospel or Christian missions.

21. **We affirm** that God has freely chosen to relate every creature to himself, that a creature may change in his relation to God, and that by virtue of Christ God graciously effects such a change in the elect without any change of relation in himself. **We deny** that a change in the creature can bring about any change of relation in God.

22. **We affirm**, in agreement with Chalcedonian Christology and the communication of properties, that "Christ, in the work of mediation, acts according to both natures, by each nature doing that which is proper to itself; yet by reason of the unity of the person, that which is proper to one nature is sometimes in Scripture, attributed to the person denominated by the other nature" (2LCF 8.7). **We deny** that the divine nature underwent suffering or change in the passion of Christ.

23. **We affirm** that the classical doctrine of divine impassibility as expressed by the 2LCF 2.1 is founded in the Scripture, "necessarily contained" (2LCF 1.6) therein, and therefore consistent with and essential to the system of doctrine delivered to us through special revelation. **We deny** that the classical doctrine of divine impassibility as expressed by the 2LCF 2.1 is a scholastic dogma founded in philosophical and metaphysical speculation based on natural theology.

24. **We affirm** emphatically, therefore, that the classical doctrine of divine impassibility as expressed by the 2LCF 2.1 is the teaching of Holy Scripture.

Soli Deo gloria!

Appendix 1

K. Scott Oliphint,
God with Us: Divine Condescension and the Attributes of God.
Wheaton: Crossway, 2012. Pp. 302.
Reviewed by Charles J. Rennie*

Our contemporary theological context has witnessed much debate about the relationship between God's transcendence and immanence, or his absolute and relative attributes. Within the last century, theological questions have been raised that have set the agenda of the debate as theologians continue to seek adequate solutions to how we understand God in relation to the world. What underlies much of the debate is the presupposition that transcendence and immanence are opposing concepts, such that transcendence is viewed as a problem that needs to be overcome for God's immanence to be possible. How can the wholly transcendent and independent being of classical theism personally and sincerely relate and respond to creation, much less create at all, without jeopardizing his otherness? Moreover, which biblical texts should be given the priority for an understanding of who or what God is—those which emphasize God's independence and immutability, or those which imply a degree of dependence upon the creature (i.e., God's grieving, repenting, etc.)? While Open Theists have consistently given priority to God's immanence over his transcendence, it is suggested by Dr. K. Scott Oliphint that classical theism has not taken God's condescension, which is expressed by way of covenant, seriously enough (14).

In *God with Us*, K. Scott Oliphint declares the approach of both Open Theism and classical theism inadequate and therefore proposes a new way of understanding God-in-relation that he believes is "compatible" with God-in-himself. His thesis is that although God is transcendent and altogether independent, he nonetheless freely "takes on characteristics that determine just how

* This review originally appeared in *JIRBS* (2015): 163-73, and is used with permission.

he will interact with us, and with creation generally" (12). Central to his thesis is the concern to interpret fully and literally those passages of Scripture that describe God-in-relation, by way of voluntary condescension, without jeopardizing his independence. Citing WCF 7.1, "The distance between God and the creature is so great . . .," he proposes that God has voluntarily condescended to us by way of covenant by taking on certain properties that enable him to relate to us in a way that we may know him. He variously refers to these "characteristics" that God "takes on" as created and temporal properties (13, n. 8; 120; 198; 208; 209), non-essential properties (16), and covenantal properties (40). Oliphint proposes that God "takes on" these created properties in a manner analogous to the divine Son's assumption of created properties in the incarnation, without altering his *essential* properties and necessary attributes. When God asked Adam and Eve in the garden, "Where are you?," Oliphint explains, "In condescending to relate to Adam and Eve, he is, like them (not essentially, but covenantally), restricted in his knowledge of where they might be hiding in that garden" (111). Again, after rejecting the distinction between literal and anthropomorphic locutions, he writes:

> When Scripture says that God changes his mind, or that he is moved, or angered by our behavior, we should see that as literal. It refers us to God and to his dealings with us. It is as literal or as real as God being the God of Abraham, Isaac, and Jacob. But we should also see that the God who really changes his mind is the accommodated God, the *yarad-cum-*Emmanuel God who, while remaining the "I AM" nevertheless stoops to our level to interact, person-to-person, with us. His change of mind does not effect his essential character, any more than Christ dying on the cross precluded him from being fully God. He remains fully and completely God, a God who is not like man that he should change his mind, and he remains fully and completely the God who, in covenant with us, changes his mind to accomplish his sovereign purposes. (123-24)

Thus, when God takes on the covenantal properties of grief, sorrow, and ignorance, he really and literally grieves, sorrows, and acquires knowledge by virtue of those properties, though he remains independent and *essentially* unchanged. In this manner, Oliphint seeks to take God's voluntary condescension seriously, while simultaneously affirming the immutability of God's necessary and essential attributes.

In the Introduction, Oliphint outlines the theological method he attempts to apply throughout. Intent on resisting a transcendence-versus-immanence approach, he advocates what he calls

> a biblical notion of compatibility (affirmed in christology) [that] can provide a context in which we can take God's activity in relation to us and creation seriously while at the same time affirming the Reformed understanding of God's aseity. (44)

Citing WCF 1.9, Oliphint (in opposition to Peter Enns' *Inspiration and Incarnation*) affirms that, because the Bible has a single divine author, Scripture must be interpreted by Scripture, the more obscure texts interpreted in light of those places that speak more clearly and in a manner consistent with the scope of the whole, which is the glory of God. In this way, systematic theology and the unity of Scripture are given a critical role in determining the legitimate exegetical conclusions of any given text. Quoting Moisés Silva, Oliphint confesses that our "theological system should tell [us] how to exegete" (25). With the Westminster "system of doctrine" in mind, he affirms that the priority must be given to those passages that speak of God's absolute independence, what he is in himself before anything existed outside himself. "Those passages are clearer because they articulate the 'divine nature' of God; they tell us something of who he essentially is" (29). Such a priority is not intended to neglect those passages which describe God-in-relation to his creation, but to emphasize that such descriptions of God must be interpreted in a manner "compatible" with his absolute independence.

> Passages that speak of God being sorry or ignorant of historical events or of our own commitment to him automatically demand questions. They cry out for resolution because we know enough about God's 'Godness' (θειότης —

Rom. 1:20) to know that he cannot be both independent and dependent in the same way. Yet there are passages that clearly note some level of dependence. . . . [e.g.,] We rightly question how such regret coheres with God's independence. (29)

To Oliphint's credit, he offers a biblical and classical defense of God's aseity in chapter 1, as well as several divine attributes that may necessarily be deduced from it (i.e., divine simplicity, infinity, and immutability). However, his precise proposal of "compatibility" and "covenantal properties" (chapter 2), which he believes is affirmed in Christology (chapters 3 and 4), is both novel and nebulous, to say the least. The reader, particularly the one whose theological system informs his theological conclusions as Oliphint has suggested, may anticipate being left with several questions in search of coherency.

The most basic question is, "What are these so-called covenantal properties?" This question is essential to his proposal, and yet it is a concept which is never clearly defined. Perhaps, in part, this is because Oliphint assumes that it is

intuitive enough that most would see immediately what we generally mean . . . that God freely determined to take on attributes, characteristics, and properties that he did not have, and would not have, without creation. (110)

One could wish Oliphint would have relied less upon intuition and more upon definition. What is clear is that it is a concept which is proposed in order to explain God's condescension, whether it be in the form of theophany, anthropomorphism, or the relative attributes in general.

Oliphint attempts to establish the necessity and legitimacy of the concept of covenantal properties with regard to God's relative attributes in general. He repeatedly uses the example of "Creator," and asks whether it is of the essence of God. Because Creator is predicated of God *relative to creation*, Oliphint argues that it cannot be an essential property of God. Otherwise, it would have been necessary for God to create, for it is argued that God cannot be considered Creator apart from creation. Therefore, he concludes, "It would seem, then, that God has properties that are essential to him and others that are not essential to him" (17). God "takes on" these so-called covenantal properties, in addition to his essential properties, in order to condescend in creating and relating to his creation.

However, Oliphint's argument assumes what it fails to prove, that the so-called relative attributes of classical theism are called such because they are ontologically relative in God. The novelty of this assumption needs to be pointed out. Zanchi, for instance, addresses the question very differently. He writes:

[H]e cannot be changed . . . by any passive potency which is in himself. For he is a most simple and perfect act; and therefore cannot be in potency to anything, be it essential, or accidental. All other things may be changed by his power, by which they are, and upon which they depend. (*Life Everlasting*, 73)

God possesses an uncreated active potency, that is, a power to create which belongs only to a Creator, whether he chose to create or not. God's power is a from-eternity-active power. In other words, God is pure *act*, all-potent, an ever-living, always active agent with the active potency to effect change outside of himself, without any passive potency whatsoever to undergo change within himself. Thus, Zanchi concludes:

Those names which argue a relative respect betwixt God and his creatures, and the names Creator, Lord, Redeemer, &c. are indeed in time given to him, and not from eternity, yet so as that no new thing is added to him, neither is there any change in him. (*Life Everlasting*, 20)

The name Creator signifies an absolute *reality* belonging to God from eternity. Yet, it is a *name* which is given to him relatively by us, insofar as it signifies a new relation established *in the creature* relative to the ever-existing immutable Creator. Unlike the relative attributes of classical theism, Oliphint's newly-proposed covenantal properties are non-essential, ontologically relative, created realities in God that are assumed to be necessary, not only for God to be able to create, but also for him to be capable of relating to his creation.

Moreover, Oliphint maintains that this notion of covenantal properties is "affirmed in christology." The incarnation is the quintessential example of God's condescension. In the incarnation, the eternal, divine Son of God took on a human nature without ceasing to be what he essentially was. It was not the union or confusion of two natures, but the assumption of a human nature by the second person of the Trinity. One person with two natures, that is, with created covenantal properties and essential properties, without confusion, change, division, or separation. According to Oliphint, Christology provides the paradigm for theology and for our understanding of all forms of divine condescension. Just as God the Son took on human covenantal properties without changing what he essentially was, so also God has taken on created covenantal properties from the foundation of the world without changing what he essentially is. Oliphint uses the Reformed *communicatio idiomatum*, that the properties of each nature of Christ may be communicated to the person, to explain how God can be said to repent, grieve, and so on, without ceasing to be the eternal, immutable, and independent God. For example, just as the Scripture states that the Son grew in wisdom, according to his human nature, without implying any change of wisdom in his divine nature, so it may be really and truly said that God, according to his covenantal properties, repents without implying any change in his divine essence. In short, God has taken on created properties from the foundation of the world in the same way that the Son of God took on created human properties in the incarnation. "What is true of the incarnation is true also of other 'incarnations' of God in Scripture" (192). Therefore, covenantal properties are created, "incarnational" properties and attributes that God really and truly takes on prior to the incarnation in order for him to relate to that which is not himself.

Such a proposal raises several unhappy consequences. For instance, are we to apply the concept to each person of the Trinity, or just the Son? On the one hand, if it is consistently applied to each, we must conclude one of two things.[1] Either we are to conceive of

---

[1] It is altogether unclear whether Oliphint is arguing for a third option, and it is equally unclear what that could be.

these properties accidentally, and therefore reject divine simplicity, or they are to be conceived of substantially. Oliphint appears to prefer the latter, arguing that in the incarnation, the Son of God did not merely take on accidental properties, but rather assumed a substantial union of two natures in one person (152-54). If this is so, then we are led to the unfortunate conclusion that all three persons have had two substantial natures, one created, and one divine, from the foundation of the world. It would seem difficult, therefore, to escape the conclusion that all three persons, to a greater or lesser extent, have been incarnate at one point or another.

On the other hand, it could be argued that Oliphint's emphasis appears to limit the concept to the person of the Son. However, doing so would fail to take into account *all* of the relative and anthropomorphic language of Scripture. According to his proposal, in order for Israel to really and truly "grieve His Holy Spirit" (Isa. 63:10), the person of the Spirit would also have to take on created covenantal properties. Likewise, are we to assume that only the second person of the Trinity took on the property of Creator? As an aside, it must also be concluded, contrary to Oliphint's insistence (186), that God would have to assume these pre-incarnate properties permanently. Otherwise, the Father would cease to be Creator and the Spirit could not be said to be capable of grief in the Old and New Testaments alike (cf. Eph. 4:30). Therefore, in order for his proposal to accomplish what he intends, it must apply equally and personally to each person of the Trinity, both in the New Testament as well as the Old — an untenable position indeed!

However, assuming for sake of argument that the concept may coherently be applied exclusively to the Son, the redemptive-historical consequences are no less concerning. It seems Oliphint's desire is to interpret every relative attribute of God, theophany, and anthropomorphism as the Son of God's pre-incarnate incarnated assumption of human properties. Therefore, the theological significance of the pre-incarnate "incarnations" of the Son of God needs to be considered. The incarnation is no doubt a divine act of condescension toward man, but it must also be considered as part of the Mediator's obedience rendered to the Father according to the eternal covenant of redemption. Jesus described his coming down from heaven in terms of "doing the will of Him who sent Me" (John 6:38), Paul spoke of the incarnation of the Son as an "obedience unto death" (Phil. 2:8), and Hebrews 10:5-7 says:

> Therefore, when He came into the world, He said: "Sacrifice and offering You did not desire, But a body You have prepared for Me. ⁶ In burnt offerings and *sacrifices* for sin You had no pleasure. ⁷ Then I said, 'Behold, I have come — In the volume of the book it is written of Me — To do Your will, O God.'" (Heb. 10:5-7)

Surely the Son's mediatorial work as surety precedes his incarnation, but his actual accomplishment of redemption does not. Oliphint, however, unwittingly provides us with reason to make the further conclusion that the Mediator's pre-incarnation "incarnations" were no less part of his active and passive obedience than his actual incarnation. Perhaps this is where his biblical theology not only runs roughshod over systematic theology (all theology becomes Christology), but also woefully fails to account for the progressive nature of redemptive history itself.

Indeed, Oliphint repeatedly states that the actual incarnation is *sui generis*, that is, one of a kind, but saying it is so is not the same as showing that it is so. By making the actual incarnation the consummation, not only of God's redemptive-historical revelation, but of an entire incarnational process since the beginning of the world, Oliphint deprives God of his glory and the incarnation of its wonder and uniqueness.

Perhaps a more fundamental question can be posed: Why do we need to invent new theological categories in the first place? The answer to this question seems to lie in at least two assumptions made by the author. First, it appears that in Oliphint's quest to take the relative attributes and anthropomorphisms seriously, he has assumed that language about God must either be univocal or equivocal. This implies that it either has to mean the same thing for God as it does for us, or else it has no meaning at all. Committed to the former, he has sought categories that would affirm both God's aseity and his ability to really and truly grieve, suffer, repent, and so on. Finding his univocal core in Christ, the God-man, he concludes that what may be predicated of Christ incarnate may also be really and truly predicated of God apart from the incarnation. For instance:

Christ, the Son of God in the flesh, suffered; he died, and he did that as the God-man, the quintessential covenant person. Since that is true, there must be some real and fundamental sense in which God can have or experience passions. (87)

We may wonder how far he would have us press this formula. Hunger, temptation, exhaustion, death, and the like are all predicated of Jesus. Are we to assume that there is "some real and fundamental sense in which God can have or experience" such things? For a Reformed theologian of his caliber, it is perplexing that he has little of consequence to say about analogical predication as it has been historically understood, which would both affirm the text's meaning and properly distinguish between the Creator and the creature. This is further evidence of what becomes clear throughout—that he is not engaging in a dialogue from within his own tradition, historically and confessionally understood, but from without.

Second, contrary to Oliphint's stated intent, his proposal assumes a problem-solution approach, wherein God's transcendence is a problem that needs to be overcome before he is able to relate to anything that is not himself. He would insist that this is not the case, for God's so-called covenantal properties do not alter his essential properties. "He limits himself while remaining the infinite God" (188). However, the case remains that, for Oliphint, God cannot relate to his creation, much less create, in his transcendence. It would seem that the incarnation was as necessary to overcome an ontological problem that is no less his than ours, as it was to overcome a sin problem. God neither does nor can relate to us *as God*, but only as he has ontologically condescended *as a creature* by virtue of created properties. Thus, for all of Oliphint's insistence that his proposal preserves God's independence and essential immutability, his particular solution has the unfortunate consequence of making God, *as God*, equally irrelevant.

According to this view, God's transcendence poses a relatability problem that must be overcome by taking on created properties. "Once he determines to relate to us, that relation entails that he take on properties that he otherwise would not have had" (188). As we have already observed, in order for God to be Creator, he had to ontologically condescend by taking on created covenantal properties. At this point, it should be asked how God, in his transcendence, related himself to the very first covenantal properties that enabled him to create as Creator, for he would need to create covenantal properties to do so. Likewise, he would need to create covenantal properties in order to relate himself to those created properties. There would be an infinite regress of covenantal properties, and thus the *reductio ad absurdum* of Oliphint's proposal.

Why do we need new theological categories in the first place? In *God with Us*, K. Scott Oliphint proposes a novel solution to a theological problem that has been posed by modern liberals and open theists. As is too often the case, the older tradition is dismissed and the presuppositions of the liberals are granted without argument. Early in the book, in an argument against an opposing view, Oliphint states, "One of the questions that should be asked in this regard is why the orthodox tradition did not see the need to posit such things" (77). This is precisely the question Oliphint should have asked the open theists, and we must now ironically ask of Oliphint. Why should it be taken for granted that there is a problem that needs to be solved? Why didn't the orthodox tradition see the need to posit created covenantal properties of God apart from the actual incarnation? Wouldn't a closer examination of the Reformed tradition suggest that much of the contemporary debate assumes a false dilemma between God's transcendence and immanence? Can we even assume that they were asking the same questions? And if not, why not?

Much of the discussion found in this book tends to reveal that the contemporary theological agenda has more or less to do with a desire to affirm the God of Open Theism without a total abandonment of the God of classical theism. And yet, the failure of Oliphint's project reminds us that if we accept their assumption that God's transcendence is a problem that needs to be overcome, then we must also accept with them the conclusion that it is a problem that cannot be overcome. As open theists have declared all along, once their version of relatability is more or less affirmed, the God of classical theism cannot merely be revised; he must be abandoned altogether.

Appendix 2

Rob Lister,
God is Impassible and Impassioned:
Toward a Theology of Divine Emotion.
Wheaton: Crossway, 2013. Pp. 333.
Reviewed by James E. Dolezal*

The long-held doctrine of divine impassibility has come under intense criticism in the past century. It is not only process theologians and radical passibilists such as Jürgen Moltmann who have abandoned the doctrine, but many evangelicals as well. Rob Lister has written this volume with the aims of correcting many modern misconceptions and caricatures of the classical doctrine, of reestablishing its theological truth and importance, and of winning back numerous of its misguided dissenters. I shall briefly summarize Lister's argument as it unfolds through the volume, point out some of its strengths, and conclude with a consideration of some of its significant deficiencies.

The book is divided into two parts, with Part 1 (chs. 2-6) focusing on the historical context of the doctrine, and Part 2 (chs. 7-10) making a contemporary case for Lister's central thesis that God is both impassible and impassioned. Lister understands impassibility to be a doctrine about God's perfect voluntary control over his emotions. "[I]n the main," he explains, "the classical tradition simply sought to preserve the notion that, as the self-determined sovereign, God is not subject to emotional affects that are *involuntarily* or *unexpectedly* wrung from him by creatures" (33). God is impassible, not in the sense that he cannot be emotionally moved, but only in the sense that he cannot be moved against his will. Indeed, God's "impassionedness," as Lister terms it, means God "may be affected by his creatures, but as God, he is so in ways that accord rather than conflict with his will to be so affected by

---

* This review originally appeared in *WTJ* 75, no. 2 (Fall 2013): 414-18, and is used with permission.

those whom, in love, he has made" (36). The author then proceeds to make his case that this "two-pronged" understanding of God as both impassible *and* impassioned is precisely what the orthodox Christian tradition historically taught.

Lister opens his historical section with a helpful consideration of the common passibilist accusation that impassibility entered the Christian tradition by way of unbiblical Hellenistic influences on the early church and that it tended to render God cold, unloving, and unconcerned about the world. In order to show that such charges are misguided, Lister examines passages from numerous Christian impassibilists who also affirm that God is loving, joyful, angry with sin, and so forth. His survey encompasses patristic theologians (including Irenaeus, Tertullian, Origen, Gregory Thaumaturgus, Lactantius, and Augustine), medieval schoolmen (Anselm and Aquinas), reformational theologians (Luther, Calvin, and Charnock), and modern impassibilists (including Richard Creel, Thomas Weinandy, and Paul Helm). Lister interprets their affirmations of the reality of God's affections as proof positive that the mainstream Christian tradition affirmed the two-pronged belief in God's impassibility and impassionedness. Impassibility does not mean God does not undergo emotional changes, according to Lister, but only that he does not undergo them involuntarily or unexpectedly. This, he concludes, was always the main concern of the core impassibility tradition (167). God's impassionedness, for its part, is accounted for as his "perfect control of his feelings" (88; citing J. K. Mozely). Lister denominates this as God's "emotional sovereignty" (167) and "sovereign emotional lordship" (168).

Lister's voluntarist proposal of impassibility as a doctrine about God's emotional self-control is positively developed in Part 2. In chapter 7, he makes a persuasive case for drawing metaphysical conclusions from biblical data (172-75) and for the need for analogical predication (182-88). He also sets forth an understanding of redemptive history in which God freely involves himself with creation and finds new outward expressions for his intra-trinitarian passion in the voluntary outgoing of his love toward creatures. While God exhibits emotional changes through his involvement with the world, he is in control of his emotions and is "not subject to any necessity distinct from himself" (177; citing Karl Barth). In chapter 8, Lister examines a number of biblical passages that teach

God's invulnerability, helpfully explaining biblical affirmations of divine transcendence, self-sufficiency, omniscience, sovereignty, and immutability. He also explores biblical evidence for the reality of God's affections, offering useful interpretations of passages touching on divine immanence, intra-trinitarian love, jealousy, anger, steadfast love, joy/delight, repentance/regret/relenting, affliction, and desire.

In chapter 9, the author draws together his interpretation of the Christian tradition and the biblical data into a grand argument for his thesis that God is both impassible and impassioned. It is clear that, for Lister, God's involvement with creation is not to be understood merely in terms of revelational condescension in which he progressively and variously discloses his eternal divine attributes to creatures. His condescension is also ontological and is seen in "certain divine attributes and in certain dispositions of passion that God takes on in respect to his creation" (225). This accrual of divine attributes and dispositions occurs in God's "unfolding experience . . . in the temporally progressive covenantal context" (230). These new realities in God are temporal, whereas his essence remains timeless. Lister roots this double affirmation in what he calls "the biblical duality respecting the doctrine of God" (226). In this connection, he states, "I would maintain that part of God's accommodation of himself to us is his taking on the property of acting in time" (231). This new property of temporal action is what the author believes clears the way for new temporal emotional dispositions in God. Again, because God has eternally foreordained all these new emotional experiences and is in perfect control of them they "do not come upon him as ours come upon us" (238; citing J. I. Packer). This perfect divine self-control is precisely where Lister locates the dissimilarity between God's experience of passions and the human's experience of them. He concludes the volume with an insightful chapter on Christ's human emotions in which he explains them according the Chalcedonian understanding of Christ's two natures.

Some beneficial features of the volume should be mentioned. First, Lister helpfully debunks the passibilist charge that the impassibility doctrine is overly dependent on Greek thought and too little built upon biblical data. He also effectively puts the lie to the accusation that impassibility undermines God's love and concern for his creation. As he shows, the leading impassibilists throughout history believed quite the opposite. Second, he provides a valuable internal critique of the inadequacies of modern passibilist teaching on doctrines such as the incarnation, the cross, theodicy, biblical interpretation, and divine love. Third, he rightly stresses the need for an analogical understanding of divine affections and of eschewing all univocal theologizing with its anthropocentric construal of God's affections. Fourth, he offers a sound Christological explanation for why the human suffering of Christ does not wash back into his divinity.

Unfortunately, the helpful aspects of this volume are outweighed by its deep defects. We shall observe three of the most significant.

Interpretation of the historical evidence. Lister's interpretation of the Christian tradition appears to be mistaken in two important respects. First, he gratuitously concludes that the various impassibilists he surveys must believe God is "impassioned" simply because they affirm that God loves, is joyful, angry with sin, and so forth. Lister seems unable to imagine that such affirmations could refer to anything other than passions in God. Yet many of the theologians he cites explicitly deny that God has passions, and none of them (with the possible exception of Tertullian) plainly affirm passions or sensations in God. It seems likely that the reason they denied divine passions while affirming divine love, joy, wrath, and the like is because for them "passion" was properly understood as denoting the *manner* or *mode* in which a subject possesses affections—namely, as an *undergoing*. Passions are emotive experiences that subjects "undergo," and since God is identical with all that is in him, per the doctrine of simplicity, none of his perfections can be properly understood as passions. God doesn't undergo an experience of himself. This conviction of divine simplicity, which prompted so many generations of theologians to confess that God is without passions, is completely ignored by Lister.

Second, Lister's voluntarist interpretation of impassibility is simply not borne out by the historical texts he considers. He incorrectly surmises from the denial that God is emotively moved or constrained by the will of creatures that God must be emotively moved and controlled by his own will. Thus, he understands the tradition to teach that God is emotively sovereign over himself by the act of his will. For most in the Christian tradition, though, the opposite of God's being controlled by creatures is not voluntary self-control; rather, it is God's pure actuality. As purely actual in all his perfections, God is not determined in any sense, not even by his own will. Lister never considers this non-voluntarist alternative in his interpretation of the historical data.

Divine immutability and atemporal eternity. While Lister maintains that God cannot be involuntarily moved by creatures or changed in his "intrinsic nature" (206), he does not believe that God is immutable in the traditional strong sense of the doctrine. It is a centerpiece of his argument that God wills intrinsic emotional changes for himself in response to his creatures. These movements and changes do not merely occur in God's works *ad extra*, but also in God himself. Lister is clear that God's responsiveness to his creatures involves "a transition that occurs in God" (179). This transition supposedly occurs when God takes on new relational properties. The question then becomes, not whether God eternally wills to alter his responses to creatures in his unfolding dispensations toward them, but whether the alterations of response correspond to some alteration *in God.* Lister affirms that they do, while the classical Christian tradition, especially the Augustinians, would disagree. God can change his dispensations and the manifestation of his countenance toward creatures without undergoing intrinsic changes of actuality. Given the author's softened understanding of God's immutability, it is not surprising that he also opposes Augustine's and Paul Helm's doctrine of God's atemporal eternality (106, 230-31). The classical view disallows the possibility that God might bring about new emotive states of actuality in himself. Lister wants to make room for just such emotive becoming in God. One can only conclude from this that Lister means to affirm that there are divine attributes in God that are in the process of coming to be and are not identical with the eternal divine nature. This leads to a final set of concerns.

God's pure actuality and simplicity. The model of God as self-determined and impassioned, which lies at the heart of this book, directly conflicts with the classical doctrines of God's pure actuality and simplicity — doctrines about which Lister says almost nothing. His disapproval of Thomas Weinandy's denial that God experiences inner emotional changes of state (157) is rooted in his commitment to Barthian actualism. Barth's view is not of a God who is *purely* actual in all his perfections, but who is "moved and touched by Himself" (177; Barth's words), who controls and guides the unfolding dynamics of his inner life. Lister's voluntarist interpretation of impassibility is wholly in line with Barth's rather extreme voluntarism. Interestingly, Barth understood his voluntarism to conflict with impassibility and so denied the classical doctrine. Lister thinks Barth could have retained impassibility if he had only appreciated that the mainstream Christian tradition can be read as affirming a voluntarist understanding of the doctrine—a rather dubious reading of the tradition, as noted above. As for divine simplicity, the "emotional complexity" (236) of Lister's impassible/impassioned God will not allow one to confess that God is without parts. Inasmuch as God takes on new non-essential divine attributes, and these are located in God, one must conclude that, for Lister, there is a distinction in God between his eternal essence and his temporal accidents of relation. On this account, not all that is in God is God from eternity; rather, some realities in him are the effects of his will and are actualized only in time. For Lister, God is composed of essence and accident, and this strikes at the very heart of the simplicity doctrine upheld by nearly all classical Christian impassibilists.

The author's insistence to the contrary notwithstanding, it seems appropriate to characterize the position advanced in this volume as a qualified passibilist doctrine rather than qualified impassibilist. For those in the Reformed tradition, Lister's voluntarist account of divine emotion will not allow the confession that God is infinite in being and perfection, without parts, without passions, immutable, and most absolute.

Scripture Index

Name and Subject Index

Glossary of Technical Terms and Theological Phrases[*]

accidental properties: An incidental or non-essential quality or characteristic of a substance. For example, the color of a human being's hair is incidental; one's hair color may undergo change without altering the essence or whatness of being human.

accommodatio: The accommodation, adjustment, or condescension of God in the use of human words and concepts in order to reveal his will to man. This refers to the manner or mode of revelation, not to its quality or the matter revealed. Revelational accommodation or condescension entails no change in God.

act-potency: A way of accounting for both permanency and change, or being and becoming. A thing *in act* is that which exists or is actualized. A thing *in potency* is that which has the potential or capacity for further perfection or actuality. For example, a marble slab is *in act* as a marble slab, but it is also *in potency* for becoming, or has the potential or capacity to be further actualized as, a marble sculpture. All things, God excepting (*actus purus, q.v.*), are composed of act-potency and, therefore, have capacity for change.

actus purus: Pure act or perfect actualization, free from all potency for change or potential for greater perfection. It is of the essence of God to be *actus purus* because he is infinite in perfection and self-existent, whose inner divine life is eternally and fully realized.

ad extra: The external works of God or the divine activities of creation, providence, and redemption.

ad intra: The internal works of God which are eternal and immutable. The internal works of God are further defined as either essential or personal.

---

[*] This glossary is *highly* dependent upon the definitions found in Richard A. Muller, *Dictionary of Latin and Greek Theological Terms*. Readers are encouraged to own and use this essential reference work.

affections: Motions of the mind and will relative to an object perceived as good or bad.

analogia entis: The analogy of being, or the imperfect resemblance, without identity, between things in being, especially finite and infinite being.

analogical predication: The affirmation of a similarity between two different things. While the predication does not imply an identical sense for both things, neither are they unrelated; there is a similar sense proportionate to the mode of each being.

anthropomorphism: Figurative language which predicates human form to God.

anthropopathism: Figurative language which predicates human feelings, affections, and passions to God.

apophatic: Predicating things of God in terms of denial or describing God by way of negation based on the incomprehensibility of God. For example, Scripture asserts that God "is not a man" (e.g., Num. 23:19) and that he is *in*visible and *im*mutable.

aseity: The divine attribute of uncaused existence. It is the essence of God to exist.

communicatio idiomatum: The acknowledgement that the properties of each nature of the incarnate Son of God are communicated in the unity of the person of the Son of God. The interchange of attributes takes place at the level of the person not between the natures.

divine felicity: The inner life of God which is one of infinite delight, rest, and satisfaction in his own perfection.

divine spirituality: God is essentially, eternally, and necessarily immaterial. Though angels and human souls are immaterial, they derive their being from God and are thus neither eternally nor necessarily immaterial.

ens a se: Being from itself, which can only be predicated of God because he and he alone is self-existent, necessary, and non-contingent being. All other being is from another.

equivocal predication: A word used in an unrelated way with regard to two or more beings. For example, the ram of a computer and the ram used to break through a wall are not only different but unrelated in sense and meaning.

figurative: A figure of speech or symbol that points beyond itself to another thing.

homoiousios: Of like substance.

homoousios: Of the same substance.

immensity: The immeasurability of God, indicating his freedom from all limit of space or measure apart from all created space. This is distinguished from omnipresence by the fact that omnipresence refers to the repletive presence of God in all created places.

immortality: An attribute of all spiritual being, meaning not subject to dissolution. The immortality possessed by angels and men is contingent because they have it by derivation from God. Thus, God and God alone is absolutely and eternally immortal.

immutability: The eternal and perpetual identity of the divine essence with all its perfections, free from all mutation of being, attributes, place, or will, and from all physical and ethical change.

impassibility: That divine attribute whereby God is said not to experience inner emotional changes, whether enacted freely from within or effected by his relationship to and interaction with human beings and the created order.[1]

---

[1] Weinandy, "Impassibility of God," in *New Catholic Encyclopedia*, 2nd ed., 7:357.

improper predication: An analogical predication (*q.v.*) wherein the thing predicated exists figuratively in one of the analogates. For example, eyes may be predicated of God, although not properly, for the form, or nature, of an eye does not exist in God. However, there is something in God, figuratively and improperly, that corresponds to the likeness of a man's eye, such as his omnipresence and his watch care over his people. SEE anthropomorphism; anthropopathism; proper predication.

incomprehensibility: God is always infinitely greater than the revelation (i.e., words or names) of himself. He is knowable but only as a revealed mystery; the more we know God, the more we understand that his essence cannot be comprehended by any but himself. SEE *via causalitatis; via eminentiae; via negationis.*

incorporeality: Without material or bodily existence.

ontology: The study of the nature of being or existence.

passions: Motions of the mind and will relative to an object perceived as good or bad. Sometimes inordinate motions, or motions contrary to nature, reason, and morality.

patripassianism: The heretical view that that Father vicariously suffered through the Son at the cross.

perichoresis: The coinherence of the persons of the Trinity in the divine essence and in each other.

potency, active and passive: Active and passive power. Active potency refers to the power to effect a change, or actualize the potential, of something else. Passive potency refers to a thing's potential to be affected and undergo change. Pure uncreated active potency, or power unmixed with any passive potency or potentiality, is pure actuality (*actus purus, q.v.*); God alone has the power to affect change without being changed. Therefore, God does not have the power to be other than he eternally and immutably is.

predication: To affirm or assert something of the subject of a proposition.

prolegomenon: A formal introduction to a treatise enunciating basic principles and premises.

proper predication: An analogical predication (*q.v.*) wherein the thing predicated exists formally in both analogates. For example, life is predicated properly of God and man because life exists formally (i.e., essentially) in both, though always in a manner proportionate to the mode of each being.

qua: as or in the capacity of

quiddity: The whatness or essence of a thing; the answer to the question "What is it?"

simplicity: Having an uncompounded or noncomposite nature which, referring to God, asserts that he is absolutely free of composition physically, rationally, or logically. Because of divine simplicity, we assert that all that is in God is God.

supra ens: Above being. God is not non-being, but rather of such an entirely different order of being from the creature that he may be said to be above being itself. When speaking of God, even superlatives become diminutives, or inadequate descriptions of the being and essence of God.

theopassianism: The heretical view that teaches the suffering or death of God at the cross.

univocal predication: A word used of two or more beings in an identical way and with the same sense. For example, "Bill is a human," and "Fred is a human." Humanness is predicated of both, and what it means for Bill to possess humanness is identically the same for Fred.

via causalitatis: The way of causality, or the premise that we may know something about the cause (i.e., God) from the effect (i.e., creation). The *via causalitatis* provides the foundation of all our language about God; the knowledge of the effect (i.e., creation) provides a foundation for an analogical knowledge of the cause (i.e.,

God). SEE *analogia entis;* analogical predication.

via eminentiae: The way of eminence, or the premise that the cause is infinitely greater than the effect (*via causalitatis, q.v.*), and God is infinitely more perfect than all that we can conceive. The *via eminentiae* raises the perfections attributable to the creature and attributes them to God in an infinitely more eminent way.

via negationis: The way of negation, or the premise that God is more unlike than like the creature, and that we may know more of God by what he is not. The *via negationis* removes the imperfections attributable to the creature, or those creaturely perfections that would be imperfections in God, and attributes the negation of those imperfections to God. For example, God *is not* finite, but infinite. SEE apophatic.

Bibliography of Works Cited

1. Books

Adams, Thomas. *The Workes of Tho: Adams*. London: Printed by Tho. Harper, 1629.

Ainsworth, Henry. *Annotations upon the first book of Moses, Called Genesis*. Amsterdam: Imprinted by [Giles Thorp], 1616.

Alexander, Joseph Addison. *Commentary on the Prophecies of Isaiah: Unabridged*. Two volumes. 1875; reprint, Grand Rapids: Zondervan, 1970.

Allen, Michael and Scott R. Swain. *Reformed Catholicity: The Promise of Retrieval for Theology and Biblical Interpretation*. Grand Rapids: Baker Academic, 2015.

Ames, William. *The Marrow of Sacred Divinity, Drawne out of the holy Scriptures, and the Interpreters thereof, and brought into Method*. London: Edward Griffin, 1642.

_____. *The Marrow of Theology*. Translated by John Dykstra Eusden. 1968; reprint, Grand Rapids: Baker Books, 1997.

Aquinas, Thomas. *Summa Theologica*. Translated by Fathers of the English Dominican Province. Notre Dame, IN: Christian Classics, 1981.

_____. *The Power of God*. Translated by Richard J. Regan. New York: Oxford University Press, 2012.

Ashley, Timothy. *The Book of Numbers*, The New International Commentary on the Old Testament. Edited by Robert L. Hubbard, Jr. Grand Rapids: Wm. B. Eerdmans Publishing Co., 1993.

Athanasius. *Against the Arians*, in *Nicene And Post-Nicene Fathers*. Second Series. Volume four. Edited by Philip Schaff and Henry Wace. 1891; reprint, Peabody, MA: Hendriksen Publishers, Fifth printing, 2012.

Augustine. *De Trinitate,* in *Nicene And Post-Nicene Fathers*. First series. Volume three. Edited by Philip Schaff. Translated by Arthur West Haddan. 1887; reprint, Peabody MA: Hendrickson Publishers, 2012.

Bahnsen, Greg L. *Always Ready: Directions for Defending the Faith*. Edited by Robert R. Booth. Texarkana, AR: Covenant Media Press, 1996.

Baron, Robert. *theologi ac philosophi celeberrimi, Metaphysica generalis accedunt nunc primum quae supererant ex parte speciali : omnia ad usum theologia accommodata, opus postumum, ex muséo Antonii Clememtii Zirizaei.* London: R. Danielis, 1669.

Barth, Karl. *Church Dogmatics.* Edited by Geoffrey W. Bromiley and T. F. Torrance. Translated by T. H. L. Parker, W. B. Johnston, Harold Knight, and J. L. M. Haire. 1957; reprint, Peabody, MA: Hendrickson Publishers, 2010.

Bavinck, Herman. *Reformed Dogmatics.* General editor John Bolt. Translated by John Vriend. Four volumes. Grand Rapids: Baker Academic, 2003-2008.

Beale, G. K. *We Become What We Worship: A Biblical Theology of Idolatry.* Downers Grove, IL: IVP Academic, 2008.

Beale, G. K. and D. A Carson, editors. *Commentary on the New Testament Use of the Old Testament.* Grand Rapids: Baker Academic, 2007.

Bebbington, David. *Evangelicalism in Modern Britain: A History from the 1730s to the 1980s.* Grand Rapids: Baker, 1989.

Beilby, James K., and Paul R. Eddy, editors. *Divine Foreknowledge: Four Views.* Downers Grove, IL: IVP Academic, 2001.

Bennett, Arthur, editor. *The Valley of Vision: A Collection of Puritan Prayers and Devotions.* 1975; reprint, Edinburgh; Carlisle, PA: The Banner of Truth Trust, 1989.

Berkhof, Louis. *Systematic Theology.* 1939; reprint, Edinburgh; Carlisle, PA: Banner of Truth Trust, 2003.

_____. *Systematic Theology.* 1939; reprint, Grand Rapids: Wm. B. Eerdmans Publishing Co., 1986.

Bobik, Joseph. *Aquinas on Being and Essence: A Translation and Interpretation.* Notre Dame: University of Notre Dame Press, 2004.

Boston, Thomas. *The Complete Works of The Late Rev. Thomas Boston.* Twelve volumes. Edited by Samuel M'Millan. 1853; reprint, Stoke-on-Trent, UK: Tentmaker Publications, 2005.

Botterweck, G. Johannes, Helmer Ringgren, and Heinz-Josef Fabry, editors. Fifteen volumes. *Theological Dictionary of the Old Testament.* Grand Rapids: Wm. B. Eerdmans Publishing Company, 1974-2006.

Boyce, James P. *Abstract Of Systematic Theology.* 1887; reprint, Hanford, CA: den Dulk Christian Foundation, n.d.

Bridge, William. *Bridge's Remains, Being VIII Sermons*. London: Printed by John Hancock, 1673.

_____. *The Works of the Rev. William Bridge*. 1657; reprint, five volumes in 1845; reprint, Beaver Falls, PA: Soli Deo Gloria, 1989.

Bullinger, Heinrich. *Fiftie Godlie and Learned Sermons, Divided Into Five Decades, Containing The chiefe and principall points of Christian Religion, written in three seuerall Tomes or Sections*. Translated by H. I., student in divinity. London: Imprinted by Ralph Newberie, 1587.

_____. *The Decades of Henry Bullinger*. Two volumes. Edited by Thomas Harding. Grand Rapids: Reformation Heritage Books, 2004.

Burgess, Anthony. *A Treatise of Original Sin. The First Part.* London: n.p., 1658.

Burroughs, Jeremiah. *An Exposition of the Prophesy of Hosea*. 1863; reprint, Grand Rapids: Reformation Heritage Books, 2006.

Byfield, Adoniram, Charles Herle, and Henry Robrough. *The Proceedings of the Assembly of Divines upon the Thirty nine Articles of the Church of England.* n.p., 1643.

Callen, Barry L. *Clark H. Pinnock: Journey Toward Renewal.* Nappanee, IN: Evangel Publishing House, 2000.

Calvin, John. *A Commentarie of John Calvine, upon the first booke of Moses called Genesis*. Translated by Thomas Tymme. London: Printed by John Harison and George Bishop, 1578.

_____. *Calvin's Commentaries*. Twenty-two volumes. Various translators. 1870; reprint, Grand Rapids: Baker Books, 1993, 2003.

_____. *Commentaries on the Four Last Books of Moses Arranged in the Form of a Harmony*. Volumes 3 and 4. Edinburgh: The Calvin Translation Society, 1860.

_____.*Sermons on Deuteronomy*. Translated by Arthur Golding. Reprint, Edinburgh; Carlisle, PA: Banner of Truth, 1987.

_____. *Sermons on Genesis, Chapters 1:1-11:14*. Translated by Rob Roy McGregor. Reprint, Edinburgh; Carlisle, PA: The Banner of Truth Trust, 2009.

_____. *The Covenant Enforced; Sermons on Deuteronomy 27 and 28*. Edited by James B. Jordan. Tyler, TX: Institute for

Christian Economics, 1990.

_____. *The Institutes of the Christian Religion*. Edited by John T. McNeill. Translated by Ford Lewis Battles. *Library of Christian Classics*, volumes 20-21. Philadelphia: Westminster Press, 1960.

Cameron, Nigel M. de S., editor. *The Power and Weakness of God*. Edinburgh, Scotland: Rutherford House Books, 1990.

Carson, D. A. *How Long, O Lord?: Reflections on Suffering and Evil*. Grand Rapids: Baker Publishing Group, 2006.

_____. *The Difficult Doctrine of the Love of God*. Wheaton, IL: Crossway Books, 2000.

_____. *The Gospel According to John*. Grand Rapids: William B. Eerdmans Publishing Company, 1991.

Carson, Thomas, and Joann Cerrito, editors. *New Catholic Encyclopedia*. Second edition. Fifteen volumes. Detroit; Washington D.C.: Thomson/Gale, 2002.

Charnock, Stephen. *The Existence and Attributes of God*. Two volumes. 1853; reprint, Grand Rapids: Baker Book House, 2000.

Christensen, Duane L. *Deuteronomy 21:10-34:12*. Word Biblical Commentary. John D. W. Watts and James W. Watts, editors. Dallas: Word Incorporated, 2002.

Clark, R. Scott, and Joel E. Kim, editors. *Always Reformed: Essays in Honor of W. Robert Godfrey*. Escondido, CA: Westminster Seminary California, 2010.

Coxe, Nehemiah. *Vindiciae Veritatis, Or a Confutation of the Heresies and Gross Errors of Thomas Collier*. London: Nath. Ponder, 1677.

Currid, John D. *A Study Commentary on Exodus: Exodus 1–18*, vol. 1, EP Study Commentary. Darlington, England; Carlisle, PA: Evangelical Press, 2000.

Dabney, Robert L. *Systematic Theology*. 1871; reprint, Edinburgh; Carlisle, PA: The Banner of Truth Trust, 1996.

Danker, Frederick, William, editor. *A Greek-English Lexicon of the New Testament and other Early Christian Literature*. Chicago: The University of Chicago Press, 2000.

Davidson, A. B. *Hebrew Syntax*. 3rd ed. 1901; reprint Edinburgh: T&T Clark, 1958.

Day, William. *An Exposition of the Book of the Prophet Isaiah*. London: G.D and S.G., 1654.

Dodds, Michael. *The Unchanging God of Love: Thomas Aquinas &*

Contemporary Theology on Divine Immutability. Washington, D.C.: Catholic University of America Press, 2008.

Dolezal, James E. *God Without Parts: Divine Simplicity and the Metaphysics of God's Absoluteness.* Eugene, OR: Pickwick Publications, 2011.

Edwards, Jonathan. *Our Great and Glorious God.* Compiled by Don Kistler. Morgan, PA: Soli Deo Gloria, 2003.

_____. *The Works of Jonathan Edwards.* Reprint, Edinburgh: The Banner of Truth, 1976.

Fairbairn, A. M. *The Place of Christ in Modern Theology.* New York: Charles Scribner's Sons, 1893.

Feinberg, John S. *No One Like Him: The Doctrine of God.* Wheaton, IL: Crossway Books, 2001.

Fenner, William. *A Treatise of the Affections.* London: Printed by R.H., 1642.

Feser, Edward. *Scholastic Metaphysics: A Contemporary Introduction.* Germany: Editiones Scholasticae, 2014.

Frame, John M. *The Doctrine of God: A Theology of Lordship.* Phillipsburg, NJ: P&R Publishing, 2002.

Fuller, Andrew. *The Complete Works of the Rev. Andrew Fuller.* Three volumes. Edited by J. Belcher. 1845; reprint, Harrisonburg, VA: Sprinkle, 1988.

Gavrilyuk, Paul L. *The Suffering of the Impassible God: The Dialectics of Patristic Thought.* Oxford: Oxford University Press, 2006.

Gill, John. *A Complete Body of Doctrinal and Practical Divinity.* Reprint, Paris, AR: Baptist Standard Bearer, 1995.

_____. *Exposition of the Old and New Testaments.* Nine volumes. Reprint, Paris AR: The Baptist Standard Bearer, Inc., 1989.

Gonzales, Jr., Robert R. *Where Sin Abounds: The Spread of Sin and the Curse in Genesis with Special Focus on the Patriarchal Narratives.* Eugene, OR: Wipf and Stock Publishers, 2009.

Goodwin, Thomas. *The Heart of Christ in Heaven Towards Sinners on Earth.* Volume four. *The Works of Thomas Goodwin.* Edited by Thomas Smith. Edinburgh: James Nichol, 1862.

Goris, Harm, Herwi Rikhof, and Henk Schoot, editors. *Divine Transcendence and Immanence in the Works of Thomas Aquinas.* Walpole, MA: Peeters Leuven, 2009.

Gouge, William. *A Plaster for the Plague, in God's Three Arrows:*

Plague, Famine, Sword. London: George Miller, 1631.

_____. *Commentary on Hebrews.* Two volumes. 1866; reprint, Birmingham, AL: Solid Ground Christian Books, 2006.

Grudem, Wayne A. *Systematic Theology: An Introduction to Biblical Doctrine.* Grand Rapids, MI: Zondervan, 1994.

Gundlach, Bradley J. *Process and Providence: The Evolution Question at Princeton, 1845-1929.* Grand Rapids: Eerdmans, 2013.

Harris, R. Laird, Gleason L. Archer, Jr., and Bruce K. Waltke, editors. Two volumes. *Theological Wordbook of the Old Testament.* Chicago: Moody Press, 1999.

Haykin, Michael A. G., editor. *The Life and Thought of John Gill (1697-1771): A Tercentennial Appreciation.* Leiden: Brill, 1997.

Haykin, Michael A. G. and Kenneth J. Stewart, editors. *The Advent of Evangelicalism: Exploring Historical Continuities.* Nashville: B&H Academic, 2008.

Henry, Matthew. *Commentary on the Holy Bible.* Six volumes. New York: Funk & Wagnalls Co., n.d.

Henry Ward Beecher as His Friends Saw Him. New York: The Pilgrim Press, 1904.

Hodge, Charles. *Systematic Theology.* New York: Charles Scribners, 1871.

_____. *The Church and its Polity.* London: Thomas Nelson, 1879.

Hodges, Thomas. *A Glimpse of Gods Glory.* London: Printed for Iohn Bartlet, 1642.

Holladay, William L. and Ludwig Köhler. *A Concise Hebrew and Aramaic Lexicon of the Old Testament.* Leiden: Brill, 2000.

Hoogland, Mark-Robin, C.P. *God, Passion and Power: Thomas Aquinas on Christ Crucified and the Almightiness of God.* Walpole, MA: Peeters Leuven, 2003.

Horton, Michael S. *Covenant and Eschatology.* Louisville: Westminster John Knox Press, 2002.

_____. *Lord and Servant: A Covenant Christology.* Louisville, KY: Westminster John Knox Press, 2005.

_____. *The Christian Faith: A Systematic Theology for Pilgrims on the Way.* Grand Rapids: Zondervan, 2011.

Huffman, Douglas S. and Eric L. Johnson, editors. *God Under Fire: Modern Scholarship Reinvents God.* Grand Rapids: Zondervan, 2002.

Hughes, Philip Edgcumbe. *A Commentary on the Epistle to the Hebrews*. 1977; reprint, Grand Rapids: Wm. B. Eerdmans Publishing Co., 1993.

Hutchinson, Roger. *The Image of God or Layman's Book in The Works of Roger Hutchinson*. Edited by John Bruce. Cambridge: The University Press, 1842.

Joüon, Paul, and T. Muraoka. *A Grammar of Biblical Hebrew*. Roma: Pontificio Istituto Biblico, 2006.

Kapic, Kelly M. and Bruce L. McCormack, editors. *Mapping Modern Theology: A Thematic and Historical Introduction*. Grand Rapids: Baker Academic, 2012.

Keating, James F. and Thomas Joseph White, editors. *Divine Impassibility and the Mystery of Human Suffering*. Grand Rapids; Cambridge: William B. Eerdmans Publishing Company, 2009.

Keil, C. F., and F. Delitzsch. *The Pentateuch*. Volume one. *Commentary on the Old Testament in Ten Volumes*. Translated by James Martin. 1949; reprint, Grand Rapids: Wm. Eerdmans Publishing Co., 1983.

Kelly, J. N. D. *A Commentary on the Pastoral Epistles*. 1963; reprint, Grand Rapids: Baker Book House, 1981.

Kistler, Don, editor. *The Puritan Pulpit: Jonathan Edwards*. Morgan, PA: Soli Deo Gloria, 2004.

Klein, Ralph W. *1 Samuel*. Word Biblical Commentary. Edited by John D. W. Watts. Dallas: Word Incorporated, 1998.

Knight, III, George W. *The Pastoral Epistles: A Commentary on the Greek Text*. The New International Greek Text Commentary. Grand Rapids: William B. Eerdmans Publishing Company, 1992.

Leigh, Edward. *A Systeme or Body of Divinity*. London: Printed by A. M. for William Lee, 1662.

_____. *A Treatise of Divinity Consisting of Three Books*. London: John Downham, 1647.

Letham, Robert. *The Westminster Assembly: Reading its Theology in Historical Context*. Phillipsburg, NJ: P&R Publishing, 2009.

Lindsay, James. *Recent Advances in Theistic Philosophy of Religion*. Edinburgh: Blackwood, 1897.

Lister, Rob. *God Is Impassible And Impassioned: Toward A Theology Of Divine Emotion*. Wheaton, IL: Crossway Books, 2013.

Lombard, Peter. *The Sentences: Book 3 On the Incarnation of the Word*. Medieval Sources in Translation 45. Translated by Giulio Silano.

Toronto: Pontifical Institute of Medieval Studies, 2008.

Mackay, John L. *Isaiah*, An Evangelical Press Study Commentary. Darlington, England: EP Books, 2009.

Macleod, Donald. *Christ Crucified: Understanding the Atonement*. Downers Grove, IL: IVP Academic, 2014.

_____. *From Glory to Golgotha*. Fearn, Ross-Shire, Scotland: Christian Focus Publications, 2002.

Manning, Bernard. *Essays in Orthodox Dissent*. London: Independent Press, 1953.

Manton, Thomas. *An Exposition of the Epistle of James*. Reprint, Grand Rapids: Associated Publishers and Authors, Inc., [no date].

_____. *The Works of Thomas Manton*. Twenty-two volumes. Birmingham, AL: Solid Ground Books, 2008.

Mason, A. J. *The Faith of the Gospel: A Manual of Christian Doctrine*. New York: Dutton, 1891, revised edition.

McGinnis, Andrew M. *The Son of God Beyond the Flesh: A Historical and Theological Study of the* extra Calvinisticum. T & T Clark Studies in Systematic Theology, vol. 29. Edited by John Webster, Ian A. McFarland, and Ivor Davidson. London: Bloomsbury, 2014.

Moo, Douglas J. *The Epistle to the Romans*. The New International Commentary on the New Testament. Grand Rapids: Wm. B. Eerdmans Publishing Co., 1996.

Mosely, Nicholas. *Psychosophia: Or, Natural & Divine Contemplations of the Passions & Faculties of the Soul of Man*. London: Printed for Humphrey Mosley, 1653.

Motyer, J. Alec. *The Prophecy of Isaiah: An Introduction & Commentary*. Downers Grove, IL: InterVarsity Press, 1993.

Mozley, J. K. *The Impassibility Of God: A Survey Of Christian Thought*. Reprint, Cambridge, UK: Cambridge University Press, 2014.

Muller, Richard A. *Dictionary of Latin and Greek Theological Terms: Drawn Principally from Protestant Scholastic Theology*. Grand Rapids: Baker Book House, 1985.

_____. *Post-Reformation Reformed Dogmatics*. Four volumes. Grand Rapids: Baker Academic, 2003.

_____. *The Unaccomodated Calvin*. Oxford: Oxford University Press, 2001.

Mullins, E. Y. *The Christian Religion in Its Doctrinal Expression*. Philadelphia: Roger Williams Press, 1917.

Murray, John. *Epistle to the Romans*. 1959, 1965; reprint, Grand Rapids: Wm. B. Eerdmans Publishing Co., one-volume edition, 1984.

_____. *Redemption Accomplished and Applied*. 1955; reprint, Grand Rapids: Eerdmans Publishing Company, 1987.

Musculus, Wolfgang. *Common Places of Christian Religion*. Translated by John Man. London: Henry Bynneman, 1578.

Nazianzen, Gregory of. *To Cledonius the Priest against Apollinarius* in *Nicene and Post-Nicene Fathers*. Second series. Volume seven. Edited by Philip Schaff. Translated by Charles Gordon Browne and James Edward Swallow. 1887; reprint, Peabody MA: Hendrickson Publishers, 2012.

Noll, Mark, editor. *Eerdmans' Handbook To Christianity In America*. Grand Rapids: Eerdmans, 1983.

Norton, John. *The Orthodox Evangelist*. London: Printed for John Macock, and Henry Cripps, and Ludwick Lloyd, 1654.

Oliphint, Scott K. *God with Us: Divine Condescension and the Attributes of God*. Wheaton, IL: Crossway Books, 2012.

Oswalt, John N. *The Book of Isaiah, Chapters 40-66*. The New International Commentary on the Old Testament. Grand Rapids: Eerdmans Publishing Co., 1998.

Owen, John. *The Works of John Owen*. Twenty-three volumes. Edited by William H. Goold. Reprint, Edinburgh; Carlisle, PA: Banner of Truth Trust, 1965-1991.

_____. *Vindiciae Evangelicae Or, The Mystery of the Gospell Vindicated, and Socinianisme Examined*. Oxford: Printed by Leon. Lichfield, 1655.

Perkins, William. *A Golden Chain or the Description of Theology*. Edited by Greg Fox. 1597; reprint, Puritan Reprints, 2010.

Pinnock, Clark H. *Most Moved Mover: A Theology of God's Openness*. Carlisle, PA: Paternoster, 2001.

Pinnock, Clark H., Richard Rice, John Sander, William Hasker, David Basinger. *The Openness of God: A Biblical Challenge to the Traditional Understanding of God*. Downers Grove, IL: InterVarsity Press, 1994.

Placher, William. *The Domestication of Transcendence: How Modern Thinking about God went Wrong*. Louisville, KY: Westminster John Knox Press, 1996.

Pool, Jeff B. *Against Returning to Egypt: Exposing and Resisting*

Credalism in the Southern Baptist Convention. Macon, GA: Mercer University Press, 1998.

Poole, Matthew. *A Commentary on the Holy Bible.* Three volumes. London: The Banner of Truth Trust, 1962.

Pringle-Pattison, A. Seth. *The Idea Of God In The Light Of Recent Philosophy.* New York: Oxford University Press, 1920.

Renihan, Samuel, editor. *God without Passions: A Reader.* Palmdale, CA: RBAP, 2015.

Reymond, Robert L. *A New Systematic Theology of the Christian Faith.* Nashville: Thomas Nelson, Inc., 1998.

Reynolds, Edward. *A Treatise of the Passions and Faculties of the Soul of Man.* London: Printed for Robert Bostock, 1656.

Ridderbos, Herman. *The Gospel of John: A Theological Commentary.* Grand Rapids: William B. Eerdmans Publishing Company, 1997.

Robertson, O. Palmer. *The Books of Nahum, Habakkuk, and Zephaniah.* New International Commentary on the Old Testament. Grand Rapids: Eerdmans Publishing Company, 1990.

Rocca, Gregory P. *Speaking the Incomprehensible God: Thomas Aquinas on the Interplay of Positive and Negative Theology.* Washington, D.C.: Catholic University of America Press, 2004.

Sanders, John. *The God Who Risks: A Theology of Providence.* Downers Grove, IL: InterVarsity Press, 1998.

Scott, Thomas. *The Holy Bible, Containing the Old and New Testaments, with Explanatory Notes and Practical Observations and Copious Marginal References.* Three volumes. New York: W. E. Dean, 1846.

Simeon, Charles. *Horae Homileticae, Or Discourses Now First Digested Into One Continued Series and Forming a Commentary Upon Every Book of the Old and New Testament.* Twenty-one volumes. London: Holdsworth and Ball, 1832.

Skinner, Quentin. *Visions of Politics: Regarding Method.* Volume one. Cambridge: Cambridge University Press, 2002.

Spurgeon, Charles Haddon. *Metropolitan Tabernacle Pulpit* 34. London: Passmore and Alabaster, 1888.

Tennent, Gilbert. *Discourses, on Several Important Subjects.* By Gilbert Tennent, A.M. Minister of the Gospel in Philadelphia. Philadelphia: W. Bradford at the Bible in Second-Street, 1745.

Thaumaturgus, St. Gregory. *To Theopompus, on the Impassibility and Passibility of God* in *The Fathers of the Church: St Gregory*

Thaumaturgus Life and Works. Translated by Michael Slusser. Washington, D.C.: The Catholic University of America Press, 1998.

Torbet, Robert G. *Venture of Faith: The Story of the American Baptist Foreign Mission Society and the Woman's American Baptist Mission Society 1814-1954*. Philadelphia: Judson Press, 1955.

Towner, Philip H. *The Letters to Timothy and Titus*. The New International Commentary on the New Testament. Grand Rapids: William B. Eerdmans Publishing Company, 2006.

Trinity Hymnal. Philadelphia: Great Commission Publications, 1961.

Trueman, Carl R. *The Claims of Truth: John Owen's Trinitarian Theology*. Carlisle: Paternoster, 1998.

Turretin, Francis. *Institutes of Elenctic Theology*. Three volumes. Edited by James T. Dennison, Jr. Translated by George Musgrave Giger. Phillipsburg, NJ: P&R Publishing, 1992-97.

Ursinus, Zacharias. *Commentary of Dr. Zacharias Ursinus on the Heidelberg Catechism*. Translated by G. W. Williard. 1852; reprint, Phillipsburg, NJ: P&R Publishing, 1985.

Vanhoozer, Kevin. *First Theology: God, Scripture, & Hermeneutics*. Downers Grove, IL: InterVarsity Press, 2002.

_____. *Remythologizing Theology: Divine Action, Passion, and Authorship*. Cambridge: Cambridge University Press, 2010.

VanGemeren, Willem, editor. *New International Dictionary of Old Testament Theology and Exegesis*. Five volumes. Grand Rapids: Zondervan Publishing House, 1997.

van Asselt, Willem J. with T. Theo J. Pleizier, Pieter L. Rouwendal, and Maarten Wisse. *Introduction to Reformed Scholasticism*. Translated by Albert Gootjes. Grand Rapids: Reformation Heritage Books, 2011.

van der Merwe, Christo H. J., Jackie A. Naudé, and Jan H. Kroeze. *A Biblical Hebrew Reference Grammar*. Sheffield: Sheffield Academic Press, 1999.

Vermigli, Peter Martyr. *Life, Letters, and Sermons*. Volume five. Edited and translated by John Patrick Donnelly. *The Peter Martyr Library*. Kirksville, MO: Thomas Jefferson University Press, 1999.

_____. *The Common Places of the most famous and renowned Diuine Doctor Peter Martyr*. Translated by Anthonie Marten. n.p., 1583.

von Harnack, Adolph. *What is Christianity?* New York: The

Knickerbocker Press, 1902.

Waltke, Bruce K. and Michael Patrick O'Connor. *An Introduction to Biblical Hebrew Syntax*. Winona Lake, IN: Eisenbrauns, 1990.

Ware, Bruce A. *God's Lesser Glory; The Diminished God of Open Theism*. Wheaton, IL: Crossway Books, 2000.

Ware, Bruce A., editor. *Perspectives on the Doctrine of God: Four Views*. Nashville: Broadman & Holman, 2008.

Warfield, Benjamin Breckinridge. *The Person and Work of Christ*. Edited by Samuel G. Craig. Philadelphia: Presbyterian and Reformed, 1950.

Watson, Thomas. *A Body of Divinity*. Reprint, Edinburgh: The Banner of Truth, 1957.

Weemes, John. *The Portraitvre of the Image of God in Man*. London: Printed by T.C., 1636.

Weinandy, Thomas G. *Does God Suffer?* Notre Dame, IN: University of Notre Dame Press, 2000.

Wells, David F., editor. *Reformed Theology In America: A History Of The Modern Movement*. Grand Rapids: Baker, 1997.

Wenham, Gordon J. *Genesis 1–15*. Volume one. Word Biblical Commentary. Dallas: Word, Incorporated, 1998.

Wilson, Douglas, editor. *Bound Only Once: The Failure of Open Theism*. Moscow, ID: Canon Press, 2001.

Witsius, Herman. *Sacred Dissertations on the Apostles' Creed*. Two volumes. Translated by Donald Fraser. 1823; reprint, Phillipsburg, NJ: P&R Publishing, 1993.

Woodbridge, John, Mark Noll, and Nathan Hatch. *The Gospel In America*. Grand Rapids: Zondervan, 1979.

Wright, Joseph. *Folly Detected*. London: John Harris, 1691.

Wuellner, Bernard. *Summary of Scholastic Principles*. Chicago: Loyola University Press, 1956.

Young, Edward J. *The Book of Isaiah*. Three volumes. Grand Rapids: Eerdmans Publishing Company, 1972.

Zanchi, Girolamo. *De Natura Dei seu de divinis attributis. Lib. V.* Heidelberg: Jacob Mylius, 1577.

Zanchius, Jerome. *Life Everlasting: or, the True Knowledge of One Jehovah*. Cambridge: John Legat, 1601.

2. Articles

Barcellos, Richard C. "*Scopus Scripturae*: John Owen, Nehemiah Coxe, our Lord Jesus Christ, and a Few Early Disciples on Christ as the Scope of Scripture." *JIRBS* (2015): 5-24.

Dolezal, James E. "Eternal Creator of Time." *JIRBS* (2015): 127-58.

_____. "Review: *God is Impassible and Impassioned*." *WTJ* 76 (Fall 2013): 414-18.

_____. "Still Impassible: Confessing God without Passions." *JIRBS* (2014): 125-51.

Duncan, J. Ligon. "Divine Passibility and Impassibility in Nineteenth-Century American Confessional Presbyterian Theologians." *The Scottish Bulletin of Evangelical Theology* 8 (1990): 1-15.

Erickson, Millard J. "God and Change." *Southern Baptist Journal of Theology* 1/2 (1997): 38-51.

Greenleaf, Andrew. "The Problem of Pain." *The Church: A Journal of American Churchmanship*, VI:3 (November, 1898): 38-39.

Hart, David Bentley. "No Shadow of Turning: On Divine Impassibility." *Pro Ecclesia* 11.2 (2002): 184-206.

Helm, Paul. "B. B. Warfield On Divine Passion." *WTJ* 69:1 (Spring 2007): 95-104.

Hodge, Charles. "Adoption of the Confession of Faith." *The Biblical Repertory and Princeton Review* (October 1858): 692-721.

_____. "The General Assembly." *The Biblical Repertory and Princeton Review* (July 1858): 533-70.

Hospes. "On the Immutability of God." *The American Baptist Magazine and Missionary Intelligencer*, New Series, Vol. 1 (1817): 14-15.

Muller, Richard A. "Incarnation, Immutability, and the Case for Classical Theism." *WTJ* 45 (1983): 22-40.

_____. "Not Scotist: Understandings of being, univocity, and analogy in early-modern Reformed thought." *Reformation & Renaissance Review* 14:2 (2012): 127-50.

Renihan, James M. "Theology on Target: The Scope of the Whole (which is to give all glory to God)." *RBTR* II:2 (July 2005): 36-52.

Robison, Olin C. "The Legacy of John Gill." *The Baptist Quarterly* 24 (July, 1971): 111-25.

Ware, Bruce A. "An Evangelical Reformulation Of the Doctrine of the Immutability of God." *JETS,* Vol. 29, No. 4, (December 1986): 431-46.

Warfield, Benjamin B. "The Presbyterian Churches and the Westminster Confession." *The Presbyterian Review* 10:40, (1889): 646-57.

Wolterstorff, Nicholas P. "Does God Suffer? Interview with Nicholas P. Wolterstorff." *Modern Reformation* Vol. 8, No. 5 (Sept./Oct. 1999): 45-47.

3. Internet Links

Allen, Michael. "The Promise and Prospects of Retrieval: Recent Developments in the Divine Attributes." http://zondervanacademic.com/blog/common-places-the-promise-and-prospects-of-retrieval-recent-developments-in-the-divine-attributes/#citation1. Accessed 20 October, 2014.

Gonzales, Jr., Robert R. "The Passionate Impassible God: Toward a Biblical View of Divine Emotions." http://drbobgonzales.com/2012/biblical-balance-affirming-gods-emotivity-and-his-impassibility/. Accessed 23 March 2012.

Jonathan Edwards Center at Yale University. *Sermons, Series II, 1729 (WJE Online Vol. 44).* http://edwards.yale.edu/archive?path=aHR0cDovL2Vkd2FyZHMueWFsZS5lZHUvY2dpLWJpbi9uZXdwaGlsby9nZXRvYmplY3QucGw/Yy40Mjo3LndqZW8=. Accessed 26 March 2015.

Oliphint, K. Scott. "Theological Principles from Van Til's Common Grace and the Gospel." Lecture delivered at the 2014 Reformed Forum Theology Conference, Gray's Lake, IL, October 2014. http://reformedforum.org/rf14_08/. Accessed 30 March 2015.

Russell, Bertrand. *Is There A God?* www.personal.kent.edu/~muhamma/Philosophy/RBwritings/isThereGod.htm. Accessed 30 March 2015.

Sproul, R. C. "Did God Die on the Cross?" http://www.ligonier.org/blog/it-accurate-say-god-died-cross/. Accessed 2 August 2014.

Stanford Encyclopedia Of Philosophy. "James Ward." http://plato.stanford.edu/entries/james-ward/. Accessed 30 March 2015.

"Subscription, Full." See Appendix #1 of the Constitution of the

Association of Reformed Baptist Churches of America. http://www.arbca.com/arbca-constitution. Accessed 31 March 2015.

Weinandy, Thomas G. "Human Suffering and the Impassibility of God." *Testamentum Imperium* Volume 2, 2009: 9. http://www.preciousheart.net/ti/2009/52-111_Weinandy_Human_Suffering_Impassibility.pdf. Accessed 9 February 2015.

Contributors

Ronald S. Baines, Ph.D. candidate, University of Maine, is co-pastor of Grace Reformed Baptist Church, Brunswick, ME. Ron co-authored *Jonathan Edwards, A God-Centered Life, An Enduring Legacy*, with Michael A. G. Haykin. He has written journal articles and reviews in both theology and history. Ron also serves as Associate Editor of the *Journal of the Institute of Reformed Baptist Studies* (*JIRBS*).

Richard C. Barcellos, Ph.D., is pastor of Grace Reformed Baptist Church, Palmdale, CA. He is author of *The Lord's Supper as a Means of Grace: More than a Memory, Better than the Beginning: Creation in Biblical Perspective*, and *The Family Tree of Reformed Biblical Theology: Geerhardus Vos and John Owen – Their Methods of and Contributions to the Articulation of Redemptive History*. Rich has contributed articles and book reviews to various theological journals. He is also Managing Editor and Book Review Editor of *JIRBS* and a member of the Evangelical Theological Society (ETS).

James P. Butler, Th.M., is pastor of the Free Grace Baptist Church, Chilliwack, BC, Canada. Jim has contributed to two books and has contributed two book reviews for *JIRBS*.

Stephen Garrick, B.A. (Theology) from Baptist Bible College, Springfield, MO, is pastor of Emmanuel Reformed Baptist Church, Georgetown TX.

James M. Renihan, Ph.D., is Dean and Professor of Historical Theology at the Institute of Reformed Baptist Studies at Westminster Seminary California, Escondido, CA. He also serves as a pastor at Christ Reformed Baptist Church, Vista, CA. He is the author of *Edification and Beauty*, *True Confessions*, *True Love*, and several other works. He is the editor of *JIRBS* and has published articles in many scholarly and popular periodicals. He is a member of the Baptist Historical Society and ETS.

Stefan T. Lindblad, Ph.D. candidate, Calvin Theological Seminary, and M.Div., Westminster Seminary California and the Institute of Reformed Baptist Studies. He is a pastor of Trinity Reformed Baptist Church, Kirkland, WA. In addition to published articles and book reviews in popular and academic journals, he has several forthcoming essays on various aspects of Reformation and post-Reformation Reformed theology. His doctoral research focuses on the doctrine of Christ's office of Mediator in the era of confessional orthodoxy (16th - 17th centuries).

Michael T. Renihan, Ph.D., is pastor of Heritage Baptist Church, Worcester. MA. He is also an adjunct professor of history and political science at Worcester State University. His doctoral thesis on the antipaedobaptism of John Tombes was published in 2000. Mike has edited a number of volumes in print and penned chapters for a handful of works. He is also a member of the New England Reformed Fellowship and ETS.

Samuel Renihan, Ph.D. candidate, Free University of Amsterdam, and M.Div., Westminster Seminary California and the Institute of Reformed Baptist Studies. Sam is a pastor at Trinity Reformed Baptist Church, La Mirada, CA. He is the author of *God without Passions: A Reader* and *God without Passions: A Primer* and has contributed articles to *JIRBS*.

Charles J. Rennie, M.Div., Westminster Seminary California and the Institute of Reformed Baptist Studies, is pastor of Sycamore Baptist Church, East Moline, IL. He has contributed to *JIRBS*.

Brandon F. Smith, B.A. in History from Macon State (University of Georgia System), is a pastor of Trinity Reformed Baptist Church, Jackson, GA. He is co-author of an upcoming book on Georgia Baptist Church History, *The Gospel Heritage of Georgia Baptists: 1772-1830, Who were they and what did they believe?*

www.ingramcontent.com/pod-product-compliance
Lightning Source LLC
Chambersburg PA
CBHW062355090426
42740CB00010B/1281